HIROHITO
EMPEROR OF JAPAN

By
Leonard Mosley

Prentice-Hall, Inc., Englewood Cliffs, New Jersey

To D.

Introduction

In his vivid and scholarly account of the last phases of the Pacific war, *Japan's Decision To Surrender*, Doctor Robert C. Butow writes of the termination of the conflict:

"It was the nation's [Japan's] good fortune that, in spite of the existence of a hard-headed and strong-willed corps of fanatics, the men responsible for the movement to terminate the war were finally able, under the circumstances of 1945, to give the fullest possible effect to the depth of appeal in the voice of the man who is the supreme symbol of Japanese life and thought."

He is, of course, referring to the voice of Hirohito, Emperor of Japan, the sound of which, broadcasting an Imperial Rescript without precedent in the history of the Japanese Empire, brought the war in the Far East to an end on August 15, 1945.

This is the story of the events, environment and influences which led him to this climactic—and quite unexpected—moment of his life. It is the story of a gentle introvert, scholarly and civilized man of peace who found himself Emperor of a nation bent on war and conquest. It is the story of how he found the courage and the resource, in spite of military fanatics and palace conspiracies, to outwit the plotters and end the war.

It is, of course, much more than that, as I hope the reader will discover, in that it seeks to trace the path of Japan and the Japanese people and Government through the past sixty-odd years, as well as Hirohito and his family. When the present Emperor of Japan was born, the Western powers still had extra-territorial rights in the land, jinrikshaws

vii

ran through the streets, and the prostitutes sat for their clients' inspection in the cages of Yoshiwara. The eyes of the East turned enviously Westward and coveted Occidental achievements—steam engines, gaslamps, cameras, telegrams, lightning conductors, newspapers, postcards, steamships and hansom-cabs (according to a children's song popular in 1901). Women were chattels. Amaterasu was the Goddess of the Sun and the Emperor of Japan was her direct descendant, the Son of Heaven.

Hirohito has spanned the life of his nation from the last of the samurai and the Knights of Bushido through the fanatics of Shintoism and Kodo to the democracy and neutralism of today. He has worn well—in many ways better than his people.

To assemble the facts of his story, I have spent some considerable time in Japan talking with close associates of the Imperial Family and with those survivors of the war (and the International Military Tribunal, Far East) who played any part in the development of the Imperial role. I have also delved deep into the treasures of the National Archives in Washington, where are to be found the records of interviews by teams of United States investigators of practically everyone who mattered in Japan and was still surviving in 1945.

In a biography of this kind I think it is essential to say quite clearly that it is not authorized. Neither the Emperor nor any of his advisers will have any idea of what I say about him, and of the criticisms I make of his conduct, until they read this book. I have, however, spoken to many of them and have acknowledged their contributions wherever they have allowed me to do so. A number of them have specifically asked not to be identified, and I have respected their confidences. In every case, the opinions expressed—particularly about the part played by the Emperor in the coming of the Far East War—are strictly my own, though I hope that the facts I produce in association with them reinforce their impact. No one in the palace entourage has tried to exert any undue influence upon me, and all of them have listened to my criticisms and tried to answer them.

Of necessity, the names of quite a number of sources with whom I have spoken have had (at their request) to be omitted. Others have asked that, if acknowledgment be given, I do not specify what information or background material they provided. I think, therefore, it is best if I give a blanket list of names of those to whom I talked and to whom I am particularly indebted for their help. They include:

Doctor Edwin O. Reischauer, U.S. Ambassador to Japan; Sir Francis Rundall, H.M. Ambassador to Japan; Admiral Katsunoshin Yamanashi, K.B.E., C.M.G.; Prince Tadatsugi Shimazu; Marquis Osanaga Kamroji; Baron Kyoichi Usui; Mr. Hiroshi Takashima, M.D., Ph.D; Doctor Joseph Roggendorf, Sophia University; Mr. Den Takase; Mr. Shiro Sumikura; Mr. Shinzo Yoshimoto, N.H.K.; Baron Sukemasa Iriye; Mrs. Elizabeth Vining; Mr. Lewis Bush; and Captain A. J. ("Jock") Petrie-Hay, H.M. Naval Attaché, Tokyo, whose advice and "contacts" I found unfailingly useful.

They have my warmest thanks. So have Lt. Col. C. V. Glines, USAF, Office of the Secretary of Defense; Mr. Burnet Hershey, a veteran foreign correspondent who dug up some invaluable photographs; and Mr. John Taylor and Mr. Will Nigh of the National Archives in Washington, both of whom worked indefatigably on my behalf.

Finally, I should like to acknowledge my warm thanks to two authorities on Japan and Japanese affairs who have been kind enough to read this book in manuscript form and give me the benefit of their knowledge of the land, people, history, language and culture. The first is Doctor Ivan Morris, at present Professor in the Department of Chinese and Japanese at Columbia University, author of *The World of the Shining Prince,* a study of Court life in ancient Japan, and *Nationalism in Postwar Japan;* and the second is Mr. Don Cyril Gorham, who was educated in Japan, graduated from Tokyo Imperial University in 1941, and later became an acknowledged specialist on Japanese affairs. His mother was the tutor of Emperor Hirohito's youngest brother, Prince Mikasa.

I would point out that they helped me to correct my mistakes but are not responsible for my opinions.

A list of documents, interrogations and books consulted will be found at the end of this book.

Sidlesham, Sussex,
September, 1965.

ix

Chapter One

The doyen of the *corps diplomatique* in Japan in 1900 was Baron Albert d'Anethan, Belgian envoy extraordinary to the Court of the Emperor Meiji, and on May 10th of that year he and his wife had an official engagement. The Baroness (who, incidentally, was the sister of Rider Haggard, the English novelist) wrote about it in the diary which she kept of her life in Japan.

"Today was the wedding day of the Crown Prince of Japan and Princess Suda, daughter of a *kuge* [Court noble] family. Their marriage took place in the Imperial shrine in the palace grounds at eight in the morning. Both bride and bridegroom were dressed in ancient court dress, but only Japanese were present and only two people outside the family witnessed the actual ceremony behind the curtain of the holy of holies. These two were the Grand Master of Ceremonies, Baron Sannonomiya, and a lady-in-waiting. The bride and bridegroom changed into European dress for the drive back to the Prince's palace [at Akasaka, some three miles away] and Albert and I witnessed the procession of the many magnificent Court carriages. At 4:30 we were due at the [Imperial] Palace in uniform and evening dress, but no court train was worn. After we had been detained for some time in rooms put aside for the *corps diplomatique*, we were received in audience, Albert and I being received first. Albert presented his message from the King of the Belgians to H.I.M., which came the day before. Both the Emperor and the Empress spoke to us, but the Crown Prince and his bride merely shook hands and bowed at our felicitations. The bride is only sixteen,

1

but she looks full of life and strength, and she possesses a pleasant and intelligent face." [1]

It was from this union of Crown Prince Yoshihito and Princess Sadako (to give her the name by which she was usually known at the time) that, almost twelve months later, on April 29, 1901, a male child was born. He was named Hirohito, and he was the first of three sons the Crown Princess was to bear in the next four years.

It is the custom when a son and heir is born to a prince of the Japanese ruling family that he be separated as early as possible from his parents and the court. It was done in pre-Meiji times to safeguard the boy from unscrupulous uncles or concubines with sons of their own who could become heirs themselves should the infant prince expire. Officials of the Imperial Household are apt to explain the custom nowadays as being intended to divorce a young prince early in life from environmental influences which might feed incipient vanity, or soften character by pampering and flattering. While this may be the effect of court life on a boy in the later years of his childhood, it is hardly likely to happen to him when he is three months old, which is the age at which Hirohito was taken from his mother. The truth is much more likely to be that the Emperor Meiji and his advisers feared for the baby's health so long as he remained with his mother at the Togu-gosho, the Crown Prince's palace at Akasaka. Despite his mother's robust appearance, the stock from which he sprang could hardly be described as sturdy. His grandfather, the Emperor, made a great show of sexual activity and ostentatiously dropped a silk handkerchief each evening before one of the Court concubines whom he had chosen as his bed companion; but he did not seem capable of fathering virile babies. Four half-brothers of Yoshihito had died young from ill health, and the Crown Prince himself (the offspring [2] of Meiji and one of his ladies-in-waiting, Yanagiwara-no-Naruko) had been sickly in his early teens and would become much more than that later.

[1] Baroness d'Anethan, *Fourteen Years of Diplomatic Life in Japan*, London: 1912.
[2] Until the Meiji Era the Japanese Imperial line, "unbroken from ages eternal," was kept so by frequent adoptions from within the royal family. From Meiji onward the rule has been that only descendants of the blood can succeed; though this has never been allowed to bar an illegitimate son of the Emperor from the succession.

2

Hirohito was alarmingly puny at birth; the atmosphere at the Togu-gosho was enervating in the extreme; and his mother would be unlikely to enlist any expert or effective medical help (and definitely no surgery) should he fall ill. For princely bodies were sacrosanct in those days and no doctor could touch them, let alone give them injections. According to Professor Matsumoto, the son of one of Meiji's favorite admirals, Hirohito's removal from the palace to the care of foster parents probably saved his life, for his condition was so frail that he would undoubtedly have succumbed to the bouts of dysentery, fever, typhoid and smallpox which periodically swept through the court. Matsumoto spent much of his time during childhood with the young Hirohito, and remembers being told about the infant prince's puny condition.

"I had my first audience with Hirohito when I was one year old," he said (in a conversation with the author). "I climbed across the same tatami [straw mat] in the house of his foster parents, and although we were approximately the same age—I was about a month older—it seemed that I was a much bigger and brawnier child. Apparently I crawled over and tried to steal one of the future Emperor's toys, and I was pulled away. I was told later that the remark was made at the time: 'Look how much bigger this little upstart is than the Prince. He needs building up or he'll never grow up to sit on the throne.'"

But if separation from his parents was good for Hirohito's health, it lost him the opportunity of enjoying the only period in life when most Japanese can be uninhibitedly free and happy. Childhood is the time of indulgence in Japan, when for a few years a child is allowed, even encouraged, to be an individual, to make mischief, to have tantrums, to show off, to laugh too loudly, to cry too easily, to be a bully or a coward. By the time he is aged ten or eleven, he will have to begin learning how to conform to the restrictive behavior patterns of grownup Japan, and he will never again be forgiven for lapses from the rigid rules of conduct upon which social life is based—unless, of course, he happens to be drunk. But until that time Japanese children are allowed to be the spoiled and pampered darlings of the household and are punished for only one sin: failure to show proper respect to their father.

This happy interlude of irresponsibility was denied the infant Hirohito. From the moment he could understand what was being said to him, he was made aware of his position and the awesome nature of his future. He would one day inherit the Imperial throne of Japan and become the divine ruler of his people, and that he must never be allowed to forget.

From the age of three months until November, 1904, when he was three-and-a-half years old, his guardian was Count Sumiyoshi Kawamura, a vice admiral in the Imperial Navy. It was in his household that Matsumoto first met Hirohito and it was here that they were joined, in 1902, shortly after his birth, by a royal brother, Prince Chichibu. Whether any memories reaching as far back through a man's lifetime as sixty-odd years can be trusted is doubtful, and Matsumoto's memories of life in the Kawamura mansion may well be colored by what he was told afterward rather than what he experienced himself; but he has a remarkable mind, and he certainly remembers Count Kawamura with affection and his household with considerable warmth. He says that he and Chichibu were allowed the run of the household and never checked in their exuberances, but that from the first Hirohito was a child apart, sensitive, withdrawn, acutely aware of the special deference his guardian and staff displayed toward him, and conscious, too, that questioning eyes were always upon him.

It was even worse when he moved back to the palace at Akasaka at the beginning of 1905, for then his education began in earnest. Though he and his brothers (the third prince, Takamatsu, had now joined them) were to spend the next few years living in the precincts of the Crown Prince's palace, they rarely saw their father and were allowed only weekly visits with their mother. They had their own quarters with a wet nurse for Takamatsu, their own maids and male retainers, and a new guardian in the person of Mr. Kinsaku Maruo, who was something of a disciplinarian and only too well aware that he had a future Emperor of Japan in his hands, his character ready for shaping. In addition to his brother, Chichibu, Hirohito was joined during class and play periods by four and sometimes five boys of similar age who were the sons of court officials or members of the peerage. They were quick to note that Hirohito rarely was allowed to escape from the vigilance of Mr. Maruo or one of his minions, and that playtime with him was almost inevitably bound to be interrupted, or even halted, by an adult. Matsumoto recalls the time when Hirohito climbed on to a three-foot wall and was followed by his classmates; but as he was about to jump, Mr. Maruo appeared and cried "Stop!" He put up his hands and helped the prince

4

down, at the same time pointing out that it was unseemly for a future Emperor to be indulging in such antics; and the crestfallen Hirohito had to stand by and watch his companions jump from the wall, scramble up and jump again. It is perhaps not surprising that the schoolboys turned from Hirohito and rallied round the much more gregarious and extrovert Chichibu as leader of their fun and games. It was the beginning of a strained relationship between the two brothers which was to have important repercussions later. Meanwhile, Chichibu, too young to understand the reason for it, grew increasingly scornful of what seemed to him Hirohito's timidity; for even when he was goaded into disobeying his tutors, he was usually hesitant and maladroit. (There would come a time later in their youth when Chichibu would wound his brother deeply by saying, in his hearing: "The trouble with Hiro is that when he falls down, he doesn't know how to get up!") But unlike Chichibu, he was already learning—at the age of seven—to mask his emotions and give no sign of any mortification he might feel, and Mr. Maruo reported to the Emperor Meiji that he was acquiring swiftly the art of comporting himself like a true prince of the Imperial line.

It is possible to judge what manner of a boy he was growing to be from an incident which happened at this time. The boys had strayed, after lessons, into one of the pavilions in the palace grounds and, squatting on the tatami, were indulging in a favorite Japanese childhood prank—poking their fingers through the paper windows. It was one of the older pavilions in the grounds and the corridors had "nightingale" floors which means that they had built-in warning systems which whistled when anyone tried to tiptoe along them. The boys heard the squeak of an approaching adult and incontinently fled—all, that is, save Hirohito. His tutor found him squatting in the corridor beside the tell-tale windows and listened while the Prince gravely confessed full responsibility for the damage and absolved all his companions from blame. He may not have liked it that he was treated so differently from other boys of his age, but he was already conscious of the responsibility of his position. Perhaps even a little proud of it.

And then, in 1908, he found the father figure to replace the real father whom he so seldom saw. It has been mentioned earlier that Crown Prince Yoshihito had been sickly in his teens; his ailments were, in fact, mental as well as physical, and shortly after the birth of his second son he had begun to show signs of the eccentricities that would eventually turn to madness. He did not help his condition by a life of self-indulgence. That he had little time for his wife once she had produced him sons was not unusual in Japan, where wives are hardly kept for pleasure or companionship; but it was more unusual that he showed hardly any interest in the sons, sometimes letting weeks pass by without seeing them and not seeing them at all in winter, when he left the chills of Tokyo for the balmier airs of Southern Kyushu, at the other end of the Inland Sea.

It was true that if Hirohito needed a symbol to look up to, he could always think—or even pray—to his grandfather, the Emperor Meiji. Like every other little Japanese boy, he was taught to revere the Emperor as a god, to bow low in his direction each morning and evening, and to know by heart the Imperial Rescript on Education, which bound every child to the service of his divine ruler. As third in line to the Imperial throne himself, he also possessed the awesome privilege not only of being able to look at the Emperor but also of being touched by him. On the rare occasions when Meiji left the Imperial Palace, the crowds in the streets bent their heads and stared at the ground, the more superstitious because they feared that the sight of their divine ruler would kill them, the patriotic because they believed it unseemly to look upon such an august presence, and the rest because the police—their backs to the Imperial carriage—were watching the crowd for those "insolent" enough to stare. All windows above ground floor level along the Emperor's route were shuttered, so that no one might commit lèse-majesté by looking down on him. But Hirohito saw the Emperor three or four times a year, had once even been hoisted on his shoulder and patted on the head. What more did a boy need than this—the personal interest of His Imperial Majesty?

The answer is that Hirohito needed what every other Japanese boy needs if his childhood is to be happy and his future to be assured—a father around the house whom he can look up to and admire. (It is for this reason that, even today, an orphan or a fatherless child has small chance of success in Japan.) He was too young to appreciate the attentions of Count Kawamura, and Mr. Maruo was too much the bloodless disciplinarian. But when he was seven years old, he came under the care of a remarkable man named Nogi, and so far as Hirohito was concerned no man ever again measured up to him.

It was in April, 1908, that Hirohito was enrolled in a special class which was formed for his benefit at the Gakushuin, the Peers' School, a sort of Japanese Eton or Groton run solely for the education of the sons and daughters (there was a separate section for girls) of the Japanese aristocracy. Twelve boys of his own age were chosen to share his lessons with him, including two princely cousins; and he embarked on an intensive course of study of geography, science, English, handwriting and drawing—the last two, vital subjects in Japan—as well as singing, manual training and gymnastics.

The headmaster of the Gakushuin was Count Maresuke Nogi, and he was in many ways the living embodiment of the faith, loyalty, bravery and fanaticism of the Japanese. Nogi was born in 1849 and he fought, and was twice wounded, in the battles against the Tokugawa Shogun which ended in the restoration to power of the Imperial line, the removal of the young Emperor from Kyoto to Tokyo, and the inauguration of the so-called Meiji Restoration in 1868. Thereafter he was welcomed into the ranks of the new Imperial Army and rose rapidly—from a major at twenty-two to the rank of general in 1893, when he retired. But he was back again the following year, when the Sino-Japanese War broke out, accepting the rank of brigadier in order to get a fighting command. It was his brigade which captured Port Arthur from the Chinese after some bloodthirsty and decimating battles. Once more he retired, first as Governor of Formosa, then with a post at the Embassy in Berlin, until the Japanese made war upon Russia in 1904, when he returned to lay siege to Port Arthur in command of the Third Japanese Army.

The Russians fought well but were confronted with an enemy willing to use its men as expendables, "human bullets" to be hosed upon the Czarist troops like so many rounds of ammunition. The Order of the Day for the battle included these words: "No man must hope to return. Every officer whatever his rank shall appoint his successor. The attack will be chiefly effected with the bayonet . . . and officers are authorized to kill those men who, without proper reason, straggle behind or separate themselves from the ranks, or retreat."

Port Arthur was taken, but at enormous cost. The dead included General Nogi's own two sons, and in the midst of sorrowing over them, he seemed almost glad that their lives had been taken. To an Englishman, D. H. James, who watched the fighting from the dugouts ringing the city, "he explained his reactions after the death of his remaining son on 203-Metre Hill in this way. He was now heirless, and his bereavement answered the clamoring souls of the departed men he had, by unhappy

7

duty, sent to their death." [3] And when the fighting was over, he built a shrine, gathered his surviving troops before it, and read an address to the departed spirits of the dead:

"On the 14th of January, in the 38th year of Meiji, I, Nogi Maresuke, Commander in Chief of the Third Japanese Army, have caused this fete to be celebrated with saké and food, in honor of the officers and men who have fallen. For over 210 days and nights you have bravely battled, facing death by fire, sword and disease—and you were killed. But your efforts were not in vain, for the fleet of the enemy was destroyed and the fortress forced to surrender. This was but the reward of your sacrifice. But I and others swore death or victory, and I surviving have received the Imperial thanks, and now unworthily monopolize the glory. And I beseech you who are gone to the hereafter, share with me this glory! Fate ordaining, sadly places me in command of these hills, these streams and forts, all so stained with your life's blood. Here before this altar raised on consecrated ground, I invoke your spirits to partake of this humble offering."

Now Count Nogi's martial days were over, and he was spending the evening of his life inculcating in the sons of the aristocracy the spirit of Bushido, the Way of the Samurai, on which he himself had been raised. It seemed unlikely that such a vintage warrior, so scarred by war that he had sword, arrow, bayonet, bullet and shrapnel wounds on his face and body, should attract so retiring and temperamentally pacific a boy as Hirohito; but Nogi had gentle qualities too. He was adept at calligraphy, the cultivation of bonsai (miniature trees), ikebana (flower arrangement) and the tea ceremony. But perhaps most important was the fact that, as the young prince may have sensed, he was a father who badly missed his sons just as Hirohito was a son who felt the lack of a father.

A relationship grew up between the two which, for four years, made life almost happy for the young prince. It was, of course, in no sense the same sort of relationship as one finds between an American or British father and son, for that is not the way it works in Japan. There was no comradeship between the two—but fondness, and, of course, deep respect and admiration from the boy to the man, and a profound desire to protect

[3] D. H. James, *The Rise and Fall of the Japanese Empire*, London: Allen and Unwin, 1951.

8

and influence by the man toward the boy. From 1908 onward General Nogi saw Hirohito almost every day and took an intense personal interest in his progress, reports of which he presented regularly to Meiji. His Emperor was Nogi's ideal. He had spent most of his life serving him and hoping to die for him, and he took pleasure and pride now, in the years of his retirement, in the thought that he might yet shape Hirohito into his divine master's image.

The years of Hirohito's boyhood coincided with Japan's emergence as a world power, and everywhere throughout the land there were signs of it. It was difficult to believe that little more than fifty years had passed since Commodore Perry's "black ships" had sailed into what is now Tokyo Bay to demand, at gun point, commerce with a nation which had deliberately isolated itself from the rest of the world for more than two centuries. It was even more difficult to realize that, until thirty-three years before Hirohito's birth, an Emperor of Japan was no more than a puppet living on a pension in Kyoto, while the Tokugawa shoguns (or tycoons) ran the government from their stronghold in Edo (as Tokyo was then called).

In 1868 the iron grip of the shogunate was broken by a practically bloodless revolution in which the leaders of the anti-Tokugawa clans roused the people with the battle cry of: "Restore the Emperor and expel the barbarians!" The "barbarians" were, of course, the Americans, British, French and Russians whom the Tokugawas had allowed into the country after Commodore Perry's ultimatum. The shogun fled into retirement and Hirohito's grandfather, then a boy of fifteen, moved with his advisers from Kyoto to Edo, which was renamed Tokyo, or Eastern Capital. It was the beginning of the so-called Meiji Restoration, and most of those who had helped to bring it about believed that its object was to hold progress and modernization in check rather than accelerate it. The shogunate had allowed dangerous "outside" influences to penetrate Japan and threaten her feudal system. The young Emperor, his prestige restored, would rid the land of the hated gaijin (foreigners) and once more turn Japan into a guarded fortress which no barbarian would be allowed to enter, and no Japanese, on pain of death, be allowed to leave.

Or so they thought. In fact just the opposite happened. The oligarchy of able young men who had brought Meiji to Tokyo dropped the phrase: "Expel the barbarians!" the moment the shogunate was destroyed, for they knew only too well that the barbarians would refuse to be pushed out and that Japan was in no condition to insist. The isolation of the past two centuries meant that most modern developments, particularly in the arts and weapons of war, had passed Japan by. Japan, by shogunate decree, had no ships bigger than coastal vessels (to prevent the natives from traveling outside the country) and her guns were small and antiquated. The Westerners had already demonstrated how much bigger and more effective were their ships and the guns they carried aboard them: British warships had leveled the capital of the Satsuma clan at Kagoshima because they had murdered an Englishman, and combined British, American and Dutch ships had shelled Shimonoseki because its puny batteries had dared to fire upon their merchantmen passing through the straits. Until Japan had ships and guns of her own, she must learn to live with the barbarians.

Not only learn to live with them, but she must learn from them too. When the young Emperor Meiji recited what was called "The Charter Oath" on April 6, 1868, he included in it a sentence which read:

"Knowledge shall be sought for in all parts of the world in order to strengthen the Imperial system."

In the next three decades, imitation of all things European spread like a fever through Japan. Embassies of young men with acquisitive minds were sent abroad to seek knowledge of modern developments, and to bring back Americans, Britons, Frenchmen, Germans and Dutch to work for them—as engineers, engine drivers, pilots, schoolteachers, bankers and lawyers, military and naval instructors—and to teach them the secrets of the technological developments which had passed them by. It is a measure of the all-pervading passion for copying or acquiring European discoveries that in the 1880's Japanese schoolchildren, playing ball, counted the bouncing of the ball by singing a song called "Civilization Ball Song," which enumerated the ten most desirable amenities coveted by the Japanese: steam engines, gas lamps, cameras, telegrams, lightning conductors, newspapers, schools, mailing services, steamships and hansom cabs.[4]

Even the Imperial Court itself underwent a profound change and the Emperor urged his courtiers to think progressively. Electric light was

[4] Sir George Sansom, *The Western World and Japan,* New York: Alfred A. Knopf, Inc., 1950.

installed in the palace (but never used because of the danger of fire); Court ladies were exhorted to speak aloud instead of whispering behind their hands, as they had done since the days of the ancient courts at Kyoto; and if the ladies were loath to adopt Western dress, the men were more than eager. Mrs. Grace James, whose naval officer husband was attached to the court at the beginning of the century, remembered that "the ladies were astonishingly picturesque in their ancient and traditional costume, wearing the scarlet hakama and sweeping sleeves long to the ground. Their hair smooth and black as raven's feathers, curved away from the head over the ears in a wing-like dressing. Over the back the hair was flattened and lay on the shoulders as broadly as a mantle, and the ends were gathered and confined in a white paper wrapping." [5]

But not so the men. "The gentlemen attending His Majesty's Court, other than those wearing uniform, were less happily garbed. It must be remembered that this was in the earliest days of the adoption of western civilization, culture and style of dress. Occidental taste had as yet had no time to develop and even ordinary knowledge was lacking. Many of the gentlemen had donned their dress suits with more goodwill than good management. Almost all the garments were readymade and far too large for their wearers. Trousers were pushed at their extremities into elastic sided boots with red or yellow tags well pulled out. Ruffled top hats were pulled down over the owners' ears, or alternatively worn jauntily on the back of the head, and, queerest of all, instead of the more usual collar and tie, there was a prevailing feeling for a smallish bath towel wound muffler fashion about the throat." [6]

For a time a wave of self-consciousness swept the land about something which had never concerned the Japanese before—their own bodies. Learning that Occidentals were prudish about sex and shocked by casual Japanese nakedness, it was decreed that mixed bathing be abolished. No longer could a Japanese be seen striding naked down the street, still steaming from the bath, clothes over his arm. The sexes were not consigned to separate baths, but they were driven to opposite sides of the same one, with a curtain hung between; and for a time a pleasant and innocent rendezvous for gossip between the sexes was lost, though only for a time. As for sex: the brothel areas were by no means closed, but

[5] Grace James, *Japan: Recollections and Impressions*, London: Allen & Unwin, 1936.
[6] *Ibid.*

11

the prostitutes were no longer paraded outside in cages for prospective customers; photographs were substituted.

That the Japanese sometimes aped the Europeans too slavishly is beyond doubt, as also is the fact that they sometimes seemed to pick the wrong advisers for the purposes they had in mind. From France they chose advisers for the new conscript Army, from Britain they brought in engineers and officers for the Japanese Navy, from Belgium they solicited advice on banking and fiscal reform; but it was from Germany that they got their inspiration for the Constitution of 1889. They considered the German pattern of government most suitable for adaptation to Japanese usage, and it was to have baleful consequences in the years to come: Japanese statesmen and militarists learned, like Bismarck, how to govern behind the backs of the elected legislators.

The beginnings of Meiji's reign had not been without their teething troubles, particularly once the diehard traditionalists realized that the Meiji Restoration meant the end of everything they hoped to cherish.

By the beginning of the new century, however, the rifts had been healed and Japan made whole by a nationalistic fervor which rallied the whole nation behind the Emperor, to whom all credit was given for the country's renaissance. The latter half of the nineteenth century had been characterized by a greedy grab for colonies by the European powers in Asia, Africa and elsewhere, and this too was an Occidental custom which Japan felt it desirable to acquire. Across the water, in China and Korea, weak and corrupt administrations were in power, but it was not until 1894 that Japan considered herself powerful enough to provoke the wars which, if won, would provide colonial spoils.

The Chinese were provoked into making war for the control of Korea and were swiftly driven from that country. The Japanese Army occupied Southern Manchuria, seized the Chinese port of Wei-hai-wei and annihilated the Chinese naval forces. The subsequent peace treaty gave Korea complete independence, ceded Formosa, the Pescadores and the Liaotung Peninsula to Japan, together with a considerable indemnity in cash. The European powers, impressed by this show of strength, gave up the extraterritorial rights they had hitherto enjoyed in Japan, and gradually began to loosen the tariff treaties by which they had bound the Japanese economic system. But it was not until 1902 that recognition was given to the new Japan as a world power; in that year Britain, the most powerful naval power of the day, signed a treaty of alliance with

Japan and bound herself to come to Japan's aid should she, while at war with one power, be attacked by another. The pact opened the way for Japan to begin hostilities against Russia, whose encroachments in Korea and Manchuria she increasingly resented. Hitherto a war with Russia might have brought other European nations (particularly Russia's ally, France) against her. Now they would not dare to move, knowing that Britain was pledged to intervene.

The Russo-Japanese War began in February, 1904, with a Japanese attack of a kind which was to be repeated in 1941. She broke off diplomatic relations with Russia and then sent torpedo boats out to attack the Russian fleet outside Port Arthur. Only after crippling a number of ships did she then declare war. But there was little of the indignation expressed at the time as was heard after Pearl Harbor. *The Times* of London merely commented:

"The Japanese Navy has opened the war by an act of daring which is destined to take a place of honour in naval annals. On Monday night, February 8th, Japanese torpedo-boats surprised the Russian squadron in the outer roadstead at Port Arthur, and delivered their attack with such good effect that two of the best battleships in the Russian squadron and a cruiser were disabled."

Russia was far stronger than Japan, but her men and supplies were at the end of the single-track Trans-Siberian Railway, thousands of miles away from Russia proper. Moreover, revolution was brewing in St. Petersburg and Moscow, and troops had to be kept behind to keep order. The fanatic Japanese conscript army accepted casualties of a size that would have panicked a European force into defeat and gradually drove out the Russians from Manchuria or bottled them up in their strongholds.

But the Russians were still the stronger force and the Czarist Navy, despite the damage done by the Japanese torpedo-boats at the beginning of the war, was believed to be more than a match for anything the enemy could put to sea. The Russian European fleet sailed on the long voyage halfway around the world to meet the Japanese Navy in the climactic encounter of the war. Admiral Togo and the whole of the Japanese fleet were waiting for the Russians between the Korean mainland and the Japanese islands, knowing that they were weary from the voyage and short of supplies. The Battle of Tsushima which followed was the greatest naval victory since Trafalgar.

"The destiny of our Empire depends upon this action. You are all

13

expected to do your utmost!" Togo signaled to his men, and the ships moved into range. In the subsequent clash, only two of the Russian fleet of thirty-eight ships escaped. Six battleships and five cruisers were sunk, and the Russian Commander in Chief, Admiral Rojestventsky, and his flagship were captured.

It was the beginning of the end for Russia and a few months later she accepted, along with Japan, the good offices of President Theodore Roosevelt, who found a formula for ending the war. The Japanese people, hardly realizing how overstretched were their resources and how unprepared they were for a long war, were dissatisfied with the peace terms, which they believed let off Russia too lightly. There were outbursts of anti-Americanism in Tokyo and other big cities, and the seeds of antipathy toward the United States were sown and would begin to grow in the coming years. But the Japanese had, in fact, little to grumble about. The world was impressed by their prowess and, like America, every European nation now accepted Japan as a major power. King Edward VII of Britain made Admiral Togo a member of the Order of Merit, the nation's most distinguished award, and in 1905 he sent H. R. H. Prince Arthur of Connaught to Japan to invest the Emperor Meiji with the Order of the Garter. It was to be the occasion of Hirohito's first public engagement, for he was taken to Shimbashi Station as a member of the Emperor's entourage. Meiji had decided to stress the increasingly close ties between his country and Britain by leaving his palace to meet his royal guest as he descended from the train bringing him from Yokohama. Hirohito had a tiny Army officer's uniform made for him especially for the occasion.

The system of education which General Nogi superintended for the royal princes at the Peers' School was not very much different in its curriculum from the one drawn up for the ordinary schools which had been set up in Japan. An almost miraculous achievement of the Meiji Restoration had been the establishment of schools throughout the land and their success in ending illiteracy. Although there had been an educational system under the Tokugawas which was surprisingly efficient, it was by no means universal. Within four years of the Restoration, schools were opening in every town, city and hamlet and education was mandatory for both sexes, from the age of six to fourteen. From being a nation 75 percent illiterate in 1860, Japan had 95 percent of its population able to read and write by the beginning of the twentieth century.

The mastery of the difficult Japanese written language was not, however, the sole—or even the primary—purpose of the Japanese educational system. The advisers behind the throne used the schools for another, less altruistic, purpose—to instill nationalism in the young and rally them fervently behind the Emperor. The motive behind this policy was carefully thought out and had the virtue of necessity behind it. Under the Tokugawa shoguns, for more than two hundred years the Japanese people had little sense of nationhood or patriotism. The peasants paid tribute to their local daimyos and knew little or nothing of the Shogun in Edo or the Emperor in Kyoto. The samurai swore allegiance to, and fought for, their lords rather than the shoguns. Only the daimyos themselves acknowledged the overlordship of the shogunate, and that often enough only because they had left behind in Edo their wives and sons as hostages for their loyalty. As for the Emperor, they politely acknowledged his existence and paid lip service to his regality, but he really did not count.

But with the abolition of the shogunate in 1868, followed shortly afterward by the abolition of the feudal estates and the disbandment of the samurai, the Japanese masses needed someone or something to take the place of their regional masters. So in place of a feudal chief, the men behind the throne gave them a national god, their Emperor. The Constitution of 1889, written by one of the Imperial advisers, the Marquis Ito, stressed that the Emperor was "sacred and inviolable" and that Japan "shall be reigned over and governed by a line of Emperors unbroken from ages eternal." And in the schools the process began of teaching Japanese children that Meiji was of divine origin, and was to be worshiped as a god. There would come a time during Hirohito's reign when a Japanese professor would question the beginnings of the Japanese Imperial line (and, in consequence, be threatened with assassination), but during his boyhood there were no sceptics, and the legend of the Imperial origin was accepted as history. Japanese children were told that, a long way back in the past, the god Izanagi and the goddess Izanami were hovering in the clouds above the world when drops of moisture fell from Izanagi's spear and congealed on the surface of the globe to form an island. The gods descended to have a look and circled the island in opposite directions. When they met halfway round, Izanami said: "I am overjoyed to meet such a handsome man." Izanagi was furious that a female should have had the effrontery to address him first, and he forced his companion to make another circle of the island, after which he said the first words: "I am overjoyed to meet such a lovely woman." From their subsequent embraces (whose technique, incidentally, they learned from studying two love birds) a son and a number of islands were born. These islands were Japan and for long years they were the only islands to exist on the globe, until flotsam and jetsam floating in the sea solidified to form the rest of the world.

The legend as it is read by grownups proceeds from this point to embark on uproariously obscene incidents, but the school version as taught to Hirohito and his contemporaries was somewhat more sedate. Izanami was burned to a cinder giving birth to fire, and Izanagi went on to beget from himself (like a godlike oyster) the three principal gods of the Japanese pantheon—Amaterasu, the sun goddess, from his left eye, Tsuki-no-kami, the moon goddess, from his right eye, and Susanoo, the sword god, from his nostril. Susanoo is also sometimes known as the Impetuous Male, from his appetite for wenching and his habit of cutting down with his sword anyone he suspected of the merest slight upon his honor. In Japanese mythology (which was taught as history during Hirohito's boyhood) Susanoo's appetites goaded him into violating his sister, Amaterasu, who at once retired to a cave in a dudgeon, vowing never to come out again. Since she was goddess of the sun the whole world was at once plunged into darkness; but the groans of dismay which she expected to hear were not forthcoming, and instead she heard delighted laughter; for the warriors outside, as a stratagem, had persuaded one of their number to dance for them. When Amaterasu demanded to know what was going on, she was told that a beautiful goddess was entertaining the warriors, and when she asked to see her the warriors held up a mirror to Amaterasu's own face. She was so jealous of the beauty of her supposed rival that she at once emerged from the cave, brought light back to the world, and produced Susanoo's son. The son's son, Ninigi, descended to the earth and became its ruler, and from his grandson the first Emperor of Japan, Jimmu, was born and ascended the throne in 660 B.C. His mother was a crocodile, but his great-great-great-great grandmother was Amaterasu, and he was therefore the Son of Heaven, God of the Sun, and divine, as all his forebears have been ever since. The Emperor Jimmu was founder of the Japanese Im-

16

perial line "unbroken from ages eternal," and the Emperor Meiji was his descendant.

The Constitution of 1889 stressed the divine origin of the Emperor, and the school system of Japan had as its primary objective the inculcation of implicit obedience to his will. In 1890 an Imperial Rescript on Education was issued in Meiji's name and henceforward, until the defeat of Japan, it was the writ by which Japanese were expected to rule their lives. Each morning at the Gakushuin there was a ceremony presided over by General Nogi in which Hirohito and his fellow pupils took part. They bowed for sixty seconds toward the Imperial Palace in the ceremony known as "worshiping at a distance," after which they repeated the Rescript on Education, which they were expected to know by heart. It went as follows:

"Know ye, our good and faithful subjects! Our Imperial Ancestors have founded our Empire on a basis broad and everlasting and have deeply and firmly implanted virtue. Our subjects ever united in loyalty and filial piety have from generation to generation illustrated the beauty thereof. This is the glory of the fundamental character of Our Empire, and herein also lies the source of our education. Ye, our subjects, be filial to your parents, affectionate to your brothers and sisters; as husbands and wives be harmonious, as friends true; bear yourselves in modesty and moderation; extend your benevolence to all; pursue learning and cultivate arts; and thereby cultivate intellectual faculties and perfect moral powers; furthermore advance public good and promote common interests; always respect the Constitution and observe the laws; should emergency arise offer yourselves courageously to the State; and thus guard and maintain the prosperity of Our Imperial Throne coeval with heaven and earth. So shall ye not only be Our good and faithful subjects, but render illustrious the best traditions of your forefathers. The Way here set forth is indeed the teaching bequeathed by Our Imperial Ancestors, to be observed alike by Their Descendants and the subjects, infallible for all ages and true in all places. It is Our wish to lay it to heart in all reverence, in common with you, Our subjects, that we may all thus attain the same virtue."

After this, General Nogi led them in the singing of the national anthem and then asked them:

"What is your dearest ambition?"

To which they all replied:

17

"To die for the Emperor!"

To die for the Emperor!

In the ears of young schoolchildren it rang romantically, a clarion call to patriotic sacrifice. But what did it mean in fact? Each day the children of the new Japan were stirred by their teachers' stories of brave men who had given their lives for their country with the words, "Long live the Emperor!" on their lips. Yet it was a period when the nation was no longer engaged in wars but was, instead, consolidating the gains of earlier campaigns, and the heroes were intangible, almost mythical beings whose deeds stirred the senses but did not convey anything of the pain involved. They were, moreover, heroes who had died in war, spurred on by their comrades, conscious of the honor their sacrifice was bringing upon them and their family; and to a Japanese child, the posthumous rewards of valor seemed to make sudden, or even protracted, death an easy price to pay.

In 1912, however, Hirohito learned how a subject could love his Emperor to the point of death even when no war was involved and when the Emperor would have no need (at least in this world) of his sacrifice. In September of that year the Emperor Meiji died. He was fifty-nine years old and in the forty-four years he had ruled over Japan the nation had moved from the Middle Ages into the modern world. Exactly how much of the miracle was due to the personality and foresight of Meiji himself and how much to the shrewd statesmen who surrounded him from the age of fifteen will probably never be known. To the Japanese the Emperor Meiji will always be regarded as a strong and enlightened monarch who, singlehandedly, by stimulating his advisers, steered their country into the modern world. But historians would dearly like to have proof that this was so, and so far they have not discovered it, for the documents do not exist. The Imperial rescripts which shaped the mental attitudes of the Japanese during the renaissance were ascribed to Meiji's pen, but were merely issued under his personal seal and there is no clue to prove that he was responsible for them. The Constitution of 1889 was definitely not written by him but composed by Marquis Ito with a team of advisers, and based on European, mostly German, models. Did Meiji inspire or merely approve? Surrounding him throughout his reign was a remarkable team of farsighted men, almost all of them former members of the Satsuma or Choshu clans, who between them plotted Japan's path to world power. There were the two rivals, Prince Ito of the Satsumas (assassinated by a Korean in 1909) and Prince Yamagata of the Choshus; there were Prince Saionji and the other elder statesmen (or Genro) like Matsukata, Oyama and Inouye, whose advice had guided the Empire's destiny through the first decade of the twentieth century. But was it the Emperor Meiji who had galvanized them, or they who had used him as a convenient Imperial seal for their adventurous policies?

It is unlikely now that anyone will ever know. But at least, in the final stages of his illness, the Japanese people were in no doubt. They flocked to Tokyo and knelt to pray in their thousands outside the Imperial Palace, and when the announcement came of his death a convulsive sigh of regret expressed the feelings of the masses.

It was not only the simple-minded Japanese peasants who felt the loss of Meiji. Among the officers of his Army, too, there were those who believed that his death left a gap in the life of Japan that no other Emperor could fill. Among them was General Nogi.

The great state funeral of the Emperor was to be held on September 13th, 1912, and on the evening before it General Nogi called Hirohito to see him at the Gakushuin. He had before him as he squatted on the tatami a copy of the Prince's calligraphy lesson for the day, and for the next thirty minutes they discussed it. There followed a long catechism which lasted for three hours, during which the General covered the whole range of the Prince's studies and questioned him closely on what he had learned. During all this time, man and boy sat motionless on the tatami, and Hirohito knew that it would have hurt and disappointed his master had he betrayed for a moment that he was uncomfortable. Finally, General Nogi nodded his head to indicate that the session was over.

"I am not dissatisfied with your progress while I have been away," he said.[7] "Please remember that my physical presence is not necessary for me to be with you in your work. I shall always be watching you and your welfare will always be my concern. Work hard, for your own sake and for the sake of Japan."

He bowed his head again, to show that the time had come for Hirohito to go. The prince bowed himself out of the room.

[7] There had been a break in the association of Nogi and his charge during the previous year, while the General accompanied Admiral Togo to London to attend the Coronation of King George the Fifth.

Shortly afterward General Nogi returned to his house. His wife was waiting for him and they bathed together before donning ceremonial kimonos. Then they squatted before the tokonoma in which a picture of Meiji had been placed, and Nogi-san passed her husband a cup of saké, from which he sipped. After which he took a dagger and dispatched his wife with it, and then ripped open his bowels with his short sword in an act of sacrificial seppuku (ritual suicide). It was his last service to the Emperor he adored.

Hirohito was eleven years old—old enough to know that he was not allowed to display any emotion when they came to tell him the news. He heard them impassively and gave no sign of the pain and desolation which consumed him.

Chapter Two

There is no interregnum between the death of an emperor of Japan and the accession of his heir—though there is a ceremony of enthronement later—and Crown Prince Yoshihito became Emperor Taisho the moment his father died. To each new emperor's reign a name is given by which the holder will be known after his death, and the new regime was called the era of Taisho because it means Great Righteousness.[1] The behavior of the new monarch gave little hope that he would be the inspiration of righteousness among his people.

The Imperial line of Japan has produced some extraordinary occupants of its throne, weaklings, tyrants, decadents, debauchers and fools, but, as Sir George Sansom remarks, most of them, even in their emptiest follies, were moved by considerations of refinement and governed by a rule of taste which inspired "certain standards of personal behaviour and aesthetic judgments which are the source, or it might be better to say the foundation, of Japanese social life."[2]

Taisho had nothing of the kind to offer his people, amid his pathetic feebleness, by way of an example. He had grown to be a fop and a dandy who considered Kaiser Wilhelm of Germany the monarch he would most like to emulate, and he waxed and curled his moustaches

[1] Meiji (which means Enlightened Rule) was known as Prince Mutsuhito until he acceded. Hirohito's reign is known as Showa—which means, ironically enough, Enlightened Peace.

[2] Sir George Sansom, *A History of Japan*, California: Stanford University Press, 1958, 1961, 1963.

and liked to gallop around on a horse while wearing a uniform not un-like the Death's Head Hussars. He carried a riding crop with which he was wont to whip anyone who displeased him (and most people did). He was given to sudden fits of eldritch laughter or outbursts of ungov-ernable rage; he had childish tantrums which all too often ended in tears; he was terrified of assassination (especially after Ito, who had be-come one of his mentors, was murdered in 1909); he had inherited his father's appetite for concubines without any sense of moderation (though his wife, the Empress, kept herself well-informed of his peccadilloes and saw to it that there were no male bastards left around the court to challenge the inheritance rights of her own sons). He was completely uninterested in being emperor except in so far that it, occasionally, allowed him to dress up.

It was a moment in Japanese history when the nation needed a force capable of welding the people together and imbuing them with some sense of national purpose. The great achievements of the Meiji Era had slackened off during the last years of the regime, and there had been a surge of disturbing scandals and intrigues. Rivalry between the two ruling clans around the throne, the Satsumas and the Choshus, had flared up as the older members of the oligarchy tired and were replaced by their sons and nephews, more interested in personal aggrandizement than national revival.

Taisho was so totally devoid of the qualities needed in an emperor that the very lack of them could be an advantage. So long, that is, as there were strong-minded and patriotic advisers around him to turn him into a useful tool of a new and regalvanized administration. But did they exist? Would the right men come forward? It was in the knowledge of the needs of this situation that General Nogi had so formally and cere-monially committed seppuku just before Meiji's funeral. It was the act not simply of a loyal Oriental servant following his beloved master into the beyond. Nogi left a testament behind in which he lamented the corruption and lassitude of the latter years of the Meiji reign, of the loosening of the ties of duty which had formerly bound so many Jap-anese to their emperor and to the cause of their country. His suicide was a gesture designed to jolt the people back to a sense of patriotic service, particularly those ruling aristocrats to whose caste he had belonged. He had much hope of his young protégé, Hirohito, but none in Taisho; and in the years while the boy was trained for the throne, he urged the best brains at the palace to manipulate the stopgap Emperor for the best interests of Japan.

But who were the men who would pull the strings of the imperial puppet, and were they capable of coping with the problems?

In the latter part of Meiji's reign, some of the brilliant men who had engineered the restoration had formed themselves into a group of unofficial advisers called the Genro, or Elder Statesmen. Most of them came from the two clans which had brought the young Emperor from Kyoto to Tokyo, the Satsumas and the Choshus; most of them were originally soldiers, though afterward the Satsumas monopolized the higher ranks of the Navy and the Choshus did the same in the Army; and all of them had been prime minister at least twice. So far as the government was concerned, they had no official function; but in fact they were the most powerful men in the Empire. It was they who chose the premier and the members of his cabinet, and they who decided policy. But in 1912 their strength had been sapped either by death or illness. Prince Ito, a dynamic, precedent-breaking character of great enterprise,[3] was dead of an assassin's bullet. Prince Matsukata and Marquis Inouye were old, sick and weary of politics. Only a fierce and arrogant oldster named Prince Yamagata and a younger but even more distinguished aristocrat, Prince Saionji, seemed capable of deciding what was best for Japan, and their ideas, unfortunately, were contradictory. In the first few months of the Taisho era they clashed, and the results were disastrous. Since Yamagata was a soldier and Saionji a scholar and calligraphist, it is perhaps not surprising that their collision was concerned with military affairs.

Japan in 1912 had an Empire but, not for the first time, the Army guarding it was trigger-happy about its neighbors and eager for more troops and armaments—ostensibly to strengthen the defense of Korea. Prince Saionji was Prime Minister and realized that the economic burden of providing more armaments to "live up to the obligations of Empire" were threatening the country with bankruptcy, and to the clamant demands of the generals

[3] He overcame all disapproval and married—not just took into concubinage— the tea-house girl who hid him from vengeful samurais by stuffing him in the rubbish hole and squatting on top of him.

23

for the raising of two extra divisions his answer was a blank refusal. He was supported, moreover, by all the members of his cabinet save one—the Minister for War. But that was enough to mean his downfall.

General Uehara, the Minister for War, resigned his post in the Saionji government and the premier could not find a replacement. The government fell, much to Yamagata's satisfaction. At his urging, the Emperor was asked (and, of course, he did as he was told) to make Prince Katsura premier in Saionji's place; it seemed a safe Army choice, since Katsura, like Yamagata, belonged to the Choshu clan and was an Army man. But Katsura had ambitions; not simply to become premier but to make use of Taisho's feebleness and the weakness of the Genro to step back into the past, reviving the duarchy of the pre-Meiji era with himself as a latter-day shogun. To signalize his breach with Yamagata, he procrastinated over the Army's demands but made a quiet deal with the Navy for an expansion of the Imperial Fleet that would eventually cost 350 million yen ($1,400 million at the then rate of exchange). In doing so, he brought the wrath of Yamagata, the Diet and the newspapers down upon his head. The Diet met to protest and was prorogued by decree of the government, but when the news spread crowds assembled outside the building. Opposition members had prudently pinned white flowers to their yukatas or the lapels of their coats, but the rest were pulled from the rickshas and beaten by the mob. Soon there were riots all over the city, buildings were burning and the angry mob had turned the fire hoses on firemen and police instead of the fires.

By this time Saionji and Yamagata, autocrats never really comfortable when on the side of the people, were alarmed at what was happening. They swallowed their mutual antipathies and joined forces. When Premier Katsura, who was now beginning to panic, produced a "message" from the Emperor "ordering" them to fix up some sort of a compromise with the administration, they quickly did so. Anything to put down popular revolt. But the events of the previous days had stimulated the opposition, and there was now no holding them. When the Diet met again a vote of "no confidence" was put to the Chamber, in the course of which one of the opposition leaders, Mr. Yukio Ozaki, made a speech which shocked all Japan by daring to include a mention of the Emperor. Whose was the responsibility, he asked, for advising the Emperor to summon Katsura to the premiership—thus involving him personally in such a *mistake?* There was uproar in the Chamber and cries of: "Blasphemy! Treason! How can an Imperial message be mistaken?" To this Ozaki replied with a further attack on those who stooped to masking their sinister designs behind Imperial commands.

"There are people," he said, "who always mouth 'loyalty' and 'patriotism' and who advertise themselves as the sole repositories of these qualities, but what they actually do is hide themselves behind the throne and fire at their political enemies from this secure ambush. The throne is their ambush. Imperial Rescripts are their bullets."

For the time and place, it was a bold and a brave speech to make, for even to mention the Emperor except in laudatory terms set patriotic hearts burning with a sense of outrage. An attempt was made to make Ozaki guilty of *lèse-majesté* by "persuading" the official stenographer to alter the transcript of the speech. When this failed (Wakabayashi was sacked for his honesty) the Katsura group formed a League for the Protection of National Institutions and issued a manifesto which said, in part:

"Our Constitution definitely states that the Emperor is divine and superhuman, and the fact of his sanctity cannot in its nature depend on the responsibility of Ministers of State. . . . If such imprudent words and immoral actions be left unquestioned, the country will be shaken to its foundations. We appeal with tears to all patriotic hearts and hope they will make earnest efforts for the sake of the country."

It was a blatant appeal to some fanatic to come forward and assassinate the man who had "insulted" the Imperial ruler, and there were some anxious moments for Ozaki when it seemed likely that an unbalanced student might come forward, gun in hand. Part of the attack made upon him in the manifesto had mentioned his alleged disloyalty during his term, during a previous administration, as minister of education. Ozaki could hardly forget that he had taken the post because his predecessor, Viscount Mori, had been murdered—because he moved a curtain of an Imperial shrine with his stick. The murderer later had his own shrine erected to his memory by approving patriots.

Fortunately for Ozaki, before the campaign against him could be properly whipped up, Yamagata and the Genro once more withdrew their patronage from Katsura, and he was forced to hand in the resignation of his cabinet. He died at the end of 1912, no doubt from disappointed ambition. Or was it disappointed greed? Shortly afterward, during the administration of his successor, Admiral Yamamoto, rumors of corruption in administrative and military circles came to a head. A German named

Richter had undergone trial in Berlin during 1913 on a charge of black-mailing two Japanese officers, Admiral Fujii and Captain Sawasaki, on the grounds that they had accepted bribes from Siemens, Schuchert and Company in return for contracts for the supply of radio equipment. Soon there were other rumors, this time from Britain, that the great armaments firm of Vickers, in association with the Mitsui Company, had paid out large sums to naval and political personalities in return for a contract to build the cruiser *Kongo*.

Once more there were riots and scenes in the Diet. Admiral Yamamoto and his colleagues handed in their resignations and a number of arrests were made. Yamamoto was put on the retired list. A rear admiral and a vice admiral were given terms of imprisonment and fined 409,800 yen and 368,306 yen, the exact amount of the bribes they had received; and a number of others, including two directors of Mitsui, two Englishmen and a German, were either imprisoned or heavily fined.

Fortunately, the hands of the two princely Genro, Yamagata and Saionji, were clean; and they made a mutual resolve never to precipitate a scandal again by taking the opposite sides. (It was a resolve which, later on, was almost to cost Hirohito his wife.) In the meantime, as a sop to the masses, as well as to the Diet and the press, they recommended the election as the new prime minister of one of the grand old characters of Japanese politics, Marquis Okuma. Okuma was well into his seventies, lived in great luxury, and liked nothing better than to relax with a jug of saké and an armful of beautiful young concubines. He was known as the Sage of Waseda because he had founded the university of that name, but was apt to make light of learning. The same young fanatic who killed Viscount Mori had also thrown a bomb at Okuma and blown off his leg, but the new premier was so eccentric that he had cheerfully subscribed to the building of the assassin's memorial. "He was a great patriot. He meant well," he said.

Those qualities could also be ascribed to Okuma himself. More important, he was completely honest.

The ceremony of enthronement of Emperor Taisho was due to take place in the autumn of 1914, after the prescribed period of mourning had passed for the death of Meiji. But in April of that year the Empress-Dowager Haruko died, and for the court it was a most untimely moment to expire—if not for her. She could hardly have relished the prospect of attending, or even being alive at the time of the enthronement ceremonies, since the new Emperor, though Meiji's son and heir, was not of her body; for though she had provided Meiji with fourteen children, all four of her sons had died in childhood and five of her daughters not long afterward. To see him, a concubine son, enthroned, would have been too much, and she must have been happy that death had forced her to refuse the engagement.

In dying, however, she caused no little inconvenience to the Imperial Household Agency, which was intensively engaged in arranging the elaborate enthronement ceremonies at Kyoto. For one thing, the Empress-Dowager did not die in her own quarters in the Imperial Palace but at her pleasant estate in the country. Custom in Japan demands that a member of the royal family die in his or her own home, and if death insists on rudely overtaking a royal personage while he or she is abroad, the fact is ignored and death considered strictly incognito until arrangements can be made. In the case of Haruko it was simply announced that the Empress-Dowager was returning to Tokyo, and the journey by special train to the city and thence by carriage to the palace was carried out as if she were still alive. Only when the carriage crossed the royal moat was her death officially announced.

She was buried with her husband in the Imperial shrine at Momoyama, outside Kyoto, and it was the first time she had lain with him for twenty-nine years.

Hirohito had just completed his preparatory school course at the Gakushuin, and he journeyed with his father and mother in the special train to Kyoto for the funeral services. As a result of the funeral and the period of mourning that followed, the enthronement ceremonies, due to take place in the autumn, were postponed. It was just as well, for a month before they were due to take place World War One broke out and Japan, as ally of Britain, hesitated for three weeks and then declared war on Germany. It was a decision which was to produce rich dividends for Japan.

The knowledge that the heavy and irksome duties that would be demanded of him by the enthronement ceremonial had been put off for a year, together with the exciting news of a Japanese victory over Germany on the Chinese mainland,[4] seemed to drive the clouds from Taisho's brain

---

[4] A Japanese force overran a weak German garrison and occupied Tsingtao.

27

for a time. In the next few months he had a period of combined lucidity and euphoria which wrought a radical change in his nature. In the next few months, Hirohito saw more of his father than at any other time of his life, and he enjoyed the experience. Taisho even took to visiting his young wife, Sadako, again, and the Imperial household, not least the concubines and court ladies, boiled with steamy gossip as the Emperor repeatedly retired to his wife's quarters. This too produced its inconveniences for the court agencies concerned with the enthronement; for the ladies of the wardrobe, checking on the elaborate ceremonial gowns the Empress would wear, soon discovered that she had grown too big for them, and grown too big with child too. As the date drew near it became obvious that the enthronement and the accouchement were going to coincide. In fact, when Emperor Taisho departed for Kyoto on November 9, 1915, he left the Empress behind in labor. She gave birth a few days later to her fourth son and her first child for ten years. He was named Prince Mikasa.

The enthronement went on without her. And it might have provided some consolation to the dead Empress-Dowager to know that at least one of her family took part in the ceremonies that began on November 10, 1915. For the substitute chosen to accompany Emperor Taisho through the elaborate rituals was Taisho's half sister, the Empress-Dowager Haruko's indubitable daughter.

By the time his father was enthroned as Emperor of Japan, Hirohito was fourteen years old and what little boyhood freedom he had previously enjoyed was now at an end. Since for him childhood pranks and exhibitionistic displays had almost always been taboo, he found it less difficult than the average Japanese boy to settle down to the restrictions and circumspections expected of an adult. Among other things, General Nogi had schooled him hard to be austere and to toughen himself, physically and mentally, for the tasks he would face and the responsibilities he would have to shoulder when he succeeded his father. Count (now Mr.) Osanaga Kamroji, who is now head of the Meiji shrine in Tokyo, was a contemporary of Taisho and saw a good deal of Hirohito during these years. He remembers him as a frail-looking, earnest boy who never laughed and never, although he was always taking exercise, seemed to play. "Later on in life, after the Emperor was married," Mr. Kamroji

28

recalled,[5] "he relaxed and even revealed that he liked playing practical jokes, though until this time they had been performed only in his mind. I learned about this one day when I received as a gift from the Emperor a huge and most delicious-looking melon. It was very hot in Tokyo at the time, and I put the melon in the refrigerator to get cold, thinking that it would be most pleasantly thirst-quenching later. I must mention, by the way, that I am inordinately fond of melon—I even went on eating one rather than lose it during the Tokyo earthquake—and His Majesty knew this. Later that day the Emperor called me into audience with him and, after we had dealt with other matters, asked me with a slight smile what I thought of the beautiful melon he had sent me. I told him I was saving it up. He told me to repair at once to my quarters and eat it immediately. It was not until I got back, obediently took out the melon, and started to cut it, that I realized why he was so eager. I was holding up the joke! The melon was not a melon at all, but a pumpkin!"

But that was after he was married. "I remember," said Kamroji, "the day when I was out skiing with the Emperor and his bride one day. I am a poor skier and I am also a wicked old man with the worst collection of bad language in Tokyo. Once when I fell down I cursed my ineptitude with every single bad word I had ever learned. His Majesty came up to me and looked down at me, and he said, very sadly: 'Sensei [teacher], I wish I knew words like those.' But, of course, he was never allowed to mix with the boys or play the games that would have taught them to him." Kamroji shook his head. "I think perhaps that we were a little too austere. But as a boy, it hardened him, physically and mentally. I used to go on winter walks with him or be with him when he exercised. He was never allowed to wear anything but the thinnest clothing. On one occasion, on a visit to Nikko, his gym master, Mr. Naito, made him stand for fifteen minutes under one of the waterfalls as part of an endurance test. There was snow and ice all round, but he did not flinch and, when he was waved out of the water, came back to his tutor quite slowly and bowed before taking the towel." The aged high priest touched his leg beneath his gown and said: "I am eighty-five years old and I have never worn wool next to my skin in the coldest weather. Nor has the Emperor."

In April, 1914, Hirohito moved into the Takanawa Palace and a special

[5] In a conversation with the author.

29

department called the Togu-gogakumonsho was established for his education. To call the Takanawa a palace is something of a misnomer, for it was merely a pavilion in the grounds at Akasaka with no more facilities than the humblest Japanese house and certainly just as drafty in winter. There were two stewards (Baron Takanao Hatano and Baron Arata Hamao) attached to his household as well as a staff of servants, but except for the formal functions which it was now necessary for him to attend, they had little looking after to do. He rose at six each morning and, after kneeling before the Imperial shrine, ran around the grounds. Then he ate a bowl of brown, unpolished rice and went off to his lessons.

The Togu-gogakumonsho had as its president a more distinguished personage than even General Nogi had been. The Genro had appointed none other than Japan's most illustrious hero, Admiral Togo, victor of the famous sea battle with the Russian fleet, to teach the young Prince Imperial the virtues and duties of Bushido. He took his position as President of the Togu-gogakumonsho seriously and dutifully reported each year to the Emperor to read a report on the progress of his son—a subject in which, after 1915, Taisho was hardly capable of taking an interest. But Admiral Togo's heart was at sea with the Japanese fleet, and but for ill health he would have been there; and though he dutifully read military histories to Hirohito and painstakingly recounted, with humble apologies for immodesty, the great Battle of Tsushima by which he had won the Russo-Japanese War, there was little rapport between him and his pupil. No doubt he sensed in the young Prince an antipathy to war and military valor which was to grow increasingly obvious in the years to come. But he did provide one excitement which Hirohito was always to remember from his early youth; in October, 1915, Admiral Togo accompanied the Prince aboard a cruiser which sailed out of Tokyo Bay with the First Squadron on a gunnery exercise.

The target turned out to be an old battleship called the *Iki* and when Togo looked at it through his glasses, he started. As the shells began thudding home the prince noticed that the Admiral's excitement became intense and he could hardly prevent tears from running down his cheeks. It was not until later, when he asked about it, that Hirohito discovered that the *Iki* was none other than the old flagship of the Russian fleet, *Nicholas I* from which Togo's old adversary, Admiral Rojestvensky, had run up the flags X G H, meaning "I ask to negotiate," thus conceding defeat in the Battle of Tsushima.

For most of the next few years, however, Hirohito saw much more of his tutors than he did of Togo, and there was much to learn. Each morning from seven-thirty until six in the evening, with only a short break for lunch, he squatted on the tatami and gravely listened as his mentors droned on. There was Mr. Gugo Sugiura to teach him ethics, Mr. Kurakichi Shiratori to teach him history, Professor Kunitsugu Ishii to teach him mathematics, Mr. Naokata Yamazaki to teach him geography, Mr. Takuji Yoshii to teach him science, Professor Tadao Iijima to teach him Japanese and Chinese literature, Doctor Hirotaro Hattori to teach him natural history, Doctor Isaburo Wada to teach him physical science, Viscount Masanao Tsuchiya to teach him French, Judge Cho Shimazu to teach him law and economy, and Professor Seiichi Taki to teach him the history of fine arts.

The curriculum was a punishing one and the amount of study was too much even for one of Hirohito's grave and dogged temperament. He struggled as best he could with the multifarious subjects which had been set for him, and his nights were knitted up with homework. But he found some of the information he was given impossible to absorb, sometimes because of an inherent scepticism about the nature of the subject matter he was being taught, sometimes because of inadequacy in one or other of his tutors. At first he made little progress in the study of ethics, principally because the tutor chosen for him was a sort of Samurai-*manqué* whose idea of a moral character was a brassy admixture of Bushido and blind patriotism, and the example of the Forty-seven Ronin an ideal to be striven for.[6] To Prince Hirohito, still aching from the death of General Nogi, whose act of seppuku he considered to be both misguided and disastrous for Japan,[7] the windy calls to glory voiced by his tutor seemed to have little to do with the attainment of a good moral character and a philosophy of life. But this was before Mr. Sugiura, a more sophisticated

[6] The Forty-seven Ronin, heroes of many a Japanese play and film, were a group of Samurai whose master was tricked at court by a rival daimyo and forced to commit seppuku. They vowed vengeance, but knowing that they were being watched spent years pretending to be misfits and debauchers. One sold his wife into prostitution, another sent his sister to be the wicked daimyo's concubine, all for the purpose of concealing the nature of the sacred mission of revenge. Finally, they trapped their victim and ordered him to kill himself. When he refused they cut off his head, placed it on their master's grave, and later fell together on their swords in a final gesture of union with their dead master, having cleansed his memory.

[7] Information from a fellow pupil who does not wish to be identified.

31

tutor, with a blander manner, took over. Mr. Sugiura proved to be much more than a teacher of ethics in the days to come.

But this was far from being the end of Hirohito's troubles.

His progress in French was hindered by the fact that Viscount Tsuchiya, though he spoke the language reasonably well, was always too timid to ask his pupil any questions or reprimand him when he made mistakes. In later life it did not help the relationship between the two of them when Hirohito discovered that his younger brother, Chichibu, spoke both English and French fluently and used his accomplishment in Hirohito's presence.

But it was about history that the young Prince clashed most seriously and fundamentally with his instructors, and it gave his advisers their first hint that the uncommunicative and acquiescent young Prince might yet prove to be not quite as amenable an Emperor as they hoped. Professor Shiratori was a doctor of literature at Tokyo University and thus might have been expected to give his young charge a broad, sober and factual view of Japanese history. He was, unfortunately, a fundamentalist. He believed in the sun goddess Amaterasu just as fervently as a Plymouth Brethren believes in Adam and Eve and Jonah and the whale, and the daily lessons were devoted to a recitation of the fabulous adventures of her descendants, of whom, of course, Hirohito was one. Word was soon conveyed to General Togo by the shocked professor that the Prince was a sceptic and had expressed doubts (admittedly polite) in the divine origin of his family, during which he suggested that many of the details of the descent were biologically unsound and most of the adventures were physically impossible. Thirty years later, when asked to make a public denial of his divinity, Hirohito is said to have asked why such a declaration should be necessary, since the world beyond Japan had never believed that he was divine. But he later acknowledged that the denial was necessary, and confessed to having been a lifelong sceptic so far as his divinity was concerned. It was no use General Togo transmitting the news of Hirohito's apostasy to the Emperor, for he was in no mental condition to receive it. Instead Prince Saionji was called in to reason with the young Prince, and no better instrument could have been chosen to strengthen Hirohito's scepticism. For this particular Genro believed as little as did the Prince in the divinity of the Imperial House. He could, had he wished, have produced just as valid a lineage as Taisho back to the Imperial beginnings and might easily have made his own claim to the

32

throne. Not that he would have thought of doing so, for he was dedicated to the service of Japan and the Emperor and would not have dreamed of upsetting either. But he was ill-suited to persuade a doubting prince to believe in fairy tales, for his own family history had taught him the foolishness of it. True, he came from one of the most ancient and noble families in Japan, no upstart peer like some of the new barons and viscounts, but a member of a Kuge aristocracy which had been associated for generations with the ancient Imperial Court at Kyoto and spurned the shoguns in Edo. His family tree, too, showed that he was descended from one of the gods of the Japanese pantheon, even if he had not sprung from the belly of the Sun Goddess herself. But like Hirohito's, his beginnings had started in the clouds of myth and had been continued by convenient adoptions. The peculiarity of Saionji's line was that, like the hero of the old folk song, his father had been a bachelor and so had most of his forebears. The family had specialized in being unmarried if not exactly celibate. It enabled each head of the family to adopt the children most suited to carry on the line, and it had not always been a bastard child who was chosen as son and heir; the by-blow had often been usurped by a vague cousin or other likely lad with the qualities the Saionji family believed in. These were not usually martial, either. They were a deeply patriotic family but believed that the soul of Japan could best be kept alive by the pen rather than the sword.

It was not likely that such a refined and worldly distillation of the spirit of old Japan would be likely to influence Hirohito to accept a set of crude and bawdy fables as the gospel truth about his own family or the history of his country. But Saionji was also a man who did not believe in stirring up controversy where it could be avoided. There was no reason why the young Prince should believe in his own divinity, so long as he did not try to persuade the people that he was merely a simple mortal. The myth was convenient and must be sustained. The Emperor was divine, superhuman, a God of the Sun, a Son of Heaven—they were convenient symbols for the Japanese masses to rally round, for schoolchildren to worship, for soldiers to die for. That, Saionji told the Prince, he must never deny for it would deprive simple believers of their faith. As for his own dilemma . . . why, he suggested mildly, did the Prince not abandon the study of history for the time being? It was a complicated and controversial subject anyway, and the further he pursued it, the more likely was he to become dangerously involved in politics. Perhaps there was some other subject

33

for which the Prince could summon up rather more enthusiasm, and he breathed a sigh of relief when Hirohito replied that he was very keen on collecting butterflies and wild flowers and studying fungi. Henceforward his history sessions were confined to harmless readings about court life among the Fujiwaras, and the natural history lessons were much increased.

Thereafter, Hirohito saw much of Dr. Hirotaro Hattori, his natural history tutor. They spent many enjoyable hours together climbing the hills behind Hayama, Nikko and Karuizawa collecting specimens for subsequent study in the little laboratory which was established for their use in the Takanawa Palace. When the Prince once or twice complained that the retinue of officials who accompanied them on their expeditions distracted his mind, Hattori suggested that perhaps the Prince might find equally fascinating specimens at sea and less interruption from the retinue, especially if the boat was small.

So began an absorbing interest by the Prince in marine biology, and a life-long friendship between Hirohito and Hattori which has continued to this day.[8] Two pearl divers were brought from Toba—a young man and his wife—and they were installed in a small house on the shores of Sagami not far from Hayama. Once a week, when Hirohito went to Hayama to pay a formal visit to his mother and his sick father, the boat was prepared and Hattori, Hirohito and the pearl divers set off from the shore into the waters of Sagami Bay for four or five hours of busy and blissful fishing for specimens. They were some of the happiest hours of the young Prince's life. The setting was a beautiful one—the smoking volcanic island of Mihara on one horizon, the floating white peak of Mount Fuji on the other, the green waters in between.

It was not long before Hirohito was sliding over the side with the naked young pearl divers and being led by the hand to the rocky depths to find treasures for himself. It was soon apparent that he was a born swimmer with spectacular breath control, and he learned to manipulate the hazards of the seabed with eel-like efficiency.

On dry land, however, different skills were necessary to avoid the obstacles that were looming large in his life at court, and just before his seventeenth birthday he stumbled against the first of them.

[8] As I write (1965) it is reported in the Japanese press that Dr. Hattori has just retired from the post of "tutor to the Emperor in biology" at the age of 89.

Chapter Three

For a few months in 1914 and 1915, the Emperor Taisho had been sane and reasonable, but the taxing duties of the enthronement ceremonials were too much for him. When he arrived back in Tokyo after having performed his devotions to his ancestors at the shrines of Ise, the imps invaded his head again and began prodding. The whisper soon spread through court and diplomatic circles that the Emperor had become more temperamental and eccentric than ever. He fell off his horse at parades or whipped soldiers he was inspecting (alternatively, on one occasion, he suddenly embraced a young officer). His advisers began the gradual retirement from public life which ended with a tragicomic farewell appearance. He rolled up the prepared speech he was supposed to read to the assembled members of the Diet and used it as a telescope through which he owlishly observed them. Could it have been a last gesture of derision rather than a manifestation of insanity? The members of the Diet at the time were certainly not worthy of much respect, since they were little more than a rubber stamp for the decisions of the Genro. But Taisho's contempt for them was interpreted as the final stage in his disintegration. Thereafter he was retired to the palace on the beach at Hayama and his household put under the control of the Empress, who treated him not unkindly and catered to his whims to the last.

So began Hirohito's emergence as the royal figure upon whom the limelight increasingly fell, as his father was drawn back into the shadows. On November 3, 1916, his picture appeared in all the Japanese news-

35

papers in the uniform of a naval captain, together with the official announcement from the Imperial Palace that he had been installed as Crown Prince. He was fifteen and a half years old. He was tall for a Japanese and for his age (five feet six) and not unhandsome, even if his glasses were thick and his sight myopic. The Imperial Household Agency leaked the news to the newspapers that he liked tennis—though it never mentioned with whom—and his favorite foreign book was Aesop's Fables.[1] He was also said to have a favorite poem:

> The light of the Sun
> And Moon
> Withholds no favors;
> They shine equally
> Upon all.

There was no mention of any plans to get him married, though there was much unofficial gossip about it, and even more activity behind the scenes. From the point of view of the Genro, the elder statesmen, the sooner the young Prince Imperial had a consort and children, the better it would be for the stability of Japan. They detected signs in the Prince of a grave restlessness very different from the youthful ebullience which they had expected and could easily have managed. Hirohito was no rebel. Unlike Chichibu, his younger brother, he would never go overboard for socialism or go mad over Western ragtime music or collect pictures of London stage stars. At the time of the death of General Nogi, Taisho had realized, in a moment of clarity, what distress the faithful fanatic's gesture might have caused his son and heir, and his anodyne for the pain was to send to Hirohito—who was eleven at the time—a young concubine from his own court with instructions to comfort him. It is a measure of the young Prince's difference from all other Japanese of his age—including his brothers and fellow pupils—that he alone was totally ignorant of the full significance of her mission, though not necessarily shocked by the subsequent demonstrations of sympathy.

But the danger to the Genro, who had grown pleasantly accustomed by

[1] He revealed later that the one which made him laugh most was the fable called "The Man and his Two Wives," of a certain husband with a young and gay spouse and an old and grave one. The first pulled out his white hairs when she saw them so that he should appear young, the second pulled out his black hairs so that he should appear no older than she. In the end, they made the poor man quite bald.

Taisho's madness to the continuous exercise of power, was that Hirohito's sporadic outbreaks of revolt against the established pattern of Imperial education seemed to be neither reckless nor feckless, but well thought out, the result of deep and considered decisions, and therefore the mental processes of someone with his own ideas of the functions of power. Was the shy, quiet, incommunicative Prince another Meiji silently engorging knowledge and experience, or could he be fitted into Taisho's clothes?

Not for the first time, either in Japan or elsewhere, the men behind the throne decided that a wife might provide the distraction calculated to take the edge off Hirohito's ambitions, real or imagined. Prince Yamagata, as the most powerful of the Genro, had no doubt from what source the bride of the Emperor-to-be would spring. She would be a daughter of one of the five Kuge (Court noble) families which had, for generations, provided the consorts of the emperors of Japan, and since he himself was a Choshu, she would naturally be the offspring of a member of that clan. His favorite was a clever and strong-willed young princess named Asa, the daughter of Prince Ichijo, whose family had in previous generations provided several Empresses of Japan. There was also a young daughter of Prince Nashimoto, who had become friends with Hirohito many years previously during a holiday at Karuizawa, and had grown up to be an extremely beautiful girl—and a Choshu, of course.

There were other candidates from the eligible families, and Prince Yamagata had no doubt whatsoever that one of them would fill the necessary requirements. It was not, of course, a question of satisfying the Crown Prince, for it was presumed that he would accept the choice made by his advisers. Even the Emperor Meiji had taken the bride chosen for him by his court officials, and Taisho had not even seen Sadako before their betrothal was announced.

He was astonished, therefore, if not yet alarmed, when he heard a rumor from the court that Viscount Osanari Ogasawara, the Secretary of the Togu-gogakumonsho,[2] had procured a number of photographs of all the eligible girls and had allowed the Crown Prince to study them. He began to be concerned when he learned that the Empress had come back to Tokyo from Hayama in order to entertain the eligibles at tea in the Imperial Palace, and Hirohito, it was said, had been given opportunities of studying them from a secret vantage point. He was aroused at last when

[2] Imperial Palace School.

he discovered that the Empress and Professor Gugo Sugiura, the Crown Prince's ethics master and confidant, had been conferring together. The Empress, of an obscure if noble family, had no particular liking for the Choshus and no love at all for Prince Yamagata, whose cavalier treatment of her sick husband she had always resented. Professor Sugiura considered the two most eligible Choshu consorts to be far too lacking in sympathy and understanding to suit his charge. And they had found an unexpected ally in the Lord Privy Seal, Count Makino, who was ambitious to break Prince Yamagata's hold on the power behind the throne, was moreover a Satsuma, and had a relative with a suitable daughter and an urgent need of royal patronage.

To the fury of Yamagata and to the surprise of practically everyone else, it was to this young, fifteen-year-old girl that the Crown Prince's engagement was announced on February 4, 1918.

Princess Nagako was the eldest daughter of Prince Kuniyoshi Kuni, one of the most amiable rascals in the Japanese aristocracy. His father, Prince Fushimi, was an old adversary of the Choshu clan, having backed the wrong side at the time of the Meiji Restoration. Meiji had forgiven him but the Choshus had not. His son, Prince Kuni, had not by any means mollified them by marrying a princess of the Satsuma clan— Nagako's mother. Not that he confined the procreation of his progeny to one woman. He and his father had been willing to accept Meiji's edict about monogamy but had never let it interfere with their extramarital activities, from which Kuniyoshi had produced no less than eighteen sisters and brothers for Nagako, only three of them by her mother.

It made for a happy household but also a hungry one. Prince Kuniyoshi was constantly short of money, and far too busy in other directions to participate in Japan's wartime business boom. He lived on the profits from a small estate, plus loans from friends and relatives, and with these he had managed to give Nagako an education in the girls' section of the Gakushuin (the Peers' School), where her sparrow brightness and shrewdness in class had first caught the attention of Professor Sugiura. He had engineered a meeting between her and the Crown Prince and not failed to see that Hirohito was attracted by her inherent simplicity of manner. From that moment on he had worked hard to enlist the aid of powerful influences at court who, like Sugiura himself, wished to see the influence of Yamagata if not of the Choshus broken.

Nagako learned the nature of her future and the identity of her future spouse one afternoon a month before the formal announcement, when she emerged from the Gakushuin and found her father awaiting her in a carriage instead of the jinrikshaw which usually took her home to Shibuya. That evening she met her fiancé formally at the Imperial Palace and they were allowed to wander in the grounds together for half an hour, no romantic idyll, since it had rained shortly before and the paths were muddy and Nagako was terrified that the puddles would rise above the level of her wooden geta and dirty her spotless white socks. They met again three weeks later for a series of official betrothal photographs which were, however, not issued at the time.

Thereafter, Nagako saw her husband-to-be only nine times in the next seven years, and never once alone. It was the beginning of the unhappiest period of her life, not even relieved by a certainty that the outcome of it would be happy.

Not that she had any doubts at the beginning. The preliminaries to the engagement had been a series of medical examinations of a nature which would never have been allowed had she already been a member of the royal family. Doctors took her pulse and her blood count, sounded her chest, tapped her head, fingered her body and measured her hips. They finally pronounced her to be what she undoubtedly was, a bouncingly healthy girl eminently fit to be the receptacle for royal babies.

Once these preliminaries were over, she moved back to the bosom of her family. But not to the same happy-go-lucky life. No longer was she allowed to go each day to the Gakushuin, and no longer was she allowed to share games and secrets with her playmates. As the future spouse of the Crown Prince, she was moved into a sort of private incubator from which a royal bride would be hatched. Prince Kuniyoshi enthusiastically embarked on the superintendence of his daughter's transformation, dividing his time equally between her and his latest concubine. There was no lack of money in the household now, and the prince's quarters rang with girlish merriment, but not from Nagako. A special pavilion was built for her in a corner of the grounds and there she studied, under a series of seventeen different tutors, for her role as a future Empress. She had two former schoolmates to keep her company, and there were annual trips to Karuizawa in the summer and Kyoto at New Year's. But otherwise it was the hard grinding study of "suitable subjects" which kept her pinned to the tatami before her masters and mistresses each day, and the fact that the subjects were such congenial ones as ikebana, the tea ceremony, calligraphy, Chinese and Japanese classics, deportment, dancing, singing and playing the samisen did not make the discipline any easier. Mrs. Sugimoto has given a picture of the ordeals of learning for a well-born Japanese girl in her book, *A Daughter of the Samurai*, when she writes:

"Throughout my two-hour lesson he [my tutor] never moved the slightest fraction of an inch except for his hands and his lips. And I sat before him on the tatami in an equally correct and unchanging position. Once I moved. It was in the midst of a lesson. For some reason I was restless and swayed my body slightly, allowing my folded knee to slip a trifle from the proper angle. The faintest shade of surprise crossed my instructor's face; then very quietly he closed his book, saying gently but with a stern air: 'Little Miss, it is evident that your mental attitude today is not suited for study. You should retire to your room and meditate.' My little heart was almost killed with shame. There was nothing I could do. I humbly bowed to the picture of Confucius and then to my teacher, and, backing respectfully from the room, I slowly went to my father to report as I always did, at the close of my lesson. Father was surprised, as the time was not yet up, and his unconscious remark, 'How quickly you have done your work!' was like a death knell. The memory of that moment hurts like a bruise to this very day."[3]

It was not possible to deflate the natural exuberance of the young bride-to-be for very long: she had, in fact, many of the qualities of her future mother-in-law, the Empress—strength of character, solid good sense and instinctive shrewdness—plus a bubbling sense of humor which did not allow her to take even her setbacks too seriously for too long. But there were crises approaching which would all but break even Nagako's indomitable spirit.

After the official announcement of the Crown Prince's betrothal everyone who knew him waited breathlessly to see what Prince Yamagata would do. The failure to consult him in the choice of Hirohito's bride, together with the selection of a daughter of the Satsumas, was much more than a personal rebuff. It was a challenge to his own influence as an arbiter of government policies, it was an insult to his clan, the Choshus, which had always presumed that they would provide the royal bride, and it was a blow to the prestige of the Army as well as a fillip to the Navy.

[3] Etsu Inagaki Sugimoto, *A Daughter of the Samurai*, 1926.

For, of course, the Choshus still controlled the Army, whereas the Satsumas still ruled the sea.

Prince Kuniyoshi and his allies at the Imperial Palace were not by any means relieved of certain anxieties when Prince Yamagata sent formal and frigid felicitations, and joined with Prince Saionji and the Prime Minister, Hara, in wishing the young couple well. The semipurdah into which Nagako retired after the official announcement was not simply to keep her in a condition of concentrated training for her marriage; it was also to protect her from any dangers which might threaten her. No one suggested that Yamagata, fierce old autocrat though he might be (he was eighty-one in 1916), would resort to the stratagems of his youth in dealing with the situation. In those days, at the court in Kyoto, a princess carrying a child which might alter the succession only too often tripped on an unexpected obstacle, and an inconvenient wife or bride-to-be had been known to die unexpectedly of the colic. But this was 1916, and such schemings were a thing of the past. Or so everyone hoped. But just in case, Nagako was guarded night and day and all her food was tasted.

As the months passed, however, and the old Prince gave no sign of overt hostility toward the match, tension relaxed. Both Nagako and Hirohito pressed on with their studies, while their relatives and advisers discussed the official announcement of the engagement and the date of the marriage. The crisis appeared to be over and the humiliated Yamagata under control.

He was not. He was simply waiting for the right moment to retaliate, the right excuse for intervention; and when he found it, it was neither with booby traps nor phials of poison that he attacked Nagako, but with something much more subtle—an article in a magazine.

The article appeared in a medical journal published in Tokyo in 1920. Whether it was deliberately "planted" in the journal by Yamagata will never be known, though the timing of its appearance and the nature of its subject would suggest that it was hardly fortuitous. For the article, written by a doctor specializing in heredity, dealt at some length with color blindness in the Shimazu family and set out to show that it was a weakness passed from generation to generation in the family. Princess Nagako was a member of the Shimazu line on her mother's side.

By a coincidence as fortuitous as the first, it so happened that the article was read by Doctor Hirai, who had formerly been surgeon-general to the Imperial Army and was now (what else?) family doctor to Prince

41

Yamagata. He drew the attention of the Prince to the article and together they "discussed the general principles of hereditary diseases," to use Hirai's own subsequent words. Prince Yamagata "saw his duty at once, and called a conference of leading Japanese medical specialists, including the vice president of Tokyo Imperial University." He also summoned Baron Nakamura, Minister of the Imperial Household and the premier, Mr. Hara. They were shown the results of a discussion among the medical men, Mendelians all, which confirmed the color blindness in the Shimazus and the likelihood of its transmission through the generations.

Prince Yamagata faced his two kinsmen, Nakamura and Hara (both of them were Choshus) with an appropriate expression of sorrow on his face. It grieved him, he said, that he should have to be the medium through which the secret of the Shimazu family's congenital weakness should have been revealed. He had earnestly hoped that the facts as they were originally reported would prove groundless. He was especially sorry that they had been confirmed since they endangered the future happiness of Princess Nagako. She was a dear child of whom he was extremely fond; it was he who had acted as her protégée in her early days at court, bringing her to the attention (and ultimately into the affectionate regard) of the Empress-Dowager and the Empress; and no one had been gladder when the news of her betrothal to the Crown Prince was announced. But what was a young girl's happiness measured against the security of the Imperial line? He had his duty to do on behalf of his Emperor and Japan.[4]

Prime Minister Hara asked what the Prince proposed to do. He was most anxious to avoid a public scandal. At all costs any suggestion that the Imperial family had made a mistake must be avoided, and no word of the contretemps which had now developed must be allowed to leak out to the public.

Prince Yamagata had a simple solution—or so it seemed at the time. He had, he said, appealed to Prince Kuniyoshi's sense of patriotism. He had written to him and enclosed a report from the doctors about the color blindness of the Shimazus. He had asked him, in the circumstances, to think of his Emperor and his country and to cancel the engagement for the sake of the preservation of a flawless Imperial line. To reinforce his argument, he sent Kuniyoshi's own father, Prince Fushimi, to see him,

[4] Summary of the entry in the diary of a former court official who does not wish to be quoted.

having first persuaded the old man that there would be a scandal if he did not keep his son's imperial ambitions in check.

Kuni was not impressed. He regarded the charge of color blindness as a Choshu pretext to get the betrothal annulled for purely dynastic reasons, and he quickly made it clear that he would fight to the bitter end to protect his own interests and those of his daughter. When his own father upbraided him for lack of humility and sincerity, he turned upon him and replied:

"Do you come from the Empress? Have you brought a message from the throne? Do they wish the engagement to be cancelled? Is this what Yamagata has arranged?"

When the old man fumbled for something to say (for, of course, he was in no position to answer), Kuniyoshi went on:

"It was not I who gave my daughter to the Crown Prince. It was the Royal Household which asked for her. It is they who must annul the arrangement. And I warn you, if they do, I will take my dagger and I shall kill Nagako, after which I shall commit seppuku for the insult which has been done to my family and my line."

Whether the Prince intended to kill himself and his daughter is questionable. Certainly he was determined to fight first before taking any step to destroy himself, and though the Throne for a time preserved a noncommittal silence, he rallied allies who were not afraid to make their opinions heard. One of them was Professor Sugiura, the Crown Prince's tutor in ethics, who had latterly been coaching Princess Nagako in the same subject. At the height of the agitation for the rupture of the betrothal arrangements, Prince Kuniyoshi appealed to him for his opinion. It seems a little bizarre that a professor of Oriental ethics should have been asked for his opinion on a question of eugenics, but no more so than the identity of some of the opinions being canvassed on the other side. After cogitating for a few days, Sugiura not only stated that color blindness in a distant relative was far from being justification for the cancellation of Nagako's engagement; he also announced his resignation from the faculty of the Gakushuin if the engagement should be cancelled. "What is the use of teaching ethics," he stated, "if such an event as a royal engagement, based on mutual confidence, can be broken?"

It was not broken—yet. Kuniyoshi was determined that it should not be, and was prepared to summon every possible ally to his aid. And use every possible stratagem.

43

First of all he sat down to write a letter to the Emperor (well knowing, of course, that it would be read by the Empress first). He enclosed with it a series of doctors' reports about the state of his daughter's health and the condition of himself and his wife. After which he went on:

"I need not stress that I took every precaution to test the state of health of my daughter and my family before accepting the royal offer. So far as color blindness is concerned, I came to the conclusion that the trait is virtually nonexistent. When I found that the papers brought to my attention by the minister of the Imperial Household through Prince Fushimi were concerned with the problem of color blindness, and its transmissibility, I could not help suspecting that the papers were an indirect recommendation that we cancel our daughter's engagement. On reflection, however, the papers seemed to suggest a revision of the old conscription law designed to conform to new medical findings. On further reflection the papers seemed to be the reflection of various doctors' opinions on the question of color blindness in answer to the Imperial inquiry. I am now quite at a loss as to how to interpret the meaning of the papers. Only two situations would move me to cancel my daughter's engagement to the Crown Prince: first, if Their Majesties the Emperor and the Empress or the Crown Prince himself deemed it better to do so, or, second, if I were sure that the marriage would bring weakness to the Imperial line. Herewith Your Majesty will find a complete set of scientific reports about the nature of the color blindness in our family and its transmissibility. I pray that Your Majesty give me the privilege of his advice and I pray for Your guidance." [5]

The letter was circulated to officials at the Imperial Palace and thus reached Minister Nakamura, who at once sent copies to Premier Hara and Prince Yamagata. The Prime Minister told his colleagues in the Cabinet that he considered the letter to be a shocking piece of bad form, unworthy of a prince. At the same time he counseled his colleagues to secrecy and took steps to keep the controversy out of the newspapers, for he knew on which side the populace would be if the quarrel became public, and it was certainly not the one on which he had ranged himself. As for Prince Yamagata, he took his pen and sat down on December 16, 1920, to compose a long letter [6] in which he said, in typically magisterial prose:

[5] Papers in the National Archives, Washington.
[6] Family sources confirm that the scroll was nearly four meters long.

44

"Of course Prince Kuniyoshi is right in insisting that the engagement should be adhered to once entered into. But it should not be forgotten that the engagement was arranged, so to speak, behind our back. If we had been advised of the negotiations, we would have been able to offer our humble point of view beforehand. We are deeply distressed at the way in which things have turned out. I feel it my duty, however, to point out in the accompanying paper that there are several contradictions in the so-called scientific report which Prince Kuniyoshi has sent. Are these contradictions due to careless copying or to faulty investigating methods? As this is a most important question, may I suggest that you look into the matter again? We would appreciate it if you would inform us of the name of the doctor who carried out the investigation as well as that of the official who received the information about the hereditary traits of your family. In the last part of your memorandum you say that if you were convinced that the marriage would be to the detriment of the Imperial family you would gladly cancel your daughter's engagement to the Crown Prince. That is the best witness to your loyalty to the Imperial family and the cancellation of the engagement would certainly bring public applause. Your reconsideration is sincerely urged."[7]

But Prince Kuniyoshi would not budge. How could he? His whole future, financial and social, was now hitched to the wagon of an Imperial marriage. The Choshus were not slow to realize that money was an important consideration and Prince Fushimi was once more engaged to point out that the Kuniyoshi family would suffer no hardship if they now backed down. But this was not enough. Kuni was now enraged by the machinations of his adversaries and announced that his giri, his honor, was involved in the contretemps. He must win or he would be disgraced forever and would be forced to wipe out the humiliation by an act of immolation. In this resolve he was now joined by Professor Sugiura, who also let it be known that he would commit seppuku if the engagement were broken.

No one, of course, thought of consulting the two people whose lives would be so momentously affected by the controversy which was now raging. Hirohito knew what was going on but was never asked for his advice or opinion. Nagako was not even told about it; not by her family, at least, though she undoubtedly learned of it from gossiping with her

[7] Papers in the National Archives, Washington.

45

servants. But both of them were helpless to affect the outcome, except that Hirohito—with typical mildness—continued to remind his stewards that he preferred Nagako to all other candidates and would be most reluctant to accept an alternative.

Professor Sugiura was not so helpless, and now that his own giri was so deeply involved he was determined to use every stratagem to ensure that the engagement was confirmed, if only to humiliate Prince Yamagata. Once upon a time Sugiura had been Yamagata's protégé and his path to professional eminence had often, in earlier years, been smoothed by Choshu influence. Now former patron and protégé had become bitter enemies, less concerned now with an Imperial betrothal than with a question of personal "face."

Sugiura had resigned his position at the Gakushuin in December, 1920, and to those old pupils or professorial colleagues who saw the official announcement and wrote to ask him why, he replied guardedly, hinting that there was a plot against the royal marriage and mentioning his determination to commit seppuku if it did not take place. At once his friends and supporters flocked to Tokyo to urge him to reconsider his decision; and there, once they heard all the details of the Yamagata "plot," rallied behind him in his determination to "outwit the evil men behind the throne." Among these adherents was a mild-looking, bespectacled gentleman named Mitsuru Toyama.

Toyama, whose name will appear several times more in this story, was possibly the most feared man in Japan. He was the nation's most pervervid patriot and also a super-gangster. He organized and operated the most powerful and effective secret society in the land, the Kokuryu-kai, sometimes known as the Black Dragon Society.[8] He controlled a vast network of bullies who, under the guise of keeping Japan "pure" and her prestige high, were prepared to carry out any dirty work from breaking up labor strikes to assassinating politicians. He had many friends (or, at least, willing tools) in high places, and he had only one answer to anyone who, even by inference, insulted the divinity and infallibility of the Emperor—death.

Toyama interfered in the dispute over the royal engagement for two reasons. He believed that, by trying to get the betrothal annulled,

[8] "Kokuryu-kai (kai means society) is thought of as the Amur Society in Japan, though the same ideographs also translate as Black Dragon—the rather more sinister name adopted outside Japan.

46

Yamagata had "insulted" the Emperor who had already agreed to it. He also knew that Yamagata was the prime mover behind a scheme for sending the Crown Prince on a trip abroad, to Britain and Europe. This, to the Black Dragon chief, was anathema. He had always been an enemy of the white races; he believed that an Emperor of Japan should never venture beyond the sacred frontiers of his own country; and he felt that the tour being organized by Yamagata "to enlighten the Crown Prince and broaden his mind" would, in fact, demean him by forcing him to associate with lesser breeds incapable of appreciating the inherent superiority of the Japanese.

When he heard that Prince Yamagata's latest move in his campaign against the marriage was to speed up the Crown Prince's journey ("I can work much more effectively when he is out of the way," the Prince is reported to have said), Toyama rushed to Sugiura and enlisted himself as his ally. Sugiura was not unwilling to accept him. If the Crown Prince were allowed to leave the shores of Japan without any official confirmation of the engagement, everything might well be lost, for all the precautions in the world could easily fail to ensure Nagako's safety. So all through January the leader of the Black Dragon Society flitted from meetings with Sugiura and Prince Kuniyoshi to conferences with his shadowy henchmen.

If Prince Yamagata, not an easy man to frighten, was unmoved by the conspiratorial goings-on, the government certainly was. Prime Minister Hara [9] nervously read reports from his "thought police" and began to wish that he had never heard of color blindness. The police agents (not a few of whom were members of the Black Dragon Society themselves) reported that sinister plans were about to be put into operation. The silence in the newspapers was abruptly broken not by any factual details of the controversy but by a rash of articles mentioning "a delicate situation" which had arisen "between the Imperial family and the Minister of the Imperial Household." The Minister was Yamagata's henchman, Baron Nakamura, and the inference was that he had dared to question a decision of the royal family—a grave matter indeed in Japan.

There was also a spate of articles attacking the Crown Prince's visit to Europe. Some wrote that it was "unseemly" for the heir to the throne to leave while his father was ill. Others stressed the dangers he might

---

[9] Who was assassinated by secret-society killers later that year.

face from Japan's enemies, especially roving Korean assassins. Yet others maintained that to allow the Crown Prince to visit Occidental countries would be to lay him open to ridicule. ("If he eats and drinks like a true Japanese,[10] they will not understand and laugh at him," one article said.)

All these articles had the effect desired by Toyama of arousing speculation in the country and fraying the nerves of the government. Premier Hara had his own bodyguard doubled and put a horde of police around Prince Yamagata's mansion at Odawara, until that arrogant old man drove them away with his stick, angrily denying that he needed protection. Thereafter, a number of his fellow clansmen took turns to keep watch on the old man's safety, but from a discreet distance. They reported that strange prowlers had been seen around the mansion but that, so far, no one had tried to break into the grounds.

Typically enough, the Black Dragon leader reserved his most effective form of blackmail for February 11, 1921. February 11th is National Foundation Day, anniversary of the birth of the Emperor Jimmu in Japan. Jimmu was Japan's first Emperor and, until all such patriotic celebrations were abolished by General MacArthur, his day was observed with great ceremonial and mass visits to the Shinto shrines to pray for the aggrandizement of Japan. Toyama chose it as the occasion to send his henchmen through the swarming crowds handing out pamphlets asking the people's blessing on the betrothal of the Crown Prince and Nagako and bitterly denouncing those who were trying to wreck it. So that the populace should have no doubt whatsoever who were the wreckers, he had bands of students parade through the wet streets—it was raining—crying "Death to Yamagata!" and "Nakamura insults the Emperor!"

The response to the agitation came more rapidly than even Prince Kuniyoshi could have hoped for. Prime Minister Hara called Nakamura to an urgent conference at which he dwelt at length on the dangers of the situation both to individuals and to the government. At his suggestion Nakamura hurried back to the Imperial Palace—where the Emperor was temporarily in residence for Empire Day—and asked for an immedi-

[10] Japanese occasionally slurp appreciatively as they drink and belch after eating, but rarely do so in the presence of foreigners—although one Court official and one famous industrialist always did so when taking tea with the author, who returned the compliment.

ate audience. When he was shown into the royal presence he flung himself down in front of Taisho and said:

"I must ask abysmal pardon for the failure of the Imperial Household Agency in omitting to discover that there is color blindness in the family of Princess Nagako. But now it is generally known, what is your Imperial Majesty's wish?"

There was a heavy silence. Nakamura grovelled on the tatami and waited. Then he heard whispering and shuffling, after which silence descended again. Presently he looked up and saw Taisho staring vacantly ahead. He turned to the Empress, who was watching him with a gleam of humor in her keen brown eyes. To her now he started to repeat himself. But he was interrupted. For suddenly the Emperor spoke, in a high, constrained, detached voice.

"I hear," he said, "that even science is fallible."

Silence again. Was this the end of the audience? Nakamura looked up and saw the Empress gesturing for him to go. He crawled out, bowing. An hour later he was back with Hara at Odawara to report to Prince Yamagata. They did not need to tell him. The old Prince knew that the day was lost. But he listened to them while they excused themselves, producing evidence that his life was in danger. Finally he looked at his colleagues and said, frigidly:

"Could it possibly be, gentlemen, that you are equally worried for your own safety as you are for mine? If so, I must take cognizance of it. If protecting my own unworthy life will ensure the preservation of your so much more valuable persons, then I must give way. You may tell Prince Kuniyoshi that I withdraw my objections."

The battle was won. The same night the engagement of the Crown Prince and Princess Nagako was officially confirmed from the Imperial Palace. So was the resignation of Baron Nakamura as Minister of the Imperial Household. He had, said an announcement from the Home Office Police Bureau, withdrawn "because of his apprehensions over mistaken manifestations of public indignation toward him."

In a dispatch on February 11, 1921, to *The New York Times* and the London *Times,* the staff correspondent of the two newspapers also appeared to believe that it was "popular opinion" which was responsible for the successful suppression of Prince Yamagata's plot. A dispatch from the correspondent said:

"A very remarkable demonstration of the power of public opinion in

Japan is revealed in an announcement issued today by the Imperial Household and the Home Department to the effect that the betrothal of the Crown Prince with Princess Nagako would be publicly announced. This is the official reply to the sudden outburst of public indignation against the intrigues in powerful political quarters aiming at breaking off the betrothal. Signs of opposition to the intriguers have long been apparent. Yesterday [February 11 in Japan is February 12th in America and Britain], a great national holiday, was chosen by the agitators for a dramatic call to the people. Hundreds of thousands of handbills were distributed from motor cars, calling on the people to offer prayers to the spirit of departed Emperors, notably to appeal to the spirit of the Emperor Meiji. Though the handbills were couched in guarded language, according to custom in all matters affecting the Imperial Family, the official announcements made plain the cause of the popular upheaval."

The dispatch went on:

"So effective was the sudden opening of the floodgates of public opinion that General Baron Nakamura, Minister of the Household, resigned, together with the Vice Minister. It is significant that a statement issued from the Home Office Police Bureau says that the resignations result from the fear of the consequence of popular indignation."

But, of course, popular indignation had had little to do with it, and the Black Dragon everything. What the Imperial Household Minister, Nakamura, was afraid of was an assassin from the Black Dragon Society, and what Premier Hara feared was a campaign directed by Toyama that would drive him and his cabinet from office.

On February 14th an official announcement from the Imperial Palace confirmed the engagement of the heir to the throne and Princess Nagako. At the same time the whole Imperial machine went into action to try to repair the damage to the Establishment which had been caused by the great controversy. Prince Yamagata offered to resign from all positions he held at the palace, but they were ostentatiously refused. No one wished to cause further humiliation to the old man now that he had been defeated. At the same time both Prince Kuniyoshi and Professor Sugiura, both more than satisfied with the outcome, withdrew their objections to the Crown Prince's forthcoming visit to Europe and went to work to persuade Toyama to join with them. He pretended to hesitate, but in fact did so only to mollify his more fanatic followers and to demonstrate his "serious concern for the welfare of the Imperial line." On February 20th

50

the Imperial Household Agency issued a statement to the press, saying:

"Reliable circles consider the court affair definitely closed with the official confirmation of the betrothal of the Crown Prince. The affair was restricted to matters touching on questions of blood and inheritance of the dynasty which vitally concerned the Japanese people. Although it is true politicians and mischief-makers tried to make it appear that the question at issue involved intrigue connected with the Choshu and Satsuma factions to obtain influence at Court, Government circles wish to say that such contention is groundless. Agitation for the postponement of the trip of the Crown Prince, which is continuing, arises from apprehension of danger to him abroad by Korean malcontents."

To take advantage of the euphoric atmosphere which had been created by the official confirmation of the engagement, it was thought better to get the Crown Prince off on his travels as speedily as possible. The British Government was astonished to receive a cable telling them that Hirohito would be coming a week early and would spend even longer in Britain than had previously been announced. There was a flurry of re-arrangements.

He sailed from Yokohama on March 3, 1921, on the first visit abroad ever made by the heir to the throne of Japan.[11] He was to be away for six months.

It is typical of the cold-blooded attitude of the Japanese toward marriage that not once during the blazing controversy did Hirohito visit his bride-to-be nor send her any words of comfort through what must have been painful months of doubt and distress.

Nor was she allowed to see him off when he sailed away. But Prince Kuniyoshi was there, and so was Professor Sugiura.

There is one ironic footnote to the great controversy. Throughout the whole affair, no one appears to have taken the trouble to find out whether Princess Nagako herself was color-blind. They would speedily have discovered that she was not. From early childhood she had been a keen painter, and by the time she was seventeen—when the great debate began—she had developed an excellent sense of color.

[11] Prince Yoshihito, his father, had not been made Crown Prince when he traveled abroad.

Chapter Four

At the only press conference he has ever given,[1] Hirohito was asked by a reporter if he could look back over his life and decide when he had been happiest. He replied, without hesitation:

"During my visit to England."

The Grand Tour of Europe which he undertook in 1921 could hardly have come at a better moment for the Crown Prince, and though he could not have guessed at the time that it would be the first and the last time he would ever be allowed to leave his own country, he embarked on every moment of it with a determination to enjoy himself—in his own particular way. All the circumstances combined to make it both an adventure and a relief. He was twenty years old. He had just completed seven years of arduous and often tedious study at the Gakushuin. He had been forced to sit back in silence and show no emotion while the men behind the throne attacked his future wife. The bloodless efficiency with which he had been schooled almost from birth had taught him to accept the fussy life of formality and protocol which was lived at Court, but during recent months even he had found the meticulous routines irksome. On the night of March 3, 1921, the 12,000-ton battleship *Katori* anchored three miles out from Hayama while its attendant destroyers retired further out to sea. In his admiral's uniform, Hirohito came up on deck and was left there alone by his entourage, who dis-

[1] In 1946, to correspondents attached to General MacArthur's headquarters in Tokyo.

52

appeared through the companionway. The Crown Prince stared through the darkness and then bowed low toward the land, toward the spot on the Hayama shore where his father, the Emperor, was restlessly eking out the winter at his beach palace.

For five minutes he continued to bow. Then he turned, there was a signal from the bridge, and the *Katori* began to push her way through the Inland Sea toward Hong Kong. The period of release had begun.

"March 3rd will probably be regarded," wrote the *Times* of London in a leader printed on that date, "as one of the most memorable days in the history of Japan as today H. I. H. Prince Hirohito starts his journey from Yokohama to visit this country. Never before in the annals of Japan has the heir to the throne left his native shores, and the precedent thus created marks an epoch in the history of the most ancient dynasty in the world almost equal to the Restoration in 1867. One of the Crown Prince's greatest assets as heir to the throne of Japan is his striking resemblance both in person and character to his grandfather, the great Emperor Mutsuhito of the Meiji Era. This resemblance has been the subject of much comment during the last two or three years when, owing to the ill health of the Emperor, the Crown Prince often took his place at the reception of foreign ambassadors and other Court functions. It is related that many of the Court dignitaries were moved to tears by the striking resemblance of the Crown Prince's appearance and deportment to that of his grandfather."

It was true that the physical resemblance to Meiji was definitely there, though it was hardly remarkable in the circumstances, but otherwise there was little similarity between the Crown Prince and his illustrious grandfather. There was none of the pugnacity of Meiji's facial expression in Hirohito's rather diffident features, and he was not and gave no sign of ever becoming the womanizer and hard drinker that his grandfather was from his early twenties until his death. Two of his entourage, Count Yoshinori Futari and Mr. Setsuzo Sawada, kept a diary of the royal tour, which they prefaced with a description of the Crown Prince as they found him on the journey. "We found in him a prince worthy of our admiration and wholehearted devotion," they wrote. "His lofty and noble character, his manliness, his intellectual brilliance, his manifold interests, his sympathetic mentality, his wonderful memory, his fine sportsmanship, his most natural and unassuming attitude, his peace-loving disposition and charming demeanor, his strength of will, the happy union of all these fine qualities never elsewhere found together was revealed to us in full light. Thus we found in him a noble prince of whom the whole nation could well be proud. We found in him a most attractive prince whom we could serve well and whole-heartedly. We found in him a great prince whom the whole nation could well look upon as its leader in shaping the destiny of the country."

Perhaps the best summing up of Hirohito's character at this time can be given by saying that he would not have recognized the paragon described in the foregoing paragraph as referring to himself, and would have been embarrassed when he realized it. The diarists get nearer to the truth when, in a later entry, they detail a typical day in his life aboard ship, studying French and English in the morning, reading about the French Revolution and the reign of Queen Elizabeth in the evening, and relaxing at deck golf in the afternoons: "We note with interest and pleasure how our Prince manifests a rare sportsmanlike quality of being a good loser."

He bathed in the open-air swimming pool on the battleship's deck and conducted the ceremonies to mark the death of his ancestor, Emperor Jimmu. He had more immediate deaths to mourn a few days later when a tube in the boiler room of the *Kashima*, an accompanying warship, blew up and three of the stokers were killed.

"April 4. The *Kashima* and the *Katori* stopped at 8:30 P.M. and we witness the sad ceremony of the burial at sea of the three stokers who died at their posts. The flags were lowered to half-mast. The entire crew of both warships lined the sides as the bodies were offered to the deep. The prince made offerings in memory of the victims. April 7. It was only a few days ago that three stokers were killed by an explosion of a tube aboard the *Kashima*, and now a similar accident has happened aboard the *Katori*, resulting in injuries to four stokers, in the case of two to fatal effect. April 8. The squadron stopped once more to perform the funeral service. Both the princes again made offerings to the deceased.[2] The lives of both these men have been given in the service of their country. April 10. We sailed through the Red Sea near Aden. The sides of our ship, heated by the burning rays of the sun, makes it uncom-

[2] The Crown Prince was accompanied by his uncle, Prince Higashikuni.

fortable at night. More and more we are tempted to stay on deck at night."

But not Hirohito. "The Crown Prince retires regularly at 9:00 P.M. Moreover he never makes use of the electric fan fixed in his cabin."

On April 12 the Crown Prince and his staff, all clad in boiler suits, "visited the engine room. . . . In spite of the heat (over 130 degrees F.) the princes, covered with oil and perspiration, clambered up and down the hot iron ladders. They made inquiries concerning the whereabouts of the spot where the stokers had been scalded to death. This visit from Their Highnesses stimulated and encouraged the crew to an unimaginable extent."

Field Marshal Allenby, the conqueror of Jerusalem and Damascus in the First World War, gave a garden party in Cairo for the Crown Prince and the event was made for him, even if it spelt ruin for the ladies, when one of the biggest sandstorms of the year, a choking blackout of a haboob, descended on the British Embassy grounds. He liked the chaos which resulted. At Malta he visited the theater for the first time in his life, and, accompanied by Prince George (later King George the Sixth), heard a touring Italian opera company perform *Otello*. (His diarists make no comment about his reactions.) At Gibraltar, the Governor (General Sir H. L. Smith-Dorrien) invited the Crown Prince to his first race meeting. The diarists write:

"Commander Niblack [a U.S. naval attaché] in his typical jovial American way, promptly arranged a sweepstake for our benefit. This sweepstake as it happened resulted in an easy win for the horse His Highness was presumed to have backed, whereupon the jovial commander rendered unto Caesar that which he considered to be Caesar's, and congratulated the Prince on his first success on the turf. An awkward situation! Not only is it not customary for the members of the Imperial family to handle money themselves but the Japanese are rather shy of participating in a wager. Our Prince hesitated for a moment and then laughingly consented to receive the money. He subsequently handed it to Admiral Oguri in order that it might be properly dealt with."

From many points of view, it could hardly have been a more awkward time for a State visitor to arrive in England. 1921 was a black period for Britain. The wartime boom had collapsed and there was hunger and misery throughout the land. The unemployment figures were up to an agonizing 1,800,000. The Welsh coal miners, whipped to a resentful fury by their volatile leader, A. J. Cook, had begun the longest strike in the history of industrial Britain. There was a partial stoppage of the trains. But Britain set great store by the Anglo-Japanese Treaty and was determined to do the Crown Prince proud. The British fleet (at that time without rival as the biggest and most powerful in the world) put on a Spithead Review for the visitor from Japan and he was afterward met at the gangplank by the Prince of Wales.

In later years the Prince of Wales became for Hirohito the ideal of all a crown prince should be. They had next to no conversation with each other, for Hirohito was, in spite of his lessons, too shy to speak English and the Prince of Wales did not even venture a word of Japanese. They appeared at banquets and receptions together. They rode through the streets of London. They even played a game of golf.[3] But what for Edward Windsor must have been a series of tedious chores (for he was going through his own first chafing experiences of the demands of royal duty) were a revelation to the Japanese Crown Prince. Here was the way for a crown prince to live! He could doff his uniform and go out into the city to enjoy himself, and no one was arrested if he failed to prostrate himself. He could visit the theater. He could dine in restaurants and play games in public. He could go out alone without an entourage of nervous officials and hangers-on. He could wear plus fours and go out hunting and drink champagne in night clubs and dance with pretty girls and swear out loud. It seemed to the introvert Crown Prince to be a life of blissful freedom, and he envied it even if he knew he would never be able to emulate it.

The diarists dutifully record their admiration for the behavior of the populace which greeted Hirohito's arrival, "such a great crowd of people entirely uncontrolled by the police." They were also struck by "the parental attitude of the King and Queen toward our prince, the way they attended to his comfort and welfare, treating him as if he were one of their own children. The fact that they had sons of approximately his own age must have contributed in no small way to the sympathetic and cordial atmosphere which marked his stay at Buckingham Palace." What his entourage do not record is the state of shock into which they were

---

[3] As a result of which, Hirohito's advisers agreed to build a nine-hole golf course in the grounds of the Imperial Palace on Tokyo, a trailblazing beginning to Japan's present-day passion for the game.

thrown on the first morning of that stay, when King George the Fifth suddenly walked into Hirohito's suite at breakfast time. To the horror of the Japanese equerries he was only half-dressed, wearing trousers, braces, carpet slippers and an open shirt, and he walked straight up to the Prince and slapped him on the back.

"I hope, me boy," he said, "that everyone is giving you everything you want while you are here. If there is anything you need, just ask. I'll never forget how your grandfather treated me and me brother when we were in Yokohama. I've always wanted to repay his kindness." He chuckled. "No geishas here, though, I'm afraid. Her Majesty would never allow it." [4]

Most of the equerries attached to Hirohito's suite never quite got over the informal (to their way of thinking) manner in which he was treated by his royal hosts, and by the casually cheerful attitude toward him of the British people. They were shocked when the College Chronicle at Eton used the occasion of the Crown Prince's visit to the school to print the following verse:

> Banzai!
> Gaude, gaude gaudete,
>   Rejoice aloud indeed!
> For soon Prince Hirohito
>   Will tread our verdant mead!
> And may no Thames mosquito
>   Be rash or indiscreet O,
> And bite the Prince's suite O,
>   To satisfy her greed.
> Henceforth to Alabama
>   We'll no more want to go
> But yo ho for Yokohama
>   Where the hari karis grow!
> And we'll sing I'm off to Asia
>   By the Nippon Yusen Kaisha
> To see my little Geisha
>   Way down in Tokyo.

[4] The future King of England and his brother, the Duke of Connaught, visited Japan during Meiji's reign as midshipmen in the Royal Navy.

They protested not against the quality of the doggerel, for which the writer surely deserved to feel the swish of a master's cane, but at the *lèse-majesté* involved in referring to the Crown Prince in such frivolous terms, and they were considerably and painfully surprised when they were told that it was impossible for the government to have the magazine suppressed and other newspapers forbidden to reproduce the verses.

There was one newspaper article written during the visit which did cause the British Government considerable, if temporary, embarrassment. It appeared in, of all newspapers, the *Church Times*, organ of the established Church of England, and it began:

"Who is the bespectacled young man from Japan whose visit to this country has aroused so much interest?" and went on: "Newspaper correspondents gave graphic accounts of the almost fanatical opposition to the proposal that the Crown Prince of Japan should demean himself and Japan by going on a visit to any foreign and barbarous nation. Pilgrimages to shrines, processions and all manner of demonstrations were designed to stop it. . . . Among those in England who know Japan there is a growing feeling that the present visitor is not the actual Crown Prince at all. They see nothing improbable in the rumour that the Japanese Government have sent someone else to personate the Crown Prince, since the opposition to the visit came very much from the bureaucratic set which, the Emperor being practically imbecile, rules the throne. Some colour is given to the suggestion by the fact that, for some time before our visitor left Japan, all photographs of the Crown Prince were withdrawn from sale in Japan by the police."

Luckily the Prince of Wales saved the day for them with that one. On the way back from Windsor he said to Hirohito: "I hear you aren't really here. It's the first time I've ever been out with a ghost. May I touch you?" The Crown Prince laughed and the equerries decided that they must have misinterpreted an example of peculiar English humor.

It should be added that though the Crown Prince himself was simply delighted by what, from a Japanese standpoint, was the easy informality of his stay, the British advisers attached to his suite seemed as desperately anxious as his court officials to put starch and ritual into the proceedings. Their attitude is typified by Major General F. S. G. Piggott, C.B., D.S.O., a former military attaché in Tokyo who was seconded to the Crown Prince's party during the visit. Charged at one point with getting Hirohito hurriedly fitted with British Army uniform for a march-past at Aldershot, the Army's chief depot, he corralled the leading fitters from his own tailor, hatter and bootmaker. He writes:

"Picture, then, a royal car driving through the gates of Buckingham Palace with myself and three representatives of the clothing and outfitting trades, whom I introduced to each other as we drove along. In the anteroom of the Japanese apartments I again impressed on them the importance of doing the job well, and also the honour of being allowed to take the measurements of the future Emperor's person. . . . I had forgotten to find out the dates of the foundation of the three firms, so settled precedence by the age of their representatives. In this arrangement the bootmaker came first. He was in fact quite elderly, and having to deal with the Prince's feet it was natural to take up a position of extreme obeisance, indeed prostration, while performing his functions. This went well, though I had some difficulty in the matter of his withdrawal, as he tried to carry this out on his knees without rising." [5]

So circumscribed had his life been in Japan that even the official program mapped out for his European visit seemed to Hirohito to be both novel and free and easy, and he even found Lord Curzon (then H. M. Secretary of State for Foreign Affairs) "an amiable and affable host." The banquet which Lord and Lady Curzon threw for him at Carlton House Terrace included a performance of *Le Mort du Cygne* danced by Pavlova, who had been brought specially from Paris, but the Crown Prince made no comment about her and his diarists merely refer to her as "a dancer from France." He lunched at the Guildhall and at the Bank of England, where, his diarists note:

"An example of the British character was shown during His Highness' visit to the Bank of England. The employees of the Bank did not leave their desks but simply lowered their heads when His Highness passed them. After the luncheon was over, however, when His Highness

[5] F. S. G. Piggott, *Broken Thread,* London: Gale & Polden, Ltd., 1950. General Piggott in the same book gives a perfect example of what two royal personages with nothing in common save regal expectations are apt to say to each other at odd moments. He was talking to Hirohito in Japanese when the Prince of Wales joined them and listened. "Then His Royal Highness said: 'Tell the Prince that when I was on the staff of XIV Corps under Lord Cavan you were in the 20th Division of the same Corps, and that you lent me your horse one day.' After I had translated this, to the obvious interest of the Crown Prince, the Prince of Wales remarked: 'Splendid. One of the star turns of the evening!' "

59

was about to leave the building the employees came out in full force to give him a royal sendoff. We realized that the reason why the employees had not left their desks when His Highness entered the Bank was because they were on duty at that time, but that they were able to show their warm sense of welcome during their own luncheon hour."

He visited the Tower of London and the British Museum and Oxford. He talked to the Prime Minister, Lloyd George. His diarists note:

"His Highness has shown great skill in conducting conversations with the great statesmen of England. The way in which he talked with Mr. Lloyd George was something which could hardly be emulated by professional diplomats. His Highness first of all said that he was delighted to meet a statesman of such a world-wide reputation. He expressed his great sympathy to Mr. Lloyd George over the great industrial crisis through which England was then passing. The Prime Minister minutely explained the cause of the coal strike and its actual situation. His Highness then referred to the friendly relations existing between Japan and England and expressed his appreciation that the two nations had contributed in no small measure toward the peace of the Orient as well as the whole world. His Highness also spoke with appreciation of the visit he had paid to the House of Commons on the previous day. In parting His Highness said: 'I am told you are frightfully busy these days. I hope you will take very good care of yourself not only for the good of this country but also in the interests of the rest of the world.' The British Prime Minister was deeply moved by these words of His Highness."

They may not have been the words of a great statesman, but they could not have been better calculated to appeal to the British, who grew increasingly fond of his modest demeanor. "The head is small with remarkable development above the eyes, showing, I believe, great powers of observation," wrote Lord Riddell. "He was pleasant and unassuming—in fact no one could have been more courteous and appreciative." [6]

One of the writers of the time, anticipating Isherwood, compared the Crown Prince during his tour with "a Japanese camera loaded with film and snapping enthusiastically every impression in view." There are still rumors in Japan that during a part of his tour he disappeared from

[6] Lord Riddell, *Intimate Diary of the Peace Conference and After, 1918-1923.*

60

official ken for at least twenty-four hours and sampled the entertainments provided by British geishas.[7]

This was not, however, the kind of souvenir for which he was looking, not because he considered it improper but because it would have been quite inappropriate to his nature. His diarists describe how, when his ship called at Gibraltar, he watched some of his naval officers preparing to go ashore for a day in Algeciras. He asked them what they were going to do and, when they told him that they would merely be sightseeing in the town, remarked:

"It was at Algeciras where the conference on the Morocco question was held. The delegates met at the Town Hall. If I were you, I should take advantage of this opportunity to visit the historic room."

It was what he would have done himself and it never occurred to him that the officers would sooner have visited a bullfight or a bodega.

There were no Scottish geishas awaiting him when he crossed the border on May 21, 1921, but there was Britain's nearest approach to a Japanese daimyo in the shape of Scotland's oldest feudal peer, the Duke of Atholl. He and his wife lived in the spectacular castle of Blair Atholl, a frowning and formidable stronghold whose household appurtenances included Britain's only remaining private army of eight hundred kilted Highlanders. Though they were kept solely for ceremonial purposes, the men of Atholl were a sturdy and impressive bunch and they put on a braw show of caber-tossing, piping, dancing and drilling for the Crown Prince, and fifty of them were detached as his personal bodyguard.

His diarists write:

"In the evening, the Prince was entertained with Japanese music. The 'Kimigayo'[8] was played by a band of pipers and the Duchess played a selection of Japanese airs. For the first time Japanese music was played on the pipes and heard in the wilds of the Scottish highlands. Knowing the Prince had had a strenuous series of entertainments since arriving

---

[7] The idea that the geisha system prevails in Britain caused the Crown Prince's former tutor, Admiral Togo, some moments of discomfort during his visit in 1912. Visiting Scotland with his aide, he was given a double room in an Edinburgh hotel and his aide a single one next door. Togo took one look at the double bed and forced his aide to change over. "If they are going to provide a Scottish geisha," he said, "then I would sooner she entertained you than I."

[8] The Japanese national anthem.

in Britain, the Duke made it a point not to draw up any set program during his stay. He had arranged for fishing excursions, sightseeing tours, musical entertainments, dances and other diversions, leaving it to the Prince to choose. . . . On May 23rd a farewell banquet was given at Blair Atholl. According to Scottish custom, the song of farewell was sung at the end with the ritual peculiar to the occasion. This banquet was followed by a dance which appears to have left a very deep impression upon our Prince. It would not be amiss to add a few words here as to why His Highness was particularly delighted to see this dance. The Duke's castle is a huge place. There must be a large staff of servants employed. In reply to an inquiry put by one of the Prince's servants on this occasion as to how she could secure so large a domestic staff, when everybody in England was said to be troubled by the servant problem, the Duchess said that ordinarily she and her husband lived in a small cottage adjacent to the castle and required no large staff, but on such an occasion as that of the visit of our Prince the village people, men and women, young and old, vied with one another in coming to place their services at her disposal. Her difficulty therefore was not in getting the number of required people but in making a choice of suitable ones."

The *amour-propre* of the entourage was once more jolted by the discovery that half the dancers at the ball which followed the banquet were, in fact, these villagers-*cum*-domestics come to join in the fun. "They looked on at first but later," the diarists write, "they joined in at the invitation of the Duke, a countrywoman dancing gaily with the Duke, and a farmer-like man with the Duchess. These were supposed at first to be villagers come to pay respects to our Prince, but it was later found out that they were the Duke's temporary servants."

They add, with a hiss of amazement that can almost be heard between the lines:

"A genuine democracy without class distinction! Hence perfect harmony between the people and their chief. This impressive sight explained of itself why the Duchess experienced no servant difficulty. Just at the time when the largest and longest coal strike which has ever broken out in England was at its height, here at Blair Atholl there was no vestige of conflict between Capital and Labour, but a picture of mutual confidence and goodwill."

Hirohito was impressed. "Appreciating most highly his little visit to

Blair, His Highness used to refer to it with a special fondness during the remainder of his European tour, and even after his return to Japan."

He visited Manchester and Glasgow (where shipyard workers refused point-blank to bow to the Crown Prince but insisted on shaking his hand), he had his picture painted by Augustus John, and he played golf at Addington. At the end of the month he left on a visit to France, during most of which he traveled incognito—Marshal Pétain took him on a tour of the Western Front battlefields—except for two major engagements. One was a lunch and reception given him by President Millerand at the Palais de l'Elysée, the other a banquet at the Japanese Embassy for the President, the Government and most of the notables of France. It was here that the Japanese Embassy made a monumental gaffe. Ambassador Ishii fixed the date of the banquet for the evening of June 6th and dispatched his invitations. Twenty-four hours later the chief of protocol of the French Government came to him wringing his hands. It so happened that an American theater company under the direction of Mr. James Hackett had recently arrived in England, where it had given a most impressive performance of *Macbeth*, so impressive that the French had invited the company to repeat the performance in Paris. June 6th had been chosen for a gala performance in aid of French refugees made homeless by the war. President Millerand had promised to attend. What was to be done?

Since the visit to the theater was a prior commitment, *Macbeth* would have seemed to demand presidential preference. On the other hand, Mr. Hackett was only an actor and Hirohito was a future Emperor of Japan. But then again, a cancellation of the theater visit by the President might well be seen not so much as a slight to a group of wandering players as a snub to the United States. In that case, however, what about the Japanese, who took snubs so much more seriously than Occidentals? As the Japanese Ambassador had now sent out the invitations, the "face" of his Emperor was obviously involved should the President send his regrets, and who could guess what might follow—an act of ritual suicide by Mr. Ishii at least.

In the end, however, a solution was found. Since Birnam Wood could obviously not come to the Embassy banquet, a method had to be discovered of getting the Embassy banquet (or, at least, the distinguished guests) to Birnam Wood. Hirohito's diarists write:

"His Highness was also informed of this matter, and regretting that the President was prevented from honoring the performance by his presence, commanded his attendants to make arrangements whereby the President should go to the Odeon [the theater where the performance would take place]. He expressed his willingness to accompany the President and his wife to the theater after dinner if agreeable to the President. So steps were immediately taken through proper channels to ascertain the President's convenience. Finding that the President was only too keen to see the Hackett performance after dinner if His Highness was ready to do so, it was arranged that His Highness and the President should proceed to the Odeon after the banquet. Mr. Hackett was much pleased at the presence of so many distinguished personages at his performance and highly appreciated the kind thought of our Prince which made it possible for them to be present on this occasion."

He was indeed. He came round to the Crown Prince's headquarters three days later to convey his thanks in person and to say he had sent a cable to the President of the United States in which he described the audience at his play (at which the American and British Ambassadors were there, along with the Crown Prince and the French President) as "the realization of a Four-Power Intellectual Entente." What Hirohito thought of *Macbeth* his diarists do not reveal; his English was not good enough for him to have understood much of it, but he must have recognized in its plot some vivid parallels with the history of his own country.[9]

There was a visit to Versailles, a night at the Opèra, though no record of what he heard (it was certainly not *Madame Butterfly*), a tour of a diamond factory in Amsterdam and a visit to the Rijksmuseum—where he saw "the painting by the famous Dutch artist Rembrandt, *The Nightwatch*" and "stood before it long, admiring it and listening to the explanations." After his battlefield tour with Pétain "who took him through a bayonet trench" he embarked for Naples and an official visit to Rome. It was high summer now and hot indeed. Hirohito was now beginning to tire from the demands of his tour. But not enough to relax. His diarists write:

"July 14. 12:30 P.M. The Crown Prince partook of lunch at the [Quirinale] Palace with His Majesty [King Victor Emmanuel] and the

[9] As did the Japanese film director, Kurosawa, many years later in his film, *Throne of Blood*, based on the *Macbeth* story.

Duc d'Aosta. Owing to the high summer temperature the citizens of Rome usually close their doors in the afternoon till about four o'clock and take a siesta. Accordingly one of the authors of this diary went into the presence of His Highness, who was at a desk writing, and suggested he should take a rest until about four P.M. because of the high temperature. 'I have no such leisure time,' replied the Crown Prince, and continued, 'I have to write to Princes Atsu and Takamatsu and in addition I have many things to do.' The author however had been advised by the Crown Prince's court physician that he must ask that the Prince take best care of himself because of the high temperature in Italy, and also as the Crown Prince was to lead a life on a warship again for about two months after leaving Italy. Consequently he repeated his advice to the Crown Prince, saying, 'Besides the high temperature, the program of Your Highness is rather crowded. In addition there is the journey aboard the *Katori* yet. Therefore I hope Your Highness will take a rest lest Your Highness be affected by the weather.' The Prince appeared rather embarrassed and said, 'Oh, that's all right. I only mean to do as much as I can. As I have no time of my own, I can't take a rest. Really, I have no time. Why, you know I have no time, don't you?' The Prince put down his pen and looked at him with a bright countenance as if expecting an affirmative answer, and the author could say nothing further to His Highness."

He visited Pope Benedict XV on July 15th and saw President Masaryk of Czechoslovakia (who happened to be in Rome) the same afternoon, and in seventy-two hours managed to fit in a sightseeing tour to the top of St. Peter's, the Forum, the Coliseum, two museums and the Villa d'Este, after which he journeyed south for a visit to Pompeii. Possibly because he found it less spectacular than the eruptive products at home, he did not attempt to climb Vesuvius.

By the time he sailed with the Japanese naval squadron from Naples on July 19th, his diarists could boast that he had indefatigably toured five European nations, received the heads of eight different states, and had never missed an appointment either from fatigue or through illness. They did not add that he had also used money for the first time, when he bought a ticket on the Paris Métro, or that his greatest pleasure was to go on a foursome dinner to La Perouse in Paris (he ate snails; his entourage protested that he had demeaned himself by "eating worms").

He had won a reputation as a gentle and thoughtful prince and the image of Japan abroad had been burnished by his presence. His behavior had been impeccable. He had made many friends and committed no errors whatsoever—not even, as some of his countrymen feared, slurping his food when he ate. That he himself was quietly confident that he had done well, and hoped that this would be the beginning of many such trips, is indicated by the interview he gave to Mr. Wilfred Fleisher, the representative of the United Press of America, in Paris on June 8, 1921. In it he said:

"I am fully aware of the fine spirit of patriotism and the noble ideals upon which the American nation has been founded, and I have long cherished a desire to visit the United States and to meet and learn to know her people. I would have gone on this trip had the time at my disposal not been so limited. I greatly regret that I am unable to carry out my wishes on this occasion, but since it is only a fortnight's trip from Japan to the United States, I hope it will only be a deferred pleasure. I know to what point justice and freedom are valued in America and that no efforts are ever spared by her people in the cause of humanity. I hope that America and Japan may always be found working hand in hand not only to our mutual benefit but to ensure lasting peace throughout the world." [10]

He wrote the statement himself and he meant every word of it. He had no inkling that his first and last journey out of Japan was over and done with, and that he would never see the United States.

There was a great crowd to greet him at Tokyo Central Station when he arrived back on September 3, 1921, and there were those among the reverent concourse who dared to look at him and shout: "Banzai!" When those in the vicinity noticed that the police guard left the offenders unmolested, and, not only that, even smiled at their demonstrations of enthusiasm, a murmur ran through the throng and swelled into a cheer.

There was no doubt that the emotion which the crowd now displayed towards the heir to the throne was no longer awe but affection. Hirohito smilingly acknowledged it, and was pleased. But that was far from being the reaction of the men behind the throne.

[10] Wilfred Fleisher, *Volcanic Isle*, New York: Doubleday, Doran, 1941.

Chapter Five

He was still twenty years old, and only six months had passed since he had left Japan, but Hirohito had grown from student to man during his absence. Neither the Genro nor the militarists were quite sure that they liked his new maturity, and after he had been back for a few months they were sure that they did not.

Later on Prince Saionji, now the most influential of the Genro, was to say that the Crown Prince had returned from Europe "filled with dangerous delusions of liberalism." This is to exaggerate the state of mind which his experiences, particularly in England, had developed. True, his outlook had been broadened by what he had seen and done—it had been pathetically narrow before his departure—but to suggest that Lloyd George, Curzon, Millerand, Queen Wilhelmina and Pope Benedict XV had filled him with dangerous or even vaguely liberal thoughts was ridiculous. Had he returned at any other time but the autumn of 1921, it is unlikely that Saionji would have been anything but pleased by the increased flexibility of the Crown Prince's mind.

But Saionji was afraid, both for the future of his country and the safety of the throne. Japan since the end of the war had been passing through a period of increasing unrest among the workers in the industrial plants and the farmers in the countryside. The wartime boom was over and there was unemployment and want in the land; labor unions were gathering in recruits but were running into trouble from the police; and there was agitation for the repeal of the notorious police regulations

67

which forbade unions to call meetings and urge strikes, both of which were put down with great brutality.

There was agitation on the left—and a certain sympathy toward it by some of the more enlightened members of the government. The Prime Minister was even believed to be in favor of a repeal of certain laws which would enable unions to organize and to use the strike as a weapon in dealing with employers.

But agitation on the right, too—and this was much more to be feared, in Saionji's view. During the squabble over Hirohito's engagement to Nagako, the Choshu clan (which dominated the Army) had temporarily split with the Satsuma (which dominated the Navy), and Mitsuru Toyama, the evil eminence behind the bully-boys of the Black Dragon Society, had thrown his weight decisively on the Satsuma side. But now they had closed their ranks in face of the threat of "liberal" ideas which they called bolshevism, and they let it be known that they would kill anyone who sought to weaken the Constitution or disseminate "dangerous thoughts." As far as the armed forces were concerned, the threat came from those who might try to diminish their influence by cutting military budgets, disbanding troops, or undermining military control of policy by weakening their influence in the Cabinet. But these were aims not likely to gain mass approval from a nation which was short of money, over-taxed, and well aware that Army adventures in Russia and China were wasting hundreds of millions of yen.[1] The veneer of popular appeal was provided by the Black Dragon Society, which stood for the preservation of "purity" in Japan, the suppression of "modernism" and female emancipation, the banning of jazz and other manifestations of Occidental society, the hatred of all foreigners and foreign ideas, the aggrandizement of Japan (Hakko-ichi-u)[2] and the worship of the divine Emperor (Tenno Heika). It was a platform which appealed to the conservative-minded, mainly middle-aged minority who possessed the vote and feared universal suffrage; who hated the "mogas" (modern girls) who had begun to appear in the streets with their boyfriends, the "mo-bos," both clad

---

[1] Long after the other Allied Powers abandoned their abortive attempt to overturn the government of the U.S.S.R., Japan retained her Army in Siberia and did not withdraw it until the end of 1922. The expedition by that time had cost Japan $280,000,000.

[2] Hakko-ichi-u means "The eight corners of the world under one roof," the roof of course belonging to Japan.

in European dress; whose instinctive xenophobia had been whipped up by American laws against Japanese immigration and citizenship, and anti-Japanese articles in the U.S. press (where one writer called them "varnished barbarians"); and who believed that Japanese salvation rested on their Emperor, a powerful army and navy and colonies for her surplus population.

It was they who provided the money with which Toyama recruited his bully-boys to break up meetings and intimidate politicians; and they did not withhold their tacit approval even when he resorted to death by assassination. Just a month after Hirohito's return to Japan, the Prime Minister, Mr. Hara, was traveling to Kyoto by the train from Shimbashi Station in Tokyo when a young man dashed toward him and thrust a dagger into his back, fatally wounding him. The killer was a railway worker named Konichi Nakaoka, and he gave himself up to the police immediately after the stabbing, calmly informing police and officials that he had acted in the name of patriotism because the Prime Minister had "defiled the Constitution." The premier's crime, it turned out, had been to take over himself the portfolio of Minister of Marine in the Cabinet while the actual holder of it, Admiral Koto, went to Washington for the Naval Conference. According to the Constitution, the post even pro tem should have been given to a serving naval officer, whereas Mr. Hara was a civilian. It soon became apparent, however, that even if a fanatic like Nakaoka believed that his mission was to uphold the Constitution, those who had incited him to the crime—Toyama in particular—were inspired by quite different motives. Hara could easily have been removed from office either by invoking the law and appealing to the Emperor to have it enforced, or by asking the Army Minister to resign, thus bringing down the government. Mr. Hara was removed from life because it was known that he secretly sympathized with the idea of universal suffrage and the right to strike. It was decided to make an example of him; and though Nakaoka went to jail for the murder (but not for long) no suggestion was ever made that Toyama, who had incited him, should be put in the dock.

It was in these circumstances that Hirohito came back to Japan matured by his journeys abroad and anxious, like any youth of the same age in the same circumstances, to invigorate his people and change at least some of their ideas. It is unfortunate that his first attempt to emancipate himself from royal protocol turned out to be a disaster. It

69

has been mentioned earlier in this story that the Prince of Wales had greatly impressed the Crown Prince as the ideal of how an heir to a throne should be allowed to behave both as a public image and a private person. He could be seen in public. He went to parties and race meetings and the theater. He visited night clubs. Above all, he was allowed to show that he was enjoying himself.

In his heart, Hirohito must have known that he was not the type to emulate the Prince of Wales, for he was much too serious a character; but at the age of twenty you have your idols and you do your best to imitate them. The Crown Prince decided to throw a party of the kind he heard the Prince of Wales gave (though he had never been to one himself) with no protocol, no bowing and scraping to superiors, and plenty of drink, music and dancing. Now, it had caused shock enough in Britain when the Prince of Wales gathered his friends together, put on the phonograph, danced the Charleston with short-skirted debutantes, and told everyone to call him Edward. A more sophisticated prince than Hirohito would have realized that to attempt a similar social revolution in Tokyo was asking for trouble, or a shambles. He got both.

The party he gave in his quarters inside the Imperial Palace in Tokyo in December, 1921, was meant to be a homecoming celebration for a number of his fellow pupils at the Gakushuin. Not even Hirohito in the flush of his successful tour dared to make it anything more than a stag party to which a number of geishas were invited, but he did stipulate that there would be no formalities throughout the evening and that his guests should forget for an hour or two that he was a crown prince. It was asking too much. A Japanese is schooled from the age of ten to think of his contemporaries in terms of rank and social class. The exact place in the social scale of each person he meets determines the lowness of his bow, the form of his speech, the humility or the arrogance of his attitude. To expect Hirohito's guests to forget he was a crown prince was obviously beyond them, sober. But for Japanese shyness and inhibition there has always been an accepted remedy, a lubricant to ease the stiffness of formal life, alcohol. When the Japanese wish to get drunk and release their tensions, they can do it on a very few cups of saké; it is almost as if they will themselves into a state of inebriation, the weakness of their heads being less of a reason for it than their desperate urge to get themselves into a state when they can no longer be held responsible for what they say or do.

70

At the Crown Prince's party there was not saké but whisky, served from a keg of Scotch especially distilled for the Duke of Atholl and brought back from Scotland by Hirohito as one of the souvenirs of a memorable forty-eight hours in the Highlands. His guests for the most part drank it straight, and it was potent. There were the latest records from London and Paris playing on the phonograph. Soon Hirohito's wish had been fulfilled and no one in the room was worried any longer about the awesome dignity of their host. They felt nothing but fraternal feelings toward him; and only those who have seen the Japanese with their minds unbuttoned can have the faintest glimmer of what it must have been like.

It was inevitable that word of the party should reach Prince Saionji; one of the court chamberlains told Count Makino, the Lord Keeper of the Privy Seal, who passed it on to the Old Genro. Saionji was shocked. He realized that a Crown Prince, even an Emperor, must be allowed to relax sometimes (though hitherto Hirohito had shown less tendency to do so than any of his forebears), but he must do it in strictest privacy, surrounded by only the most trusted of courtiers, none of whom must ever forget his position vis-à-vis his august master. He was not interested in whether there had been any wild fun and games at the party, as an elderly Occidental might have been on hearing about such an uninhibited party; his concern was over the "appalling familiarity toward the person of His Imperial Highness" which had been shown by many of the guests, and he was angry with Hirohito for having allowed it. He took the train from his country home and went to the Imperial Palace to voice his sternest disapproval. Hirohito listened to him in abashed and sheepish dismay; he was a great admirer of Saionji's wisdom and judgment and he was appalled to think that he had earned the old man's rebukes. He apologized fervently and promised that he would never try such an experiment again.

It was not quite the end of his rather pathetic attempt to be another Prince of Wales. He had a nine-hole golf course built inside the Imperial Palace and regularly played there, in a suit of plus fours with the same tweedy patterns that the British prince wore. He still played his gramophone records, but in private. And when the Prince of Wales himself arrived in Japan on an official visit in 1922, he happily went beyond the call of politeness to make it evident to the Prince how welcome he was. And there was one Occidental habit he resolutely refused to give up—a

71

bacon-and-egg breakfast of the kind he had been served at Buckingham Palace.

If Hirohito had brought no burning liberal ideas back with him from Europe, there was one ambition he hoped to fulfil which had also, like his admiration of the Prince of Wales, been stimulated by his contact with the British royal family. The life that they lived in 1921 seems, nowadays, to have been one of rigidly regulated boredom; but compared with the strict protocol and isolation of life for a Japanese Emperor, it must have seemed like freedom.

A few months after his return home, the elder statesmen met to consider the state of the monarchy and decided that it was time to make the general public aware of the seriousness of Emperor Taisho's condition. It was now obvious that he would never recover, and inevitably Hirohito would be called upon to deputize for him even more frequently than before. It was agreed that his assumption of this increased responsibility should be recognized by his elevation to the distinction of Prince Regent to signalize to the public that he was now Emperor in all but name.

To Hirohito it seemed an admirable moment to acquaint his advisers with his idea of how monarchy should present itself to the people now that a new reign was dawning. It was time, he told them, for the image of the Emperor to be refurbished, for many of the old myths and shibboleths to be repudiated, and for a closer and warmer contact between Emperor and people established. He had in mind, of course, a similar sort of relationship to that between King George the Fifth of England and the British people, where the distinction between ruler and subject, between royalty and the common people, was recognized and acknowledged, but the emotion felt by the masses toward their king was love rather than awe, loyal affection rather than superstitious fear.

In the conditions prevailing in Japan at the time, nothing was more likely to alarm the military diehards and their cohorts in the secret societies, for both of them were sustained by their claim to be the apostles of the divine Emperor, the instruments of his infallible will. Were the monarchy suddenly to become a merely constitutional institution, fallible, human, willing to listen to the people and obey the decisions of the Diet, as the King of England did, their activities could be called in question and their domination of policy thus jeopardized, for they could no longer claim to be acting in accordance with divine commands. Constitutional monarchy meant democracy, and democracy was a condition they least wished to see, for they rightly suspected that it would be suspicious of the Army and Navy, reluctant to finance their adventures, pro-peace, pro-disarmament, pro-appeasement of the peoples of those parts of the Asia mainland, particularly China, where the military had plans for Japanese aggrandizement. The last thing they wanted was a "human being" on the throne; to produce the kind of awesome respect most conducive to an obedient populace, they needed a god for whom they carried the sword. It would spell death to their plans if the new Emperor came to be regarded as just another pleasant young man; and they grew alarmed when Hirohito accompanied the Prince of Wales during part of his tour, waved his hand in acknowledgment of the cheers of the crowd, and was even seen to be smiling. It was bad enough for a prince regent to be seen walking with a foreign prince and chatting and smiling; but it would be shameful if such conduct continued after he ascended the throne. Vague criticisms began to appear in the newspapers, planted by the assiduous disciples of Toyama, the chief of the Black Dragon Society, muttering that the Prince Regent's advisers were remiss in allowing him to demean himself by hobnobbing with foreigners and other inferiors. Responsible people realized, the critics went on, that international relations demanded that a royal guest from Britain be received by the Prince Regent and treated with politeness, but was it necessary to walk with him and smile at him? Was this not making the Imperial family seem obsequious? And Toyama let it quietly be known that a young man who had blown himself up with a homemade bomb in front of the Imperial Palace in March, 1922—three weeks before the Prince of Wales' visit—was a member of the Black Dragon Society. He had killed himself as a gesture of protest against attempts to sully the purity of the Imperial family by forcing the Prince Regent to mix with foreign (and therefore inferior) royal persons on terms of equality.

Had Prince Saionji and Count Makino, the two most senior advisers of the Prince Regent, been less concerned for a quiet life and an absence of political conflict, they would have advised Hirohito to face up to the objections of the military clique. It may be taken as certain, from a reading of their background, that they too would have been appalled by the diminution of the Imperial influence and the encouragement of the idea that the Emperor was a constitutional monarch rather than a descendant of the gods. But neither of them wished to see Hirohito become a puppet manipulated by the extremists. Had they been wiser they might well have utilized his eagerness to popularize himself as a weapon against both the Army and members of the Black Dragon Society, judiciously using him and his successful European tour as a means of building up his persona and turning him not from a divine prince into a human being, but from a remote and mystic god-who-is-feared into a god-the-people-know-and-trust. In other words, this was the period when he could have been encouraged to assert his independence. It could have been so easy. The public was on his side. The Army was unpopular. The secret societies would never have dared to oppose him, dedicated as they insisted they were to the protection of the divine Emperor and the propagation of his Imperial will. It was a moment when there were strong enough forces in Japan to have rallied round him had he insisted on a showdown with the militants and the fanatics. Alas, Saionji and Makino were too effete to grasp the opportunity. They counselled caution and advised the Prince Regent to pay attention to the Army and treat the Black Dragon Society with respect. Perhaps they were afraid of Toyama's dedicated assassins, the ones who had threatened Prince Yamagata with death during the crisis over the royal engagement, and feared for their own lives as well as that of the Prince Regent. Whatever the reason, their advice was such that Hirohito, still chastened by his failure to free himself as a person, was now persuaded to circumscribe his activities as heir to the throne. One wonders if he would have revolted had he realized that it was the first step by the Army to immure him in the Imperial Palace and turn him into the puppet behind whom they could plan the policies that would lead to world war.

In all this time, preparation for the wedding of the Prince Regent and Princess Nagako had been making progress, and a date had actually been chosen for the ceremony in 1923. In fact Hirohito had seen his bride-to-be infrequently during all this time and had written no letters to her while he had been away.[8] They had been engaged for nearly five years, and Nagako made it quite clear to her friends—and to her father, Prince Kuniyoshi, for that matter—that she was weary of waiting. The years of preparation had not been easy for her, and not only because of the intensive course of education which she had undergone. The Choshu

[8] Though he did bring back a present for his future father-in-law—a set of bagpipes.

clan had been bested in their attempt to break the engagement, but this had not stopped them from doing what they could to make life unhappy if not unbearable for Kuniyoshi and his family; and the campaign of slander which they had had to endure even included a successful attempt to sabotage the marriage plans of Nagako's sister. (Emissaries from the Choshu presented her husband-to-be with indubitable evidence that she was no longer a virgin.)

But now it was all over. The wedding date was set. Nagako put her books and paintings aside and began to concentrate on the fittings for her wedding dress. As if to emphasize that there were no more obstacles to be overcome, Prince Yamagata, the most determined opponent of the engagement, expired at his country home. The Choshu could not stop the wedding now.

An earthquake, however, could.

Chapter Six

No one who lives in Japan for very long can fail to be aware that the country is a series of vast ouija boards which are liable to tremble and shake at any moment with messages of doom and disaster. The surface of the land is pitted with seething or suppurating springs of sulphurous mud or boiling mineral water, and many of the smaller islands are active volcanoes rumbling with terrestrial indigestion and belching great clouds of garlic into the air. The bowels of the earth beneath Japan are in a mess and at regular intervals they heave with discomfort; not for long, usually, just for a few seconds in which the trees sway, all the buildings in sight strain out of perpendicular, and the walls of the houses creak and groan as if in need of lubrication. Earthquakes, even minor ones, are something one never gets used to, for not only is the surface of the ground beneath one's feet upset but so is one's mental equilibrium. *Solid earth* is suddenly seen to be capable of crumbling and *keeping one's feet on the ground* no longer means that one is playing safe, being stable, keeping one's sense of balance.

Japan experiences two or three hundred earth tremors, or tremblors, every year, most of them not serious enough to put a ripple on a cup of green tea, but several of them bad enough to buckle railway lines. The Kanto dai-shinsai (or Great Kanto Earthquake)[1] of 1923 was probably, in the measurement of its convulsions, not the worst one the country has ever had, but its results were certainly the most devastating in recorded history,

[1] Kanto is the region containing Tokyo, Yokohama and the great plain stretching along the shores of the Inland Sea.

76

for it could not have happened at a more unfortunate moment.

September first is usually called ni-hyaku-tohka in Japan, meaning the 210th day since the ending of winter, and is regarded by superstitious natives rather like Friday the thirteenth is to Occidentals, fraught with dire possibilities. The day lived up to its evil reputation; just before noon, lamps and lanterns hanging from walls and ceilings began to sway and the Great Kanto Earthquake had begun.

It is the time of day in Japan when rice is being cooked and tea boiled, usually on charcoal braziers (hibachi). Most Japanese houses, particularly in those days, were flimsy structures of wood and paper with no foundations, no fireplaces or chimneys, and built close together with only narrow alleyways between; the flimsiness of the dwellings being intended to make them resilient in the event of earth tremors. In the case of minor terrestrial disturbances, it was an arrangement which worked; the majority of houses survived the shaking while those which did not could easily be reassembled and there was little furniture—only tatami on the floor, a few pots, a small table or two—to be damaged. But this was no minor earthquake but a major upheaval of the foundations upon which Japan rested. Professor Akitsune Imamura, a well-known Japanese expert on seismology, was at the Seismological Institute in Tokyo when the first quivers came. He wrote later:

"At first the movement was rather slow and feeble, so that I did not take it to be the forerunner of so big a shock. But soon the vibration became large and after three or four seconds from the commencement I felt the shock very strongly indeed. Seven or eight seconds passed and the building was shaking to an extraordinary extent, but I considered these movements not yet to be the principal portion. When I calculated these movements the twelfth second from the start there arrived a very big vibration which I took at once as the beginning of the principal portion. Now the motion, instead of becoming less and less as usual, went on to increase its intensity very quickly, and after four or five seconds I felt it to have reached its strongest. During this epoch, the tiles were showering down from the roof, making a loud noise, and I wondered whether the building could stand or not. I realized the direction of the principal movements distinctly and found them to have been about northwest or southeast. During the following ten seconds the motion, though still violent, became somewhat less severe and its character was gradually changing into slower but bigger vibrations. For the next few minutes we felt the undulations like those we experience on a boat in windy weather, having now and then

77

been threatened with severe after-shocks. After five minutes from the beginning, I stood up and went over to see the instruments."[2]

The series of violent spasms rolled across the surface of the Kanto plain as if it were a carpet with a draught under it, toppling houses and spreading disaster as it came. Epicenter of the turmoil was the Sagami Bay area, some sixty miles south of Tokyo, and it was here that, proportionately, most damage was done. Tidal waves (tsunamis) rolled in from the sea smashing houses and harbor works, flooding rivers, collapsing cliffs and uprooting trees; the principal towns of the Japanese Riviera, Ito, Atami and Kamakura, were almost completely destroyed. At Kamakura the giant Daibutsu, the great bronze statue of the Buddha, was toppled from its pedestal. At Ito three hundred wooden houses were carried out to sea.

But it was in the thickly populated centers of Yokohama and Tokyo itself that the full horror of the disaster was felt. The tremors flattened houses and dropped their flimsy, tinderwood walls and roofs (it was last of summer in Japan and the weather was hot and dry) on to the charcoal braziers still cooking the midday meal. The fires began. Gas mains broke and quickly caught fire. At the great naval base of Yokosuka, outside Yokohama (where the U.S. Navy now has its Far East base) oil tanks with enough fuel to keep the Japanese Navy afloat for two years broke, spilled rivers of highly inflammable gasoline into the streets, and then caught fire. In Yokohama, the liners *Empress of Australia* and *André Lebon* were preparing to sail as the earthquake struck, and crowds of sightseers on the piers beside them were tipped into the sea.

The great conflagrations had started in Tokyo and Yokohama. The flames ripped down the narrow streets, burning up air and causing a series of violent whirlspouts which the Japanese call tatsumaki (or dragon's tails), which ripped off roofs and balustrades and beams and hurtled them through the air in a cosmic blizzard of flying and burning missiles. The twelve-story Tokyo Tower, the highest edifice in the city, swayed like a reed and then collapsed in a heap of rubble. In Yokohama, where nine-tenths of the city was now blazing, the populace had taken refuge in the sea, but for thousands of them it was an appointment in Samarra. The rivers of burning oil slopped over the shoreline into the water and set the sea alight, frizzling those who had not already been drowned by the tidal waves. It was a scene of horror which the most devilish works of man have

[2] Akitsune Imamura, *Theoretical and Applied Seismology*, Tokyo: 1937.

so far failed to equal, for not even the heaviest raids on London, Berlin, Dresden, and Tokyo, nor the atom bombs on Hiroshima and Nagasaki, produced such fiery disaster. The cities blazed. The dragon's tails twisted in furious black columns across the Kanto plain. The seas heaved and flooded, and the air was filled with the snarl of rushing winds and flying debris.

By the time the conflagrations were brought under control (and that took days), three-quarters of Tokyo had been destroyed and four-fifths of Yokohama. Tokyo's list of dead and missing amounted to 107,000 and Yokohama's 33,000, most of them victims of what Tokyo's residents, who have suffered from them ever since their city was known as Edo, cynically call Edo no hana, the Flowers of Edo—fires.

Edo also had a slogan about the result of earthquakes which Tokyo's residents would now need to heed: Nana korobi, ya-oki (fall down seven times, get up eight). Most of their city was now flat on the ground.

It was only by a twist of fate that Emperor Taisho was not one of the victims of the disaster. Usually in the summer he spent much time at the seaside palace at Hayama, which is only a few miles from Kamakura and Yokosuka. But it so happened that he found the heat and humidity at the seaside made him fractious and nervous, and he was taken by the Empress to an Imperial residence at Nikko, where he could solace himself in royal shrines or gloom through Tokugawa mausoleums, and be refreshed by the cool air of the hills. It was just as well. The Hayama seashore palace was badly damaged. Taisho watched from his open window the glow in the sky as Tokyo burned. Three days after the disaster, all communication with the devastated area having been broken, a small plane wheeled over the Imperial residence and dropped a note to say that Hirohito was safe.

For the Prince Regent had been in Tokyo awaiting the deliberations of the newly appointed Prime Minister, Admiral Count Gompei Yamamoto, who was in process of forming his Cabinet.[8] He had an appointment to receive the premier at the Imperial Palace at four in the afternoon, but never made it. He was about to eat lunch at the Akasaka Detached Palace, his official residence (which is, incidentally, a small-scale model of the palace at Versailles) when the convulsions began. Most Japanese know in-

[8] The Admiral, who was presiding at a conference in the Navy Club in the capital, was injured by a falling wall and put out of action for twenty-four hours.

79

stinctively what to do when there is a violent earthquake, and Hirohito and his companions quietly but with no slouching left the room for an open space where there would be no fear of falling masonry. Because of its site and its structure, however, the Akasaka Palace easily rode the turmoil with only minor cracks to its walls and a few broken flower urns; which is just as well for Baron Osanaga Kamroji, one of the Prince Regent's guests, who, as has been mentioned earlier in this story, loved watermelon more than his life and stayed behind to finish the slice on his plate.

The meeting with the new Prime Minister had been arranged to take place at the Imperial Palace in the center of Tokyo, and had Yamamoto been available it would still have been possible. Instead the investiture took place at Akasaka next day. The buildings inside the Imperial moat, in fact, stood up to the earthquake well and sustained only minor damage. The thick stone walls, deliberately fashioned out of huge rocks piled atop each other, with no adhesive in between, absorbed the shocks and remained intact. In fact the district of Marunouchi and Chiyoda-ku, in the center of which the Imperial Palace stands, emerged comparatively unscathed from the holocaust, thanks mainly to the architectural skill of an American and and Englishman. Most of the buildings in the Marunouchi district were designed by or copied from the plans of a British architect, Josiah Conder, and were thick, solid, steel-reinforced. The biggest of them was the Mitsubishi Building and all of them survived the earthquake. But the pride of Tokyo was the Imperial Hotel, designed by the famous American architect, Frank Lloyd Wright, which also rolled with the primeval punches of September 1, 1923, and still stands intact today.

Elsewhere in Tokyo, however, the devastation was complete and soon physical disaster was followed by mental and emotional disintegration. Here was a moment when the people of the devastated areas needed to see, or hear, or read some rallying call from their leaders. In the first forty-eight hours of the crisis they behaved with the discipline and fortitude which are two of the principal Japanese virtues. There were countless acts of bravery during the actual earthquake and the fires. There was a spirit of community purpose and mutual aid in the hours which followed; and though open spaces like Ueno Park and the Meiji Park were filled with acres of burned, broken and bleeding bodies, there were no cries of anguish heard and no one complained because the scanty medical teams took days to look them over. But for the great hordes of homeless, hungry, thirsty and bereaved, a message of cheer and encouragement was needed—and it did not come. There was no radio service. All the newspapers had been put out of action. The Kanto Plain was cut off from the rest of Japan by road and rail, and from the rest of the world by cable. The populace inevitably became prey to all sorts of rumors and fantasy fears. A visit from the Emperor would have sent some sort of word-of-mouth message of good hope through the city, but he was still in Nikko and too sick, anyway. The Prince Regent would have been an even more popular substitute, but Prince Saionji, who might have advised the government to send Hirohito out to be seen in the public places, was at his country estate; and the government showed no initiative of its own. The Prince Regent, too chastened by this time to take any initiative, fretted at the Akasaka Palace waiting to be told what to do; and it was days later before they got around to utilizing his power for good, by which time the damage had been done.

It needs to be mentioned at this point that Korea, on the Asiatic mainland, was in 1923 a protectorate of Japan whose inhabitants received short shrift from their masters. The conditions in their homeland persuaded thousands of Koreans to cross the water in search of jobs in the Japanese cities, where they congregated in ghettoes not unlike the Puerto Rican areas of New York, the West Indian settlements in Notting Hill and the Pakistani slums of Bradford. The Japanese despised them not simply because they thought their habits unwholesome, their food smelly and their proclivities immoral (many Koreans drifted into crime, pimping and prostitution), but because they considered them an inferior race. It was not simply poverty or the humbleness of their jobs which drove them into ghettoes—there were plenty of poor Japanese, too—but because the Japanese would not mix with them. There was no social contact. Intermarriage was simply unthinkable.

In the miserable days which followed the earthquake, the Japanese, bewildered, hungry, thirsty and in pain, looked around for a scapegoat. They could hardly blame the Koreans for the earthquake, for most superstitious Japanese knew who was responsible for that—the great catfish, Namazu, which inhabits the waters of the archipelago and whose restless convolutions cause the islands to shake. But they found in many of the fires and explosions which followed an excuse to turn upon the loathsome immigrants in their midst and wreak a bloody vengeance on them.

There is some suggestion that the anti-Korean riots which broke out in Tokyo and Yokohama in the early days of September, 1923, may have been incited by a member of the outgoing Japanese Cabinet, Mr. Rentaro

81

Mizuno, the former Home Minister. Mr. Mizuno had once been an official —and a well-hated one—in the Japanese administration in Korea and had been severely wounded in a bomb-throwing attack in Seoul in 1919. It was said that this had exacerbated an already lively dislike of the Koreans. Because of the earthquake and the delay in swearing in the new Cabinet, Mizuno was still Home Minister on September 2nd and it was his last act as a Minister to declare martial law in the Kanto area. On the same day he had a long conference with the chief of the Tokyo police in which he instructed him on how his men should deal with riots, disturbances, recalcitrant elements and looters. It may or may not have been significant that September 2nd happened to be the fourth anniversary of the bomb-throwing incident in Korea.

Whatever the reason, an ugly series of anti-Korean riots began in Tokyo. They were inspired by rumors that bands of Korean looters were wandering about the city; and these may, of course, have been true, for there were hordes of homeless Koreans with no food and, even worse, no water—for their wells had been destroyed. Soon, however, the rumors grew wilder. It was said that an army of Koreans had assembled on the banks of the Sumida River and were planning to capture the city. Where the "army" had come from and in what circumstances no one stopped to think. It was enough for the word to go around, and so circumstantial did it sound that even normally levelheaded Japanese became prey to exaggerated fears. Mr. Tetsuzo Inumaru, now the distinguished chairman of the company owning the Imperial Hotel, at that time merely the manager, has written a pamphlet about his experiences during the days following the earthquake. His hotel had been open for only a few days when the earthquake happened, but word swiftly spread among the diplomatic corps that Frank Lloyd Wright's design had admirably withstood the tremors and Inumaru's emergency activities had kept food and services going. An influx of foreign ambassadors and rich Occidental tourists resulted. Inumaru took great pains to make them comfortable but was afraid for their safety once the rumors began. He writes:

"The first night there had been the danger of fire. The second night there was the scare about the raiders. There were thousands of refugees in Hibiya Park, just across the street. [And though Mr. Inumaru does not mention it, large numbers of them were Koreans.] What would they do if they could not get food? Or if it should rain? There had been no rain for several days. The weather was still warm enough to sleep out of doors. The day after the earthquake, there was some fighting and raiding in the city, and wild rumors began to go around—of large bands of raiders on the march. A Japanese official whispered to me that they would aim at our hotel—now the commercial and political centre—and at Tokyo Station to cut off all communications. Some reliable reports of trouble came to me. I have a friend who is a sort of Robin Hood and he brought his men to help me protect the hotel. With several ambassadors here and many other foreigners, we had to take special precautions. Our whole staff armed themselves with whatever they could find and kept guard all night. In the evening I sent a letter to the Captain of the Guard asking for soldiers to protect the hotel. His answer was that soldiers are not sent by the request of private persons but by order—that they would be sent if the military authorities thought it necessary. So I went and said: 'Well, how do they find out if it is necessary? If they find out the necessity it is too late. In home affairs we can suppress things but if an affair is international it goes by wireless to foreign countries. For this international affair why can't you send soldiers? It is not my business to keep guard.' I could not get soldiers so I went to the Foreign Office and the next morning they sent thirty right away and more later. That night I slept." [4]

If a character of the caliber of Mr. Inumaru, of whose calmness and resource I can testify, was moved to such measures by the rumors (and, incidentally, the Imperial Hotel was never attacked), it is possible to imagine how the more ignorant members of the populace reacted. With the encouragement of the police, district householders formed themselves in vigilante groups, ostensibly to "protect" their ruined homes from the "invaders." But soon these groups, seething with complicated emotions, psychologically receptive to incitement, eager to find those responsible for their sufferings (whether they were genuinely culpable or not), began wandering the streets looking for Koreans.

When they found them at first they took into custody only young Korean men, and these they gravely tried for their supposed crimes before mock courts. After finding them guilty, and they always found them guilty, they forced them to their knees and beheaded them. But in the days that followed the thirst for blood grew and the vigilantes grew less discriminating. Soon they no longer bothered about trials, or about the sex or the age of those they caught, so long as they were Koreans. Since Koreans,

[4] Quoted by Noel F. Busch in his book *Two Minutes to Noon*, a brilliant reportage of the whole sequence of the Great Kanto Earthquake and Fire.

83

especially children, are indistinguishable from Japanese in appearance, the victims were given a simple verbal test of words which only native-born Japanese can pronounce correctly. Those who failed, men, women and little children, were cut down, mistreated and tortured, clubbed to death (in many cases by soldiers) and otherwise massacred in their hundreds— simply because they were Koreans. It was the particular crime of the new government that it made little attempt to halt the atrocities nor showed any eagerness, once they had stopped, to punish or condemn those who had committed them. It was yet one more crime against their race by the Japanese which the Koreans cite to explain the hatred and suspicion with which they regard them to this day.

It was not only the Koreans who fell victims to man-made violence in the aftermath of the great earthquake. Mr. Mizuno had counselled the police chief in Tokyo to beware of all "trouble-makers and recalcitrants" and his successor endorsed the instruction. To the kempeitai, the "thought police," it seemed an admirable opportunity to wipe out those "dangerous elements" which had been causing the military and the secret societies so much cause for concern in recent months. Using the emergency as an excuse and the martial laws as a justification, the "thought police" swooped on hundreds of labor leaders and known Socialists.

Lewis Bush writes: "Typical of the 'dangerous thoughts' hysteria of authority was the arrest of over one thousand known Socialists who it would appear were blamed for any untoward event. At a police station at Kameido, Tokyo, where nine leftists persisted in singing revolutionary songs, the military police were called in who stabbed them all to death and flung their bodies down a well. But the most terrible crime in the name of patriotism was committed at this time by a certain captain of the gendarmerie named Amakasu who, after strangling to death the extremist Osugi, who had been arrested with his wife and his seven-year-old nephew, then dealt with the woman and the child in like manner. Later, Amakasu was sentenced to ten years' imprisonment, hailed as a hero by one newspaper, turned up in Paris a few years later under an assumed name. During the Pacific War he served in a position of authority in Manchuria where he committed suicide just after Japan's surrender in 1945."[5]

They were days of savagery during which the so quiet, so polite, so care-

[5] Lewis Bush, *Land of the Dragon Fly*, London: 1959.

84

fully controlled Japanese people went wildly berserk, and were incited and encouraged by Army and police, while their government pretended not to know. It was a small but sinister rehearsal of more appalling things to come.

It was days before Hirohito was allowed out of his palace to see for himself the carnage which the unstable earth, the unpredictable elements and the ill will of man had wrought between them. He donned Army uniform and rode on horseback with a small escort on a series of tours of the city, along the wrecked Ginza, through the ravaged slumlands of Asakusa, and into the huge Ueno Park, which had proved a haven for men and animals alike; for it had provided a refuge for thousands of homeless streaming in from the blazing communities which surrounded it, and the collection in the Ueno Park Zoo had also survived intact through forty-eight hours of fear and panic.

The Prince Regent's appearance among his people, though too late to halt the riots, did have at least one good psychological effect: it made it clear that the emergency, if not the misery, was over. And amid all the discomforts and privations through which they were passing, the populace found time to sympathize with their young prince when it was officially announced that his wedding had been postponed until times were more fitting for such a happy celebration.[6] They had solid reasons for being grateful to him, as well, for he had already announced that he was contributing ten million yen ($2,500,000) from his privy purse toward the emergency relief fund which had been started, a gesture which did not fail to increase his popularity. In many parts of the city the reception he received from the crowd was even more spectacular and enthusiastic than had greeted him upon his return from his European tour, a fact which did not go unnoticed among some of the Army and police officers accompanying him. It reinforced their conviction that such a popular Prince Regent might, as Emperor, develop into a monarch whose sway over the people could prove dangerous, at least for those who wanted to keep control of him for their own purposes; and they were more than ever determined to have a remote god-king inside the Imperial Palace rather than a popular hero on the streets for all to see and cheer.

[6] Princess Nagako and her family were all unharmed by the earthquake.

In view of Hirohito's mounting influence with the ordinary Japanese people, it is hard to explain the happening of December 27, 1923. If one accepts the official version of what took place, that is.

On that day the Prince Regent drove to the Diet to open a special session, and it was needed, for in the three months since the Great Kanto Earthquake the government's plans for the reconstruction of the capital had gone awry. Grandiose schemes had been mooted, some for moving the capital away from Tokyo, others for constructing a great port to rival or even replace Yokohama, others for the building of wide streets and new tremor-proof ferroconcrete edifices to contain flats and offices. But while the planners talked and the Cabinet debated, the ordinary people got on with piecemeal replacement of what had been there before. Up went the same kind of wooden shacks, as inflammable as ever. Soon Tokyo and Yokohama mushroomed with a series of shanty towns into which the citizens huddled in the same old clusters. Since hundreds of thousands of refugees had left the city to find accommodation with relatives in the country, there was a shortage of labor; and when the government tried to press on with state-backed building schemes, they could find no one to dig the foundations or lay the bricks. An ardent social reformer and campaigner for women's rights called Mrs. Kaji Yajima (a dragoness for justice though she was ninety years old) could have told them why, and did. Among the most devastated areas left behind by the post-earthquake fire was the Yoshiwara district of Tokyo, the famous brothel area, where every house was devoted to the exploitation of thousands of young women sold by their parents into prostitution. The Yoshiwara had been all but demolished by the fire and five hundred of its inmates burned alive. The brothel keepers, however, were not worried about the supply of new girls; the disaster was already creating such hunger and want that needy parents were already clamoring to sell their daughters, and the bottom had dropped out of the market for pretty young virgins. What was urgent was the rebuilding of the red-light district with houses to put them in; and labor touts were ranging the city, offering high wages for work in Yoshiwara. The government, unable to compete, was dropping out. It had convened a special session of the Diet, under the premiership of Admiral Yamamoto, on December 27 to pass a measure cutting their contribution to the rebuilding scheme by two-thirds.

It was on his way to the Diet in his State carriage that the Prince Regent was attacked. From the cheering crowd dashed a young man with a re-

86

volver who fired at the royal carriage and missed. He was seized by the police and carried away.

The nation was horrified by the notion that anyone would dare to attempt the assassination of the Prince Regent, and astounded that anyone should want to. Why? Who was the would-be assassin and what were his motives?

It was here that the mystery began. The young man gave his name as Daisuke Namba, but no more than that. It was claimed later at his trial that he had confessed to being a socialist who blamed the Prince Regent for the failure to make a utopia grow out of the ashes of the devastated capital. He was sentenced to death and hanged the following year, and it was said that as the noose was fastened round his neck he cried: "Banzai for the workers!" But though he must have had accomplices to help him plan his crime and find the assassination weapon, none was ever produced in court, no associates were arrested, nor would Namba say one word about the attempt except to admit his responsibility for it. But the police were assiduous in spreading the word that it was the leftists, busily sowing "dangerous thoughts" among the workers, who were the real culprits.

At this stage the truth will never be known, for the records were burned during the Tokyo fire raids of 1945. But to say the least, it seems unlikely that any left-wing organization in 1923 would have planned Hirohito's murder, for it would have alienated their own people, with whom his popularity was at its height.

What is certain is this: it was the right wing in Japan, the militarists in particular, who got most benefit out of the assassination attempt. They were able to use it as a weapon with which to influence the Imperial advisers, already nervous and fussy enough, into deprecating and discouraging any further public appearances by members of the Imperial family, particularly the Prince Regent. It was the first move in a campaign to immure him in the Imperial Palace, like one of the puppet Emperors under the Tokugawas; and the pressure would increase as the months went by.

Meanwhile the Yamamoto Cabinet resigned en bloc and an administration entirely composed of peers of the realm took its place.

"With all the picturesque but subdued Shinto setting, before the ancestral shrine within the moated Palace of the Emperors, and with the ancient ceremonial and costumes, Princess Nagako today became the bride of the

87

Crown Prince Hirohito, Prince Regent of Japan," wrote the correspondent of *The New York Times* and the London *Times* on January 26, 1924. "The witnesses numbered some 700, including all the Imperial princes and princesses and Court and Government officials, all wearing the costumes or uniforms of their rank."

It had happened at last, after nearly five years of waiting and the royal bride was not the only one who rejoiced at the ceremony. There is nothing better for stimulating the taste buds of a nation than a royal marriage, and Japan went *en fête* in celebration. January is not the best time of the year in Japan—March and April are more spring-like, October is more sentimentally balmy and golden—but the people were badly in need of a holiday from the gloomy and disastrous winter, and what better to revive them than a union of two young people whose marriage was a triumph over opposition? The ceremony was designed to extract the utmost public euphoria from the occasion, and a holiday was proclaimed throughout Japan as a salute to the royal couple. The condition of his health kept the Emperor away, fortunately for everyone concerned, for he might have made an exhibition of himself; and of the seven hundred guests, all were relatives of Hirohito himself or the Choshu and Satsuma clans, with no gaijin to sully the proceedings; all foreign diplomats having been informed that the celebrations but not the ceremony would be the time for them to offer their felicitations.

"Prince Kujo, Master of the Rites," wrote the *Times* correspondent, "performed the main ceremony, which lasted 45 minutes, concluding with the exchange of the sacred wine cup. At a quarter of 11 the first of a salute of 101 guns from the battery at Miyake Hill announced the completion of the ritual; it was taken up simultaneously by the warships in Shinagawa Bay and other warships and forts throughout the country. The whole nation is making holiday in the brilliant sunshine. Public entertainments are being held everywhere, while here in the capital quaint costumed processions are being carried through in a spirit of merrymaking which is entirely lifting the pall of depression and apprehension which has been a marked feature of life in Tokyo for the last four months."

Nagako had been fetched from her father's home in Shibuya, now so enlarged that it could with some justification be called the "Kunis' Palace," at eight A.M. and driven by Viscount Iriye, the Lord Chamberlain and Imperial Messenger, to the Imperial Palace. She was wearing what was described as "a wonderful four-fold silk marriage kimono, her hair done in old-time looped style." The Prince Regent meanwhile made his way from the Akasaka Detached Palace through a cheering crowd to the same palace, but not yet to join her, for both had their respective robing rooms.

"The Regent, dressed in full ceremonial marriage costume," wrote the *Times* correspondent, "emerged carrying a sceptre and joined the Princess, who carried a Hinoki Court fan. The massive doors of the outer shrine swung back, and as the imposing gathering stood facing the approach to the inner shrine, Prince Kujo recited in a monotone the Shinto scripture messages. Then the inner shrine was opened and the bridegroom approached and paid homage to the altar, afterwards reading a report to his ancestral shades. Then the couple retired to the outer shrine, where Prince Kujo filled and handed the cup of sacred wine first to the Regent and, after he had drunk, to the bride."

When the guns reported the solemnization of the marriage, there were celebrations of the event in Japan of a kind which were unusual in that they were genuinely spontaneous. The day had begun with formal obeisances to the royal bridegroom and polite felicitations to the happiness of the royal couple; but as the day wore on, the banzais and deep bows of respect gave place to genuine effervescences of sentimental joy. There is very little romance in Japanese life, and there was even less in those days. Japanese got married because their spouses had been chosen for them by their parents; the union would be for the practical purpose of sealing a solid business arrangement; sexual connection was mainly designed for the production of children. But though little had been said in the newspapers, the people knew that in the case of these nuptials the personal preferences of the principals had been involved. Powerful influences had tried to stop the marriage, but they had been bested. It seemed that the Prince Regent had insisted on doing something which every Japanese boy dreamed of achieving, marrying the girl he loved, rather than the one his parents had picked for him; and that Princess Nagako had proved that a kind Satsuma heart was worth more than a Choshu coronet, that even in Japan a Cinderella could win.

The happy couple retired for their honeymoon to the palace of Hirohito's uncle, Prince Takamatsu, at Okinajima, boating on the lake which lapped the terrace gardens, strolling along the slopes of Mount Bandai, on the opposite shore. And the Japanese public waited for the logical development. Some newspapers had informed them that among the presents they had received were "pillow books" from the Empress, which would take them diagram by diagram through the mechanics of sexual intercourse and the possible permutations of the technique.[7] Now the nation sat back to gossip and speculate about the expected outcome of the marriage. How soon would it be before Nagako produced a son?

[7] A not unusual gift for Japanese couples. They are sometimes known as "bride books."

Chapter Seven

In a land where the monarchical system insists that only a male child can succeed to the throne, the bearer of a royal baby must often feel like a traitor to her sex. For each time one of the eggs in her womb hatches a female, she must resent it; her *raison d'être* is the production of an heir, and each female she produces is an only too tangible evidence of her failure. A polite pretense is usually made by the government, by the officials of the court, even by the husband, that a daughter is welcome—and so she is if she is soon followed by a son.[1] But what if the Consort's cycle of ovulation seems to drop nothing but female eggs?

The marriage of the Prince Regent and Princess Nagako had taken place at the beginning of 1924, and the nation expected it would be celebrating the birth of a first child before the end of the year. Where love and romance are concerned, the Japanese can be sloppily sentimental, and their eyes had filled with tears as they had discussed Nagako's stormy engagement; but marriage is something else entirely, and they are coldly practical about it. A wife, particularly a royal wife, has but one purpose only, to be a vessel for her husband's children, preferably sons, and to produce them as speedily and efficiently as possible. It is not just instinctive stoicism which enables a Japanese woman to keep silent even during the worst labor pains; she knows she would lose "face" even with her own sex if she let out so much as a moan, for this is her function, and she

[1] In July, 1965, the King of Greece told reporters, after his wife gave birth to her first child, a daughter: "In our family we are polite. Ladies come first."

91

must perform it without fuss and without disturbing her husband.

The Japanese people waited for the tidings that would tell them that Nagako was doing what was expected of her, and when 1924 neared its end without any announcement that an accouchement was imminent, discussions were lively. If they are unemotional about marriage, they are also extremely practical and outspoken about sex, and when the first months of 1925 went by and still no announcement came, the whole of Japan began to speculate. At the same time the superstitious peasantry began spreading a rumor, which was soon heard at Court, that Nagako was the victim of a curse. Prince Yamagata had vowed on his death bed that she would never bear royal children and had made her barren. The hardheaded advisers around the throne brushed the idea of a curse aside (though it was surprising how many others believed it), but the potential barrenness of the Prince Regent's consort they did not so easily dismiss. For the moment they held no consultations with Hirohito, whom they rightly suspected would have reacted with some irritation, but Prince Saionji and Count Makino had a number of earnest confabulations with the old Empress. She at least did not need to be told what might happen to Nagako if her womb stayed empty, for was not Taisho himself the son of a concubine? The Empress, whose own prestige was involved in Nagako's performance, for she had been the most influential supporter of the girl against Prince Yamagata, sent for her daughter-in-law, questioned her closely, and sent her back to her husband with some wise words and some herbal infusions.

In the spring of 1925, Nagako was able to tell her husband that she was pregnant, at last. Once the fact of the seed's germination was well and truly beyond doubt, an official announcement was made and, in the next few months, the excitement began to mount. The Prince Regent and his wife spent most of that summer at the beach palace at Hayama, and it was the last time they were to have so much time together, at least until the autumn of their lives. To call it a beach palace is to flatter it, for it is a simple seaside villa with a garden running down to the sea, surrounded on the landside by a wall. Most of the rooms in the house have paper windows, Japanese style, which open to the garden and the sea, and floors covered with tatami, though there is a Western-styled study and library and, upstairs, a room with a panoramic view across the bay to Mount Fuji on one side and the fuming crater of Mihara on the other. There is also a small pavilion for the ritual of the tea ceremony, and, perched on a rock overlooking the water, a moon-viewing platform, two ceremonials in which the Prince Regent and his bride took much pleasure.

1926 was not the happiest year for Japan, for a variety of reasons. Military unrest and uneasiness were rife as the economic situation worsened and the civilians called for cuts in Army expenditure; the pride of the nation had been ruffled by the obtuseness of certain legislators in the United States in their handling of Oriental immigration questions; and there was widespread unemployment and hunger. It would be unfair to Hirohito to say that he was unaware of any of these uneasy fermentations—he was in fact, actively concerned in discussions about them—but he would nevertheless probably look back upon the summer of that year as one as near to idyllic as he has ever known it. With her pregnancy, the pressure had been taken off his wife, and he did not have to be concerned about the recurring question of their obligations for the time being. He was able to spend hours of every day out in the Bay fishing for specimens, hauling in shells and shrimps and crabs, and hours every evening examining them in his laboratory (a makeshift one at that time). The Diet had been adjourned and most of the members of the Cabinet had retired either to Karuizawa or Hakone to keep cool and escape the humid Tokyo heat. No politics. No responsibilities. Bliss.

At the end of September the Prince Regent and his consort moved back to the Akasaka Detached Palace in Tokyo and preparations began for the birth of the first royal child. It was expected in mid-November, and for the next six weeks workmen moved into the palace grounds to build a new maternity pavilion into which the princess would move when her time came. At the end of the first week in November, tents were raised in the palace grounds and reporters from the main Japanese newspapers arrived and settled in. They were assured by court chamberlains that they would not have long to wait before the good news—and the baby—was delivered.

In fact, they waited for three whole weeks. The baby did not come. Not that the newspapers worried too much about that. The delay only served to whoop up the excitement, and, of course, the circulation. With their frankness about sex, there was plenty of scope for discussion. In the meantime, the government offered bounties to all children born on the same day as the Prince Regent's child, the magazines and newspapers offered prizes for the composers of verses to hail the advent of the babe, and every town and city in the land first planned and then elaborated its

93

celebration ceremonies in anticipation. What did it matter if the November rain slashed down and turned the reporters' tenting ground into a quagmire?

Finally, on December 6th, Nagako gave birth to a girl child. The nation gulped and then politely expressed its joy. Hirohito announced that he was calling his daughter Terunomiya, or Little Sunshine, in the hope that her advent would bring rays of warmth into the life of his people. The nation bowed and said a restrained thank you, and whispered under its breath the hope that Nagako would do better next time.

The Emperor Taisho had been growing feebler every month, both physically and mentally, and now at last his time had come. His Empress had taken him to Hayama because there he could see Mount Fuji across the bay, a sight which had always comforted him, and there he expired on December 25, 1926. Christmas Day in Japan was not then the excuse for raucous and drunken celebration which it has since become,[2] and it was the end of a normal working day when the people heard the news. A day of mourning was ordained, but in fact, even had they been a race inclined to weep for the death of kings, the Japanese would have found this one hard to squeeze a tear over. Taisho for his whole life had been little more than a cipher, a shadow Emperor manipulated by the men behind the throne, not only mad but helpless.

"Immediately upon the passing from earthly life of an Emperor," a court circular pointed out, "his successor accedes to the Throne, for the Sovereign Seat can never be left vacant even for a single day." Hirohito was thus automatically Emperor in title now as well as in fact. The enthronement ceremonies would take place at Kyoto after a suitable period of court mourning, but meanwhile, inside the Imperial Palace, there was a short ceremony of accession. The Grand Master of the Rituals intoned the news that the new Emperor had come into possession of the Three Sacred Treasures of Japan, the Sacred Mirror (Yata-no-kagami) of his divine ancestress, Amaterasu, the Sun Goddess, the Sacred Sword (Ame-no-murakamo-no-tsurugi) of her belligerent and bloodthirsty brother, Susanoo, and the Sacred Jewel Necklace (Yasakani-no-magatama) of her sister, Tsuki-no-kami, the Moon Goddess. He prayed to his ancestors in

[2] The Japanese reverse the order compared with the West, celebrate (loudly and publicly) at Christmas, but observe New Year's Day with religious services and family devotions.

94

the palace shrines for guidance, and then retired with his advisers to find a name for his regime and to write the Imperial Rescript which would signpost the path his regime intended to follow.

On December 28, 1926, it was announced that he had called his reign Showa, which means Enlightened Peace, a choice that was most sincerely meant by Hirohito even though it was to prove so ironically inept in the years to come. In his Rescript issued on the same day he said:

"Having succeeded, through the benign influence of our Imperial ancestors, to the Throne of a lineal succession unbroken from ages eternal, and having assumed the power to reign over and govern the Empire, We have now performed the solemnity of the ascension to the Throne. It is our resolve to observe the fundamental rules of the State, to cultivate the inherited virtue, and to maintain intact the glorious tradition set by Our ancestors."

After which traditional preamble, he went on:

"With Our limited gifts, We are mindful of the difficulty of proving ourselves equal to the great task which has devolved upon Us. The world is now in a process of evolution. A new chapter is being opened in the history of human civilisation. This nation's settled policy always stands for progress and improvement. Simplicity instead of vain display, originality instead of blind imitation, progress in view of this period of evolution, improvement to keep pace with the advancement of civilization, national harmony in purpose and in action, beneficence to all classes of people, and friendship to all the nations of the earth: these are the cardinal aims to which Our most profound and abiding solicitude is directed."

Hirohito was twenty-five years old. Since so many of his father's Rescripts had been written and even sealed without the poor mad Emperor ever having seen them, Hirohito wrote the first of his own reign in his own words, and he meant every one of them. He was still a shy and diffident young man, and marriage had not changed him, for Nagako was not yet experienced enough nor sufficiently confident to give him the stiffening he needed. His advisers had urged him to call his new reign a restoration rather than a mere succession, to symbolize the new spirit of dedication which he would devote to the welfare of his people and his people to the welfare of Japan. From Hirohito's standpoint, Showa expressed all he hoped from the future—enlightened peace.

But there were others who had different interpretations. For only a naïve optimist of twenty-five could have looked at what was happening in

Japan and in the world and believe that the future was golden. In Japan itself the Army was restless, because the economic pruners were abroad with their axes, lopping large branches off the military tree and, in the view of at least the younger members of the staff, threatening the very future of the land forces. The Navy's future had been settled, at least for the time being, by the 1922 conference in Washington at which Admiral Kato had secured a measure of agreement about the building of new warships; for the moment there was no longer any risk of frenetic competition between the three major naval powers, Japan, America and Britain. But the Army was subject to no such limitation by international agreement, and in the years just before the Great Kanto Earthquake liberal and leftwing elements, despite harassment by the police and the secret societies, had campaigned for a reduction in the Army's expenditure and a harder and closer look at its plans by the government supposed to control it. It was a campaign which had some success before the earthquake, but considerably more afterward, when the need to economize became urgent. Just before the Emperor's accession, the War Department bowed to the agitation and the Minister for War, General Kazushige Ugaki, brought in a scheme for the scrapping of four whole divisions of the Imperial force, a move which infuriated the younger members of the Army to the point of mutiny. They were not mollified by the announcement that the destruction of two Army corps was to be counterbalanced by the expansion of the air force, the establishment of an armored corps, and the creation of an antiaircraft section. Nor did they take much comfort from Ugaki's plan to institute a system of compulsory military service which would begin in the schools with an intensive curriculum of military education.

But Ugaki knew what he was doing. In the early 1920's, particularly just after the earthquake, the unpopularity of the Army had reached such a pitch that it could be dangerous for a soldier to walk on the streets in uniform after dark. By a widely publicized policy of retrenchment—which was, in fact, no more than a windowdressing operation—the Minister of War took the heat off the Army for the time being. But shortly after Hirohito's accession, he began the campaign to rebuild its popularity. What better way to do it than to play on the fears and the resentments of the people, by persuading them that the rest of the world—particularly the Occidental world—was against them. To do this was not difficult, for the United States had handily provided a potent excuse for whipping up antigaijin propaganda.

96

It was one of Ugaki's fellow generals, Kojiro Sato, who had once described Japan as "a potted plant" desperately seeking for room for its roots and food to feed it as it grew. Britain had its roots, he said, stretching to India and Africa and the Antipodes. The United States (with a population density of thirty-one per square mile compared with Japan's four hundred) was nurtured by the arrangements in the Americas. France, Belgium and Holland all had their feeding grounds.

But what of Japan? What was Japan to do about her hungry and thirsty roots? Where was she to feed them? If the colonial powers and the United States denied her the right to have colonies, feeding grounds, too, surely there could be only one alternative—to allow her to send her surplus population to the places where there was room for them to live and work; in other words, to open the gates of Canada, Australia, Latin America, New Zealand and the United States to Japanese immigration.

Canada, Australia and New Zealand had already made it clear that they were operating a "whites only" policy, and it was difficult for the Japanese propagandists to concentrate resentment against them, for they were Dominions of the British Empire for whom Britain, the mother country, acted as spokesman; and, in this case, speaking as an old ally of Japan, the British said how much they disagreed with the whole thing, but what could they do? South America shrugged its shoulders at any protests.

But from the United States the people of Japan—if not the government—expected rather more sympathy. There were large colonies of Japanese in Hawaii and in the western states of the Union, and they wrote home to say that opportunities were boundless—land waiting to be tilled, homes to be made, crops to be grown by those willing to work hard enough. Did not the message on the Statue of Liberty say to the world: "Give me your poor and oppressed"? And had not the United States responded with unprecedented generosity to the emergency of the Great Kanto Earthquake, showing her friendship with munificent gifts of money, clothing and food? So now, as Japan's economic situation grew worse, surely she would accept the immigrants who might otherwise starve.

It so happened, however, that the United States in the mid-1920's was going through a psychological crisis about immigration not unlike that which afflicted the people of Britain in 1965. There was economic retrenchment in the United States, too, and a feeling that there were too many foreigners around threatening the job security of native-born

97

citizens. Vague resentment against competition from white immigrants boiled over into racial hatred so far as the Asiatics were concerned, and there had already been some clashes in California between whites and yellows in the truckfarm areas, where the Japanese laborers were accused of cutting wages and the Japanese growers were accused of cutting prices. In 1924 a bill was introduced into both Houses of Congress limiting immigration from all countries to 150,000 a year, the quota from each country to be decided by the number of natives of that original nationality already settled in the United States.

That would have been bad enough for the Japanese, for their quota would not have amounted to more than 150 in any one year. Some of the sponsors of the bill, however, were out to show that they were not only keeping out immigrants but also keeping the country "American," and they inserted a completely unnecessary and gratuitously insulting clause into the bill specifically excluding "Asiatics" from any part of the quota whatsoever. Since the Chinese were already banned under a previous law, the clause could only be—and was—meant to discriminate against the Japanese and make it clear that they were not wanted. That was bad enough. But what happened subsequently was worse. Secretary of State Hughes, well aware of implications of the bill and what might be its effect on American-Japanese relations, did his best to lobby opposition to the Exclusion Clause and called in the Japanese ambassador, Mr. Masakao Hanihara, to discuss the question with him. Their talk ended with Hughes suggesting that Hanihara should write him a personal letter outlining the serious effect the passage of the clause might have in Japan, and this he did, stressing the consequences which might ensue from passing a bill which implied that his countrymen were "undesirables." The letter was circulated in the Senate with an explanation of how it had come to be written; but this did not stop Senator Henry Cabot Lodge, a brahmin diehard and isolationist, from speaking in the subsequent debate and characterizing it as "interference" in American domestic affairs. The Japanese ambassador had used the phrase "serious consequences" to describe what he thought might be his country's reaction to the clause. Did this mean, asked Lodge rhetorically, that Japan was threatening war?

The bill was passed and the shutters clanged down on Japanese immigration into the United States. That was not the most serious result of the bill, but the way it had been handled in the Senate. This evidence of Occidental antipathy, even contempt, for the Japanese gave the military in Japan just the propaganda weapon it needed. In his Rescript, the new Emperor had called for "friendship to all the nations of the earth." But what was the use of offering friendship to those who were so obviously intent on spurning the proffered hand? Must Japan continue to truckle to those who despised her? Was it not better to realize the facts of the situation—that Japan was surrounded by those who hated her, who might attack her at any moment?

And so the propaganda began that was to convert Hirohito's reign from one of Enlightened Peace into one of planned belligerence. That the new Emperor believed in peace and would personally abhor any policy that led to illiberalism at home and aggression abroad was of no importance to the Doiharas and the Tojos, who were now rising in the military machine. It was merely a question of keeping him under control, so that he would have no opportunity of conveying his own opinions to the people; of suppressing his personality as a popular monarch and building up his persona as the divine symbol of a new Japan, dedicated to loyalty, obedience and sacrifice.

A rash of articles began to appear in the newspapers about the divine heritage of the Imperial line, combined with exhortations to the people to dedicate their lives to the new Emperor's service and die for him if necessary. And very soon a number of them did. A schoolboy immolated himself, clutching the Emperor's picture to him, when the school building housing it caught fire and could not be rescued in time. A young Army lieutenant fell on his sword when he made a slip of the tongue while reading an Imperial Rescript to his men. These and other incidents were hailed in the newspapers as "happy manifestations" of love for the Emperor, and Japanese temperament being what it is, these pathetic martyrdoms swelled the hearts of the people rather than depressed them. The unpopular militarists of the early 1920's rapidly came into favor again as soldiers of the Emperor, crusaders for what was soon to be known as Kodo, the Imperial Way.

It was the first successful stage in the Army's plot to transmute a young and modern king into a shadowy god hidden behind a moat and a wall.

In 1927 it was announced that the Empress was pregnant with her second child, and all over the land loyal subjects gathered in front of their Shinto shrines and clapped their hands to call attention to their prayers that this time Nagako would be allowed to produce an heir. She wasn't. A second daughter was born, who fell ill a few months after birth from a wasting disease which subsequently killed her at the age of two. But if she brought scant comfort to the Emperor and Empress, she did achieve one useful thing in her short life. Her illness was a painful one, and Nagako found it hard to bear the sight and sound of her sufferings. Finally, she could stand it no longer. It was a rule of the Imperial House that royal persons were never to be subjected to "medical molestation," and such things as hypodermic injections were strictly forbidden. Nagako pleaded with her husband to have the rule rescinded so far as her ailing daughter was concerned, and he agreed to call in the doctors and allow pain-killing injections to be given. It was the beginning of a new regime for the royal children; thereafter they were able to receive full medical treatment whenever it was thought necessary.

But there were no pain-killing drugs to comfort Nagako, only too well aware that the nation blamed her for failing once again. It can have given her no comfort at all to be present, the following year, at the marriage of the Emperor's brother, Prince Chichibu. The Prince had escaped all his life the rigid supervision which had been Hirohito's lot since childhood. He had been allowed to go to Oxford. He danced and played tennis. He was gay and gregarious; another Prince of Wales, the Emperor must have thought. And no one had stood in his way when he chose his own bride, the pretty and cosmopolitan Setsuko Matsudaira, daughter of the Japanese ambassador to Britain. As she watched the wedding ceremony, Nagako must have wondered anxiously whether the popular younger brother and his new bride might cause even more heartache for her—by producing a male child first.[3]

A month after the wedding, the nation gave itself over to three weeks of pageantry and celebration. The period of mourning for Taisho had passed, and the time had come to ceremonially enthrone the new Emperor. For the Army it could not have been more opportune, for it took the pressure off them. There were rumors of a grave political crisis over Japanese policy in China, where the pro-Japanese warlord, Marshal Chang Tso-lin, had been killed by a mine which blew up his special train. The government, with Hirohito's concurrence, had called for stern measures to punish the murderers, for the old marshal was an ally of the Japanese; but now, it seemed, the murderers were none other than mem-

---

[3] They didn't. There were no children of the marriage.

bers of the Japanese Army, acting as agents provocateurs. What could the government do? They had been deceived themselves and had, in turn, deceived their Emperor. As a smoke screen to cover their embarrassment, the enthronement could not have come at a better moment, and they poured government money into the task of making it an extravagant panoply of ancient ceremonial such as Japan had not seen since the days of the Heian Empire.

"Rarely can a State ceremony have had a more beautiful setting than that of the Emperor's departure today for Kyoto for his enthronement," wrote the *Times* of London correspondent on November 6, 1928. "When the first figures of the Imperial procession appeared at seven A.M. on the upper bridge at the Palace entrance, the sun had just risen above a low bank of clouds and was pouring a soft light full on the scene. The broad sanded spaces of the foreground were framed in solid masses of troops whose bayonets flashed in the light, and behind rose the famous double bridge winding into the castle through the deep green banks of the moat and the cyclopean walls of the ancient Palace fortress."

These were the days before television and the correspondents could let themselves go. They had plenty of material to work on. For once the court was anxious to secure as much publicity as possible for the ceremonials, for they were deliberately designed to emphasize from start to finish the divinity of the monarch taking part in them. So reporters and foreign diplomats, who were allowed to see at least part of the ceremonial, were loaded down with booklets and prints designed to explain to them the sacred nature of what was taking place. The *Times* of London commended its readers to look at *The Golden Bough* for parallels and devoted eight columns to its descriptions. One need only read it, together with the official handbook issued by the court, to realize that if it was a colorful spectacle for the onlookers, it was an ordeal for the Emperor.

He had arrived in Kyoto with the Empress from Nagoya on the evening of November 9, 1928, and there was not much sleep for either of them, for their gowns were elaborate, his a ceremonial robe of white silk damask, hers a complicated damask gown with train and elaborate hairdo spiked with ornamental pins. In the morning they paraded before the assembled guests, Japanese and foreign, to worship before the Kashiko-Dokoro, or Imperial Sanctuary, to inform the Sun Goddess, Amaterasu, of the Emperor's ascension, and afterward to offer food to the goddess to the accompaniment of prayers and ritual music. In the afternoon, Hirohito

101

now clad in orange robes (the color of the rising sun), the formal en-thronement took place "to inform the living world of that which in the morning was announced to the world of spirits." The heralds signaled the coming of the Emperor and his Empress, curtains were pushed aside so that the assembly could see them sitting on their canopied thrones, and to the accompaniment of drums and cymbals and gongs, Hirohito an-nounced himself as occupier of the throne of Japan and everyone bowed profoundly before him. But it was not over yet. There followed a day of ritual bathing, of elaborate dances and the ringing of bells to summon the Emperor's ancestors. After which, on the third day, followed the mysterious and sacred rite of Daijosai, or Thanksgiving Festival, which Dr. Minobe has called "the arcanum of initiation into the duties of king-ship." From this ceremonial all foreigners were excluded. Two sacred huts had been built in the grounds of the Imperial Palace and would be destroyed once it was over; huts of plain pine with the bark left on, their boards tied together with the tendrils of wild vines. The timbers had been cut with Shinto rites by workmen first purified by a Shinto priest. The first tree felled had been burned as an offering to the god of wood, and the rest drawn through the streets of Kyoto by peasants bedecked in ancient costume.

Hirohito took a bath in an ordinary square Japanese tub, to wash away all impurities, and then once more donned a robe of white. His hands were ritually cleaned by a priest, and he was now ready "by all the high and ancient rites of Shinto to enter as High Priest of the Nation into com-munion with the great kami [goddess] of the food ritual." After the sing-ing of harvest songs and ancient dances, torch bearers (for it was evening) took their place at the entrance to the first of the sacred huts.

The *Times* reported:

"The Emperor entered in a sacred procession. The sword and jewel were carried on his right and left. The central part of the corridor was reserved for the Emperor alone who 'walks between heaven and earth.' His feet were bare, and, as he passed, a mat of rushes was rolled up behind him so that no other foot may tread upon it. This, no doubt, is a survival of the ancient belief that ground on which the naked feet of the ruler has trod become taboo. Over his head was held an umbrella made of reeds and suspended from it the beak of a brazen phoenix. He entered the sacred hut; the Empress and the princes retired; the musicians withdrew. . . . The curtains were drawn; the Emperor was alone. He made his obeisance before the elevated seat of the unseen goddess; then, after a few moments of composure, began his acts of devotion, which consists of placing the offerings [of food] before her. He waited on the invisible Princess and partook of the same food and drink. Every utensil employed, the furniture, the building itself, take him to the remotest antiquity. Centuries were eliminated in his sight. Fully four hours were spent in this reverent communion. After an hour's interval, the Emperor entered the second room to repeat the same sacrament, retiring only with the coming of the dawn."

The *Times* correspondent added:

"Is it possible for any mortal to forget an experience like this? Will not the remembrance of devotions so unique follow him through life? This is ancestor worship pure and simple, fidelity to the past pledged to the duties of the present and the service of the future. . . . It is a solemn form of oath by which the new Sovereign binds himself to observe the laws of his fathers."

Chapter Eight

Professor Ivan Morris, the great authority on the Heian Period (784-1156) in Japan, has described "the love of life of the Heian aristocracy" at the Court of Kyoto as being "marked by a curious mixture of depravity and decorum" and "a high degree of promiscuity."[1] James Kirkup calls the ladies of the court during the same period as a collection of "tittering snobs" whose sexual peccadilloes in the frail pavilions of the Imperial Palace reduced them to a state of "nerve-racked rapture." On the other hand, the ladies of the court in Hirohito's day lived lives which were less circumscribed and therefore did not palpitate with such dangerous but delectable temptations. It was made clear to them at the beginning of the new Emperor's reign that the system of royal concubinage, so popular with his father and grandfather, was abolished and they need no longer expect to be summoned for amorous duty according to their Emperor's whim; a decision which, in the circumstances, caused not as much relief as an Occidental might have imagined. It was made plain that life at court should strive for a condition of respectability and circumspection; and the ladies were urged to be sedate and well-behaved at all times. But one appetite they shared with their ancestors at Kyoto, and this no court edict could curb—a passionate love of gossip, the more scandalous and malicious the better.

The Empress was giving them plenty to gossip about. In 1929 it was

[1] Ivan Morris, *The World of the Shining Prince*, New York: Alfred A. Knopf, Inc., 1964.

announced that she was with child again, and for the third time she gave birth to a daughter. True, the national disappointment was tempered with sympathy for Nagako, since the death of her weakly second daughter occurred about the same time, and word was spread that the Empress regarded the new child, named Takanomiya, as a "divine substitution" for the dead baby.

But three daughters in a row! Word quickly spread among the ladies of the court that the Imperial advisers were worried. In particular, Prince Saionji, the old Genro, was said to have taken the matter much to heart and had been engaged in solemn consultation with Count Makino, the Lord Keeper of the Privy Seal, and Count Tanaka, a venerable court official who belied his eighty years of age by great physical and mental energy. It was soon common gossip around the court what was being discussed, and a quiver of anticipation was to be discerned among the ladies-in-waiting, more especially among the younger ones. Should the Emperor be urged to sire an heir through one of them?

The Imperial Succession Law is quite clear about what should happen in the event of an Empress failing to produce a son. The succession to the throne can pass only to a male; and in the days before Meiji, it was always possible for an Emperor to adopt a suitable young relative from among the families at Court. Meiji brought this custom to an end, and made it mandatory that the heir be of the Emperor's blood. He did not need to be legitimate (bastardy has never been of itself an impediment in Japan). Should the Empress be barren, or should she, as in Nagako's case, persist in spawning females, then the royal concubines were at the disposal of the Emperor to breed him an heir, and it was his duty to utilize them. The first to produce him a son could well be the mother of the next Emperor of Japan.

But would the Emperor be prepared to do his duty?

It is a measure of Hirohito's character (and their realization that he was "different" from most Japanese) that the three old statesmen [2] hesitated before approaching the Emperor on the subject. To the great majority of Japanese, there was nothing strange in the custom. Meiji himself had fathered so many royal bastards that he never saw half of

---

[2] Only one of whom, incidentally, Count Tanaka, was the legitimate son of his parents. Saionji was illegitimately sired by his father, a bachelor, and then adopted by him. Count Makino was also adopted.

105

them after they were born. The one he did see, Taisho, had succeeded him on the throne. The average Japanese wife knew only too well that, after the first year or so of marriage, the husband sought his sexual pleasure outside the home; and many a young married woman was regarded as a spent force by the age of twenty-five, expected to sublimate her own sexual needs while her husband found his elsewhere, with geishas if he could afford them, or with prostitutes if he could not. If Hirohito turned away from Nagako now (or so the court ladies reasoned, as excitement began to mount) what had she to complain about? She was now nearly thirty years old, and had tried and failed three times to produce a son. She was no stranger to the habits of royalty. Had not most of her own father's nineteen children been born of concubines?

It was not until 1930, however, that a positive move was made by the three elderly statesmen to bring the matter of the succession before the Emperor. It was Prince Saionji who reminded him of his duty to the state, doing so in a long letter written from his country home in which no direct reference was made to the question of taking a concubine; the old man was far too subtle for that. Instead he spoke of the nation's great love for the Emperor and its ardent desire to see him fulfil their dearest wishes by giving them his son to continue the line. He made a reference to the beloved Nagako and the three daughters she had borne. She too must wish to see her beloved husband become the father of a son, no matter how great a test it might be of her fortitude and courage.[3]

The Emperor cannot have missed the purport of the missive, but whether he replied to it is unknown. What does seem to be certain is that he made no mention of it whatsoever to Nagako. She, however, did not need to be told. Her servants brought back to her the gossip among the ladies of the court, and they were agog. Count Tanaka had been talking to some of the older ladies-in-waiting and had given them instructions; soon, amid titters of quaking excitement, the whisper spread among the young ladies that they were to dress in their finest kimonos and to go as far as seductive glances and honeyed words could to show their adulation for the Emperor whenever he came among them. The days of concubinage were not over after all. A son was needed for Japan— and the one with the warmest glances might well set the sweet trap that could capture the Emperor. The young ladies trembled behind their fans

[3] Information supplied by a former official of the court who does not wish to be identified.

in a tizzy of emotion. The Emperor was young and handsome, and they knew their duty. Here was an appeal to their patriotism that they found quite irresistible.

And then suddenly—at least for the moment—the tensions slackened, and in the ladies' pavilion at the Imperial court the smiles on the pretty faces turned to pouts. It was announced in 1931 that Empress Nagako was once more pregnant, for the fourth time.

Surely, this time it would be a boy. If the spirits of the court ladies slumped at the news, those of the Japanese people rose. As her time drew near, excitement began to boil throughout the land and crowds of loyal subjects came in by every train to gather outside the palace, in the Imperial plaza beside the moat, to bow toward the unseen Emperor, to keep vigil until the child was born, and to pray that he would be a boy. In the newspaper offices arrangements were made for special editions to be rushed on the streets the moment news was received—exultant panegyrics under joyful headlines if it were a male child, flatter and less enthusiastic displays if it were a girl. Just across the moat, sirens had been erected; they would sound once for a girl, twice for a boy.

When Nagako's labor pains began, a telephone call went out to Prince Saionji at his country home, and he made one of his increasingly rare journeys to the capital. With Count Makino, Count Tanaka and Baron Yuasa, Minister of the Imperial Household, he went into the anteroom of the maternity pavilion. He did not have to wait long. Four hours later, he was seen leaving the anteroom and climbing into his car, which took him to the railway station. He looked old and dispirited.

Shortly afterwards the sirens on the palace walls began to sound. One blast. Would it be followed by another to signal a boy? But no, it stopped short. And silence followed. The crowd turned to look at each other, and only a few scattered "banzai's" were heard.

Nagako had given birth to her fourth daughter. Now the Emperor would *have* to take a concubine.

It was now five years since Hirohito had ascended the throne of Japan, and he had found the going rough not only in his domestic life. The pressure was increasing to force him to obey in the council rooms of the state as well as in the boudoir. Had the acquiescence which was demanded of him come simply from his government or from the elder statesmen who acted as his advisers, he would have found no strain in conforming; his nature and training were such that he was naturally inclined to bow before the judgment of those who were older and therefore must be wiser; and though the government of the day had its faults, at least it came nearer to a democratically elected regime than ever before in Japan's history. Perhaps one day manhood suffrage would be both universal and fair, as it was in Britain, whose system he so much admired, but in the meantime the government was doing the best it could (or so he believed); and at least in Japan, where exports were booming and industrialists were making profits, conditions were better than in the United States, blighted by the Depression, and in Britain itself, racked by vast unemployment and want.

In fact, however, the government of Japan was in a sorry mess, and repeatedly gave the secret societies an excuse to claim, not always unjustly, that the administration of the country was in the hands of exploiters. Towards the end of the 1920's several of the members of these secret associations banded together into a society called Nikkyo, otherwise known as the All-Japan Patriots Society, which dedicated its members to fight against corruption in government, against the overt influence of the zaibatsu (that is, the big industrial cartels), against the "evil effect" on the Emperor of the advice of the Genro, and against the general perversion of the Imperial rule by men of ill will. They had points in their favor. The two main parties which took turns to govern in Japan were indeed financed and almost certainly controlled by the great industrial cartels—the Minseito Party by Mitsubishi, the Seiyukai Party by Mitsui. There had been many scandals about bribery and corruption in government.[4]

The members of the Nikkyo rallied under the banner of a fervent patriot named Doctor Uesugi to remove "malign influences" from the government and promote the "divine will" of the Emperor. They called their policy Kodo-ha, or the Way of the Emperor, and they insisted that their only object was to "purify" Japanese life and bring it back to dignity and respect. To find the word Kodo as well as another phrase, Hakko-ichi-u, which they also used as a slogan, the secret societies had delved back into the mythical past of Japan for an Imperial Rescript said to have been issued by the Emperor Jimmu in 660 B.C. The two expressions had been used in that Rescript. Kodo meant literally "the Im-

[4] It was said that Mitsubishi and one of their pet politicians had made fortunes when Japan left the gold standard during the 1931 crisis.

perial Way" and Hakko-ichi-u "the eight corners of the world under one roof" and, in their context, signified respectively, the benevolence of the Emperor and the brotherhood of man.

Even the Nikkyo maintained that by following Kodo-ha this was what they were trying to promote. One of the principal activists of the Nikkyo [5] wrote, "The meaning of the word Kodo signifies the correct path of conduct for the Japanese nation and the correct position of the Emperor. The ideology of Kodo has never included the ideology of aggression."

It all depends what you mean by aggression, of course. The campaign of "purification" which the patriotic societies conducted in the late 1920's and early 1930's used the Emperor's name to assassinate a prime minister, a financier and an industrialist. The prime minister, Hamaguchi, they killed because he had accepted the "humiliation" of the 5-5-3 ratio for the navies of Britain, America and Japan at the London Naval Conference. The minister and the industrialist were murdered for their attempts to block the departure from the gold standard during the 1931 economic crisis—proof, the plotters said, of their entanglement with foreign banking interests in the West. But if the secret societies killed, they did so for domestic reasons, to further sincere, if misguided, efforts to end domestic corruption and decadence.

Bad enough. But it was not until the militarists, who had so far only egged them on from the sidelines, swamped the secret societies and actively adopted Kodo as a slogan for themselves that the "Way of the Emperor" became a synonym for world conquest, a camouflage for aggression, an excuse for foreign adventures which the Japanese people might otherwise have refused to stomach.

But before setting the feet of the Japanese along the Imperial Way, it was necessary for the military to make sure that the Emperor himself was willing to tread it first; and despite his mildness of manner and amenability to reason, they doubted if his present circumstances made him a willing traveler along the road they had chosen for him. For Hirohito had shown that he was deeply perturbed about the activities of

[5] Yoshio Kodama. A member of several secret societies before joining Nikkyo, often imprisoned for anti-Government activities, but later a Government agent in China. Kodama was arrested in 1945 and accused before the International Military Tribunal, Far East. He was given a nominal sentence and released.

the Japanese Army in China, and had made it clear to his ministers that further adventures on the Asiatic mainland were to be curbed, even at the risk of incurring the displeasure of the Army. For the moment, the militarists were willing to believe that this hostility on the Emperor's part was due more to misguided advice given him by his "decadent" and "defeatist" advisers than to any inherent dislike of overseas adventures; and the plot they formulated in March, 1931, was designed purely and simply to "purge" him of the influences which stood in the way of his understanding and sympathy for the Army's intentions. As has been mentioned, a member of the Nikkyo had shot the Japanese Prime Minister, Hamaguchi, on the platform of Shimbashi Station—a favorite spot for such deeds—the previous year, as a reprisal for his "humiliating" acceptance of the London Naval Treaty. The militarists, who wanted him and his Cabinet out of the way for other reasons, waited for the fall of the government that should have automatically followed, especially since the assassin was hailed as a hero by most of the newspapers. But Hamaguchi did not immediately expire; he lingered on, though gravely wounded; and so did his Cabinet.

Thereupon, the activists in the Army decided that if the Cabinet refused to give up its seats, then something must be done to overturn them. The middle-rank members of the Army General Staff in Tokyo were in close touch with their senior officers in Manchuria, and knew that a coup was being planned that would lead to the annexation of that country. They rightly suspected that the Hamaguchi Cabinet, well aware that Japan was a member of the League of Nations and pledged to eschew aggression under the Briand-Kellogg Pact, would never accept the coup, and that a new and more militarily aligned government was a prerequisite for the annexation.

Thereupon a certain Colonel Hashimoto, aided by a militant civilan named Doctor Okawa (they were both members of a branch of the Nikkyo called the Cherry Society) planned a domestic coup of their own which they believed would drive the already panicky Hamaguchi Cabinet from power. A session of the Diet was planned for March 20, 1931, at which foreign affairs would be discussed. Hashimoto and Okawa thrashed out a plan whereby the doctor would provide demonstrators who would gather in front of the Diet at the appropriate moment and clash with the police, sufficiently violently to provoke the need for military reinforcements. Then Hashimoto and a number of Army officers (al-

110

ready in the plot) and their men would arrive to take over. Martial law would be declared. The Diet would be prorogued. War Minister Ugaki —a serving Army officer—would take over as premier, and a pro-Army administration would be in power ready to approve the plans for conquest in Manchuria. It would all, of course, be done in the name of Kodo, the Imperial Way.

Hashimoto had already secured the agreement of the chief of the military affairs bureau, the vice chief of the general staff, the chief of the intelligence bureau and several other high officers to his plan. They in turn contacted War Minister Ugaki and came away satisfied that they had secured his acquiescence, if not active participation, in the plot. This was not unusual, of course, in Japanese affairs; the language is made for inferences and circumlocutions which might be taken as agreement or disagreement, one can never be sure. At any rate, the plan went ahead and Hashimoto actually delivered to Doctor Okawa some two hundred small practice bombs which his demonstrators were to use to create the utmost confusion in front of the Diet.

And then something went wrong. Whether it was that War Minister Ugaki backed out of the plot at the last moment, or whether he had never agreed to it at all, is not now clear. But the plot fizzled out without the general public ever hearing about it. Okawa called off his demonstrators, and, temporarily, retired from the terrorist business. So did Colonel Hashimoto. But not for long.

On September 18, 1931, the Kwantung Army in Manchuria independently embarked on the annexation of that country, ignoring opposition to their plans in Tokyo. As usual, they manufactured an excuse for their aggression: once more, as in the case of the killing of Marshal Chang Tso-lin in 1928, a train on the line near Mukden was blown up by a mine. This time Japanese were among those killed. Once more the Japanese command in Manchuria blamed "provocateurs" in the Chinese Army and took over key points in the country as "necessary measures of self-defense" and "to protect the lives of Japanese civilians." The plot by local Army officers to seize the country had reached its climax, and the establishment of Japanese-controlled Manchukuo, with Henry Pu Yi as its puppet Emperor, was on the way.

The Prime Minister in power at the time of the coup (Hamaguchi meanwhile having died of his wounds and his administration dissolved) was an irresolute politician named Mr. Reijiro Wakatsuki. Why he had been chosen for the job at this moment in Japan's history is a mystery. The three statesmen most responsible for recommending him to the Emperor, Prince Saionji, Count Makino and Baron Harada, appear to have done so because they believed he would stand up to the Army in the matter of keeping its budget under control and exercising needed economies. But he was soon shown to be vacillating and craven-hearted (not surprisingly, perhaps, in the circumstances) when Army matters came before him.

The secretary to the Lord Keeper of the Privy Seal, Count Makino, at this time was a certain Baron Koichi Kido, who will loom larger in this story as it proceeds from now on. The office of the Lord Keeper of the Privy Seal was a key one in that it was this official who maintained a constant contact between the Emperor and his Ministers: it was through him that all audiences with the Emperor were arranged (with the important exception of the Ministers of War and Navy, who had free right of access); and it was through him that all information about what was happening in his Empire was conveyed to the monarch. If Count Makino was his Imperial master's voice, Baron Kido was Makino's eyes and ears. It was his job to act as informant of any rumors, gossip, plots and trends which came to his ears. Fortunately for the researcher into the period, he also kept a diary of his professional comings and goings, and from it a day-to-day record can be pieced together of events in Japan as seen from the Imperial Palace.

It is from Kido's record that it is possible to measure Hirohito's reaction to the coup in Manchuria and the dangerous permeation of the Army by political elements, especially among the junior officers. The evidence shows that the senior statesmen were quickly disillusioned with Wakatsuki's performance. Shortly after news of the Manchurian coup reached Tokyo, Kido realized that "unless the Cabinet now took resolute action, political power might be transferred to the Army, and it could be said that we were now in a constitutional crisis. Thus having been concerned with the permeation of the Army by political elements since the March [Hashimoto] Incident, I was most concerned at the unreliable attitude of Premier Wakatsuki at the time." [6]

Between them, Kido, Baron Harada and a brilliant young aristocrat, Prince Konoye, succeeded in putting a poker down the backbone of the

[6] Affidavit before the International Military Tribunal, Far East.

112

apprehensive premier by insisting that the policy they advocated of opposition to the Army's muscle-flexing activities in Manchuria came from the Emperor himself, who wished to see it enforced. The premier went away promising to take more energetic steps to discipline the recalcitrant and rampant militarists, and let it be known that his Cabinet were "resolute" in their disapproval. In the circumstances, it was a brave thing to do, for the Army was furious at these signs that the government's attitude was stiffening against them. Kido writes in his diary (September 22, 1931):

"Fearing for Saionji's life, Konoye, Sakaiye, Okabe and I decided that it would be wiser if he did not come to Tokyo. We were all opposed to the Army and things were so critical and military feeling was running so high that we were apprehensive of the Emperor's safety, but he was never advised of our opinion that it might be wiser for him to say nothing more about the Manchurian affair. We thought it better for the Emperor to let the Cabinet pursue its policy upon its own responsibility."

On October 1, 1931, Kido discussed with Prince Konoye the possibility of a *coup d'état* in Japan itself by the Army. "We decided on a program to guide the militarists before a national calamity should happen," he writes. "After the outbreak of the Manchurian Incident on September 19, 1931, the Army's attitude became so tough that the problem of national reform began to be discussed. At the same time there was a report that even a reform of the Imperial Household was being discussed. Prince Konoye told me of his being anxious about this problem. So we went together to Ichiki, Minister of the Imperial Household, and asked him to be most careful and deliberate lest he should fall in a trap to be laid by the Army. With regard to the strong attitude of the Army, the premier said to the Lord Keeper of the Privy Seal that the Army seemed to disagree with the Government as to the question of solving the Manchurian question through negotiations with the Nanking Government. The premier said that concerning this point the Government might come into a head-on conflict with the Army."

On October 6, 1931, Kido reported to Makino and Saionji his deep apprehension about Army intrigues in Tokyo, and on the following day he was able to tell the Lord Keeper of the Privy Seal that a plot was about to erupt. "Monday, October 7. Fine day. Went to office at 10 A.M. and in the afternoon the Lord Keeper came to his office. Harada was called up and at three-thirty he came. Harada was asked to press Prince

113

Saionji to return quickly to Tokyo in view of the acute situation. In the evening Mr. Otaira Shinichi of the Chugai Shogyo and Mr. Mori Tetsuo of the Hochi newspapers called on me. The fact that Count Kiyura called at the Lord Keeper's was an important event to both of them. They asked me various questions. At 10 P.M. called at Harada's. Just then Harada was called out to the Prime Minister's residence. He was asked by the Prime Minister to convey to Prince Saionji the Prime Minister's wish that the prince return to Tokyo quickly. On Harada's return we talked over the latest development in the situation and I left his house at 11:30."

On October 17 all the rumors Kido had been hearing became realities, and he recorded in his diary for that day:

"Saturday. Returned home towards evening. Just then the telephone rang. It was Harada at Kyoto. Was told of the arrest of several General Staff officers. Immediately I called upon Marquis Inouye [finance minister in the government] from whom I heard a story approximately as follows: leading officers in the Army, including War Minister Minami, sat in conference at the War Minister's official residence last night. It was a very important conference. It lasted until three o'clock in the morning. It was only at that hour that the final decision was reached, with the result that at four this morning Lieut. Colonel Hashimoto, Lieut. Colonel Nemoto and ten others were arrested 'for protection' by the gendarmerie. They were planning to besiege and occupy the War Department and the General Staff Office and then to carry out a *coup d'etat*. For that purpose they were going to assemble young officers at the Kaikosha this noon to give them directives. Within this defection was an Imperial Guard regiment commander, and it seems that they were well in a position to mobilise one or two companies. This is indeed an astonishing event. Called the Lord Keeper at seven and conveyed the foregoing information."

Colonel Hashimoto again. But his plot had mushroomed, and he appeared to be well aware that among those to be reckoned hostile to his designs this time were not only the advisers to the Emperor but the Emperor himself. The object of the plot, he was afterward to say, was to "convince" the Emperor that he was being misinformed and misguided by his government and by the elder statesmen, and that it was essential for the welfare of his people that the aggressive policy of the Army in Manchuria be endorsed and encouraged. The coup which he and his co-

114

conspirators had worked out this time was an elaborate one. It would, as Kido says in his diary, start by the investment of the War Ministry and the headquarters of the General Staff, and it was planned that an ultimatum be dispatched to the inmates saying: "Join us or die!" Simultaneously, another posse of officers would surround a scheduled meeting of the Cabinet, and for them there would be no choice; the orders were to kill the lot.

As for the Emperor, a curious fate was reserved for him. The revolt was, of course, to be launched in his name and with Kodo as the rallying cry; but to clear the tenno's mind of the poisons with which it had been clouded by the genro, Hashimoto planned to confront him in the Imperial Palace with none other than his old principal and tutor, Admiral Togo, who would plead with him to solve the national emergency by declaring martial law and putting an Army man (General Araki, a rising firebrand, in fact) at the head of the government. Even Hashimoto, however, seemed not too sure that this gambit would succeed, but he had an alternative in case Togo refused to plead or Hirohito to listen: the Emperor would be taken away, "purely for his own safety," to a warship anchored in Tokyo Bay, where he would remain until "the situation was resolved." Just how they planned to resolve it is indicated by one of the plotters at his trial later; he confessed that he had been told to "brandish a dagger" and "plead with his divine majesty to see reason."

Once more the plot failed; or failed in that the Cabinet ministers were not killed, the military Government was not formed, and the Emperor was not kidnapped. But otherwise it was eminently successful. Neither Hashimoto nor his cohorts were punished; they were released soon after arrest and merely posted out of Tokyo. As for the government, it wilted away out of sheer funk and made no real effort to curb the excesses of the military any longer. And the aggression went on in Manchuria and China. It was developing into what one of its participants would later on describe as "a war without a Rescript" and its excesses as "a mad carnival of debauchery carried out by gangs of ignorant bullies."[7] There would only be one more attempt to stop it before it was too late.

The strengthening of military fanaticism and the increasing outbreaks of "brainless patriotism," as Prince Saionji called the assassination

[7] Yoshio Kodama, *I was Defeated,* Tokyo: Booth & Fukada, 1946.

115

plots, had their impact upon Hirohito's private life, such as it was. His advisers were worried. They felt that if he were to continue to make it clear that he opposed military adventures in Asia, he must do so from a position of strength, as an Emperor not only revered but admired as well by his subjects. How could that be so when he had failed to give them solid evidence of his desire to serve them—by giving them a son to carry on his line? There would be emotional instability among the masses, they argued, so long as he continued to be the father of four daughters, but no male heir. The time had come to abandon his scruples and take a concubine who would provide him with a son.

It must have become apparent by this time that Hirohito was a reserved, gentle and most unbelligerent character. His idea of bliss was a sea trip into Tokyo or Sagami Bay in search of marine specimens. Whenever he could snatch a few hours away, he climbed the hills behind the beach palace at Hayama with his old tutor, Professor Hirotaro Hattori, searching for flora and studying fungi. Between them, the two were working in the laboratory at Fukiage to produce the text and photographs of a book on mushrooms in which they hoped to announce some new discoveries about diseases in fungi.[8] It is perhaps not indelicate to suggest that with the birth of four daughters, three of them thriving, he would in other circumstances have been quite content, and that he had reached the stage of relationship with his wife not of his Imperial ancestors—who met them only on formal occasions, preferring the company of concubines—but of a bourgeois middle-aged husband who had found his wife a good companion. He was only too well aware that if he were to spurn her now and turn to one of the ladies-in-waiting to breed him a son, he would not only hurt her, he would also lose her friendship; and this he had no desire whatsoever to do.

It would be naïve to say that, amid all the difficulties of the early 1930's, the succession problem made him as miserable as it undoubtedly did Nagako. In many ways, it was a tantalizing relief from affairs of state. He was just over thirty years old and no different from most men of his age in his liking for the company of a pretty woman. To have a succession of statesmen come to him and plead with him, for the sake of Japan, for the sake of the Imperial line, for the sake of his people, to bed himself down with a succession of nubile virgins must have been

[8] The book, which was actually written by the Emperor, was eventually published in 1936 with Professor Hattori's name given as author.

tempting indeed. There were probably moments in 1932, at least, when he must have most seriously contemplated having to do his duty. Certainly, during that period, it was related to Prince Saionji and Count Tanaka that the Emperor, in his free moments, often came down to the pavilion of the ladies-in-waiting and spent some time chatting with them.

It was news which sent Tanaka careening around the Imperial Palace like an old satyr, whipping up enthusiasm in the older ladies of the Court and exhorting them to set their charges to the task of seducing the Emperor. It was a year which older members of the court still talk about with a glint in their eyes, for it was a period when the Imperial Palace in Tokyo must have been, in many ways, like Kyoto during the Heian era, quivering with intrigue, palpitating with suppressed ecstasy and excitement, buzzing with gossip.

Tokyo and the rest of Japan in 1932, a decade after the Great Earthquake, had changed its shape and its character, and not necessarily for the better. Higgledy-piggledy, the buildings had gone up again, with just as little sense of planning as before. But otherwise the cities had gone modern. The great fire had destroyed most of the clothes which people wore, with the exception of what they carried on their backs, and few of them could afford to replace them; not, that is, the kimonos and yukatas which they had normally worn before the fire, for they were (and still are) expensive. So the Japanese had mostly forsaken their Oriental attire and (save for ceremonial occasions) adopted Western clothes. They were much more practical, but, especially on women, were much less attractive, for most Japanese female legs are not made for short skirts. It was more convenient to wear modern dress in crowded trains and streetcars, though it seemed all the more incongruous when a packed streetcar's complement of lounge-suited businessmen and tight-skirted secretaries bowed in unison as it rattled past the Imperial Palace. Alas, except on feast days, the streets were drab.

But behind the walls of the Imperial Palace, little had changed. Once through the great gates and you were in another world, 247 acres of woods and gardens and pavilions and pools. There was a silk worm pavilion and a concert pavilion, a ladies-in-waiting pavilion and a pavilion for the royal princesses and their maids; there were greenhouses and stables and a riding paddock; there was the nine-hole golf course built after Hirohito's return to Japan; there was an administration building; and, beside a meticulous Zen garden of streams and rocks and cryptomeria,

117

there were the pavilions of the Emperor and the Empress, connected with each other by a linking corridor through which Nagako never came unless she were summoned. On a spring or autumn afternoon, with the frenetic roar of Tokyo's traffic reduced to a murmur by the baffleboards of walls and moat, the scene was idyllic: young ladies in gay-colored kimonos teetering daintily over the ornamental bridges across the streams, butterflies and bees hovering over the banks of flowers, an occasional pheasant breaking from the undergrowth, and, in tiny pergolas dotted about the ground, more young ladies knelt prettily on the tatami learning the complicated arts of calligraphy, flower arrangement and the tea ceremony. In 1932 it could have been likened to an exotic hothouse. Prince Saionji wryly referred to it as looking "like a harem," though if so it was a harem without the one essential ingredient to make it viable, a sultan. So far.

Tanaka, the old but avid goat, had hoped that propinquity and the sheer eagerness of the ladies of the Court to be chosen would overcome the Emperor's scruples and bring his inclinations into line with his innate sense of duty. But when the general atmosphere of barely suppressed sexuality failed—or so it seemed—to stimulate His Imperial Majesty, Tanaka decided that a particular appeal might be more efficacious than a surfeit of blandishment. With a thoroughness that would have done credit to the talent scouts of Haroun-al-Rashid, he cocked his octogenarian but far from rheumy eye over the possibilities, and having found three who seemed to come up to his ideals of beauty, charm and freshness, had them photographed in their most appealing kimonos. He contrived to have the photographs brought to the Emperor's attention, having first seen to it that full details of each young girl's parentage and background was enumerated on the back of each print. The cynics at the court did not miss the fact that all three girls had been bred from Choshu stock, which meant that they all had fathers, uncles or other close relatives high up in the Army. Tanaka may have been a romantic at heart, but he was also a political realist. The birth of a son would appease the populace; but the birth of a son by a Choshu mother would appease the Army as well.

While the Emperor was studying the photographs and listening once more to his advisers calling him to do his duty, the militarists had been plotting once more. This time, however, they did not call off their plans at the last moment but carried them through; and though there was bungling and inefficiency amid the bloodshed, the results were to have a marked influence on Japan's future and, of course, on the Emperor as well.

In May, 1932, the Prime Minister of Japan was Mr. Tsuyoshi Inukai, whose Seiyukai Party had won the last election and ousted the administration of the hesitant and nervous Mr. Wakatsuki. Mr. Inukai was one of those remarkable phenomena of Japan, a man old in years who, despite a life in which wine, women and song were never stinted, seemed to grow younger every day. Goatee-bearded, mentally alert and physically energetic, he was not only extremely able but also courageous as well. His appointment to the premiership recommended once more by the old Genro, Saionji and Count Makino had been warmly welcomed by the Emperor, for in his first audience the old man had made it clear that he would brook no nonsense from the Army fanatics and would curb their ambitions in China by cutting their budget at home. In fact one of Inukai's first acts on coming into office was to dispatch a secret envoy to Chiang Kai-shek in China with the object of finding a formula with which peace talks could begin and Sino-Japanese differences resolved. That he had no intention of withdrawing troops from Manchuria or of diminishing Japan's position as "most favored nation" in China—he merely thought the goals could be attained more subtly by diplomatic than military means—did nothing to dissuade the younger members of both Army and Navy that he was working against them. They were determined to eliminate him and also the advisers at the court whose "evil machinations" had persuaded the Emperor to accept him. They chose May 15, 1932, for their day of judgment, and how they did it—a pattern of things to come—cannot better be described than by Hugh Byas, who was Tokyo Correspondent of *The New York Times* and the London *Times* when it happened.

"At five o'clock that Sunday evening, nine naval and military officers of ages between twenty-four and twenty-eight alighted from two taxicabs at the side entrance of the Yasukuni Shrine in Tokyo. The shrine is dedicated to all members of the fighting services who have died in Japan's wars. There is no holier place in Tokyo. Five white strips running along its outer wall signify that it is under Imperial protection. . . . If anyone gave a passing glance to the young officers it was only to think that they had probably been ordered to Manchuria, where the Imperial Army was then extending the Imperial Way. They worshipped at the shrine, doffing caps, clasping hands, and bowing towards the unseen mirror of the Sun Goddess in homage to the souls of the dead soldiers whose names are inscribed in the book and whose spirits dwell there. One of them bought charms from a priest and gave them to his comrades to protect them from the bullets of the police. They piled into their taxis, five in one, four in the other. In five minutes they had passed the British Embassy with its Sunday Union Jack flying and were entering the front and back gates of the Prime Minister's official residence. . . ."

The men carried revolvers and hand grenades but no one challenged them when they went inside; an officer's uniform would get you into most places in Japan in those days. But once there they were lost.

"One of the officers asked a police sergeant to show them the Prime Minister's private apartments. They pointed revolvers at him but he refused. Lost among passages and staircases, the officers wandered about, not knowing where to go. Some went upstairs and found the Cabinet room empty. A 'large man' appeared and they asked to be taken to the Prime Minister, saying they had come from the Naval Academy. Before the 'large man' had done anything a group of three or four men appeared from nowhere and ran away when a shot was fired in their direction. Then someone heard a key turning in a lock and an officer shouted: 'That must be the way to the private apartments.' They knocked. A voice called: 'Who is it there?' A naval officer burst open the flimsy door with his shoulder and they burst in."

Inside the room, calmly awaiting them, they found Mr. Inukai, the premier. "He led the officers into a Japanese room. His daughter-in-law, carrying her baby, was with him, and one of the officers, 'knowing what would happen in a few minutes,' as he said at the trial, told her to go away but she stayed. The young men were rather confused and some were impressed by the old man's calm demeanour as he asked them to take off their shoes and sit down and talk it over. He had a cigarette in his hand and he lit it. 'As I observed,' said one of the officers in his testimony, 'our leader was willing to talk with the Prime Minister.' The group that had gone to the back door burst in headed by Lieutenant Masayoshi Yamagishi, a man of action, carrying a dagger. 'No use talking,' said Yamagishi. 'Fire!' The word was shouted like an order and they all began firing. One shot hit the Prime Minister in the neck and another, deliberately, in the stomach. The Prime Minister sank on the matted floor and never spoke again.[9]

It was a senseless crime—but so were they all—and Hirohito was shocked by it. The conspirators panicked after their first murder and failed to coordinate what amateurish plans they had made; as a result of which a side-plot to kill Count Makino was never carried through, nor was the capture of police headquarters and the occupation of the Mitsubishi Bank. The Minister of War, Araki, who was known to be in sympathy with the rebels, was the first to receive news of their bungling methods and quickly found an excuse to leave Tokyo, so as not to be in hearing distance when they called for help. They were arrested and held for trial.[10] It looked as if it had been just another fizzle.

In fact it was not. The effect of it was to bring democratic government in Japan to an end for good and all. For when Prince Saionji and his colleagues—and Saionji, for one, was growing weary with the repetition by this time—began once more to search for a successor to the unfortunate Inukai, the Army made its position clear. By law the positions of War Minister and Minister of Marine could only be filled by serving or ex-service officers. A serving officer obviously had to be approved by the High Command, or he ceased to be a serving officer. Therefore, the Army and Navy pretty well, if not quite, controlled the government; by withdrawing their nominee, they forced a government to resign. By disapproving a nominee, they could do much to prevent a government from being formed. Now the Army let the old Genro know that no war minister would be nominated unless the Army approved of the new prime minister. Not only that—they would only allow him to serve in a *national* rather than a party administration.

It was a moment in history when Japan sorely needed a regime less interested in domestic politics than its position in the world, less anxious to bicker over who should grab the spoils of office than in how the

[9] Hugh Byas, *Government by Assassination*, New York: Alfred A. Knopf, Inc., 1942.

[10] Since Japanese courts respond to "political murder" as Italian juries do to *crime passionel*, the assassins came off lightly. All of them were amnestied after a few years in jail. During their trial, dozens of young men throughout Japan cut off their little fingers and sent them through the post to the court, asking to be allowed to substitute before the firing squads if the accused were sentenced to death.

121

fanatics should be disciplined; and a national government dedicated to the nation's interest rather than the selfish ends of the ministers might have produced miraculous results. It may have been that this was what the Emperor had in mind when he asked his advisers to find the prime minister to succeed Inukai. Kido wrote in his diary on May 22, 1932:

"3 P.M. Called again at Harada's. The Emperor's words to the elder statesmen were as follows: 'His Majesty desires that the Genro select as the next premier one who has no fascist leanings and about whom there has been no unsavory rumour, who is moderate in thought and who is not militaristic.'"

It was a tall order, and, in the circumstances, not capable of fulfilment, for of the few candidates whose record enabled them to measure up to the need, none possessed the courage to take the job. The Genro was forced to fall back upon an all-party administration whose premier was Admiral Makoto Saito and whose war minister was the same Araki who had sympathized, if not sided, with the rebels during the last three abortive putsches. Admiral Saito was eighty-one years old and equipped with a strong sense of self-preservation. He had neither the stamina nor the inclination to stand up to Araki, a voluble apostle of Kodo, who would storm into his presence, handlebar moustaches bristling, and hector him if he showed the slightest inclination toward liberalism.

One of Araki's first speeches after he took over the War Ministry referred to the fanatics among the military as "irrepressible patriots" and "the flowers of the Army." He had an eager ally in Mr. Ichiro Hatoyama, the Minister of Education, who demanded the immediate dismissal of a professor at Kyoto University after he had suggested in a lecture that the Constitution of Japan was more important than the Emperor. The faculty of the university threatened to resign in sympathy if their colleague was forced to go, a move which left the Minister of Education unperturbed.[11] "Let all the professors resign if that is how they feel," he said. "We do not mind closing the universities altogether."

With such a national government in power, there was little hope that moderating influences would have any say in curbing the mounting drift to totalitarianism in the Army and Navy. Manchukuo was being openly exploited as a Japanese colony, with Army generals in all the positions of power; and in Shanghai the Japanese Army and Navy had taken over

---

[11] Mr. Hatoyama became Prime Minister of Japan after the war.

all but the International Settlement and had begun to carry out what they called "a policy of seeking the sincere cooperation and friendship of our dear neighbors, the Chinese" by a campaign of murder, brutality and exploitation. At least two Japanese civilians found the activities of their countrymen in uniform horrifying and shameful. One of them, a young diplomat named Terasaki, whose name will recur in this story, wrote to the Emperor and asked to be recalled from his post in Shanghai, where, he said, he was humiliated by "the arrogance of our military, who force their so-called Chinese 'brothers' to kowtow to them in the streets, even to ordinary soldiers." And even a former terrorist, at this time a government agent in China, was disgusted at military excesses.

"Like a rotting sewage canal," he writes of the Japanese sector of Shanghai, "it has succeeded in creating a special atmosphere in the complicated environs of the International Settlement. The place is jammed with geisha houses, cabarets and dance halls packed door to door, while military automobiles were always lined up in front of the Japanese geisha houses. . . . In contrast to this, the Chinese sector and the British and French concessions have been completely destroyed by the war, and countless war refugees were living in distressful poverty and suffering. Every night I used to gaze down [from my hotel window] bright with neon lights, the street illuminations giving the impression that the sector was one large 'gay quarter.' But underneath these dazzling lights were tens of thousands of Chinese refugees, penniless, homeless and clotheless, living on the verge of starvation." [12]

There were not many like them, however, or at least not many who dared to raise their voices against the Army. The tone of the times was set by Mr. Yosuke Matsuoka, the Japanese delegate to the League of Nations, who defied the League's condemnation of his country's annexation of Manchukuo and belligerence in China with what almost amounted to a challenge. "If you don't like what we are doing, then try to stop us!" was what he seemed to be saying. He was, of course, on safe ground. Neither the United States, too busy finding work for its unemployed, nor the members of the League, too busy finding formulae for nonintervention, were willing to back condemnation with action. Matsuoka marched Japan out of the League of Nations and dared the members to do their worst, and practically every Japanese applauded the action.

[12] Kodama, *op. cit.*

123

One of the exceptions was the Emperor. Baron Kido wrote on March 3, 1933:

"Today the Minister of Foreign Affairs reported to the Throne that the Government intends to petition for an Imperial Rescript to our people to appear simultaneously with the announcement of our withdrawal from the League of Nations, now that it has been decided to withdraw therefrom. After the Minister's withdrawal, the Emperor gave instructions to the Prime Minister and the Foreign Minister through the Grand Chamberlain to the effect that when the Imperial Rescript is promulgated the following two points should be included in the text: 1. It is very regrettable that Japan should have been placed in the unavoidable position of being forced to withdraw from the League of Nations; and 2. That even though Japan withdraws from the League of Nations she will continue to cooperate and maintain intimate international relations with other powers. I visited the Foreign Minister at his official residence by order of the Lord Keeper of the Privy Seal at half-past one and delivered the Imperial intention and asked that it be delivered to the Prime Minister. I came back to the Lord Keeper immediately and reported that it was done.

"In connection with the withdrawal from the League of Nations the Lord Keeper told me confidentially of his audience with the Emperor, and this is what he said: 'The Emperor inquired of me upon my visit of our intention to resign from the League of Nations, and asked me whether the need to withdraw from the League still held in view of the favourable settlement of the Jehol problem.[13] Upon this inquiry, I said that while His Majesty's words were reasonable, our plenipotentiary was already acting in every direction in accordance with our Government's previous decision to withdraw and that the Imperial Government had already taken a firm stand on this matter, and that if we should change our minds on this matter externally foreign countries would have the impression that we are vacillating, while internally the people would become utterly confused. With the matter being so, I advised the Emperor to let the Government carry out its decision.'"

The government—or rather one of its members, Araki—did not fail to let the armed forces know of the Emperor's anxiety to discourage

[13] The Japanese Army in Manchuria had invaded and occupied Jehol Province in 1931, bringing them to the Great Wall of China. In 1933 they agreed to withdraw their forces, but only temporarily.

aggression and preserve peaceful methods of international cooperation (though he used other phrases to describe Hirohito's attitude), and the result was a new plot which was designed this time not just to "persuade" the Emperor to support the Army, but to oust him altogether.

Paradoxically enough, the campaign with which the plotters began the build-up for their *coup d'état* seemed, on the surface, to be nothing less than a great boost of the Emperor's divine authority. With Army backing, an association was formed which called itself the Shimpeitai, or Heaven Sent Troops, and pledged its members to defend the Imperial Way to the death. Its manifesto read:

"1. The Soldiers of the Gods are ready with Celestial swords to accomplish the Restoration of Showa as their life mission for the glory of the Empire;

"2. The Soldiers of the Gods denounce all institutions and activities which are based on liberalism and socialism, and aim to establish a government, an economic policy and a culture which shall be based upon the position of the Emperor; and

"3. The Soldiers of the Gods aim at the annihilation of the leaders of the financial groups, the leaders of the political parties, *the villains of the Imperial Entourage* and their watchdogs who are obstructing the progress of the Empire. They shall thereby establish the Imperial Restoration and proclaim the Imperial Rule throughout the world." [14]

But behind the propaganda of the Shimpeitai was a hard-core terrorist group of young officers armed not with celestial swords but pistols and machineguns and hand grenades; and their aim was not just annihilation of the "Imperial Entourage" but removal of the Emperor himself as a reprisal for his continued opposition to militarism at home and aggression overseas.[15]

Toward the end of April, 1933, Count Makino approached the Emperor and said that it was in his mind to resign his post as Lord Keeper of the Privy Seal. The excuse he gave to Hirohito was that of infirmity— he was half-crippled with what he described as "neuralgia of the feet," but which was probably arthritis. To Kido, however, he confessed that he was afraid; repeated rumors of attempts on his life had at last worn him down, and he was anxious to leave the court and spend the rest of

[14] My italics.—L.M.
[15] See *The Brocade Banner,* U.S. Army, GHQ, SCAP, Counter-Intelligence Sector, National Archives, Washington, D.C.

his days (he was in his seventies) in peace in the countryside. Kido's own intelligence service made him aware that the next attempt on the Lord Keeper's life could not be far away, for there were strong indications that the Shimpeitai had drawn up a plan of action and were almost ready to put it into operation. But while sympathizing with the old man's fears, Kido persuaded him to stay on temporarily and produced evidence of a nature that convinced Makino that it would be disloyal of him to go at this time. For the Shimpeitai's plot was not only to eliminate him but his royal master as well. The bolder faction among the Soldiers of God reasoned that the Japanese people would accept the usurpation (or even the death) of Hirohito provided they could defile his name sufficiently and put in his place an Emperor capable of inspiring popular support.

They believed that they had material enough for Hirohito's denigration, in Japanese eyes, at least. They could produce evidence (quite genuine) of his attempt to curb the Army's adventures in Manchuria and China, thus proving his "cowardice" and his betrayal of "Japan's sacred mission." They could easily fake evidence that he was tied up with the unpopular zaibatsu, the financial tycoons who were squeezing the peasants. They could prove (again quite genuinely) that he was anxious to secure treaties of friendship with the United States and Britain—a fact which they would not have much difficulty in twisting into a willingness to accept domination by the White races. And they would not fail to point out that Hirohito was also a weakling who bred nothing but daughters and could not even provide his people with an heir to the throne.

How could the nation not fail to welcome the elimination of such a treacherous weakling—especially if, as they planned, the prestige of the Imperial line was simultaneously restored by the apotheosis of his popular brother, Prince Chichibu, who would be made Emperor, and the formation of a government under the premiership of his uncle, Prince Higashikuni, an Army man? Let me hasten to say that Prince Chichibu had no notion until afterward of these grandiose plans and would certainly have spurned any attempt to enthrone him at the expense of his brother. The two brothers were highly dissimilar in temperament and had had their moments of jealousy in their youth, but they shared an abhorrence of war and a dislike of totalitarianism.

Such considerations have never prevented fanatics in Japan from proceeding with their plots. It is typical of them that they did not even think of contacting Chichibu or any of his entourage beforehand. Makino's reaction to Kido's revelations was to advocate immediate arrest of the ringleaders of the Shimpeitai and the disbandment of the organization, but his secretary was more cautious, pointing out that since the plotters would obviously deny any plan to murder the Emperor—for that would mean their inevitable execution for high treason—they would once more be hailed as martyrs suffering because they wished to "purify" national life and purge the Emperor of evil influences. Better, he counselled, to infiltrate the organization instead and find out exactly when it planned to carry out its coup.

Meanwhile, both he and Makino must have wished more fervently than ever that Hirohito would take a concubine and father a son. If he insisted on opposing the Army's line and risking his prestige for political reasons, at least he might try to win some personal popularity by giving the people an heir. Count Tanaka was instructed to renew his efforts to inveigle his Emperor into a concubine's bedchamber; but if he had had some hope of success in 1932, in the spring and summer of the following year he got nowhere. Hirohito returned the photographs of the three young virgins which had been submitted to him by the old man, politely remarking that they seemed eminently suitable for marriage and would, he hoped, find husbands worthy of them. There were no more visits to the pavilion of the ladies-in-waiting.

On July 10, 1933, the Tokyo police raided a number of houses and arrested forty members of the Shimpeitai, charging them with plotting the assassination of government and court officials (though no mention was made of a plot against the Emperor). On July 11th—which was the day the Shimpeitai had chosen to put their plan into operation—Count Makino quietly let it be known that Empress Nagako was pregnant again.

This time, when the official announcement came, one could almost feel the nerve ends quivering throughout Japan, and the next weeks of waiting were well-nigh unbearable. The Empress herself must have found it no less so. After ten years of marriage and four daughters, this was obviously her last chance. If she failed her husband now . . . But it was not for her own sake that she prayed for a happy outcome to her pregnancy. She was dearly anxious to give her husband a son, well aware of

127

the pressures which had been put upon him, and this time she had tried everything—exercises, herbal infusions, hours of meditation, talks with doctors and eugenists, and prayer, prayer, prayer. If sheer will power could do it, everything would be all right. And if the power of concentrated mass thought could help, she had plenty of allies on her side; practically the whole population of Japan was flocking to Shinto shrines and clamantly demanding the attention of the gods as they intoned: "Please see that you do your honorable best to give our divine tenno a son."

Curiously enough, amid all the steaming frenzy, Hirohito was one of the few who seemed calm and unworried, though he could lose a throne over the outcome. He knew by now of the Shimpeitai plot and was well aware of his vulnerability. The ringleaders had been arrested, but there were others in the background, waiting to come forward. He did not need to be told that even one of his own ministers (Araki) would not be displeased if the birth of another daughter brought him into disfavor. But his advisers found him cool and serene. There were even those who said that he did not really care whether it was a boy or a girl—that he would not be too downcast, anyway, if Chichibu took his place on the throne.

On December 22, 1933, the Empress left her apartments in the Imperial Palace grounds and walked over to the special pavilion which had been erected for her accouchement. The labor pains had begun. Two midwives helped Nagako into the silk nightgown which she would wear until the child was delivered. The midwives themselves had been bathed and "purified" by a Shinto priest. A doctor was standing by. In a box by the bed was the silken cord which the Empress would take and tug when the pains grew severe and she might be tempted to groan.

Outside the bedchamber, in a small anteroom, sat two old men, Count Makino and Baron Yuasa, the Court Chamberlain. It was their duty to see that no one entered the maternity chamber except the midwives and doctor, to examine the babe when it was born, and to certify that there had been no substitution. They had a long vigil before them. After four children it might have been thought that Nagako would have an easy time, but this was not so; the labor pains were severe and protracted. It was not until nearly twenty-four hours later that the yelps of a baby were heard. At that moment the expressions on the faces of the two old men must have been something to see—for this was a moment of truth for all of them.

Presently the door of the maternity chamber opened and the doctor came out, beckoning to Makino and Yuasa to enter. One of the midwives had just finished cleaning the babe, and now she brought it forward for them to see. Chamberlain Yuasa took one look and then spun round; the sleeves of his yukata flapping like bat's wings, he sped across the park to the Emperor's quarters, there demanding immediate audience. The Emperor was in his study and he was taken to him.

He fell on his knees at the door and bowed. "Sire," he said, "I have to tell you that our beloved Empress has given birth to an heir to the throne."

Hirohito looked at him for a long moment, and then he said:

"Are you sure?"

There was no doubt about it. It was indubitably a boy.

The news was conveyed to the waiting reporters and the special editions began to roll off the presses. On the walls of the Imperial Palace, and in every city throughout the land, sirens began to blare. Two blasts. Two blasts for a boy.

The crisis was over. Hirohito had a son. Japan had an heir to the throne.

Four days later General Araki resigned his post as Minister for War, on the grounds of ill health. He had never looked fitter.

Chapter Nine

On New Year's Day the Poetry Bureau of the Imperial Household holds its annual meeting to announce the results of the Imperial Poetry Contest. Entries have come in from all over the world—either three-line, seventeen-syllable haikus, or five-line, thirty-one syllable tankas—and the ten prizewinners are summoned to the palace to hear their poems read before the Emperor. But first they listen to the poems on the same subject which have been written by the Emperor and members of his family.

It is a creative task which Hirohito has always taken most seriously. Like his grandfather, Meiji—who wrote no less than 17,000 haikus in his lifetime—he finds Japanese poetry a medium through which he can speak from the heart, voicing through imagery and inference the sentiments, the anxieties, fears and hopes, which he cannot put into plain words.

In 1936 the tanka he wrote was:

> "As I
> was visiting
> the Shino Point in Kii
> clouds were drifting far
> over the Sea."

It was as near as he could come to letting his people know that he was apprehensive about the future. On the surface, there did not appear to be much for him to worry about, at least, that is, as far as his own personal prestige was concerned. As if to press home her triumph over her critics, Nagako (in 1935) had given birth to a second son, making the succession doubly secure.

To anyone reading the Japanese newspapers and magazines of the period, it could easily have appeared that the whole of Japanese life centered on the lightest whim of the Emperor. Dire punishment threatened anyone who dared to suggest that everyone and everything in the Imperial realm was not subject to his divine judgment. It is one of the ironies of the situation that the very people who had backed the Shimpeitai (the Soldiers of God) in their plot to wreck the government and replace the Emperor,[1] were now the ones clamoring to turn Hirohito into just the sort of divine ruler which he did not wish to be.

They found the excuse for an upsurge of royalist propaganda in the textbooks of a professor at Tokyo University named Tatsukichi Minobe. These textbooks, which had, in fact, been in circulation in the schools for nearly twelve years, made the simple claim that the Japanese Emperor was, and should be, a constitutional monarch, in that he accepted the opinions of the Government of the day. In 1935 some of the more fanatical young militarists, belatedly encountering these opinions, were outraged. They accused Minobe of *lèse-majesté*. They rallied their pet newspapers and the diehard engines of the press put on steam. Soon it was being hinted that the unfortunate Minobe—who was merely suggesting that the monarch be accepted in Japan as a human being, subject to the will of the state—should commit suicide for his crime in insulting the Emperor. When he refused to indulge in such drastic self-criticism, he was forced to resign from the House of Peers, and the assassins were put on his track. Toward the end of 1935, Professor Minobe was the subject of three denunciations to the public prosecutor for *lèse-majesté*. In October of that year he was the object of an abortive assassination, the killer (a young student fresh—or rather, soured—from an evening in the brothels of Yoshiwara) being arrested as he waited, knife ready, outside the professor's home.[2] General Araki emerged from obscurity to denounce "decadent liberals" who wished to suggest that the Japanese Emperor was like

[1] Since their plans to remove the Emperor were never mentioned at their trial, the accused were treated as popular heroes. They were commended by the judge for their "patriotic motives" and afterward acquitted "because the plot was uncovered before damage was done."

[2] Professor Minobe was seriously wounded by a would-be assassin in January, 1936.

ordinary men, or even like ordinary kings. "The Japanese spirit," he said, "is the spirit of blind devotion to the Emperor."

Hirohito, who had long been aware of Minobe's opinions of the function of the monarchy, and had always regarded himself as an instrument of government rather than the chosen of God, was suddenly embarrassed to find himself the object of an intensive campaign to deify him as even his father and grandfather had never been. The newspapers spouted with exhortations to nationalists to wipe out in blood insults to the Emperor which suggested that he was like ordinary men. That autumn a new government had come into power in Japan whose premier was Mr. Keisuke Okada, a wry and rather cynical man whose attitude to life could well have been summed up in the words: "I do the best I can—but people aren't worth it, really." He held the fanatics in the Army in the uttermost contempt, but he also liked an easy life. (Like many another Japanese politician, he was a womanizer and a drinker and one of the most famous and witty geishas in the land was his mistress; he did not often go sober or unaccompanied to bed.) He suspected that he was a fool to have accepted the premiership in the conditions prevailing in 1935 and secretly envied Count Makino, who had retired at last from his position as Lord Keeper of the Privy Seal and hobbled painfully off into retirement. Viscount Saito, the former premier, had taken Makino's place at the palace as Lord Keeper of the Privy Seal, with Baron Kido still there as his secretary.

It is a measure of the furious propaganda campaign of the militarists and their civilian supporters in this period, frenetically insisting on the Emperor's divinity, that the Okada government was forced, in sheer self-defense, to fall into line. A proclamation was issued characterizing as "disrespectful," and therefore punishable, any written or spoken statement which suggested that the Emperor was merely human, a constitutional monarch, or subject to man-made laws and customs. It was now mandatory that anyone passing the Imperial Palace pause to bow low to his unseen presence. When he traveled about, the "thought police" were on hand to see that no one was impudent enough to stare at him. Foreign visitors were hauled out of their rooms if they dared to lean out of their windows and insult the Emperor by gazing down on him as he passed by. It was a period of such fanatic insistence on Hirohito's deification that a story became current in diplomatic circles in Tokyo about two Christian missionaries. They were walking along a street in the Japanese capital one day when one of them asked the other:

132

"If you saw Jesus Christ and the Emperor coming down the street towards us at this moment, which one would you bow to first?"

The other thought for a moment, and then said:

"The Emperor. I'm sure Jesus would understand."

It need hardly be said that these disingenuous processes of deification which the militarists now espoused filled Hirohito with distaste. He had never thought of himself as divine. The whole idea that he was any different from other humans would have seemed to him arrogant and presumptive, even had its sponsors been men of sincerity, for he was a modest and unassuming person. He was resentful, too; for he did not need to be told that what the militarists wanted was someone who could be presented as a god to the multitude but manipulated as a puppet by the men in power. First they deified him; then they led the Japanese people astray, in his name. Hugh Byas has described the Army conception of the Emperor as "a divine person, a symbol of the eternity of the state; he is an automaton who accepts advice without demur when it is offered by the right person; he is a high priest, but he is not a king ruling a country."[3]

These were the same sentiments as the Tokugawas had used when they relegated the Imperial family to retirement at Kyoto and ruled the land from Edo. The neo-shoguns, clad in khaki this time, were plotting a rehabilitation of their oligarchy, and the Emperor would be their first victim.

The impetus of the movement came, however, not from the military chiefs themselves, fanatics though many of them were, but from their field-grade officers, most of them sons of the soil, their heads stuffed with martial dreams of grandeur but little formal education, their political philosophy a pungent and potent admixture of National Socialism, Fascism and medieval superstition. They dreamed heady dreams of Japan as ruler of the world, and insisted that only the machinations of the zaibatsu (big business) and the corruption of the politicians prevented it from coming to pass.

The Army leaders swayed between fear of these fanatics and secret admiration for their recklessness, and knowledge of this spread insubordination through the ranks of the young activists. Gekokujo (or rule by juniors) was growing stronger in 1936. Major General Ryukichi Tanaka, a belligerent character himself, objected to it when it was demonstrated

[3] Hugh Byas, *Government by Assassination*, New York: Alfred A. Knopf, 1942.

133

by his inferiors. "Young officers barely out of swaddling clothes," he wrote, "went so far as to call military personages as high as the War Minister by name, and to hold their own superiors in obvious contempt. . . . The rank system underlies armies and discipline all over the world, yet sly junior officers took pleasure in resisting their superiors, going over their heads and 'peaching' to their secret society bosses, and in some cases threatening the jobs of their commanders. In consequence, those unit commanders who were not particularly strong would get frightened and leave them alone. This was gekokujo at its worst." [4]

It was in an effort to circumvent these dangerous youthful machinations that Hirohito asked the new War Minister, Hayashi, who had succeeded Araki, to do something drastic about curbing their activities.

Kido writes in his diary (September 2, 1935):

"At two P.M. I visited the Lord Keeper at his residence. . . . The Lord Keeper told me that the Emperor had told the War Minister to deal with the young men more firmly, even at the sacrifice of the War Minister himself. They seem to be going too far in their conduct. The Lord Keeper also told me that the Emperor had asked Prince Kan-in [his cousin, then serving in the Army], when he was received in audience, to help the War Minister in this matter."

Alas, it didn't do any good. Kido wrote later:

"Notwithstanding the Emperor's admonition to the War Minister in 1935 to control the young militarists, the February 26, 1936, incident broke out before we knew anything about the measures taken by the War Ministry in pursuance of the Imperial command. It is true that the incident broke out suddenly, but we had discerned an ugly atmosphere long before which indicated that an untoward incident might crop up. Even now I cannot understand why the military authorities failed to take precautionary measures in advance."

But perhaps they did—which is why the trouble started. On February 20, 1936, general elections had been held for a new Diet and the results demonstrated that those candidates who had campaigned as diehard rightists and totalitarians (citing the regimes in Germany and Italy as those to be followed) and others who had canvassed for votes by waving the flag and crying: "Follow the Imperial Way!" had, in fact, lost some ground

[4] Ryukichi Tanaka, *Niho Gumbatsu Anto Shi,* Tokyo: 1947.

134

to the more moderate conservatives. It was a danger signal for the activists, who feared that at any moment a liberal virus might be germinated and spread across the land. Shortly after the announcement of the election results, the First Division of the Japanese Army—among whose officers were many perfervid followers of Kodo—received notification from the War Ministry that it was being posted to Manchukuo. The division had not served abroad since 1905 and would normally have been overjoyed at the prospect of moving to territory so close to the frontiers of the Soviet Union, whom most of them believed they would some day have to fight. But the abruptness of their posting and the circumstances of the election aroused their suspicions. The officers held a meeting and came to a grave decision. If their senior commanders could not see that Japan was in danger, that her national polity was threatened by liberalism and Communism within, by the white nations without, then their junior officers must show them the nature of their errors and put them back on the Imperial Way. They would revolt.

First of all they composed among them (though it was subsequently signed by only two, Captain Nonaka and Captain Ando, both of the Third Infantry Regiment) a Manifesto explaining the motives behind their actions. Copies were delivered early on the morning of February 26, 1936, to the offices of the leading Tokyo newspapers. The manifesto said:

"The essence of the Japanese nation consists in the fact that the Emperor, reigning through ages eternal into the farthest future, does so in order that the national glory can be spread throughout the world and all men will live happy and productive lives under the sun. This has been the aim of Japan from time immemorial until the present day. Now is the time to achieve the expansion of the power and prestige of Japan! But in recent years many persons have made their chief aim in life the amassment of wealth, regardless of the general welfare and prosperity of the people. They have infringed the prerogatives of the Imperial line and impaired the majesty of the Empire. The people of Japan have suffered in consequence, and the nation has become an object of contempt in the eyes of the world. The elder statesmen [genro], the financial magnates [zaibatsu], the Government officials and the political parties are responsible. The London Naval Agreement and the events which have occurred in the Japanese Army in recent years prove these facts. That Prime Minister Hamaguchi was assassinated, that a Blood Brotherhood was formed,

135

that the May 15th incident occurred, and that Aizawa killed Nagata last summer,[5] are but reasonable consequences."

The manifesto went on to say that these "warnings" had failed to remind the statesmen of their responsibilities:

"It is clearer than light that our country is on the verge of war with Russia, China, Britain and America, who wish to crush our ancestral land. Now Japan is faced by a crisis. Unless we now rise and annihilate the unrighteous and disloyal creatures who surround the Imperial Throne and obstruct the course of true reform, the Imperial Prestige will be destroyed. Therefore it is our duty to take proper steps to safeguard our Fatherland by killing those responsible. On the eve of our departure for Manchuria we have risen in revolt to attain our aims by direct action. We believe it is our duty to remove the villains who surround the Throne. We, the children of our dear land of the gods, act with pure sincerity of heart. May the spirit of our Imperial ancestors assist us in our endeavours. February 26, Eleventh year of Showa."

By the time the editors to whom the manifesto was addressed had read the document, the February 26 Mutiny (or Ni-ni-roku Jiken, as the Japanese call it) was upon them. The first that the civilian population knew about it was when police waved buses and streetcars to a halt and ordered businessmen, secretaries and shopgirls on their way to work, to dismount. They stood around, bewildered, in the snow—it had been snowing heavily since before dawn—wondering what was happening, but no one would tell them. Soon, however, rumors began to reach them that a cordon of soldiers had been flung around the Imperial Palace "to protect the Emperor." But this rumor was wrong. The troops were all rebels (1,400 officers and men were eventually involved) and they had cordoned off the palace not to protect him from intruders but to cut him off from his people, his government, and from the rest of the Army.

In the meantime, squads of picked fanatics had been sent out to eliminate the "unrighteous and disloyal creatures who surround the Imperial Throne," and some dark and bloodthirsty deeds were to be committed in the early hours of that day. First of all, however, a group stormed the

[5] Lieutenant Colonel Aizawa murdered General Nagata, the Japanese Army Chief of Staff, by cutting him down with his sword in the General's own office in August, 1935. Aizawa claimed that Nagata was a "traitor" to the Army for having condoned the dismissal of his rival, General Mazaki. Aizawa, like Mazaki and the rebels, was a perfervid apostle of Kodo.

house of War Minister Hayashi and occupied the War Ministry and the offices of the Army General Staff. To the War Minister (a neutral nonentity) they presented a series of demands: a) the purging from the Army of all elements opposed to Kodo, the Imperial Way; b) the appointment of General Araki as Commander in Chief of the Kwantung Army in Manchuria "for the purpose of coercing Red Russia," and c) the appointment to influential positions in the Army and the administration of Kodo-inclined officers. The frightened War Minister promised to give the demands his earnest consideration and he was allowed to leave for the Imperial Palace to report to the Emperor.

Now the killings began. Perhaps the most tragic and unnecessary of them was the murder of Viscount Saito, the Lord Keeper of the Privy Seal. He was over eighty years old, amiable, gentle almost to the point of ineffectiveness. On the evening of his death he had dined at the American Embassy as the guest of Joseph C. Grew, the United States Ambassador. Afterward the guests adjourned to another room to see a film show. Grew had chosen *Naughty Marietta* with Jeanette MacDonald and Nelson Eddy because "it was full of lovely old Victor Herbert music, beautiful scenes, a pretty, romantic story and no vulgarity whatever, almost as good as *One Night of Love*." He wrote in his diary:

"We put Viscount Saito in a comfortable armchair, knowing that if he was bored with a film he could comfortably sleep because he had told Neville that he had learned in the Navy to catch a nap at any time and under any circumstances. But I think he enjoyed it too much to sleep. We had a pause with refreshments halfway through and then continued, nearly two hours of film. Betsy Neville said that the Japanese ladies' eyes were distinctly red at the end of it, so I think they were moved at the romantic story. There was supper afterwards, but the Saitos left at 11:30 P.M., pretty late for them because they generally leave dinners punctually at 10. I saw the old gentleman out and that was the end of a friendship which began when I made my first call on him as Prime Minister and Acting Minister of Foreign Affairs in June, 1932."

The old man and his wife left for their home. Six hours later a group of two hundred soldiers, commanded by four Army officers, surrounded the house. An action group burst into the house and found their way to Saito's bedroom; he and his wife were lying side by side on the tatami in a Japanese-type bed, and the assassins immediately opened fire with revolvers at the old man. His wife awoke and threw herself over her hus-

137

band to protect him, crying out for the murderers to take her life instead. "Since we had no intention of injuring anyone but her husband," said one of the officers later, "we had to push her aside and even thrust our weapons under her body in order to get at him. We fired again and again until we were sure that there was no more life left in the old man. When a soldier entered and asked that he be allowed to fire too, we let him have several shots. We wanted to cut Saito's throat to make sure of him, but we gave up the idea because the woman refused to leave the body. Afterwards we all gathered at the front gate and gave three 'banzai' for the Emperor." They had, in fact, shot the decrepit old statesman no less than thirty-six times: and also shot his wife in the hand (where she had put it over the barrel of the gun pointed at her husband.)

To be a guest at the American Embassy seemed to have been enough to invite trouble. One of the other guests was Admiral Baron Kantaro Suzuki, an elderly and fussy statesman who had been a chamberlain to the Emperor and was known to enjoy his respect if not his confidence. A large group of soldiers descended upon his house and broke in. It was almost a repetition of Saito's murder, except that it had a happier outcome. They found the old man in bed and Captain Ando (one of the chief signatories of the manifesto) woke him up, because, he confessed later, he admired the statesman and wished to make entirely sure that his victim understood why he was being assassinated. After ten or fifteen minutes of faltering conversation during which Ando seemed to be making no leeway with his argument, Suzuki said: "Is this all you have to tell me? If this is your argument, then shoot." Ando did so, putting one shot through the old man's lung, one through his leg, and one in his head—a dispersion of fire which saved Suzuki's life. At the sound of the shots his wife rushed into the room. Ando had a dagger in his hand. He had just leaned down to feel the admiral's pulse, and now he was about to deliver the *coup de grâce*. But Suzuki's wife cried out: "If my husband must die, for the sake of my honour and that of my family, let me be the one to give him the final blow." She grabbed the dagger from the assassin, an action which so startled him that he and his cohorts immediately left the room. It was an action which saved Suzuki's life. He needed blood transfusions and he was on the danger list for several days, but he recovered. More's the pity, as it turned out.

There were other murder squads abroad. One of them invaded the home of Finance Minister Korekiyo Takahashi, who was suspected of plans to limit the military budget and known to be a former protégé of Premier Hamaguchi, who had been killed two years before. The leader of the assassins confessed later: "It was I who found my way to Takahashi's room. I pulled off the bedclothes and yelled, 'Tenchu!' (Punishment of Heaven!) When Takahashi opened his eyes I gave it to him three times with my revolver. At the same time Nakajima [another of the rebels] cut him twice with his sword, once in the right arm, once in the belly. I think he died at once."

In spite of the fact that he was now retired from Imperial service and was not even any longer in close contact with either the court or the government, Count Makino (the former Lord Keeper of the Privy Seal) had been marked down as one of the victims. U.S. Ambassador Grew, writing in his diary a few days after the rebellion, tells a romantic story of the Count's escape:

"The old gentleman was staying at a hot-spring hotel in the country when an officer and several soldiers arrived in the middle of the night to assassinate him. According to the story which reached me, and I believe it to be true, Count Makino's guard shot and killed the officer and was himself killed by the soldiers, who then set fire to the hotel with the intention of forcing Count Makino into the open. Behind the hotel was a precipitous cliff and the old gentleman was led by his granddaughter Kazuko and trained nurse up on to a ledge on the cliff from which they could climb no higher. [It is at this point, according to other versions, that Makino who, it may be remembered, suffered from excruciating pains in his feet, said: 'I cannot climb any more. Leave me to be killed.'] They were shortly lit up by the fire [from the hotel] as if a flood light had been turned upon them and the soldiers raised their guns. At just that moment, however, the little granddaughter, who was a lovely girl and a great friend of our daughter Elsie, spread her own kimono in front of her grandfather, and the soldiers, being deeply moved by this heroic gesture, dropped their guns and did not shoot." [6]

Makino subsequently made his escape. The elder statesman who was held in even more respect, Prince Saionji, was warned in time of the rebellion and he was spirited away to a place of safety. But one of the Army General Staff, General Jotaro Watanabe, who was suspected by the young fanatics of favoring caution in Army policies, was shown no mercy. The

[6] Joseph C. Grew, *Ten Years in Japan,* New York: Simon and Schuster, Inc., 1944.

assassins not only killed him but his hysterical wife and his servants as well.[7]

The main object of the rebels was to wipe out the leaders of Government and the elder statesmen who advised both them and the Emperor. They would thus, they believed, create a vacuum which only the Army could fill. A state of emergency would have to be declared, and the conditions would thus be provided for the military to take over. But to do this they not only had to assassinate his ministers and advisers, but they also had to eliminate the Prime Minister himself. The murder of Admiral Keisuke Okada was therefore one of their primary aims, and no fewer than three hundred men and three officers were assigned to the task of wiping him out. Their failure to do so should have been one of the great errors of the revolt—though, alas, it did not prove to be so. The commando group which descended upon the Prime Minister's residence in the early hours of February 26th demonstrated from the start that it intended to be ruthless and determined. Since premiers had been assassinated here before, four policemen, supposedly armed and ready for any trouble, were posted at the entrance. They were shot down at once, and the rebels swept into the house.

Admiral Okada had, it so happened, spent the previous evening with his mistress, who was, as has been mentioned, a famous geisha.[8] He was an able administrator but he was also, in his hours of relaxation, a man who liked to live life to the full, and he was in no condition to wake up fresh and alert at five o'clock in the morning. Staying with him at the time, however, was his brother-in-law, Colonel Matsuo, who heard the shots outside followed by an alarm bell, and realized that assassins were about to enter. He went over to the Prime Minister and tried to rouse him, much to Okada's irritation. When he did manage to shake him awake and tell him what was happening, Okada shrugged his shoulders and said, in effect: "Let them come!"

But Matsuo, determined to cheat the assassins, patriotically convinced that his brother-in-law was needed by Japan, decided that he would do all in his power to save him. First he bundled Okada into his yukata and

[7] Though they stayed long enough after the murders to light candles around their victims' bodies, in lieu of incense. The murderers of Saito also lit candles as a mark of respect for him.

[8] This is not unusual in Japan. Geishas, rather than wives, often act as political hostesses as well as bed companions.

pushed him along the corridor of the house to the servants' quarters, where he locked him in the benjo (lavatory), telling his bleary relative on no account to reveal himself. Then, as the rebels burst into the house, he dashed out of the window and across the garden, crying: "Long live the Emperor!" The rebels, who had never seen the Prime Minister at close quarters, had brought photographs of him with them, and they thought they recognized in the figure scampering across the lawn the victim they were seeking. (Matsuo did, in fact, bear a slight, if not remarkable, resemblance to Okada.) They opened fire and shot Matsuo down. When they turned his body over and compared the bloodstained face with that on the photograph they carried, they were convinced that their mission was accomplished, and the Prime Minister was dead.

Okada meanwhile lay low in the lavatory.

In the meantime, what was happening at the Imperial Palace? The rebels guarded every gate. Their machine guns were pointed across the moat at the posts of the Imperial Guards. The best account of the situation behind the walls is given by Kido in his diary. His entry for February 26th is as follows:

"Snowfall. Was awakened from sound sleep at 5:20 A.M. by the voice of Ichikawa telling me of a telephone call from private secretary Ono. Was instantly on the phone. Ono said: 'The Lord Keeper of the Privy Seal is now being attacked in his private residence by a company of soldiers. Both he and his wife appear to have fallen victims.' Ono added that the above report was given to him over the telephone by a houseboy of the Saito family. Knew intuitively of the outbreak of an untoward incident of great proportions. At once telephoned the police commissioner. Although I was able to contact him I could not ascertain what sort of arrangements had been made by the Metropolitan Police Board [whose headquarters had, in fact, been taken over by the rebels.] Therefore sent for a car from the office and proceeded to the Court at 6 A.M. While waiting for the car I had reported on the incident to Prince Konoye and Baron Harada [Prince Saionji's secretary]. Both of them had not known of it yet. At 6:40 telephoned to Prince Saionji about the incident at Okitsu. We felt reassured when we were told by the servant that the prince and the others were still quietly asleep. Immediately went to the office. Minister of the Imperial Household Yuasa and Vice Grand Chamberlain Hirohata were already present. Was told that the Grand Chamberlain [Suzuki],

Premier Okada and Finance Minister Takahashi had also been attacked. The car coming for me having been stopped before the Metropolitan Police Board building had to make a detour. Knowing that the Metropolitan Police Board building was already in the hands of the rebels, I also made a detour around the Department of Overseas Affairs building in order to get to the office."

The rebels appeared to be following a policy of letting those ministers and officials whose names were not on their death list pass freely through the cordon surrounding the Imperial Palace. When Kido reached the administration building he found the War Minister already there. He had been received in audience by the Emperor and reported that Hirohito was visibly angry, a rare occurrence for him. He brushed aside the word "incident" which the War Minister used, calling it a "mutiny" and refused to consider the proposals which the rebels had made. Of the rebels he said:

"Whatever their excuses are, I am displeased with this incident, which has brought disgrace on the vital essence of our national character."

Kido found the administration building full of frayed nerves and barely suppressed panic. "War councillors appeared but none of the Cabinet members had proceeded to the Court yet," he wrote. "Unless a central organization for administration was established there was no working out any remedial measures. Therefore consulted with Hirohata with respect to this matter and under the directive of the Minister of the Imperial Household contacted the Minister for Overseas Affairs Kodama by telephone asking that Cabinet members proceed at once to the Imperial Palace. Furthermore, because the Lord Keeper of the Privy Seal had been killed, we decided to ask the President of the Privy Council to come. He did so after we contacted him by telephone at three P.M."

Prince Chichibu and other members of the royal family were already there, and they called in the President of the Privy Council and told him to stand by.

"There were two different opinions among the War councillors," Kido wrote. "One held that the rebels should be disbanded by an Imperial decree. The other insisted on an enforcement of martial law. Around five P.M. the Minister of Overseas Affairs, Kodama, gave me a message that they wanted to appoint a premier *ad interim*. However, after consulting the Minister of the Imperial Household I replied to the Minister as follows: 'The official residence of the premier is now surrounded by insurgents, so we do not know whether the premier was killed or not. There-fore it is not timely to submit such recommendations to the throne.'"

If Kido's hesitation had been persisted in, the outcome of the *coup d'état* might well have been different. Hirohito himself was reluctant to see the formation of a provisional Cabinet until he was certain Okada was dead [and, of course, he was not]. He was also unhappy that martial law might be declared. But in the next few hours, both came into being. Hiro-hito was in no doubt that even when the mutiny was put down—as it undoubtedly would be, now that he had made his anger apparent to the General Staff—the outcome would be injurious to his own prestige and power. He said as much to Goto, after he had sworn him in as temporary premier.

"They [the Army] are using silken floss to suffocate me with," he said, meaning that they were embracing him with a kiss of death. "I want this rebellion ended, and I want to see its instigators punished. Go to it!"

But the politicians were too frightened to take the initiative, and the military were not yet sure they had the power to bring their junior officers to heel. They procrastinated, endlessly debating what they should do. In the meantime, activity in Tokyo ground to a halt. Telephones no longer worked. Schools were closed. No trains came into the city and no public transport worked. The capital and the nation sat and shivered, and not only from cold.

What galvanized the Army command at last and sent them into action was a piece of reckless folly on the part of the rebels—who had so far had everything their own way. The dithery uncertainty of their military superiors and the civilian authorities should have told them that they were winning, that control of the nation was drifting by default into their hands. But Captain Shiro Nonaka, one of the leaders of the revolt, ap-pears to have decided that his co-conspirators were losing their nerve and needed a dramatic boost, and he picked one for them. A young lieutenant was chosen and instructed to cross the moat to present what amounted to an ultimatum to the Emperor. There was no difficulty about securing access, for one of the companies of the Imperial Guard had been in com-munication with Nonaka and conveyed the sympathy of its commander with the aims of the rebels. The lieutenant was passed through their lines with a message which he was instructed to convey to Hirohito. He was to read to the Emperor a statement of the rebels' case; he was then to ask for his Imperial approval of what the rebels were about; and if this was not forthcoming, to take out his revolver and kill Hirohito on the spot. The officer was dispatched on his mission. That he crossed the moat and entered the Imperial Palace grounds was confirmed later in interrogations with the rebels, but what happened afterward is uncertain. One source maintains that the emissary did in fact reach the Emperor's study; but from there on, things went contrary to what had been expected. Hirohito, by this time seething with anger at the murder of his advisers, the panic and cowardice of his surviving ministers, the deviousness and stupidity of his Service chiefs, had reached the end of his tether. As the door opened and the young emissary burst in, he rose from his seat and cried:

"How dare you come in here? Do you not know that I am your Emperor?"

He spoke in Court Japanese, an archaic delivery which can sound strangled and largely incomprehensible even to the Japanese themselves. He was dressed in the uniform of an Army general. It can only be presumed that the young lieutenant, confronted by this being whom he had always been taught to revere as a god, was struck with sudden awe. He fell to his knees and bowed his head to the floor; and bowing, shuffled his way out of the Presence. After which he is said to have come back to his comrades and fallen upon his sword, apologizing as he did so for having sullied the Emperor by his intrusion.

It was far from being the end of the rebellion, but it was the beginning of the end. In the next few hours, word of the Emperor's wrath was conveyed to the Chiefs of Staff of the Army. They were also apprised of the anger of the Japanese Navy. Three of their officers, including the Prime Minister (who, as far as they knew at the time, was a victim) had been killed by the assassins. This was carrying interservice rivalry too far. The Japanese fleet sailed into Tokyo Bay and landing units stood by for action.

It was decided that the rebels should be suppressed without delay, and a message was conveyed by Kido to His Majesty to that effect. But how —without setting soldier against soldier, without provoking bloody civil war and losing "face" permanently for the Army? Several methods were tried. A message was sent to the ringleaders guaranteeing that the ordinary soldiers would be forgiven provided that their officers agreed to commit seppuku, disemboweling themselves before their troops as a sign of repentance. Captain Nonaka replied, agreeing to this proposal provided that the Army Staff would send a scroll to the Emperor containing their names and "acquainting him" of their demise—which would, in effect, have denoted recognition, if not approval, of their patriotic motives. This Hirohito resolutely refused to do. "I want them crushed, not martyred," he said.

Finally, one of the only two majors in the First Division who had disapproved of the rebellion,[9] Okubo, drafted a message to the troops and had it approved by the Emperor. It specifically excluded all commissioned officers from the appeal, and was aimed at convincing other ranks that they need have no feeling of disloyalty in surrendering, since it was their superior officer, the Emperor, who was asking them to do so:

"Hitherto you have obeyed your officers, believing their commands to be just. His Majesty the Son of Heaven now orders you to return to your barracks. If you fail to obey you will be traitors. If you return you will be pardoned. Your fathers and brothers and all the people are praying for you to return. Come back to your barracks."

The leaflets appealing to the troops were read over the radio, dropped from planes, and hung from the captive balloons from which the Japanese dangle advertisements. Hugh Byas watched the result from his house on Reinanzaka Hill. He could see where the rebels had their strongholds, for over each building they occupied they flew tablecloths as flags.[10]

Groups of them began to emerge from the Prime Minister's house and walk down the hill to the barricades where loyal troops awaited. They surrendered their arms and were packed into trucks and rushed to their barracks. At two o'clock the tablecloth over the Prime Minister's residence was hauled down. For one hour and forty minutes nothing more happened. The citizens of Tokyo were not impatient, for all of them understood the solemn pause. The generals were silently giving the rebels a chance to commit hara-kiri." [11]

But the invitation was not accepted. Had the Emperor himself ordered the rebels to kill themselves, there is little doubt that they would have done so; but Hirohito was determined not to give them that privilege. He wanted the young ringleaders of the revolt to be got rid of as quickly and quietly as possible, not in bloody glory which would make them martyrs.

---

[9] The other had already committed seppuku when the troops refused to heed his objections.

[10] A typically Japanese touch was that most of the tablecloths had been obtained by the rebel officers from the Peers' Club, and paid for—at a hundred yen a time.

[11] Hugh Byas, *op. cit.*

They were allowed to surrender to their Army comrades, and then they waited, confidently, for the usual public trial at which they could spout patriotic speeches and demonstrate the purity and high-mindedness of their motives. For one of the few times in his life, however, Hirohito was blazingly angry. The savage murder of Saito, his Lord Keeper, had appalled him, but perhaps what aroused most resentment in him was the pain and indignity to which his former Lord Keeper and friend, Count Makino, had been subjected. He told Kido:

"It is not to be forgiven."

And when the ministers came to consult him about the disposition of the rebels, he made it quite clear what he wanted. There would be no public trial, no fighting speeches, and definitely no martyrdom. Over a hundred young officers and underofficers were arraigned on charges of treason and tried before a series of secret courts martial.[12] Fifteen were sentenced to death and the verdicts at once confirmed by Hirohito. Normally it is the privilege of a Japanese officer upon being sentenced to death to have a screen of silk placed between himself and the firing squad, so that he will not lose "face" by being seen by the common soldiers dispatching him. In this case, however, the condemned were shot in batches of five, after which they were cremated and their ashes disposed of. No date was ever announced of their execution, and no ashes were returned to their relatives.

The Army command was shocked, not so much by the executions—for they were glad to get these potential rivals out of the way, as by the manner of their dispatch; but there was no arguing with the Emperor. He was insistent that condign punishment should be meted out and the younger officers taught a lesson. He might have learned a lesson from the incident, too—that when he was angry and insisted on being obeyed, even those who disagreed hastened to do as they were told, for their Emperor had spoken. Alas, the significance escaped him. Otherwise, he might have behaved differently in 1941.

Ni-ni-roku had one ironic and tragicomic outcome. It will be remembered that the Prime Minister, Admiral Okada, had escaped with his life because the murder-gang had mistaken his brother-in-law, Colonel Matsuo, for him and shot him instead. The premier remained hidden in

[12] One other officer, Captain Teruzo Ando, who had signed the original manifesto, shot himself before the trial.

146

the servants' benjo for several hours after the assassins departed. At last his secretary, Fukada, arrived at the house and found his chief "squatting motionless in the closet, clad in a kimono." He helped him out and at once the premier went over to look at the body of his murdered brother-in-law. He sighed and said, wryly:

"You know, I wasn't really worth it!"

It had by now been officially announced that the premier was dead. Fukada, who was knocking his brains together trying to think up a way of engineering Okada's escape, now received a telephone call from one of the rebel leaders telling him to remove the body of the "premier" from the house.

"Considering, however, that if the body should be taken out, whatever chance there was of helping the Premier to escape would be lost, I replied that I could do nothing in that respect on my own responsibility," Fukada said later.

But by this time the Navy had grown angry at the insult to the service which had been committed by the Army in killing so many of their ex-comrades, and a spokesman of the Navy Chief of Staff also telephoned to tell Fukada to take the body from the house so that it could be given a decent interment, adding that if the rebel troops tried to stop the removal of the body "the Navy was ready to take up the matter with the Army and enforce its will."

The secretary double-talked madly until the naval officer seemed satisfied to have the body stay where it was. In the meantime, Home Minister Goto (who had been made temporary Prime Minister) announced that a state funeral would be held for his "murdered" chief. The Emperor himself issued a public statement regretting Okada's death "in the service of the Throne and the Nation." But that meant that the body had at last to be removed to a public resting place in preparation for the funeral. Fukada, who had already gained forty-eight hours of respite for his chief, racked his brains again.

"Finally we agreed that it would be best to bring many persons into the official residence on the plea of making the necessary funeral arrangements, and to lead the Premier out with the rest of them. I then went to the residence and asked the military [the rebels] to allow me and a score of other persons to offer incense before the remains of the Premier. This request granted, I ran hastily home. I telephoned to the private residence of Premier Okada and arranged with Mr. Manabu Kagoyama, a relative, to send as many old men as possible to the house. Twelve old men arrived in three motor cars. Selecting eight old men, I went along with them to the Premier's residence. Before starting I strictly instructed them not to touch the body or to show the least surprise, no matter what happened."

Fukada ushered the old men into the room where Colonel Matsuo's body lay. At the same time, on previous instructions, a loyal gendarme cried out:

"There's a man in there who has suffered a stroke. Get him to the hospital. Where's the car?"

The faithful secretary rushed from the coffin to the benjo where Okada was still hiding, put a pair of dark glasses over the premier's eyes and—brilliant thought!—a flu mask over his nose and mouth,[13] and hurried him out to his car. He was driven away before any of the soldiers could stop him.

Now in any other country in the world, the knowledge that the Prime Minister had so miraculously escaped death would have been an occasion for national rejoicing. But not in Japan. Everyone was profoundly embarrassed. Instead of being congratulated, Okada found himself the object of a certain contempt, and even resentment. Had not the Emperor accepted the fact that he was dead? Then how dare he be alive? It was an insult to the throne! If he had any decency, it was suggested, he should commit seppuku so that the royal family would not be embarrassed by having a live premier on their hands who was officially dead.

Okada, however, refused to die simply because his demise had been announced; but so far as politics was concerned, he might as well have been dead. The nation wanted no more of him. He resigned as premier and retired into private life.[14]

[13] It is not at all unusual to see people wearing flu masks in Japan.
[14] Though he did reappear during the last stages of the war.

Chapter Ten

For Hirohito the 1936 rebellion had one, but one only, good
result. It brought about a reconciliation between him and his
brother, Prince Chichibu. There had since childhood been a
certain tension between the two of them, for the younger
brother, ironically enough, had always had all the advantages in the formative stages of their upbringing. As the heir to the throne, Hirohito had
spent almost the whole of his life (except for the brief interlude in Europe) conforming. It was Chichibu who had been allowed a foreign education, allowed to choose his own bride, allowed to speak his mind about
modern developments, and it would do no good to deny that Hirohito had
moments when he not only envied his brother but intensely resented him.
Chichibu did not help matters by occasionally referring to the Emperor as
"the slow-coach," though he did so only to his wife and a small band of
admirers.

Relations between the two had not been helped by the fact that at least
two of the *putsches* of the early 1930's had envisioned the replacement of
Hirohito by his brother. That Chichibu was entirely unconnected with
these upheavals and was never consulted about them hardly made his position much easier. He had been cast in the role of the rival, and it was hard
of Hirohito to think of him otherwise. In any case, as Hirohito was on one
occasion to confide, quite ingenuously, to one of his Court officials:

"He has so many attributes of royalty which I lack. He is a natural
leader. He has no reticence about showing what he feels. The business of

149

kingship comes easily to him. He is never in doubt about what he wants from his ministers or from his people." [1]

Sensing this rivalry, the young military elements had decided that Chichibu was their man. Once they got the strings of power in their hands, it was him, Chichibu, they planned to manipulate—in the dubious belief that he would go along with them as a "front" for the radical and fascist administration which they planned to organize. They must have been disconcerted when the first result of the ni-ni-roku was to send Prince Chichibu to his brother's side at the Palace with a pledge of undying loyalty. He also sent his wife to stay with Empress Nagako and her children.

In the aftermath of the revolution, Chichibu was much concerned to show both his brother and the nation that he was a Hirohito supporter. Extraordinarily enough, for he was one of those who had secretly backed the mutineers, a certain powerful member of the Army General Staff named General Jinsaburo Mazaki was suggested as the head of a new quasi-military administration which should take over the country following the suppression of the rebellion. Mazaki, like his fellow general, Araki, was a firebrand who perfervidly propagated the policy of Kodo, or the Imperial Way. At once Prince Chichibu decided to make his position clear. Kido writes:

"Prince Chichibu stressed to Baron Harada, Prince Saionji's secretary [Saionji had been asked to find a new premier] that it would be absolutely improper for Mazaki to form a succeeding Cabinet, following the February 26th incident. At the time persistent rumour had it that General Mazaki was behind the February 26th incident, which was nothing but the Army's *coup d'état*. My diary for the same day also shows that . . . Prince Chichibu, the Emperor's younger brother, sent his message to Prince Saionji warning him against General Mazaki and others, and that when Prince Chichibu proceeded to the palace His Highness stressed to the Emperor the necessity of dismissing General Mazaki."

Both Mazaki and General Araki (together with other high officers suspected of collaboration with the mutineers) were retired from their posts; though not, of course, permanently. But at least the nation was given a demonstration of solidarity in the Imperial family. The rebellion at least healed the breach between the Emperor and his brother; and no one afterward ever tried to suggest that one was trying to usurp the other.

[1] A source who prefers not to be identified.

150

As proof of his trust in his brother, the Emperor even proposed to appoint Chichibu's father-in-law, Count Tsuneo Matsudaira (former ambassador to Britain), as his new Lord Keeper of the Privy Seal. It was an appointment, it must be admitted, which the Prince did not particularly welcome. His wife pointed out that previous holders of the job had not exactly lived to enjoy comfortable old age. Matsudaira himself eventually overruled her objections, but meanwhile Baron Yuasa was appointed.

Meanwhile, Prince Saionji had been summoned to Tokyo to advise the Emperor on the formation of the new Government. In the all too short period of euphoria which followed the suppression of the rebellion, there were moments when Hirohito genuinely believed that some sort of decency had been restored to Japanese political life, and that an administration pledged to peace and international cooperation might emerge from the chaos and bloodshed of ni-ni-roku. Alas, he was deceiving himself. The balance was all on the wrong side. Fifteen Army officers had been executed and over eighty sent to jail or cashiered. But they were all young and there were plenty of other fanatics waiting to take their places. The seven statesmen whom they had assassinated were irreplaceable, for experienced men of their moderation were in short supply in Japan in 1936. True, two powerful elements for evil had been purged with the compulsory retirement of generals Mazaki and Araki, but everyone knew they would be back.[2] Meanwhile, the purging of the mutineers had effected nothing except to tip the balance of the Army from those who followed Kodo, or the Imperial Way, to those who belong to the Tosei-ha, or Control Faction. The apostles of Kodo believed in keeping their eyes on the north, consolidating in Manchukuo and preparing for the "inevitable" war with Russia. The Control Faction, on the other hand, were even more dangerous. They believed in the limitless expansion of Japan's hegemony into China, into Southeast Asia and the Pacific. Their hostility was toward Britain and the United States, and their eyes were upon the dominions and colonies of the British Empire, the dependencies of America like Hawaii and the Philippines. Now these men—and they not unnaturally had allies in the Japanese Navy—were in the ascendant and anxious to make themselves felt.

It seems incredible that Prince Saionji—who, once more, would recommend the new premier—did not realize this and warn the Emperor about

[2] Araki returned in 1938 as, of all things, Minister of Education.

it. For some days, however, he appears to have believed that a moderate, even liberal, even antimilitarist administration was in the cards, and his first instinct was to advise Hirohito to send for Prince Konoye, who was known to be a man of peace (as well as charm) and a believer in democracy, as well as being an admirer of Britain and the United States. Prince Konoye was a kinsman of the Emperor, young, intelligent, sensitive, but also a man who suffered from an almost Proustian dislike of getting up and going out and doing things. He maintained that he suffered from bad health and, though young, had periods when he took to his bed and simply refused to get up; or, if forced to rise, sat around looking sleepy or dozing. He was in one of these phases now and declined overtures made to him to come to Tokyo and form a government. There ensued a period of anxious cogitation. Saionji had long conferences with Count Makino (who had hobbled dejectedly into Tokyo from the scene of his escape from assassination), with Chichibu and Kido, and of course with the Emperor. Eventually the man who had been foreign minister in the previous administration, Mr. Koki Hirota, was summoned to the Palace and accepted the Emperor's mandate to form a government.

Hirota was hardly a liberal. He was a member of the Black Dragon Society and a protégé of its leader, Toyama; he got along well with the Army; but to demonstrate his willingness to pursue a path of moderation, he told Saionji that he would introduce "reasonable elements" into his cabinet in those places where they could do most to refurbish Japan's image abroad. Saionji, with a naïveté which was becoming increasingly evident as he grew older, accepted Hirota's assurances, as did the Emperor. On March 5, 1936, Hirota announced that he was in process of forming a cabinet and that he had picked his first and most important colleague, none other than Admiral Zengo Yoshida, a well-known and courageous liberal, as his Minister for Foreign Affairs. Moreover, he said, Yoshida was helping him to pick the other members of his administration.

With regard to this news, the American Ambassador (Joseph C. Grew) cabled Washington expressing his astonishment. Hirota, he cabled, "is a strong, safe man" who "will play ball with the Army to a certain extent." But the appointment of Yoshida "seemed to us precisely like waving a red flag at a bull because not only is Yoshida a pronounced liberal but he is also the son-in-law of Count Makino. But naturally the Army wouldn't accept him for a moment, and soon it was announced that Hirota had run into hot water."

152

Of course. He intended to. To secure the Emperor's backing for his administration, he needed to prove that he had liberal tendencies. The appointment of Yoshida was intended to demonstrate it. He knew that Hirohito and Saionji would be impressed, for they admired Yoshida both as an incorrupt politician and a man of wide vision and peaceful tendencies, and that they would not be able to forget that he was Makino's relative.

What Hirota realized, of course, was that the Army would never accept him. To him that was not important. He had made the gesture and shadowboxed for a few hours to show Emperor and Genro that he was not giving way easily.

"I can't imagine why Hirota made the announcement," wrote Grew, "because he surely must have known that Yoshida would be impossible and it would seem to put him, Hirota, in a weak position to have to throw Yoshida overboard and revamp his Cabinet at the Army's dictation. There must have been some deep-seated purpose in the manoeuvre, possibly to place squarely on the Army responsibility for tampering with Hirota's foreign policy."

But now Hirota could go ahead, unhampered by interfering liberals, to pursue the policy he had always intended to follow; for it soon became apparent that he must, from the start, have worked hand in glove with the Army in the tactics he adopted to deceive Prince Saionji. Four days after the mandate was handed to him at the Palace, the new premier announced a complete capitulation to the militarists. Hitherto, the rule was that the Ministers of War and Marine should be Army or Navy officers; but the civilian premier had always been allowed to consult with his Service colleagues on the result, and he could, if he wished, pick an officer from the reserve. Hirota agreed to have this altered in fact and in law. Henceforward, neither of the Service ministers would be allowed to accept their portfolios unless they were actually *serving* officers, which put the question of their choice squarely in the hands of the Army and Navy. To destroy an administration they had only to order the Service minister to resign and return to active service; to prevent an administration with which they did not agree from being formed, they had only to refuse the proposed minister permission to serve. It was on these terms that General Terauchi and Admiral Nagano came into the Hirota administration—and Yoshida went out.

The stage was set for an era of government ostensibly ruled by civilians but in fact controlled by the military. It took some time for Hirohito to realize what trickery had been effected in his name.

One of the most acute witnesses of the 1936 mutiny was the Ambassador of the United States of America, Joseph C. Grew, quotations from whose diary have already appeared in this story. He was a man of keen intellect and perennial optimism who rarely fell into the slough of despond over international affairs. He did, however, sum up the outlook after the rebellion in a cable to the State Department in which he said:

"We should not lose sight of the fact, deplorable but true, that no practical and effective code of international morality upon which the world can rely has yet been discovered, and that the standards of morality of one nation in certain given circumstances have little or no relation to the standards of another nation in other circumstances, and little or no relation to the standards of the individuals of the nations in question. To shape our foreign policy on the unsound theory that other nations are guided and bound by our present standards of international ethics would be to court sure disaster."

Not many diplomatic envoys from the West have stated the contingencies of life with the East in such succinct terms. It so happened that Grew was an ambassador of no mean order. If the government at home had really wanted peace in the Orient—and not necessarily at any price—it seems almost certain that Grew would have secured it for them. He was an urbane and highly civilized career diplomat who came to Japan in 1932, and his brief was to smooth the rough relations between America and Japan.

He arrived when suspicions between the two countries were as festering as scabs. The United States was still sponsoring (at least in Western states) a policy of banning Japanese immigration and discriminating against the yellow populations already established in parts of the Union. Japanese newspapers, egged on by the armed forces, were convinced that they had been cheated at the London Conference because Japan had been allotted a naval ration of three ships to every five of America and five of Britain, and they spread propaganda like pollen to the effect that the Japanese had been humiliated and made to appear "inferior" to the whites. All this, plus the 1936 revolt, had annihilated the liberals and prepared the ground for an Oriental fascism that would fulfil itself only when it came to grips with the forces of the West, and bested them.

154

In such circumstances, Grew's assignment was a difficult one, to put it mildly. He gave no sign that he thought so himself, and from the start went out of his way to cultivate the soil of his new bailiwick. In many ways, he might have been taken for an English diplomat of the old school; he was a dresser of meticulous distinction, proud of his good looks—tall, lean figure, sparse gray-flecked hair, a trim toothbrush moustache—and he had a crisply cheerful disposition which seemed to thrive on rebuffs and disappointments. He had come to Japan from Turkey where he had got to know Kemal Pasha well—a great favorite of the younger element in the Japanese Army—and he was predisposed to like his new territory not only because of earlier service but because his wife had been brought up in Japan, spoke the language, and was the granddaughter of Admiral Perry, whose "black ships" reopened Japan to the world in the nineteenth century.[3] (He had a daughter who was modern and vivacious and had swum the Bosphorus, and to her, too, the newspapers paid keen attention.)

Grew's initial encounters with Emperor Hirohito were unfortunate, and it took some time for the situation to be straightened out. For Grew was deaf. He used a hearing aid, but even with this the interpreters had to repeat to him in no uncertain terms what he was being told. Unfortunately, court etiquette in Japan—and the custom still pertains, alas—insists that no one shall ever raise his or her voice in the presence of the Emperor or Empress. Grew's troubles started from the moment he presented his letters of credence.

"The Emperor read his speech in Japanese in a high sing-song voice," he wrote in his diary afterward, "then according to the protocol, 'shake hands,' and the Emperor asked two or three of the usual formal questions, which I did my best to answer intelligently in spite of hearing only one word in four of Shiratori's translation (he had been told that I heard badly, but simply couldn't raise his voice in the Imperial presence)."

The United States envoy had the same trouble when being presented to the Empress. "Madame Takagi did the interpreting but much too low for me to hear, and it was fortunate that Alice [his wife] was there to re-interpret everything that was said, for otherwise I would never have answered the Empress' questions. I suppose that sooner or later they will find out that they simply have to speak up if they expect me to reply intelligently. It's an awful bore to be deaf—especially at the Japanese Court."

[3] Japanese newspapers persisted in calling Mrs. Grew "Perry's daughter," which "always made us feel so terribly old."

He did not have much difficulty in hearing the voice of the Army clamantly demanding control in the next few years. In not many months the "strong, safe man" Hirota, whom he had considered to be "a good friend of the United States" had passed through the Diet a program of financial reform which put Japan's economy practically on to a war basis, organized a naval building program to bring the Japanese Navy and merchant fleets up to parity with Britain and the United States, and initiated conversations with the Nazi Government in Berlin that would result in the signing of the Anti-Comintern Pact.

"In my talk today with the Soviet Ambassador," Grew wrote on December 3, 1936, "he spoke with considerable heat concerning the Japanese-German Agreement and said that his government possessed definite evidence that a secret military pact existed. He said that the military pact was undoubtedly directed against Great Britain and on my inquiring how the pact worked in that direction, he said that it envisaged the division of various British overseas possessions and the Dutch East Indies between Japan and Germany in case of war. He said that this was directly in line with the Japanese program for southern expansion as well as for Germany's need for colonies. He spoke ironically regarding the Anti-Comintern agreement."

Unfortunately, the period during which the pact was negotiated and signed was one in which the Emperor was all but cut off from contact with those who might otherwise have guided him and persuaded him to use his influence against it. In June, 1936, Kido resigned his post as secretary to the Lord Keeper and embarked on a short—and as it turned out, ineffective—political career. The new Lord Keeper, Yuasa, was a fusspot with no feelings other than for protocol. Baron Matsudaira, who had by this time accepted the post of Minister of the Imperial Household, had not yet arranged to take up residence in the Imperial Palace and had failed so far to establish friendly relations with the Emperor. Prince Chichibu, who might have bridged the gulf between them, was away in Hokkaido serving a term with his regiment. Prince Saionji was feeling old, infirm and dispirited. Prince Konoye was (no doubt) asleep.

So the crucial months in the aftermath of the rebellion, a now-or-never time when some semblance of democracy, or, at least, civilian rule, might have been reestablished, were wasted, through trickery on the part of the politicians, through sheer inertia on the part of the advisers to the throne, and through sheer ignorance on the part of the Emperor, who simply was not told the why and the wherefore of what was being done in his name.

By 1937 the Army had had their full use of the Hirota administration, sensing that though the Prime Minister was with them not all the members of his Cabinet shared his (and their) determination to pursue a policy of planned aggression abroad and totalitarian control at home. There were murmurs in the Diet as revelations began to leak of military pressure to control the newspapers. Most of them by now were succumbing either to Army threats or accepting Army bribes, and were beginning to fill their columns with scandal stories calculated to smear the reputations of any minister or politician who seemed likely to oppose military plans. It was no new thing for politicians to be vilified in Japanese newspapers, which were apt to enumerate the names of their mistresses, the frequency of their drunken parties, and the source of the bribes which kept them going. But hitherto the propaganda was on a knock-for-knock basis, with one party organ attacking and the other defending. Now both sides were given over to snide stories imputing decadence, dishonesty and drunkenness to all but the glorious officers of the armed forces.

It was in these circumstances that one of those who had been repeatedly traduced, a leading Seiyukai member named Hamada, made a speech in the Diet openly accusing the military of deliberately denigrating civilian government and scheming to take over power. General Terauchi, the War Minister, bounced to his feet to refute the charge and accused Hamada of "insulting" the Army. Hamada calmly replied that his attacks were not against the Army as such but against a number of unscrupulous and ambitious members of its General Staff, and then added a remark which could have been made only by a Japanese—and meant to be taken literally.

"If any remarks of mine have insulted the Army," he said, "I shall not just apologize. I shall expiate my offense by committing seppuku." And then, meaningfully turning to Terauchi, he added: "But if there are no such insults, then it should be you who commits seppuku."

There was a hush in the Chamber as the Minister for War stomped out. What to do? Fall on his sword?

Alas, no. Terauchi simply consulted his Army colleagues, and then resigned. It was the end of Hirota's administration. The Army refused to appoint a successor and the government thereupon ceased to exist.

Once more from his home at Okitsu came the gallant but flagging

Prince Saionji with the weary task of choosing a new prime minister. Once more consultations began with a procession of candidates who were beneath consideration because they were all shoddy politicians, ambitious upstarts or articled hacks of the financial interests or the military cliques. It was then that Hirohito had an inspiration—and it is worth dealing with in some detail since it was the last he dared to indulge in for many years to come. He decided to play the militarists at their own game. He went through the list of all those senior army officers who were most admired by both branches of the armed forces, who could command respect with ordinary people, and who had a record of being decent, honest, uncompromisingly incorruptible individuals.

His advisers came up with the name of General Kazushige Ugaki, known to his friends as Issei. Ugaki was—need it be said?—no liberal in the sense that he wished to see the political system of Japan reformed and a regime of wider social justice installed, but he was a phenomenon among Army officers in that he objected to civilian government being replaced by military. He therefore seemed to be Hirohito's man, and one, moreover, of sufficient stature among his fellow soldiers to make them hesitate before objecting to him.

What was objectionable about Ugaki's nomination, however, so far as the Army was concerned was his past record of sheer impartiality. It was he who had—withal reluctantly—agreed to a reduction in the armed forces during the economy campaign of the mid-1920's. He was reputed to have disapproved of the military uprisings in 1931, 1932 and 1936 because he considered them ill-timed and incapable of effecting their objectives. It did not help, so far as the General Staff was concerned, that he had turned out to be right.

Ugaki was at Atami when the summons from Prince Saionji reached him to attend upon the Emperor in Tokyo. Like most Japanese, he was an inveterate enthusiast for hot-spring resorts of which Atami was at the time one of the most luxurious.[4] He arranged at once to return to Tokyo, via Yokohama, by road in the car which had been sent for him. In the meantime, informants in the palace had let the military know of the

---

[4] It has since become one of the most garish of Japanese spas, more famous for the lubricity of its baths than their therapy. Japanese nowadays call Atami contemptuously by the name of Tatami—a reference to horizontal activities which are more concerned with "sleeping" than "bathing."

Emperor's determination to appoint Ugaki, and there was consternation. The Army chiefs decided that his appointment must at all costs be prevented from coming to fruition. But how? It would never do to come out openly against a fellow Army officer, especially since he had already received an official call from the Emperor. Some more devious method must be chosen of dissuading him.

It was. A meeting was held at the office of General Terauchi, the outgoing Minister for War, at which members of the General Staff and the commander of the military police, Nakajima, met to discuss tactics. It was eventually decided that Ugaki be met personally by an influential member of the Army and the "realities" of the situation presented to him. No one suggested that Ugaki be assassinated if he refused to recognize these "realities"—for, as will be seen, such action was not necessary—but someone used to pressuring and persuading would talk to him and persuade him to refuse the Imperial mandate. Logically enough, for he was used to strong-arm tactics, both mental and physical, the military police chief, Nakajima, was chosen for the job. He immediately put his formidable organization of agents into action, as well he need. There was little time. The Emperor was waiting at the Imperial Palace to talk with his premier-to-be. Ugaki had emerged steaming from his bath and boarded the automobile to take him to Tokyo.

After a good deal of maneuvering by military dispatch riders and the urgent telephoning of reports to Tokyo, the car carrying Ugaki was picked up as it was proceeding through Yohohama and flagged to a stop just outside the city. Nakajima emerged from a limousine parked beside the road, bowed to the general, and asked permission to step inside his car. What followed was a circumlocuted discussion in which the military police chief, urged by his superiors to be delicate, did his unsubtle best to persuade Ugaki to give up his mandate. It seemed most effective to point out to the premier-to-be that he would be putting his country in danger should he accept the Emperor's call, and when Ugaki asked why, Nakajima cited the 1936 revolt and hinted that not all the recalcitrant elements had been eradicated from the forces, and that they might well show restiveness again if they learned that the new leader of the country was a man who favored the slashing of military budgets. Ugaki at once asked Nakajima if this meant that he feared another rebellion—his inference, ill-concealed, being that if the military police chief knew about it, why was he not engaged in nipping it in the bud. Nakajima at once denied that this was the situation—only that Ugaki's appointment would cause certain disturbances which might make army discipline difficult.

It was no good, and Nakajima was shrewd enough to realize it. "Ugaki is a man who shows distinct signs of wishing to give his services to the Emperor, in spite of all his obvious disabilities," he reported later. In the meantime, he asked that the car be stopped and got down in the inner suburbs of Tokyo and strode off into the darkness. It was after eleven in the evening, but no doubt a military police car had been following and he did not have to walk home that night.

As for General Ugaki, he proceeded to the Imperial Palace, where Prince Saionji was waiting to conduct him into audience with the Emperor. There he accepted the mandate and agreed to proceed forthwith in forming a cabinet which would, as Hirohito hoped, try to bring the moderates of both the political parties and of the armed forces together. Once more the naïveté of Saionji, who had given his blessing to this move, was made manifest. Once more the lack of wise, firm and practical advisers to the throne was demonstrated. Ugaki solemnly promised his Emperor that he would go forth and produce a government that would lead the affairs of Japan back into the light.

His heart may have been in the right place, but his head was certainly not: otherwise he would certainly have realized that Hirohito was once more being deceived. For quite obviously the appointment of Ugaki was a bluff which could not possibly succeed, because the Army possessed all the aces. They had tried to dissuade Ugaki from accepting the mandate, and he had refused. What should they do now? Kill him? Start a revolution? But of course not. It was unnecessary. Thanks to the former premier, Hirota, it was now established that any new administration must have its war minister chosen (or, anyway, approved) by the General Staff—in fact, in this case, by a Committee of Three of whom the outgoing War Minister, Terauchi, was the chairman. All they had to do was sit tight and wait for Ugaki to ask for a war minister, and then say no.

This is indeed, what they did. When Ugaki asked for the nomination of an officer, the Committee of Three politely replied that no fewer than three distinguished generals had been asked to accept the job, but that they had all, for one reason or another, refused. Ugaki, realizing that he could form no government without a war minister, tried every trick that he knew to get the Committee of Three to change its mind—short of

160

promising to obey Army orders as to his policy, that is. He had smelled the sweet scent of power and wanted to embrace it, and he was livid with frustration at the tactics of his former colleagues. He decided to use what influence he had left in the Army itself, and called upon all his contemporaries still serving in the forces—plus several distinguished officers who had retired—to bombard the General Staff with petitions for support.

"Ugaki is so eager to taste the sweets of office," reported the *Asahi*, sourly, "that he has even promised to give up smoking and drinking if he is allowed to become prime minister. If he is pressed hard enough, he will even give up eating and geishas, too."

Maybe. But this must be said for Ugaki. He still would not promise to follow the military—rather than the civilian and the Emperor's—line. It was this stubborn integrity, and Hirohito's failure to back it up, which lost him the premiership. For having realized that his erstwhile friends in the Army would not be able to sway Terauchi and his two fellow members of the Committee, Ugaki had a last inspiration. He went to the Lord Keeper of the Privy Seal and asked him to intervene with the Emperor himself. He asked that Hirohito *order* the Committee of Three to appoint a war minister to join his cabinet. The Lord Keeper at the time was Baron Kuruhei Yuasa, a perfervid supporter of his royal master but that kind of yes-man who is apt to say an automatic no to everyone else. He refused to convey Ugaki's request to the Emperor. Whether Hirohito heard about it himself and considered it cannot now be discovered—one suspects that he did, but not having received a direct request weakly ignored it—but certainly the failure of the last gambit ruined Ugaki's chances.

He could have asked the Emperor himself to take action when he was received in audience to report on his failure to form a cabinet. But not even Ugaki possessed enough courage for that. He murmured his regrets, prostrated himself, and shuffled miserably out of the audience chamber.

Another general, Senjuro Hayashi, was appointed in his place and ruled the country fitfully, uneasily and inefficiently for a few weeks until general elections were held in the late spring of 1937. Once more, as in the elections of a year before, the electorate gave a mandate to the civilians rather than the military. The two main political parties—not, it must be admitted, without a little bribery and corruption—gained most of the votes, and the diehard nationalists and outright militarists who had put up for nearly one hundred of the seats were returned in less than twenty of them. It may have been, as one foreign correspondent hailed it, "a signal to the world that the Japanese still believe in democratic Government." But it was also a signal to the armed forces—Army and Navy—to raise the banners again and send their fanatics into action.

But this time it was not a rebellion at home that they initiated, but a war overseas. And this neither Hirohito nor any of his advisers would be able to deal with.

Chapter Eleven

It has been mentioned in this narrative before that one of Hirohito's greatest difficulties was to find advisers who could tell him the truth about what was going on. In 1937 and 1938, which were the years the Emperor will remember as among the unhappiest of his life, he felt more cut off from reliable information and more filled with a sense of helpless frustration than ever before.

Circumstances seem to have combined during these crucial years to deprive him of advisers he could trust, men who could inform, stimulate, inspirit and embolden him—and these were the qualities that were needed in Japan at that time. True, he could still call upon the wisdom and experience of his trusted elder genro, Prince Saionji, but though this octogenarian oracle still functioned from his delphic retreat at Okitsu, he was becoming increasingly timid. When asked for advice, the quavering voice seemed nowadays to answer nothing but: "Play safe, play safe!" The other elder statesman who had once spoken wise words to Hirohito was Count Makino, but he too seemed to have become frail and afraid, shattered by threats to himself and his royal master into a quivering jelly of appeasement. His instinct too was to urge his Emperor to eschew forthrightness of mind, to be an obedient servant of his government, to live by the constitution—a constitutional monarch "like the King of England." Whereas, of course, this was a moment in Japan's history when its Emperor could be most salutarily useful by remembering that he was not a constitutional monarch in the British sense, but, as Prince Konoye once pointed out, the head of a constitution "built on the framework of direct rule by the Emperor . . . the only person who may restrain both the Government and the Supreme Command." [1]

But there was no one to galvanize him in this direction, and he had always been a character who needed a push. Marquis Kido, who could be stimulating, if not always in the right direction, had succumbed to political ambitions for the time being and had gone into the Cabinet. Lord Keeper Yuasa and his secretary, Mr. Yasumusa Matsudaira,[2] were the ones who kept in closest touch with the monarch, and a less gentle, patient and long-suffering man would have found them infuriating. Yuasa professed to be intensely worried by what he called "whispers" against the Emperor. For some extraordinary reason, right-wing activists in the secret societies and some of the more fanatic members of the military cliques decided that Hirohito's interest in marine biology was excessive and that, in any case, "it was absurd to be studying biology in this time of emergency." The nervous courtiers, conveying this information to the master, hinted to him that he should be careful of spoiling his image as a divine monarch by engaging in "the study of natural science . . . too enthusiastically," and suggested that a well-publicized absorption in the Chinese classics such as the Confucian Analects would be more appropriate to his divine persona. Baron Harada, Prince Saionji's secretary, who mentions this matter in his diary for 1937 and 1938, also reveals that so fussy did the court officials become that one of them even prevented a batch of films about marine life and seashore flora from being delivered to the Imperial Palace, though Hirohito had particularly asked to see them. He is said to have "bawled" at Tsuneo Matsudaira, the Imperial Household Minister:

"This is no time for the Emperor to be wasting his time on such things. If they arrive, I'll have them thrown out."

Harada records that even Kido, who might have shown more flexibility of mind, felt so sensitive to right-wing criticism now that he was embroiled in politics that he remarked:

"It has to be confessed that the Emperor possesses all the excessive characteristics of a scientist, and hence has no sympathy for the thinking

[1] Fumimaro Konoye, *Memoirs*, Asahi Shimbun, 1946.
[2] Not to be confused with Prince Chichibu's father-in-law, Mr. Tsuneo Matsudaira, the Imperial Household Minister.

of rightwingers and the like. It is distressing that His Majesty is so extremely orthodox." [3]

It is an indication of his nature that the Emperor, far from laughing off these criticisms, or even of angrily dismissing them, took them very seriously indeed. It was not until after the war that his studies in marine biology won him world-wide recognition as an expert in micro-organic research, but even in 1937 he was known among biologists as a serious student. But he now began to feel so guilty about his work, so convinced that he was "neglecting Japan" and indulging himself, that he began to stay away from the laboratories which had been built in the Imperial Palace grounds, in case the sentries should report that he was wasting too much time there. He made furtive arrangements through trusted servants for Professor Hattori, his former tutor in biology, to attend upon him in the evening in his pavilion, where they studied specimens through the microscope until the early hours. Once upon a time, at the courts in Kyoto, his ancestors had opened the shutters at dawn to let a beautiful mistress slip away unseen. Now Hirohito did the same for an earnest and aged professor.

Since they told him so little, one wonders how his ministers and his critics expected the Emperor to spend his time. It was a fact that he worried himself into insomnia about the political situation, but as much about what he feared was going to happen as what had already done so. Like the civilian government, he was continually being confronted with *faits accompli*. True, he was in a better position than his ministers in that he could, any time he wished, summon his minister for war and his minister of marine and demand to know what was being planned. On two occasions in the past—when Marshal Chang Tso-lin had been murdered in 1928, and Manchuria overrun in 1931—he had angrily upbraided his military advisers for deceiving him over the first and keeping him in ignorance of the second; and he had given them strict instructions about keeping both incidents "within bounds." In each case the military had faithfully promised to obey, and then quietly ignored him. These setbacks and such incidents as the 1936 Mutiny—revealing as they did that not even the Army chiefs themselves could control their young

[3] Prince Saionji and the Political Situation. (Saionji ko to Seikyoku.) Tokyo.

165

fanatics—seem to have dispirited him. In 1937 he gave every sign of mental and physical depression; and it would grow worse.

One of the few statesmen whom he still trusted implicitly—and quite wrongly—was the aristocratic and effete protégé of Prince Saionji, Prince Fumimaro Konoye. It was Konoye whom he appointed as prime minister in 1937, in the confident hope that he would deal with the military, improve the economic situation at home and bring about a rapprochement between Japan and the West, whose leaders, particularly in the United States and Britain, were growing steadily more bitter and incensed over Japan's warmongering. With debonair elegance and unfailing aplomb, Konoye failed to do all these things.

It is astonishing, studying the record, that anyone could have been deceived into believing that Konoye was a democrat, a liberal, or even a serious worker for peace. Yet right to the end he went on bamboozling people—the Emperor himself, Prince Saionji, and many otherwise quite shrewd foreign diplomats.

Sir Robert Craigie, the British Ambassador to Japan, for instance, summed him up in words which reveal a typical reaction, half-admiring, half-sceptical, to the Prince:

"His expression denotes neither energy nor determination, but rather a sense of philosophic doubt. Calm and unruffled in all circumstances, he is by disposition phlegmatic. His eyes are his best feature, denoting intelligence and political acumen, combined with a touch of laziness. The profile is disappointing and does not bear out the promise of the striking full face. These facial contrasts fit in with his enigmatic character. There were moments when his actions showed a touch of genius. Time and again one was impressed by acts of statesmanship, only to be irritated just as often by his apparent lack of firmness in leadership and his failure at times of crises to use his strong personal position to curb the extremists. His Japanese friends were completely baffled by many of his actions, wondering whether he really stood for what he was supposed to represent—a moderating influence—or whether, unknown to his more responsible friends and followers, he was a totalitarian at heart and rather enjoyed giving the Army its long rope."[4]

It is typical of Konoye that during one of the most serious crises of

[4] Sir Robert Craigie, *Behind the Japanese Mask*, London: Hutchinson & Co., Ltd., 1945.

his premiership—in 1938—Kido could write of him in his diary (about one of their conferences together):

"Prince Konoye was composing with a brush. . . . I took over the two pieces of poetry which he had written down. These will make very fine souvenirs of the occasion."

His mind, as usual, was only half engaged with what he was supposed to be doing.

Konoye had taken over in the late spring of 1937 pledged by the Emperor to "do something" about China. Sino-Japanese relations were in a state of simmering antipathy but at least there was no open fighting for the moment; but certain elements in the Japanese Army professed to be concerned about the buildup of the Chinese armed forces (trained, ironically enough, by a German military mission and armed with German and Italian guns and ammunition), and what they termed the "pro-Russian leanings" of the Chinese leader, Chiang Kai-shek. There were some among them who were looking for any reason to crush the Chinese Army and occupy the country before she became too powerful and joined up with the Soviet Union against Japan. There were others who were simply interested in the creation of a *cordon sanitaire* in North China which would, rather more simply, they thought, achieve the same object of keeping China and Russia apart.

On July 7, 1937, both factions found an excuse to take action. Since the days of the agreements which followed the Boxer Rising, the relieving powers (of which Japan was one) had had the right to station troops in Peking and along the railway to the sea. Britain kept a few hundred, the Americans somewhat less, the French a couple of thousand, but the Japanese had by 1937 boosted their garrison to over ten thousand troops. On July 7th these troops, without giving the prior notice to the Chinese which was expected, began night maneuvers in the vicinity of the Marco Polo Bridge, just outside Peking. Shortly afterward a Japanese officer stomped his way into the headquarters of the local Chinese general to report angrily that the Japanese troops had been fired on, and that a Japanese soldier was missing. He demanded the right to enter the town of Wanping, from which the firing had come, and carry out a search. The Chinese general refused, on the grounds that the Japanese shouldn't have been there, anyway; but he did eventually agree to a joint Sino-Japanese search of the town.

In the meantime, however, the Japanese had brought up reinforcements and began shelling Wanping. They also sent their emissary back to tell the garrison commander that he must either surrender at once or be attacked. He chose to be attacked. In the next twenty-four hours he gave the Japanese rather more than they were able to give him, and their casualties were considerable.

News had reached Tokyo, and Konoye called a Cabinet meeting to discuss the situation. At the same time the Emperor summoned the War Minister, General Sugiyama, a thick-headed officer of such bovine stupidity that he was not able to conceal the truth from Hirohito, who forthwith told both him and Konoye to put a stop to the hostilities at once. Within an hour or two the Japanese authorities had received orders to settle, which they hastened to do, telling the Chinese commander—in order to save face for themselves—that they had found the missing soldier. (He had never, of course, been lost.) Arrangements for a truce and a withdrawal were made.

It was all over. A storm in a China tea cup. Or so the Emperor thought. And so it would have been had not some malcontents in the Japanese Army realized that here was the opportunity they had been waiting for. When the evacuation of the Japanese troops took place, more than half a company of them—whether by accident or design will never be known—was left behind. On July 9th they began firing at Wanping. The Chinese, not unnaturally, fired back.

At once the Army General Staff in Tokyo raised the alarm. Without waiting for permission from the Cabinet, troops from the Japanese (Kwantung) Army over the border in Manchuria came in to swell the troops already there, and they ringed the Chinese garrison. In the meantime, Sugiyama addressed a Cabinet meeting and demanded that the Japanese Army at the Marco Polo Bridge and elsewhere in North China be reinforced with more troops from Manchuria, with a division from Korea, and with three divisions from Japan itself, plus air support. Konoye agreed and then went off to ask the Emperor to find out from Sugiyama exactly what *was* happening, because his War Minister wouldn't tell him![5] It was through Hirohito that Konoye thus learned that the Chinese had, in fact, agreed to "a local settlement" of the problem. In the circumstances, Konoye felt justified in telling the Army to

[5] Later, the Army agreed to allow the War Minister to keep the Prime Minister and the Foreign Minister informed of their actions, so long as they promised not to let the rest of the Cabinet know.

withhold the reinforcements from Japan and Korea until further notice.

Once more it all seemed to have ended amicably. There were even some Japanese Army men (and certainly a great many naval strategists) who breathed a sigh of relief, for they realized that an expansion of fighting might well involve them in all-out war in China, for which they did not possess the resources in men, money, armaments and oil, especially if, as they believed, they must remain prepared for war with the *real* enemy in Soviet Russia.

But these were apostles of Kodo-ha, the Imperial Way, and they had been in the minority since the executions and purges after the 1936 rebellion. The fanatics of Tosei-ha, the Control Faction, *wanted* to be involved in China, wanted to envelop and occupy the country, even if it meant risking war with Britain and the United States. And it soon emerged that it was the leaders of Tosei-ha who were in charge around the Marco Polo Bridge. They quickly made it clear that when they asked for a "local settlement" of the incident they meant one arranged on the spot between the Japanese command and the Chinese command in Peking, with no interference from Chiang Kai-shek's government in Nanking. It was rather like a German raiding party in Lorraine insisting on settling without reference to de Gaulle, and it had approximately the same result. Chiang Kai-shek responded by insisting on negotiations in Nanking, preceded by a Japanese withdrawal. When he learned what the Japanese expected from him—an abject apology for previous Chinese assaults on Japanese subjects and property, the payment of damages, the promise to accept responsibility for *future* wrongs, together with Japanese supervision which would have been tantamount to occupation—he rejected them.

It was the moment for the Konoye Cabinet to think hard and consider before its next move. It must have been obvious to Konoye, who was no fool, what might result from a renewal of hostilities. He must surely have known that what the Japanese command were doing was insisting that Chiang Kai-shek abjectly grovel. Instead, he seems to have adopted a view which the American Ambassador, Joseph C. Grew, wryly summed up as:

"How can you expect us to compromise when you refuse to accept our views?"

On July 20, 1937, his cabinet authorized the sending to China of the three divisions which had been held back, and declared mobilization in Japan. On July 26, 1937, a Japanese ultimatum was presented to the

Chinese garrison demanding its withdrawal from the Peking area, and the next day Konoye made a speech in the Diet in which he revealed that he had just come from the Emperor, in whose name the Japanese Army was now fighting so gloriously to achieve a "New Order" in Asia.

The war with China had begun. From now on it would not matter what Konoye said, or even the Emperor himself. The Army had taken over.

Or was Hirohito now really quite helpless to influence the course of events?

There was one statesman who still believed he was not, and that was President Roosevelt of the United States. In December, 1937, he made an attempt to prove it.

The war which the Japanese had now launched against China had not only shocked the other great powers by its ruthlessness and brutality; it had also hit them in the pocketbook. The British, French and Americans had great trading interests in China which were increasingly threatened as the Japanese armies drove south from Peking and eastward from Shanghai. Even the two chief fascist powers, otherwise sympathetic to Japanese foreign policy, were heavily involved in the affairs of the Chinese government, both Italy and Germany in selling arms to the Chinese Army and Air Force, Germany alone in training the Army and even, in some cases, providing them with German officers to command the troops in the field. All these powers had a vested interest in seeing the China War brought to an end (Adolf Hitler, in fact, personally approved one attempt at mediation through his own ambassador in China). True, as the war clouds began to curdle in Europe, the fascist powers realized that Japan would be a useful ally to have in the Far East should they have to fight against Britain, and following the signing of the Anti-Comintern Pact—which was, at the time, much more like an anti-British Empire pact—Germany and Italy reluctantly divested themselves of their China commitments and pledged their support to Japan; but only in words, of course. On the other hand, America and Britain were still wholeheartedly on the side of Chiang Kai-shek and had considerable popular support for their policy of giving all possible encouragement to the Chinese, short of fighting aid.

Roosevelt was determined to have the Japanese branded before the world as aggressors, and he was utterly disenchanted with the League of

Nations' failure to take a firm line. On October 5, 1937, he delivered in Chicago his famous speech in which he likened warmakers to carriers of dread disease and called for a "quarantine" of aggressor nations. He was obviously referring to Japan as well as Germany. Grew, in Tokyo, felt that the speech went too far and complained that it hindered his peace-making efforts,[6] and there is no doubt that it ruffled the feathers of the fighting cocks among the Japanese. The slow-burning propaganda which had been a feature of the Japanese press for some months against Britain and the United States began to splutter ominously. And in China itself the firecrackers began to go off.

Before the President's "quarantine" speech most of the ire of the Japanese Army had been directed against the British in China. They were slapped and humiliated by Japanese sentries for "disrespect" as they passed through the barriers of their concessions. They were harried and even driven out of their businesses. On August 27, 1937, Japanese planes swooped low to examine a car speeding along the road between Nanking and Shanghai and must have plainly seen the Union Jacks it was flying. Nonetheless, they came back and machine-gunned it. The passenger in-side was Sir Hugh Knatchbull-Hugessen, the British Ambassador, and he was gravely wounded in the back. The British had a hard time squeezing a grudging apology out of the culprits and the Japanese Government.[7]

But after October, the United States began to suffer an increasing share of persecution, humiliation and discrimination. Early in December the anger of the Japanese exploded in their faces. The U.S.S. *Panay* was sunk by Japanese Army planes and its survivors machine-gunned and shelled by ground forces.

It so happened that, in the three or four weeks before the *Panay* in-cident, large numbers of particularly fanatical Army officers had been arriving in China from Japan. The Army had been beefed up until its strength in the drive upon Nanking, the Chinese capital, was something like 160,000 men—most of them conscripts, for mobilization was now going on in Japan. Officers were needed to handle the raw troops and

[6] U.S. Isolationists characterized the speech itself as a "warmongering" act.
[7] Sir Hugh was subsequently awarded £5,000 by the British Foreign Office for his pain and suffering, a munificent sum by that penny-pinching organization's standards. He wryly revealed later that compensation had been put "so high" because "the FO wanted to impress the Japanese with the enormity of their crime."

they were in short supply. An application was made to the Emperor for the release of at least two-thirds of the officers and noncoms who had been imprisoned after the 1936 rebellion. This he resolutely refused to allow. "I will not have it," he told the War Minister, "they are a disgrace to Japan." But the Army, without telling Hirohito, quietly recalled all the sympathizers of the rebels who had escaped trial and imprisonment but had been purged at the same time as their two chiefs, generals Araki and Mazaki. They were shipped to China without delay.

Among them was our old friend Colonel Hashimoto, who had been ringleader of most of the *putsches* of the early thirties. It could be said that his fanatical opinions had not changed one whit since the wild days of his youth, except that his horizon had widened slightly. Instead of merely wishing to wipe out liberal-minded politicians in Japan for being, as he believed, under the influence of Britain and America, he now wished to destroy Britain and America for exerting that influence. He arrived in China, making no secret of his hope that this was only the beginning, that it would lead to bigger things—such as a war with the United States and Britain. "Britain, the United States and France are the setting sun," he had once said. "The Universe will only come to life with the bright sun of glorious Japan blazing in the sky. Watch me, Hashimoto—I am no man to sit and talk."

He had his chance for action on December 12, 1937. He had been posted to a regiment of artillery stationed on the banks of the Yangtse River just outside Nanking, then on the point of falling to the Japanese Army. American and British gunboats had gone to Nanking to pick up convoys of vessels, some containing refugees of both nationalities, and escort them away from the capital. Among them was the U.S.S. *Panay* and H.M.S. *Ladybird.* When they hove into view and Hashimoto saw who they were, he ordered his batteries to open fire.

As it turned out, Hashimoto's guns were not the ones which inflicted the most telling damage on the Western vessels. He missed the *Panay,* but his shells did hit the *Ladybird,* severely damaged the superstructure, and killed one sailor. But it was a wave of bombers which sent the *Panay*—her Stars and Stripes plainly marked—to the bottom, after which the planes machine-gunned survivors from the gunboat and the Standard Oil vessels she was escorting as they swam to the bank. Altogether four were killed and several were wounded.

But if Hashimoto had the cub's share of the action, he claimed the lion's share of the credit. Everyone else hastened to assure the American government that it had all been a terrible accident, but the colonel never made more than a pretense of innocence. Years later, while all the others went on insisting that they had made a mistake, Hashimoto boasted that his actions had been deliberate and that he had seen a unique opportunity in the evacuation of Nanking to damage American and British ships and thus provoke reprisals that would lead to war.

The sinking of the *Panay* jolted Washington as nothing in the Far East had ever done so far. There the President and his Cabinet had no doubt of the deliberateness of the attack. "The President feels," wrote Harold L. Ickes, "that the Japanese were activated by two or three motives. In the first place, an arrogant assault upon the United States, if allowed to go unrebuked, would impress the Chinese with the power and strength of Japan. In the second place, Japan wants to make it uncomfortable for any Western power to stay in the Yangtse or, in fact, in any part of China. In the third place, Japan has it in mind to force all of the Westerners out of China."[8]

But what would Washington do in retaliation? The United States Secretary of the Navy, Claude Swanson, "shouted for war in his feeble old voice," wrote Ickes, and Ickes was inclined to agree with him:

"Certainly, war with Japan is inevitable . . . Pacifist though I am, I am becoming imbued with the idea that sooner or later the democracies of the world, if they are to survive, will have to join issue—armed issue—with the fascist nations. This will mean that America and Japan will be at war, and that even if this has to happen, aren't we strategically in a better position now than we will be after Japan has strengthened her hand militarily, and perhaps replenished her treasury with the spoils of China? If we should strike now, could not we put Japan in her place at a smaller cost in life and treasure than might be possible at any time here-after? It is a serious responsibility that this Government faces today. Whatever decision is made will necessarily be a grave and eventful one."

No wonder Grew, in Tokyo—with Japanese officials and civilians continually running in and out to "apologize"—wrote:

"My first thought was that this might result in a breach of diplomatic

[8] Harold L. Ickes, *The Secret Diary of Harold L. Ickes*, Three Volumes, New York: Simon and Schuster, Inc., 1954.

relations and that Saito [Japanese Ambassador in Washington] would be given his passports and that I would be recalled, for I 'remembered the *Maine.'* " [9]

But Roosevelt had another idea. Ickes writes that "he wanted the same result as I did . . . but didn't want to go to war to get it."

It was time, he believed, to force the Japanese government to get its wild military men under control. "The Japanese government continued to maintain that the whole incident had been an unfortunate mistake," wrote Secretary of State Cordell Hull. "This was the lamest of excuses. That some members of the Foreign Office had no hand in it may be true . . . But that the Japanese military leaders, at least in China, were connected with it there can be little or no doubt. *In any case, it was their business* to keep their subordinates under control." [10]

This was what the President had in mind. But he was by this time, not without justification, sceptical of the Japanese government's power to dictate to the military. He had no faith whatsoever in the enterprise or even the sympathy of Prince Konoye. But what about the Emperor? Roosevelt knew from the reports from the American Embassy after the 1936 revolt of Hirohito's "anger and shame" at the murderous activities of the younger element in the Army, and was also aware that it was the Emperor himself who had insisted on the condign punishment of the rebels and the purging of sympathizers. As Emperor, he was Supreme Commander of the armed forces. As Emperor, he was a divine being whose orders, if spoken aloud, must be obeyed. It must have seemed to the American President that here was a splendid (if hardly heaven-sent) opportunity to appeal to the Emperor to get control of his Army once and for all. Accordingly, when he called in Ambassador Saito on December 12, 1937, Cordell Hull not only instructed the envoy to let his government know of the American Government's "deep shock and concern," but also added that the President had asked that "the Emperor be so advised." [11] But this, it seems, was not all. The President also sent a personal letter to the Emperor, and it is not hard to guess its contents from knowledge of

[9] Joseph C. Grew, *Ten Years in Japan,* New York: Simon and Schuster, Inc., 1944.

[10] Cordell Hull, *The Memoirs of Cordell Hull,* Vol. I, New York: The Macmillan Company, 1948. My italics.—L.M.

[11] Report of U.S. Foreign Relations, 1937. Vol. IV. National Archives, Washington, D.C.

what was going through Roosevelt's mind at the time—his urgent desire to see Hirohito keep his wild military men in check.

But what happened to the letter? This is the mystery. In the Archives in Washington one can find references to its existence.[12] A high Japanese official in the Foreign Office in Tokyo (Mr. Toshikazu Kase) later referred to it while being interrogated after the end of the war as "Mr. Roosevelt's message to His Majesty." So did Mrs. Gwen Terasaki, the American wife of another Japanese official who later joined the Japanese Embassy in Washington. Both of them, while certain that the letter was sent, are equally certain that it never reached its intended recipient. However, they both give different reasons for the nondelivery. Kase maintains that Roosevelt made a mistake and "sent the letter directly instead of through the regular diplomatic channels." Terasaki appears to believe that it was sent via the Japanese Ambassador from Washington or via Grew in Tokyo—at any rate, that it went to Hirohito via the Japanese Foreign Office, and his wife quotes a conversation with Roosevelt himself along these lines.[13]

Whichever its method of delivery, we do know that it never got there, and a golden opportunity was lost to galvanize the Emperor into action and bring his recalcitrant Army into line. President Roosevelt never referred to his personal message, and no one seems to know what happened to it on the way.

But he was to try the same technique—with another personal letter to the Emperor—in even grimmer circumstances four years later. The fantastic story of what happened to *that* one can and will be told in its proper place.

Meantime, among the irate and outraged Americans one at least might have disapproved had the President goaded the Emperor into action, and that was the United States Ambassador Joseph C. Grew. On December 20, 1937, he discussed the possibility that American protests might jolt the Japanese government into controlling the Army and Navy, and added:

"But the question arises, *can* they exert control? If repressive measures are taken, another February 26 incident may well occur in Tokyo.

[12] See U.S. Foreign Relations, 1937. Vol. III. National Archives, Washington, D.C.

[13] Gwen Terasaki, *Bridge to the Sun,* University of North Carolina Press, 1957.

The Government, however, is between the devil and the deep blue sea.
We know, however, that the Emperor desires to take a hand in the situation, but will he be permitted to do so? Here we have one of the many paradoxes of Japan: the Army and Navy are the Emperor's 'children' faithfully serving him, subject to his every wish and order—yet arbitrarily taking the bit in their teeth, running amok, and perpetrating atrocities which the Emperor himself cannot possibly desire or sanction."

More's the pity, it would seem, that somewhere between Washington and Tokyo someone suppressed a personal appeal which might have stimulated Hirohito into condemning them.

A few days after writing that entry in his diary, Grew had the satisfaction of seeing the *Panay* incident "closed." Perhaps realizing the very real danger of war, and sensing the intense anger in the White House and the State Department, the Japanese government offered fulsome apologies and generous compensation. Grew, who earnestly desired peaceful and amicable American-Japanese relations, and sought for any means of preventing war between the two countries, was particularly pleased at the outcome. The Japanese were very clever in their tactics as they set about appeasing the indignant American public—so clever, indeed, that one suspects an American, possibly even Grew himself, had given them some cogent advice.

"Equally masterly," wrote Grew on December 26, 1937, "was the Japanese arrangement that its note should get to Washington on Christmas Eve and should be dealt with by our Government on Christmas Day (our reply was dispatched at three o'clock on Christmas Day). The Japanese could hardly have failed to realize that the Christmas spirit is strong in our country and that the thought 'Peace on earth, goodwill towards men' must inevitably color and influence our decision. I was so profoundly happy at the outcome that when I called in Hirota [Japanese Foreign Minister] I entered his room wreathed in smiles and told him that I brought good news." [14]

But not even the Christmas spirit could have allowed anyone to forgive the Japanese for what happened a few days later in Nanking.

[14] Grew, *op. cit.*

176

Chapter Twelve

There is no more miserable business than picking over the old bones of past massacres, and those who wish to read again the obscene details of what the Japanese Army did to the Chinese in Nanking after their capture of the Chinese capital in 1937 will have to turn to other books. There are plenty of them. Let me simply quote here, as a reminder of the circumstances, the summing up of the behavior of the Japanese troops by the Japanese themselves:

"By December 7 [1937] the outer defenses of Nanking were under attack, and a week later Japanese anger at the stubborn Chinese defense of Shanghai [which had slowed the Japanese advance and caused heavy casualties] burst upon Nanking in an appalling reign of terror. . . . For four weeks the streets of Nanking were splattered with blood and littered with mutilated bodies, while Japanese soldiers ran amok, causing untold suffering among the civilian population." [1]

In this riot of sack, rape and murder, it is estimated that 200,000 Chinese died around Nanking at the hands of drunken and bestial Japanese troops. Far more than such isolated incidents as the sinking of the *Panay* and the shelling of the *Ladybird,* these terrible events surely deserved the condemnation of the Emperor. For these were his "children" whom he had been taught, by General Nogi and by Admiral Togo, to regard as civilized crusaders bringing with them into foreign lands the traditions of the samurai, the knights of Bushido. From the history lectures of his

[1] *The Japan Year Book,* 1946–48.

177

childhood, delivered by the men who had been there, he had heard how the Japanese troops had behaved toward their Russian opponents in the Russo-Japanese War, even treating with courtesy and consideration prisoners of war, whom tradition taught them to despise. He cherished the story from General Nogi himself of how he had received his Russian adversary with civilized respect after the latter's surrender, allowing him to retain his sword, accepting the Russian's white charger, which was offered to him, as a "gift" to the Emperor and not to himself. He had listened to Admiral Togo describing the surrender of the Russian fleet and of the respectful salute which the Japanese sailors had given to the vanquished enemy.

Could these and the butchers of Nanking belong to the same Army?

The Emperor Meiji's Rescript put the Imperial attitude toward the armed forces with strength and clarity, and it seems appropriate to quote a short and relevant sequence from it here, for Hirohito knew it by heart and believed in it. It was his Rescript too, for he, like Meiji, was Commander in Chief.

"Soldiers and Sailors, we are your Supreme Commander in Chief. Our relations with you will be most intimate when we rely upon you as our limbs, and you look up to us as your head. Whether we are able to guard the Empire and therefore prove ourselves worthy of heaven's blessing and repay the benevolence of our ancestors depends upon the faithful discharge of your duties as soldiers and sailors. If the majesty and power of our Empire be impaired, do you share with us the sorrow? If the glory of our arms shines resplendent, we will share with you the honor. If you all do your duty and being one with us in spirit do your utmost for the protection of the State, our people will long enjoy the blessings of peace and the might and dignity of our Empire will shine in the world. As we thus expect much of you, Soldiers and Sailors, we give you the following precepts:—

"1. The soldier and the sailor shall consider loyalty their essential duty. Who that is born in this sacred land can be wanting in his service to it? No soldier or sailor can be considered efficient unless this spirit be strong within him. A soldier or a sailor in whom this spirit be not strong, however skilled in art or proficient in science, is a mere puppet, and a body of soldiers or sailors wanting in loyalty, however well-ordered and disciplined it may be, is in an emergency no more than a rabble. Remember that as the protection of the State and the maintenance of its power depend upon the strength of its arms, the growth or decline of this strength must affect the nation's power for good or for evil. Therefore neither be led astray by current opinions nor meddle in politics, but with single heart fulfil your essential duty of loyalty and bear in mind that duty is weightier than a mountain, while death is lighter than a feather. Never by failing in moral principle fall into disgrace and bring dishonor upon your name.

"2. The soldier and sailor should be strict in observing propriety. Soldiers and sailors are organized in grades, from the marshal and the admiral of the fleet down to the private soldier or ordinary seaman. . . . Inferiors should regard the orders of their superiors as issuing directly from us. . . . If you soldiers and sailors neglect to observe propriety, treating your superiors with disrespect and your inferiors with harshness, and thus cause harmonious cooperation to be lost, you will not only be a blight upon the forces but also unpardonable offenders against the State.

"3. The soldier and the sailor should esteem valor. Ever since the ancient times valor in our country has been held in high esteem. . . . But there is true valor and false. To be incited to violence by mere impetuosity cannot be called true valor. The soldier and sailor should have sound discrimination of right and wrong. This is true valor. Those who in their daily intercourse appreciate true valor should set gentleness first and aim to win the love and esteem of others. If you neglect valor and act with violence, the world in the end detests you and looks upon you as a wild beast."

That Hirohito sincerely believed in these precepts is beyond doubt. Though he had never been, and never would be, a man of war himself and would always consider a resort to arms to settle a dispute a confession of humiliating inadequacy, he nevertheless took his role as Supreme Head of his armed forces with great seriousness, and was made wretched when they failed to live up to the standards Meiji had set for them.

Why, then, did he not send for his Minister of War and demand an explanation when he heard of the atrocities at Nanking? Why were the culprits not condemned?

The Emperor's answer to that, were he allowed to make a public statement about it today, would be a simple one. *At the time* he did not know of them. If this sounds like the stock answer that the Germans used to make when asked why they condoned the concentration camps, it is nonetheless true that there were periods when the Emperor was as isolated from the truth as his people, and this happened to be one of them.

Nearly a year after the Rape of Nanking, Grew was writing: ". . . first-hand reports, supported by photographs, of the barbaric behavior of Japanese troops fill me with impotent anger. If we were not surrounded here in Tokyo with gentle Japanese who deplore these things as much as we do—even more, perhaps, because it concerns their own country and their own honor—I should find it very difficult to remain at this post. Once in a while I do break loose and openly express my feelings, to a few of my Japanese friends. I am sure they think I am being fed with Chinese propaganda and exaggerated tales because they themselves have no access to the facts. Foreign magazines such as *The Reader's Digest* are carefully stripped by the censors of all offensive articles before delivery, if delivery takes place at all. Until they go abroad, or talk with Japanese returned from abroad, they have no sources whatever from which to learn the truth. And the truth is sickening."[2]

It is true that Hirohito had advisers whose duty it should have been to tell him the truth, but there is evidence to support denials from sources close to him that they ever did. Marquis Kido, for example, who was in Konoye's Cabinet at the time of the atrocities and was later the Emperor's Lord Keeper of the Privy Seal kept, as has been mentioned, a meticulous daily diary. After the War he turned over the original to the Allied forces and it was closely examined. The entries were there for the period during which Nanking was occupied and Chinese refugees rounded up, but there is no reference to their treatment by the troops. When he was questioned later, Kido said:

"It is stated that I made no reference to the horrors of Nanking from December 11, 1937, to February 6, 1938, and that the horror and indignation of the world cannot have been unknown to me and the Cabinet, and that though I may not have been responsible for this orgy of atrocities but I was certainly to blame for its continuance. The first time I heard of the Nanking atrocities was after the end of the War from my cousin Tokinori who went to China as an officer in the Japanese Army in 1941 until after the surrender in 1945. He was the first person who told me what he heard about Nanking, although he was not there during 1937-8. If I had heard about it at the time I would certainly have tried to do

[2] Joseph C. Grew, *Ten Years in Japan*, New York, Simon and Schuster, Inc., 1944.

something about it, even though it was not a matter for Cabinet responsibility."

It seems as simple as that. Not until a year later, in 1939, when Japanese troops and soldiers came home on leave and openly boasted of their enormities, did the people in the homeland get an inkling of the crimes which had been committed in the name of the Emperor. And even these revelations were quickly suppressed by a military ordinance forbidding any further talk, or any mention of it in the press. To the Japanese the war in China was a mission, a crusade, in the spirit of Meiji. In an interview with the Associated Press Mr. Yosuke Matsuoka, who was shortly afterwards to become Konoye's Foreign Minister, said:

"China and Japan are two brothers who have inherited a great mansion called East Asia. Adversity sent them both down to the depth of poverty. The scapegrace elder brother [China] became a dope fiend and a rogue, but the younger [Japan], lean but tough and ambitious, ever dreamed of bringing back past glories to the old home. He sold newspapers at street corners and worked hard to support the home. The elder flimflammed the younger out of his meager savings and sold him out to their common enemy. The younger in a towering rage beat up the elder—trying to beat into him some sense of shame and awaken some pride in the noble traditions of the great house. After many scraps, the younger finally made up his mind to stage a showdown fight. And that is the fight now raging along the North China and Shanghai fronts." [3]

The attitude of the Japanese toward the Chinese could well be nutshelled by the sentiment that used to be ascribed to the Germans: "Be my brother—or I'll bash your head in!" Even soldiers at the front, surrounded by the torn and bleeding bodies of their victims, appeared to believe that they were engaged in a civilizing mission. "Birthplace of Peace in East Asia," said a sign in Japanese planted beside the Marco Polo Bridge, where the savage and pitiless invasion began.

One of the reasons for Hirohito's ignorance of his Army's activities in the early months of 1938 may well have been the fact that he was far from well. The Foreign Minister of the period, Mr. Koki Hirota, reported in March, 1938, that when he visited the Imperial Palace the Emperor received him in bed and looked "painfully haggard," and this news was conveyed to Prince Saionji at Okitsu. He at once dispatched his

[3] The English is Matsuoka's own. He was schooled and lived most of his formative years in the United States.

secretary, Baron Harada, to Tokyo with instructions to exhort the Emperor not to work so hard and to take a break from his state occasions by joining his wife and children at Hayama. Saionji was well aware that when things were going badly for the Emperor a holiday at Hayama was a certain anodyne for his troubles. There he lived in the utmost simplicity, gazing across the waters at Mount Fuji and smoking Mount Mihara, moon-watching from the special table among the pines by night, playing with his children on the beach. Willard Price, who lived in a house only a hundred yards away from the beach palace in prewar years, used to watch him relax.

Here, he writes, "he takes full advantage of the sense of privacy which his subjects allow him," even though "there is nothing to prevent the bathers from seeing their Emperor enjoying himself. . . . Wearing a white suit and huge floppy straw hat, he runs races with his children, digs in the sand for shellfish, clambers through narrow cracks between the ten-foot boulders at the waterline where one must time one's passage exactly to avoid an incoming wave, picnics beside the thatched rest house, lies on the grass under wind-whipped pines and reads or looks out to sea." [4]

Price adds: "He swims with a long clean stroke and is evidently able to take care of himself in the water. Nevertheless . . . a prescribed swimming area is marked off with red flags. If he goes beyond them, which he rarely does, he finds a boat respectfully in his way, and he dutifully turns back. It is said . . . that Hayama bathers must wear full bathing costumes, but this is certainly not true. Trunks alone are commonly worn by men and sometimes even by women. Soldiers stationed in Hayama to guard the Emperor march in formation to the public beach, undress in the open, don nothing but breech clouts which promptly become translucent when wet, and dress again on the beach. Respect for the Heavenly King is not shown by clothes or the lack of them. To be sure there is a sign in unsteady English to the effect that every bather must be dressed 'at least up to the knees.' Fortunately no one has yet taken advantage of this costume which would seem to approve, as a sufficient bathing costume, a pair of rubber boots." [5]

For Hirohito, however, the glory of Hayama was that it allowed him to get away from his court officials, who were always around to nag him

[4] Willard Price, *Son of Heaven*. New York, Duell, Sloan & Pearce, 1945.
[5] *Ibid.*

Emperor Meiji, grand-
father of Hirohito, and the
architect of Modern Japan.
(He died in 1912.)

Emperor Taisho, Hirohito's
father. (He died in 1926.)

Emperor Taisho attired in court robes.

Emperor Taisho, who hero-worshipped Kaiser Wilhelm of Germany, photographed while reviewing his troops.

Prince Nobuhito.

Hirohito in 1918.

Crown Prince Hirohito rides in state through London with King George V during his visit to Britain in 1921.

Hirohito (then Crown Prince) shown in this family picture with his three brothers on the grounds of the Imperial Palace, Tokyo. (left to right): Hirohito, Prince Mikasa, Prince Takanatsu and Prince Chichibu.

Emperor Hirohito and his wife on
March 12, 1924.

Hirohito in court robes, 1928.

A pre-war photograph of Emperor Hirohito on his famous white horse.

Prince Konoye shown with members of his Cabinet in Tokyo in 1941. (left to right): Prince Konoye, Yosuke Matsuoka, Jengo Yoshida and General Tojo.

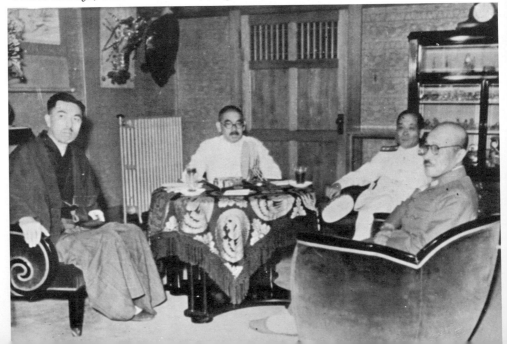

The entrance to the shelter under a hill in the Fukiage Garden.

The conference room in the Imperial air raid shelter where, in the Emperor's presence and at his behest, the history-making decision to accept the Potsdam Declaration was made in 1945. The shelter was opened to the Press for the first time in 1965, on the 20th anniversary of the surrender decision.

Entrance to Conference Hall in the Imperial Palace bomb shelter.

Emperor Hirohito inspects the damage wrought on Tokyo by one of the devastating United States air raids on the Japanese capital in 1945.

Hirohito meets MacArthur on September 26, 1945.

Marquis Koichi Kido, Lord Keeper of the Privy Seal and chief advisor to the Emperor in the final months of the war. He was charged with war crimes and sentenced to life imprisonment; he was paroled in 1955. He died shortly afterwards.

The body of Prince Konoye after his suicide in December 1945. He killed himself rather than face trial as a war criminal.

A postwar picture of Prince Konoye taken shortly before his suicide.

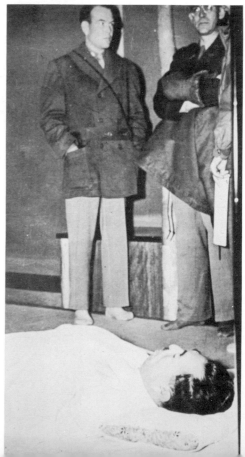

A postwar picture of Hirohito in the garden of the Imperial Palace, Tokyo.

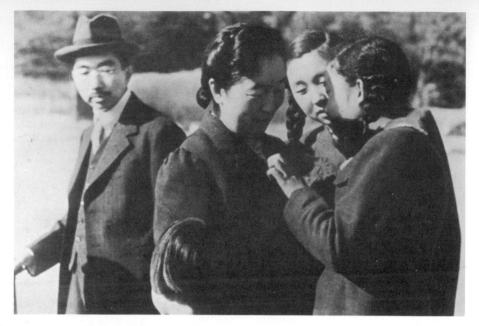

Emperor Hirohito with his wife and two of his daughters on the beach at Hayama, where he has a small palace.

Emperor Hirohito aboard the motor-launch on which he searches for underwater specimens in the waters off Hayama, near Yokohama.

Emperor Hirohito planting rice shoots in a paddy field at the Imperial Palace, Tokyo, assisted by officials of the palace wearing rice planters' straw hats. The traditional rice planting is a time-honored ceremony.

Crown Prince Akihito, Hirohito's eldest son and heir to the Imperial Throne, with Britain's Princess Alexandra during her visit to Japan in 1963. The scene is the Imperial ducknetting preserve near Tokyo.

The annual New Year's Day poetry reading in the Imperial Palace. Winners of the contest are invited to hear their entries read before the Imperial family but first they listen to poems on the same theme composed by the Emperor and his family.

The Emperor attending an art exhibition in Tokyo.

A recent picture of the Emperor on the grounds of the Imperial Palace, Tokyo.

and remind him of his duties. Gone were the times when he had been able to walk in the hills behind the beach house and collect specimens with his friend and tutor, Professor Hattori. It was now impressed upon him to go off like this was "irresponsible," and that if he must have these walks he must be suitably guarded. Since this meant hordes of police clearing out every village and posting themselves on every knoll, he henceforward eschewed the land.

But he could still go out to sea and dive and spear his specimens from his small motor launch and leave his fussy attendants behind. Willard Price, who watched him on these expeditions, writes:

"He seems as happy as a small boy. And like the small boy whose pockets are apt to contain worms, grasshoppers, and tadpoles, the Emperor nonchalantly drops algae, starfish and sponges into the pockets of his white coat. When the yacht returns to the bathing-cove it must anchor about a cable's length from shore because of underwater rocks. An ordinary unpainted fishing boat is brought alongside and the party descends into it. A boy standing on the stern manipulates the great sweep and the boat approaches the shore." [6]

But then, writes Price, "we have a strange sight. A deputation of white-suited court officials has been waiting on the beach. There is a concerted bow, followed by a march into the water until the dignified officials stand up to their hips, half on each side of the boat. Again they bow their heads to the figure standing above them. One is reminded of some scene of baptism by immersion. Then they grasp the gunwales of the fishing boat and draw it briskly up onto the beach. Again they bow as the Emperor steps out. He has returned to palace formality." [7]

These scenes, however, were watched by Price in the days before the China War had turned the nation into a totalitarian state. Now the people were being either squeezed or conscripted. Taxes had gone up to finance the war in Asia and to pay for additions to the Japanese Fleet. Mothers and fathers, like true Japanese deliberately concealing their true feelings, waved and stayed dry-eyed as their sons were shipped off to war. The people were exhorted to sacrifice themselves for their Emperor. The bright lights were dimmed. Gay kimonos were frowned on. "Dress plainly," said notices in the street, "and honor your Emperor."

But if the people had obligations to him (his captious court officials

[6] *Ibid.*
[7] *Ibid.*

183

pointed out to Hirohito), he had obligations to them. He must make his sacrifices too.

Harada discovered to his amazement and indignation that the Emperor, sick and depressed, longing for a sail in his beloved Sagami Bay, was "not allowed" by his court officials to go to Hayama to recuperate. It would be "too ostentatious at such a time," they said.

The Baron pleaded with Hirohito to ignore them, but found the Emperor, as usual, reluctant to go against the advice of his court officials. He then rushed away to Prince Konoye and to Kido, both of whom urged Hirohito to go away and relax. But each time the Lord Keeper, Yuasa, advised against it. He hinted that "the military" who were "dying on the battlefields" and the rightwingers, who were "noisy" about the Emperor's lack of enthusiasm for the China War, might become restive if they heard that their Emperor was "enjoying himself" either bathing or "wasting his time with science." So Hirohito moped in dispirited distemper around the palace all through the spring of 1938. As Harada put it:

"Even lowly civil servants and ministers take time off to relax at the weekend, recovering their vitality after their routine work. But His Majesty, who attends to affairs of State with vision and depth, is not allowed rest or diversion." [8]

Had the Emperor's work indeed required vision and depth he would not have found his enforced seclusion quite so irksome. But of course it was not. The only serious work in which he was engaged, his marine biology, had been circumscribed by his advisers and he now felt guilty about it.[9] It was not until the summer of 1938 that he felt justified in going to his laboratory again, and then only late at night. Otherwise, even after rising from his sick bed, he moped around the palace, trying to absorb himself in "affairs of State" which any competent secretary could have done. He was up at usual at six A.M. and crossed the park to pray in the shrine of his Imperial ancestors. Then to his only indulgence —his English breakfast and a perusal of his personal mail. The rest of the day was at the disposal of the state—placing his Imperial seal on documents already approved, receiving ministers and advisers, filing papers,

[8] Baron Harada, secretary to Prince Saionji.
[9] He still does, though court officials prefer the word "sheepish" to guilty. They hastily point out that he nowadays (1965) goes to his laboratory only "in the evenings or in his spare time" and "never lets it interfere with his work for his people." Times may have changed but his advisers evidently haven't.

and waiting. It was a wearying and soul-destroying routine, all the more frustrating since it went on all through Japan's crisis. He must have sighed with envy sometimes at the "free and happy life" which he imagined was the lot of the King of England, able to go out every day among his people, to open buildings, lay foundation stones, launch ships and tour factories, and all sorts of fascinating activities of that sort! Hirohito rarely went out on a public occasion now. Even when he did so, people were not allowed to look at him directly or give him a cheer. And he wasn't even allowed to smile at them.

Not that the urge to smile at anyone can have been very strong in his heart in 1938 and the years which followed. To read the controlled press, to listen to the exultant voices on the radio, to watch the gaudy parades and mass meetings of the patriotic societies, it must have seemed to the Japanese people that these were the nation's finest hours. It is true that the war in China (plus preparations for a greater war to come) was bringing hardship to the masses and inconvenience to the middle class. *The New York Times* correspondent in Tokyo, Hugh Byas, reported:

"Japan has reached the point where the length of a matchstick and and skin of a rat represent important economic factors in continuing the war with China. So do toothpaste, toy balloons, tinfoil and chocolate bars, freckle cream and caviar, bathing suits and chewing gum, bookbindings and teacup decorations, golf balls and patent medicine and a thousand and one other things which might seem far removed from the 'sinews of war.' Japan is not a nation of raw products. The materials that go into these things must be imported, paid for abroad. . . . Not even Germany of the World War [One] could have been so tightly laced as Japan is today. Chemists in the Ministry of Agriculture are tanning rat skins to find a leather substitute. Major commodities such as metals, oil, wool, cotton, leather and chemicals . . . were marked for removal from the market . . . all raw cotton and cotton cloth [removed] from domestic use. Iron is scarcer than gold. It is hard now to buy a frying pan; a month from now it will be impossible." [10]

The newspapers were full of praise for the "splendid spirit of sacrifice" of an 85-year-old ex-soldier, General Yasuyuki Nishiyama, who com-

[10] *The New York Times,* July 31, 1938.

mitted ceremonial seppuku in order that his pension could be diverted to the war effort. They also reported that the Emperor was setting an example of sacrifice at the palace by substituting "native saké for foreign wines, and Japanese cigars and cigarettes instead of foreign tobacco, on ceremonial occasions. [In fact there was no native tobacco of any significant quantity, but that didn't matter, since there were no ceremonial occasions— the annual cherry blossom viewing and the party for his birthday both being cancelled.] Henceforth Imperial gifts and cards, when absolutely necessary, will bear only silver crests instead of gold." [11]

To the Japanese people the sacrifices may have seemed worthwhile, because they believed that the war in China (or what General Matsui, the Commander at Nanking, called "the pacification of our Brother") would soon end in victory. Patriotic propaganda was beginning to have its effect. So was hate propaganda. The knowledge that increasingly large parts of the world were demonstrating their "misunderstanding" of Japan's sacred mission in China only showed how badly the rest of the world needed the attention of the propagandists of Japan. The Japanese were, on the whole, quite willing to tighten their obis and substitute geta for shoes if it meant that more soldiers and more sailors could carry the red ball of the Rising Sun to the barbarian countries where Japan's "sincerity" was so wilfully misunderstood. Toward the end of 1938, to show their oneness with Nazi Germany, they even agreed to blame the machinations of the Jews for turning the rest of the world against them, and Ambassador Grew gloomily reported that an anti-semitic propaganda exhibition in Tokyo was having something of a success with the masses, though where they were going to find the Jews they now professed to be against was something else again.

But Hirohito knew only too well what lay behind all the perfervid talk of military glory. The Army had expected that Chiang Kai-shek would be prepared to accept defeat after the fall of his capital, but he was still fighting. Some officers in the Army had suggested that since Chiang would not give in, the Japanese should begin overtures for peace; but they had been damned as defeatists by the Japanese leaders in China, and the government persuaded to "withdraw recognition" from Chiang's administration. The war went on, draining off men, materials, vital resources in a campaign that showed no sign of ever reaching a conclusion. Even so, the buildup went on, physically and mentally, for a larger war still. For

[11] *Asahi,* Tokyo, July 10, 1938.

now the Navy wanted a turn. The Army had had all the glory of combat so far. It was the turn of the sailors to be hailed as heroes of the Empire. And there were no victories for the Navy to be won in China. Theirs lay farther South, in Hong Kong and Singapore, and out in the Pacific.

"In strictest secrecy, I was informed yesterday by a prominent member of the Italian Embassy," wrote Grew in his diary in November, 1938, "that the Japanese Navy had definitely decided to declare war, presumably in the near future, as the first step toward war with Soviet Russia. My informant emphasized his opinion that he 'wouldn't give a nickel for Hong Kong.' His explanation is that the Navy feels that it has been merely a beast of burden for the Army, which has had all the glory since 1931; it is becoming restive in this role and has decided to take advantage of the present war pitch of the nation to remove Japan's opponents in East Asia and so complete her absolute domination in this sphere. England, as a result of the lag in her armament programme during the past fifteen years, is helpless, it is felt. The only fear which has so far deterred the Navy is what the United States fleet might do, but this has been removed within the last week since it is evident that the United States is determined at any cost not to become involved in the Far East." [12]

It was this impatient belligerence displayed by his military and naval ministers and the weary shoulder-shrugging of reluctance of Konoye to restrain them which plunged Hirohito into a kind of fatalistic gloom. "I am having trouble with my Service Ministers," he said to Konoye one day, "but I do not expect you can help me much with that." The Prime Minister did not dare to tell him of the true abjectness of his situation with regard to the armed forces. He was now so subservient to them that he had actually pleaded with his ministers of war and marine to take him into their confidence whenever they went ahead with yet another reckless departure from government policy. This they had promised to do, on one condition—that Konoye tell no one else in his Cabinet. And Konoye had agreed. After the War he was to tell an Allied war correspondent who interviewed him that he "fought the military tooth and nail to defeat their policy of belligerency." [13] But the teeth were false and the nails were bitten down to the quick, and they left no mark.

[12] Japanese military strategists were convinced that isolationist sentiment in the United States would effectively smother any tendency by the Roosevelt Administration toward an activist policy.

[13] Talking to William Courtney of the *Sunday Times*.

In truth, as Kido reveals in his diary, Konoye, at this time, wanted nothing better than to get out and go back to his couch or his paint brushes. He writes:

"Owing to the weakness of Prince Konoye's character, he once again expressed to me his intention to resign. However, as I believe no one except Prince Konoye could possibly settle the affair, I put emphasis on the necessity that he should summon up his courage and proceed resolutely to settle it." Konoye was also worried by threats from the right-wingers and patriotic-society bullies against senior statesmen suspected of "hindering" the expansionist plans of the military, and this was also a reason for laying down his badge of office. Kido once more dissuaded him. "Better to die," he said, "than let the Emperor down."

But in the end he was allowed to go. Even the Emperor seemed to suspect by now—though he was far from being convinced—that Konoye lacked the courage or even the will to block the ambitions of the fanatics who wanted to expand the war.

With his departure, government in Japan for the next few months was conducted more from Berlin and Rome than it was from Tokyo; and even the War Minister, when asked for information by the Emperor, could not tell him what exactly was going on. For the new government of Mr. Kiichiro Hiranuma, considerably to the right of the Konoye administration, showed itself so willing to be led by the nose that it even allowed the leading to be done by a Japanese general ten thousand miles away.

The ambassador to Berlin in 1939 was Mr. Shigenori Togo,[14] but though *persona grata* with the Nazi government he was hardly on more than bowing terms with von Ribbentrop or any other member of Hitler's administration. The Japanese in Berlin who maintained the coziest relationship with Nazi officialdom was the military attaché, Lieutenant General Hiroshi Oshima, and he reported back neither to his own ambassador or to the Gaimusho (Foreign Office) in Tokyo, but direct to the Army.

"Already at that time," Togo wrote later, "the Japanese military had established the deplorable custom of having its military attachés assigned to the Embassies in certain countries make direct contacts with the Gov-

[14] Later to be Foreign Minister both at the time of Pearl Harbor and at the end of the war.

188

ernments of the country to which they were accredited on matters of high policy." [15]

The matter of high policy in which the Army was interested was turning the Rome-Berlin Axis into a Triple Alliance, and they had in Oshima a fervid front man for their cause. Togo, on the other hand, believed that to form a military alliance with Germany at this juncture would be dangerous for Japan and inevitably involve her in war against the West. He said as much in his dispatches to the Gaimusho, at the same time vehemently protesting against Oshima's activities. The result was that Togo was withdrawn from Berlin and posted as ambassador to Moscow, and Oshima was appointed to fill his place in Berlin. From that moment on (with some powerful assistance from Toshio Shiratori, the like-minded ambassador to Italy) Oshima pushed the question of the alliance as hard as he could, several times even ignoring instructions from the Army when he considered them to be too cautious.

Even more cautious, however, was the Hiranuma administration. Despite its weight of rightwingers and Army-appeasers, it so happened that the Cabinet contained two ministers who insisted on retaining some measure of independence. One was the Foreign Minister, Hachiro Arita, and Navy Minister Mitsumasa Yonai. They had no objections to a military alliance with Germany so long as it was confined to one contingency only—war with Soviet Russia. But Hitler wanted a broadly based alliance which would involve Japan in all or any of Germany's wars should Germany demand it, and this neither the Foreign Office nor the Navy were prepared to accept at the time. All they desired was a treaty of alliance which would give Japan some security from Russia in Siberia, where, already, trouble had broken out between the Red Army and the Japanese.

The opposition to Oshima's plans was widespread in the Foreign Office, where some quiet spade work by Ambassador Grew had been going on. It was known that Grew's views on a Japanese-German alliance had also reached the Imperial Palace and Hirohito had no hesitation in acknowledging their wisdom.

"The line I have been taking with Japanese high and low—and I have plenty of evidence that my arguments have penetrated to the top—is this," wrote Grew in his diary on May 15, 1939. "If a general war breaks

[15] Affidavit to the International Military Tribunal, Far East.

out, it is almost inevitable that the United States will be unable to stay out of it; things would be bound to happen which would inflame the American people, and history has shown that the American people are among the most inflammable in the world. In such a case the pacifists and the isolationists would be in the forefront of those supporting war—at least, the great majority would be."

He went on: "If Japan were then tied up in the German camp in a general military alliance, it would be almost impossible for the United States to remain at peace with Japan. It therefore behooves Japan to look into the future and decide where her friendship ought in her own interests to be placed."

But if the Emperor was impressed and the Foreign Office and the Navy were impressed, the Army was not and they signaled Oshima to continue with his negotiations. Oshima needed no encouragement. He was prepared for an alliance at any cost.

As for Hiranuma and the rest of his Cabinet, they were abjectly eager to follow the Army's wishes, and conclude an alliance as speedily as possible. Their eagerness was not a little hastened by the knowledge that the notorious Colonel Hashimoto was on the loose again. With windy bombast, he called upon the Japanese people to forget for the moment the enemy to the North,[16] and turn South "to the real threat to Japan's future," Britain. Hashimoto wrote articles and addressed mass meetings calling for a war on Britain at once, the forging of the Rome-Berlin-Tokyo Axis, and the formation of a united fascist front against the "evil forces" of democracy and communism. And to spur on Hiranuma and his ministers, he exhorted his followers to deal death to all who dared to oppose the alliance.

To Hiranuma's intense annoyance and to the fury of the Army, not to mention Oshima, who sent sulphurous cables of enraged protest, neither Arita nor Yonai would budge. The Cabinet met seventy times in six months in 1939 in an attempt to secure a unanimous agreement to accept the alliance, and seventy times it failed. And when irate generals bullied him and Hashimoto threatened, all Hiranuma could say was: "What can I do? I can sack Arita. But with Yonai I am helpless. So long

[16] Japanese troops and planes had clashed with the Red Army at Chang-kufeng-Lake Khassan on the frontiers of Manchuria and Outer Mongolia that summer and suffered a defeat whose seriousness even the government failed to minimize. Casualties were estimated at 20,000 men.

as he represents the Navy's policy, I dare not dismiss him—because the Navy will refuse to appoint anyone to take his place, and the government will therefore fall."

And Hirohito, glum though the situation may have seemed, must have got a grain of wry amusement out of it. He had told Kido after the 1936 rebellion of his objections to the "serving officer" law by which the Army and Navy had gained control of the government. It provided a slight comic relief to know that it could embarrass the Army too, which had thought it up.

All through the summer of 1939 Hashimoto and his fellow firebrands scattered sparks across the islands, and started small blazes of anti-Western feeling everywhere. The propaganda suited the Japanese mood. The British were obviously decadent, for they would otherwise not have accepted the Munich Pact. Why then should they be allowed to dominate Japan's brothers in Asia and bar the green lands of Australia and New Zealand to the sons of Japan? They rallied around in their thousands, especially during July, 1939, to demand a pact with Germany that would put them into action against the British. Weaned as they were, too, on the sour milk of anticommunism, they coupled Russia's name with that of Britain in their clamant cries for action. War on Britain! War on Russia!

In the circumstances, the announcement from Berlin of the signing of the German-Soviet pact of nonaggression threw the Japanese public on to the tatami. Like a sumo wrestler floored without warning by a fighter from his own stable, the Japanese looked around for someone to blame other than the actual culprit—and picked on the unfortunate Hiranuma. His Cabinet had no choice but to resign. An emergency administration took over for a few weeks of ineffective doodling, and was followed by a government presided over by the stubborn Minister of the Marine, Admiral Mitsumasa Yonai. Since he had wrecked the alliance with Hitler he was hardly the darling of the Army General Staff, and he became the target of their threats and vituperation when he showed signs of slanting the policy of his government toward a rapprochement with Britain. True, what he meant by "rapprochement" was that Britain, together with France and the United States, should accept Japan's position as supreme power in China and cease to help Chiang Kai-shek, in return for which Japan would promise to be friendly. But even this I'll-stop-picking-the-lock-if-you'll-just-open-the-safe attitude smacked of ap-

191

peasement to the Army General Staff. Yonai's Cabinet had come into office just after the outbreak of the war in Europe. By June, 1940, the German sweep across Western Europe had made Yonai's overtures seem even more bizarre, and he was flatly told by the Army General Staff to get out and make way for someone more amenable to the military and less amenable to the West. When he attempted to argue, the Army curtly called him to heel. They now wanted that alliance with Germany, and they wanted it while Hitler was still in the mood. While Yonai hesitated, his War Minister resigned, and, of course, automatically brought down the Cabinet.

Who was to take Yonai's place?

The Army wanted a willing tool who would do what he was told and secure for them the alliance they had set their heart on—as well as the money to beef up their forces and pour more men into China. In other words, they wanted a man who would not much mind leading the armed forces, or being pushed by them, down the road to war. On the other hand, the Emperor and the few men of good will who remained in positions of influence wanted a leader who would work for peace, who had liberal ideas, who believed in sanity in international dealings. Two such diametrically opposed needs could surely not be found in one man.

But of course they could. Emperor and Army both agreed on the man they wanted.

They sent for Prince Konoye.

Chapter Thirteen

The frail and fractious Baron Yuasa had grown too feeble for the job, and so on June 1, 1940, the Marquis Kido returned to the Imperial Palace as Lord Keeper of the Privy Seal. Six weeks later he was with his royal master at Hayama when a message reached him that the Yonai Cabinet had fallen, and he hurried into Tokyo. This time there was no question of the old genro, Prince Saionji, or the veteran statesman, Count Makino, having any real say in the choice. Saionji was ill at Okitsu and Makino was homebound at Izu, and, in any case, the time when the civilized words of the one or the liberal sentiments of the other would be heeded was now past. Instead a new advisory body had come into being to "guide" the Lord Keeper so that he, in his return, could advise the Emperor.

This was known as a council of the jushin, or senior statesmen, and on this occasion it consisted of six of the eight living former premiers—Hiranuma, Hayashi, Hirota, Konoye, Okada and Wakatsuki. (The immediate outgoing premier was not invited; the only other, General Abe, was in Nanking serving as ambassador to the Japanese-sponsored "Chinese government" of Wang Ching Wei.) The jushin knew without being told that the only man the Army would accept was Konoye, and Kido let it be known that the Emperor also would welcome his selection. He was unanimously asked to accept the mandate and, with his customary air of preoccupation, at first temporized, reaching back into Japan's past and quoting from the classics for reasons why he should refuse; and then casually accepted.

That afternoon he drove to Hayama to be received in audience by the Emperor and once more made urbane promises to pursue peace and keep a tight hold on the Army. Some weeks in the sun, many of them out at sea diving for specimens, had restored Hirohito to health again, and his questions to his new premier were vigorous. One of the dangers of the situation, he told Konoye, was the rivalry between the Army and the Navy. It made them overambitious and apt to think in terms of rash expeditions which might disturb the delicate balance of relations in the Pacific. Konoye promised to bear that in mind. That evening he told Kido he was going to the Peers' Club in Tokyo to discuss the formation of his new Cabinet with the outgoing ministers of Army and Marine in order to secure their joint cooperation. He felt that harmony between the two services might be restored if he picked Army and Navy ministers who were each liked by both the services, and he would not proceed with any further appointments until this was achieved.

He was as good as his word. He emerged from a succession of conferences with the announcement that he had chosen General Hideki Tojo as War Minister and Admiral Koshiro Oikawa as Minister of Marine. There was no doubt of the harmony existing between these two. Tojo, who had headed the military police in Manchuria and afterward become Inspector General of Aviation, believed that Britain would soon lose the war and that Japan should immediately exploit that fact. Admiral Oikawa advocated naval ventures to the south, where the Dutch East Indies was wide open with the overrunning of the Netherlands by Germany. Both of them believed that the immediate necessity for Japan was to conclude some sort of military treaty with Germany and do it urgently, before the Nazi Armies crossed the English Channel, overwhelmed Britain, and won the war. By that time Germany would have no need of Japan's support. As Sir Robert Craigie wrote: "How, they urged, could Japan expect Hitler to divide the spoils with them unless she had been actively associated in the spoliation?"[1]

With two such activists in his Cabinet, Konoye might have been expected to appoint a powerful opponent of their political thinking as his Foreign Minister, especially since he had professed to the Emperor his opposition to an alliance with Germany. Instead he chose for the post an ambitious and unscrupulous politician named Mr. Yosuke Matsuoka,

[1] Sir Robert Craigie, *Behind the Japanese Mask*, London: Hutchinson & Co., Ltd., 1945.

194

from whose lips came an unending torrent of professions of friendship for the United States and Britain, but in whose heart was a hatred of them both. Ironically enough, Matsuoka as a boy had been befriended by an elderly Scotswoman for whom he always asserted an undying affection. Unlike Tojo and Oikawa, he was a man of the world who could exude great charm and was extremely knowledgable about world affairs. To Sir Robert Craigie, "his chief outward characteristic was loquaciousness. I have never known anyone talk so much to say so little. Even at that most solemn of ceremonies, the funeral of a Japanese Imperial prince, I could hear Matsuoka whispering to his next-door neighbor throughout the proceedings." But Matsuoka was an opportunist. "Behind the smoke screen of garrulousness was an acute mind and a stubborn and determined will. . . . He started his career as Foreign Minister with two main illusions. Firstly that Great Britain was beaten; secondly that the United States could be intimidated into remaining neutral in the European War." [2]

It seemed to Matsuoka that the obvious way to exploit the situation was to get an alliance with Germany signed at once, and from Tojo and Oikawa—but with no more than a casual consultation with Konoye—he got permission to begin exploratory talks. Before doing so he evened up some old scores in the Foreign Office. There were a number of senior officials who had snubbed him in his early days as "an upstart" and "a nobody"—family background is as important in the Gaimusho as it is in the British Foreign Office—and there were others, notably some senior ambassadors, whose liberal sentiments he felt were out of keeping with the present situation. He sacked forty of them out of hand, and replaced them with his own nominees, most of them Army or Navy officers—Lieutenant General Oshima was reappointed to Berlin, Admiral Nomura was sent to Washington, and Lieutenant General Tatekawa to Moscow.

Early in September, 1940, a special emissary of Hitler, von Stahmer, arrived in Tokyo and a series of preliminary discussions for an alliance began at Matsuoka's private house. Neither Kido nor Konoye seemed to have been aware of what was going on. Kido writes:

"I and Prince Konoye were among the so-called disciples of Prince Saionji. Since I was appointed secretary to the Lord Keeper of the Privy Seal I made it a rule to call the aged prince at Okitsu once every month

[2] *Ibid.*

195

and listen to his instructive talks. The Prince was deeply concerned over the situation of Japan and repeatedly stressed the necessity, I vividly recall, of basing Japan's foreign policy on cooperation with Britain and America. I entirely agreed with him, as I approached all questions with my way of thinking, based on that. The question of alliance with Germany tormented me. I could not bring myself to approve of it. Especially I believed that the alliance would necessarily lead to a war between Japan and America. To this point of view, I drew the attention of Prince Konoye and Mr. Matsuoka, who, however, surprised me by arguing that the alliance was intended to prevent America from joining in the war, and further, that in case Japan was isolated in the Pacific without concluding the alliance with Germany, she might be attacked by America at any moment. Notwithstanding that explanation to the contrary, I could not help feeling deeply concerned as I thought the alliance might cause an antithesis [sic] with America and we would eventually have to oppose both Great Britain and the United States."

On September 16, 1940, Kido had an audience with the Emperor. "I was received in audience by His Majesty, who inquired mainly about concluding an alliance with Germany. His Majesty aired his views and I submitted my opinions to the throne. I told the Emperor on this occasion that this alliance, if concluded, would divide the world into two parts notwithstanding the opinion of the Prime Minister and Mr. Matsuoka to the contrary. I also told him the China incident was an irritant to the United States and should be concluded as soon as possible. With regard to the conclusion of the China Incident, I expressed my opinion to His Majesty that we would have eventually to oppose both England and the United States if we conclude a military alliance with Germany and Italy. Therefore we should make necessary adjustments in our relations with China as soon as possible."

Kido came away from his conferences with Hirohito convinced that the Emperor, too, shared the misgivings over a pact with Germany. He tried to put this point repeatedly to Matsuoka, but made no headway. The von Stahmer conversations blossomed into a pact. It was approved at a full-dress Imperial Conference at which Hirohito presided but said no word throughout. He was not expected to. He was there to hear what his advisers had decided, and not to give them guidance.

"Once the Government approved it," Kido wrote, "traditions scrupulously observed since the Meiji Emperor built modern Japan dictated that the Emperor approve the Government decision, since it had been submitted to the throne as national policy. Prior to that His Majesty could have expressed his views or cautioned the Cabinet to request the Cabinet to reconsider its proposed attitude thereon. In this case it may be imagined that His Majesty inwardly felt uneasy but eventually sanctioned the conclusion of the alliance with Germany."

Hirohito had no illusions about the alliance. He knew that this was the end of the road for Japan as a neutral in the European war. "His Majesty expressed his view also," wrote Kido, "that the conclusion of the alliance would necessitate an anticipation of an eventual war between Japan and America. He asked Prime Minister Konoye and Foreign Minister Matsuoka about this. In reply, however, both of them stated that the alliance was intended to avert war between Japan and America. If the alliance was not concluded, the danger of a Pacific War would be all the greater. On the strength of their contention, they petitioned the Emperor to sanction the alliance."

He did it, but he was not deceived.

It was a moment when Hirohito must have realized the helplessness of his position. The Imperial Conference which ratified the agreement for an alliance with Germany was held at the Imperial Palace, and all the delegates abased themselves before their Emperor before making their speeches. He sat on an ornamental throne before a gold screen and looked down at the politicians, the soldiers and the civil servants below him. They were so obsequious in their posture that they might have been suppliants gathered to petition his favor and fearful that, in rejecting them, he might also order their immediate execution. They sat at attention, their hands on their knees, and none of them dared to lean back. As each statesman or service chief rose to make his statement, he first bowed low and then addressed himself to the humble attention of the divine being on the throne.

One by one, they stated their opinion that the treaty of alliance with Germany be signed, and humbly begged the Emperor in his wisdom to accept it. It is a measure of the cynicism of the occasion that every delegate preceded his support of the pact with the preamble: "As His Majesty well knows," well knowing that His Majesty knew and believed exactly the opposite. But well knowing, also, that His Majesty could do nothing about it.

As Mr. Robert Butow has put it:

"Herein lay the great difference between the *actual* and the *theoretical* force of the throne. Such power as was imputed to the Emperor in the Meiji Constitution was to be exercised in accordance with the advice of his ministers, who were thus made responsible for affairs of state. It was recognized that the Emperor could not be all-knowing and that decisions of state must reflect the combined wisdom of those whose specialized training gave them collectively a competence which no individual could command. While theoretically possessing the right to do many things, the Emperor was actually allowed, for the good of the state and for the sake of the imperial institution, to do very little. He was permitted only a limited discretionary power—nothing approaching a right to veto.[3]

No right to veto. The myth of the divine monarch whose word was sacrosanct was revealed as a shabby pretense on occasions like these, and Hirohito was well aware of it. Historians of the period are apt to condone his silence at the Imperial Conference of September 19, 1940, at which the alliance with Germany was agreed upon, and to cite his silence at an even more important Imperial Conference a year later as the real occasion when guidance from him might have changed the course of nations.

If my information is correct, Hirohito does not agree. Looking back on the events which led up to the war in the Pacific, he sees the Imperial Conference of 1940 as his "moment of truth."[4] His personal conscience was involved in the policies which were being shaped by his ministers and by the Army, and he feels that he was false both to himself and to his people in having failed to make his position clear. He was practical enough to realize that there was a good chance of Britain losing the war— although he remained an optimist to the last, and felt that she would survive and eventually win.[5] He understood the arguments of those strategists who maintained that what Japan did not grab in East Asia before Germany won would be lost to Germany after her victory. But he

---

[3] Robert J. C. Butow, *Tojo and the Coming of War*, New Jersey: Princeton University Press, 1961.

[4] The phrase, as well as the information, comes from a former court official and close friend of the Emperor who does not wish to be identified.

[5] His belief in Britain's eventual victory was reinforced by a lecture given at the Imperial Palace by Mr. Mamoru Shigemitsu, former Japanese ambassador in London, who spoke movingly about the resolution of the British and the comportment of the royal family under bombing and the threat of invasion. So impressed was Hirohito that he made Shigemitsu repeat the lecture to the Empress, who was more sceptical of Britain's chances.

distrusted a Japanese-German alliance both from a practical and an idealistic point of view. He was much impressed by a statement from one of Japan's oldest statesmen, Viscount Ishii, who warned his people that no one except the Germans themselves ever benefited from an alliance with Germany; he reminded them of Bismarck, who said that international alliances demanded that there be one horseman and one donkey, and that Germany must always be the horseman. No good, he felt, would come of the alliance even in tangible things.

It was, however, the principle involved in the alliance rather than the prizes it promised which filled Hirohito with revulsion. The underhand nature of the transaction seemed to him to be demeaning to Japan. He told one of his chamberlains, Mr. Tsuneo Matsudaira, that he despised Italy for her "stab in the back" attack on France during the last stages of the 1940 campaign in Europe. Was Japan to imitate these contemptible tactics? Was she, in a phrase he used later over the Japanese occupation of Indochina, to act "like a thief at a fire"?

He believed that when Matsuoka sponsored and Konoye condoned the Tripartite Pact he should have intervened and pointed out to them the error of their ways, and emphasized that they were besmirching the honor of Japan. He blames himself that he did not do so, and believes that his silence led to the great disasters of policy in 1941.

"For the Emperor successfully to have intervened," writes Butow, "in such a way as to direct affairs along lines more in accord with his personal conscience would have required him to be a man of less retiring personality, with a very practical grasp of political affairs. Moreover, he would have needed the support of an enforcement machinery capable of coping with powerful dissidents, and the encouragement of advisers who believed a more active, personal participation by His Majesty to be necessary and desirable." [6]

Alas, once again in a time of crisis, the elements were lacking which might have galvanized Hirohito and goaded him into following his instincts. It so happened that one of those who had been exhorting him to make a stand was his younger brother, Prince Chichibu. There was also Prince Saionji, who, earlier in the year, had warned him through Harada that the time was approaching for him to exercise his influence "forthrightly and fearlessly"—unusual advice from one normally so concerned

[6] Butow, op. cit.

with the constitutional *amour-propre* of the throne. But at the time of the signing of the Pact, Chichibu was abed with the first stages of the disease which would eventually kill him, and Saionji was at death's door. (He died on November 24, 1940.) There was no one else powerful enough to infuse the Emperor with the courage to resist the forces taking over the nation. He sat in silence while the Pact was accepted. He even issued an Imperial Rescript commending it to the people when it was signed.

Yet he was only too well aware of how disastrous for Japan was the alliance he was asking his people to approve. It took some months for Matsuoka himself to realize the folly of the Tripartite Pact. He recanted on his sick bed in December, 1941, just after Pearl Harbor, saying: "The Tripartite Alliance was my worst mistake. I hoped to prevent the United States from entering the war. I wanted to adjust our relations with Soviet Russia through this alliance. I hoped peace would be maintained and Japan placed in a secure position. Instead we see face to face the present calamity which indirectly resulted from the Alliance."

He burst into tears and begged the Emperor to forgive him.[7]

It now seems evident that the Emperor felt no less guilty himself, right from the beginning.[8]

On November 10, 1940, Japan celebrated the 2,600th anniversary of the founding of the Empire. It was an occasion, the government decided, to make a demonstration to the people of the symbolic power of the throne, and a pavilion for 50,000 spectators was built in the plaza before the Imperial Palace. Grew reported:

"The first was the day of ceremonial greeting and the second the day of celebration. For several months squads of men and schoolgirls have been working in the big plaza opposite to the palace, leveling it off, setting up decorative poles, laying out an enormous number of flowers, and finally

[7] Yoshie Saito, *Azamukareta Rekishi* (The Distorted History), Tokyo: 1955.

[8] Ambassador Grew's version of the situation is described in his diary entry for October 22, 1940: "I was told today on excellent authority that both the Emperor and Prince Konoye were dead against the Tripartite Alliance but that it was brought to the Emperor's attention that he might not survive a refusal and he said to Konoye: 'Well, you and I will have to stand or fall together.' This came indirectly from a member of the Imperial family." Though it accurately represents Hirohito's feelings it seems to err about Konoye's attitude. He himself wrote later: "I do not agree . . . that the Alliance with Germany . . . was necessarily a dangerous policy for Japan . . . [It] was an appropriate, in fact, the only policy. . . ." Statement to IMTFE.

200

building a big pavilion and rows of seats in front of it for about 50,000 people. They were the only people, all specially invited, who could witness the ceremony, because no one was allowed on the roofs or in the windows of the big office buildings in Marunouchi, which would have afforded observation spots for many more thousands. No one may look down upon the Emperor, and I noticed how completely vacant those roofs and windows were."

The sacred fires of pine logs had been lit in the iron braziers around the courtyard. Prince Konoye was master of ceremonies. Byas reported: "He crossed the courtyard and slowly climbed the steep old steps, preceded by a priest who showed him to his place. The hall [a 'massive temple-like structure called the Shinkaden' in which the Emperor would make peace with his ancestors] was filled with the soft glow of paper lanterns. At the head of the hall facing the entrance a Shinto altar was dressed and ready. The Court musicians sat on the floor, voluminously robed in scarlet cloaks and pointed headdresses, and fingered their archaic instruments. . . . When the Chief Ritualist had finished the prayer, the Emperor appeared. He was dressed in robes of heavy white silk and he carried in his right hand a small baton called a shaku, symbol of the priestly office. He shuffled forward on the straw matting to a lacquered chair or throne and seated himself. The musicians began a piece in which shrill discords dominated a broken, irregular theme. The ladies took offerings of new rice and rice wine from a table and placed them on the altar. The Emperor advanced to the altar, offered the wine and rice to the gods, raising them high as the priest does in a Mass. He recited a prayer of thanksgiving and returned to his seat, and the Imperial Princes, the Prime Minister, and other worshippers moved up to the altar one by one and worshipped." [9]

On the second day, when the anniversary was celebrated rather than revered, Ambassador Grew got a chair to sit down on (he had stood throughout the previous day).

"A Japanese meal was served with saké, and everything, but we were expected to take it home in a furoshiki, or big silk napkin, and of course we turned it over to our servants to whom it is always a tremendous privilege to eat 'Imperial food.' There were also a ceremonial dance and a lot of chorus singing of patriotic songs and band music."

[9] Hugh Byas, *Government by Assassination*, New York, Alfred A. Knopf, Inc., 1942.

Prince Takamatsu, the Emperor's second youngest brother,[10] read a speech to the throne and led the banzais for the Emperor. Grew, as doyen, was called on to reply. Even in the midst of aching crisis, Grew never seemed to lose his sense of humor or his sense of balance.

"It was quite an ordeal," he wrote in his diary, "to walk sedately in front of all the guests in the pavilion and then in front of 50,000 people below in complete silence, then to face the Emperor, bow, get out spectacles and manuscript, read, bow, replace manuscript and spectacles, bow again, turn backwards and pace solemnly back to my place; but it went off all right, and since I made a point of reading slowly and of carefully enunciating every word, the amplifiers enabled everyone in the crowd to hear perfectly."

Hirohito had gone through the whole of the ceremonials with a blank, completely unforthcoming expression. But it was noticed that while Grew spoke—and he spoke to a text agreed by the State Department, calling for peace and mutual cooperation for the betterment of all nations—the Emperor not only nodded at each point he made, but nodded vigorously.

"Arsené-Henry, the French Ambassador, came to see me the next day," reported Grew, "on purpose to tell me that he had watched the Emperor's face and was convinced that his nods of approval were given to impress the Government and higher officials of the Empire with his own desire for peace. Arsené-Henry was so impressed with this that he cabled the Government about it as an important political indication. Even the official Court release to the press announced that 'His Majesty seemed greatly pleased' with the speech."

But if it made its impression upon the Emperor, it did nothing to deflect the Army and the Navy from their plans for aggression. Konoye was mainly preoccupied with his plan to abolish the political parties in Japan once and for all and reconstitute them as a combined body under State control, to be called the Imperial Rule Assistance Association. He was convinced that the transformation of Japan into a one-party state would give him, as premier, the same sort of control over the nation as Hitler had through the National Socialist Party. He speedily discovered that it wouldn't work: the Army let him go ahead because they could deal better with a nation marshalled and compartmentalized. Far from being the fascist State which Konoye considered was necessary to meet the demands

[10] "Most of the Imperial princes and princesses [excepting Chichibu, who has been seriously ill with pneumonia] . . . were present," reported Grew.

of the times, the I.R.A.A. turned out to be a defense state which the armed forces could manipulate.

In the meantime, like a madcap magician fecklessly pulling ribbons out of his hair, rabbits out of his hat, and eggs out of his mouth, Matsuoka pattered on with a dialogue calculated to deceive everyone into thinking that he was in command of the situation, and that he alone could advise the Japanese on what to do next. Having ratified the Tripartite Pact with Hitler and Mussolini, he arrived in Moscow and talked Stalin into signing a neutrality pact whereby Russia and Japan agreed not to attack each other over a period lasting until 1946. Matsuoka bounced back to Tokyo to savor the triumph of his achievement—for had he not effectively secured safety for Japan's northern frontier in Asia while she pursued her ambitions to the South? A few weeks later, however, he was busy trying to stuff this particular rabbit back into the hat, for Germany had declared war on Russia and Matsuoka wanted Japan to join in at once.

"As might be expected," wrote Kido, "Foreign Minister Matsuoka began to advocate over Prince Konoye's head a military expedition to Siberia. But his contention met with disapproval not only from the Cabinet Ministers including Konoye but also the leaders of the Army and Navy. The liaison committee between the Government and the High Command met in session frequently, as a result of which it was decided to seek a settlement of the China affair by bringing pressure to bear upon China from the south, instead of pursuing the Foreign Minister's policy."

Konoye was now determined to rid himself of Matsuoka. Effete the Prince might be, but he was also jealous of his privileges. He considered he had lost considerable prestige when the Foreign Minister bypassed him to talk to the Emperor about the expedition to Siberia. "He does not know his own mind," Konoye told Hirohito, and discussed with the Emperor what tactics to be used to dispense with him. But Matsuoka provided the means for his own downfall. A week or two previously, he had called in Ambassador Grew for a discussion and asked him, in a hectoring tone, why the United States didn't do the "manly, decent and reasonable" thing and declare war openly on Germany, "since our [America's] attitude towards Germany is provocative." Grew went on to report Matsuoka as saying: "He adds that Hitler has been very patient and generous in not declaring war on the United States, but that Hitler's patience and restraint cannot be expected to endure indefinitely."

Grew reported the substance of this "bellicose" speech to the State Department and received in return an oral statement from Secretary of State Cordell Hull which implied, in diplomatic language, that the United States Government in future would find it difficult to deal with Matsuoka since they could not trust him. Matsuoka boiled over with fury. He called Hull's message a national humiliation, insulting to Japan as well as to himself. At a liaison conference held on July 10, 1941, he poured out a diatribe of hate against the United States and attacked those of his colleagues who wished to go on negotiating with her. He insisted that Hull's oral statement be returned to Washington at once and negotiations with the American Government broken off.

It was the opportunity for which Konoye had been waiting. He had already discussed tactics with Kido and the Emperor. He knew that on such an issue he could not very well sack Matsuoka, who would immediately go before the people as a martyr. But he could offer the resignation of himself and his Cabinet. Which is what he did. After which the Emperor simply sent for Konoye once more and asked him to head a new administration. He naturally accepted the mandate and picked his new roster of ministers. There was little change from the former Cabinet—except, of course, that Matsuoka was no longer Foreign Minister. His place had been taken by Admiral Teijiro Toyoda.

But for the apostles of peace, both inside and outside Japan, there was not much comfort to be gained from Matsuoka's departure. The Emperor appears to have expected a policy of "earnest negotiation for peace" to develop from the new Cabinet; but he cannot have been wholly deceived. True, he had presided at a second Imperial Conference on July 2, 1941, at which it had been decided that "for the sake of her self-sufficiency and self-defense, Japan shall continue necessary diplomatic negotiations with nations concerned in the southern regions, and shall promote other necessary measures." In other words, Japan would try to extract oil from the Dutch East Indies and bases from French Indo-China without resort to force. But the Conference decision added:

"In order to achieve these purposes, Japan shall not decline war with Britain and the United States."

And to make quite clear what contingencies were envisaged for the future, the Conference decided:

"In accordance with the established policy, every effort, diplomatic and otherwise, shall be made to restrain the United States from entering the war. Should the United States nevertheless do so, Japan shall act in accordance with the Tripartite Pact; but the timing and method of resort to arms shall be independently decided." In the meantime, "the nation shall promptly be shifted to a complete and firm war footing. Special efforts shall be made to strengthen the national defense. Concrete plans shall be separately decided."

The concrete plans had, in fact, been decided as far back as January, 1941, when Admiral Yammamoto, the Commander in Chief of the Imperial Japanese Navy, had gone into conference with his naval strategists to plan the attack on Pearl Harbor.[11] This the Emperor did not know. But he did know that war was now a prospect which his government and his armed forces were beginning to accept, the first with helpless reluctance, the second with ever-mounting eagerness.

On July 24, 1941, Japan (with German help) forced the Vichy Government in France to grovel and agree to Japanese occupation of French Indochina, from whose bases both China and Malaya would be within range of Japanese attack. The United States Government had had good prior warning of the Japanese intentions for American cipher experts had broken the Japanese code, thus enabling them to "read" code messages from Tokyo to Admiral Nomura, the Japanese Ambassador in Washington; and they also had an active agent in the Vichy government itself, none other than Admiral Darlan, who let them know what was afoot.

President Roosevelt made strenuous efforts to dissuade the Japanese Government from proceeding with its plans for Indochina. There were already those in the United States (particularly the isolationists) who were hinting that Roosevelt wanted nothing better than to inveigle Japan into war as the only way of involving the United States in the conflict with Germany. His activities in the days preceding the Indochinese occupation give no indication of this. He appears to have done his utmost to persuade Nomura to call off the Japanese dogs yapping around the heels of the cowed and beaten French. He offered the neutralization of Indochina itself from Chinese, British, American or Gaullist occupation. It was a considerable concession on his part, for it carried with it implications of American sympathy for Japan in her present dilemmas.

Not for the first time, however, a high Japanese official failed to translate a plain American offer into plain Japanese. By the time Nomura had

[11] With an uncanny sense of timing, as it turned out, Ambassador Grew sent a cable to the State Department on January 27, 1941, reporting "there is a lot of talk around town of the effect that the Japanese, in case of a break with the United States, are planning to go all out in a surprise attack on Pearl Harbor." The report was received with scepticism in the Navy Department.

rendered the President's proposal into his own language, it no longer made any sense and neither Toyoda nor Konoye could make head or tail of it. Not until July 27th, when Grew saw the Japanese Foreign Minister in Tokyo and repeated the President's offer did its meaning become clear. But by then it was too late. The Japanese government had already officially announced its decision to occupy Indochina—and it would have meant a loss of face to abandon its plans. The deed was done. It was to have momentous consequences.

The moment he heard of Japan's decision, President Roosevelt, by executive order, froze all Japanese assets and funds in the United States. The British and the government of the Dutch East Indies did the same. The armed forces in the Philippines were reorganized and placed under the control of the United States, with General Douglas MacArthur named as Commander in Chief, Far East. In China a semiofficial Military Advisory Group was established by the United States and a volunteer air regiment formed under the command of General Claire Chennault. On August first the President amplified the embargo by banning all goods except cotton and food, which meant that Japan would get no more scrap iron, and, even more important, no more oil.

In addition, Cordell Hull, Secretary of State, announced that he saw no reason for any further discussions or negotiations between the United States and Japan for the resolution of their difficulties.

The result was a surge of anti-American agitation in Japan and the urgent dispatch of a squad of special policemen to protect the United States Embassy in Tokyo. But it also brought another visitor to the Embassy, none other than the Foreign Minister Admiral Toyoda, who seemed particularly wounded by the abrogation of conversations between Japan and America.

"The Minister gave obvious indications," wrote Grew in his diary, "of being profoundly concerned at the rupture of the Washington conversations. As I have ground for believing that the Emperor had received him just before our interview, it seems to me likely that he was reflecting the concern of the Emperor."

He was indeed. News of the United States decision to impose an embargo on Japan reached Hirohito at a moment when he least wished to be disturbed by affairs of state, for he was in the midst of a family occasion. His favorite child had always been his eldest daughter, Terunomiya, though he had, according to court custom, seen little enough of her. Like all the royal children, she had been taken away from the royal

206

household shortly after birth.[12] "Princess Sunshine" proved to be an ebullient child who grew up with positive ideas and none of the humility which she was expected to display as a princess of the Crown. There were complaints from her maids and governesses that she was headstrong and arrogant, contemptuous of court etiquette, and far too "forward." It was decided that she should be pinned into her place in the royal pattern without delay, and she was betrothed to a Choshu prince at the age of ten. In the fraught summer of 1941, when she was fifteen, the engagement was officially announced. One suspects that Hirohito, who had allowed himself all his life to be so hamstrung by court usage, attended the engagement ceremonies hoping that his eldest daughter would not allow herself to be tied down as he had been. It was a moment when he had far rather been a father than an Emperor.

But that was not to be. The immediate result of Roosevelt's embargo on shipments to Japan was an exacerbation of relations between the two countries. Hirohito worried about it. He talked about it on several occasions with Kido, and on July 31, 1941, the latter wrote:

"Admiral Nagano, Chief of Staff to the Navy, was received in audience by the Emperor, and reported to His Majesty on the contingency of war between Japan and America. It became a matter of profound solicitude to the Emperor. I submitted my views to the throne refusing to share Admiral Nagano's simple statement at this date, stressing the necessity of pushing the negotiations tenaciously with America."

Nagano had expressed doubts to Hirohito of Japan's ability to win a war with the United States should it come. Like Admiral Yammamoto, he believed that chaos could be created and heavy damage inflicted on the Americans in the first phases of a conflict, but:

"If I am told to fight regardless of consequences, I shall run wild considerably for the first six months or a year, but I have utterly no confidence for the second and third years. The Tripartite Pact has been concluded and we cannot help it. Now that the situation has come to this pass, I hope you will work for avoidance of an American-Japanese War." [13]

Kido mentions that Nagano, in the course of his audience, tried to persuade the Emperor to exert all his efforts to avert war with the United States. "Supposing the adjustment of relations between Japan and Amer-

---

[12] According to a source close to the royal family who does not wish to be identified, Empress Nagako was always particularly resentful that she was not allowed to suckle her eldest son, the Crown Prince.

[13] Yammamoto is quoted as having said this to Konoye in Konoye's memoirs.

ica were impossible," Kido reports Nagano as saying, "we were cut off from supplies of oil and our oil stored up would run out in two years. In case war with the U.S. breaks out the supply of oil would be sufficient for only one and a half years. Under these circumstances there would be *no other alternative but to take the initiative.*" [14]

According to the reports submitted to the Emperor, the Japanese calculated that they would win a blitz campaign. But when Hirohito asked Nagano whether it was possible to win a sweeping victory as in the Russo-Japanese War, "he replied to the Emperor that it was doubtful whether we would even win, to say nothing as to a great victory as in the Russo-Japanese War. I was filled with trepidation by the Imperial anxiety about the danger of having to wage a desperate war."

On August 2, 1941, Konoye came to see Kido and seems to have heard about the Emperor's perturbation. He reported to the Lord Keeper that Navy opinion seemed to have hardened about the possibilities of war. Hitherto they had hesitated. Now they seemed to be facing up to the practicalities of an actual confrontation, and that there were elements who were disposed to welcome it. Kido says he told Konoye:

"It is an awfully troublesome question. It should not be hastily decided to go to war with America now. First of all, Japan's actual power is not fully studied, is it? So it is extremely dangerous. It will be necessary to have an exhaustive discussion of fundamental national policies with the ministers of the fighting services and probe the matter to the bottom without a moment's delay. Should you fail to come to an agreement of views with them after exhausting all possible means, it might be inevitable that you should quit."

Konoye looked both relieved and glum. He was eager to resign and go back to his couch and his books. But was this the opinion of the Emperor? When he gathered that it was, he said:

"It would be embarrassing if I quit. If you think that way I feel quite reassured. I will think it over carefully."

But what could be done? As Kido said, "the Army stood pat on a vigorous policy toward America on a basis of its continental policy, while on the other hand a section of the Navy advocated the necessity of opening war with America to forestall her for fear of a steady drain on Japan's oil supplies."

[14] My italics—L.M.

In fact, 28,000 gallons a day of Japan's precious oil reserves were draining away, and now there were no replenishments in view, because of America's embargo. It was not only the armed forces who felt the urgent need of a decision now, though of a different kind. The Emperor urged one on Kido and Kido urged one on Konoye. On August 6 and 7, 1941, at Hirohito's behest, he had two sessions with the Japanese premier during which he concentrated on trying to convince Konoye of the folly of going to war with America.

Kido wrote in his diary: "I told Prince Konoye that it was high time for the Government to put forward a constructive and concrete view and to learn clearly whether or not it was acceptable to the Army, with a view to checking the Army from rushing to war, and getting it to keep pace with the policy adopted by the Government. I pointed out to him the hopelessness of the situation from the point of view of oil alone. My sole thought in talking to him was to advance such positive arguments that he would be able to convince the military. I intentionally omitted what was related to humanity and peace, as these are fundamental matters. As my diary also shows, I concluded by advocating to him that we should do everything in our power to restore friendly relations between the U.S.A. and Japan. Although we were being pressed economically, I felt and told him that we should resolve to toil through ten years of harsh struggles. I also pointed out that we needed materials and that our hopes lay in the southern regions." [15]

To advocate a ten-year wait in Japan's ambitions while the nation built up its resources, was a policy not likely to appeal to the activists in the armed forces, or even to the members of Konoye's Cabinet. It was only because they came from Kido, who was the mouthpiece of the Emperor, that they got a hearing at all. But that was as far as they got.

"Prince Konoye listened to my views with evident interest," wrote Kido in his diary, "and I expected him to take a step in the direction counselled by me. Judging by the result, however, he made no development in that direction."

The Prince had a more melodramatic scheme for solving the situation. He would go to America. He would talk personally with President Roosevelt. He would bring back an agreement which would restore harmony between Japan and the United States and bring peace to the Pacific. He

[15] Marquis Kido's affidavit to the IMTFE.

had been toying with the idea for some time, feeling that such an encounter would herald a new phase in Japanese-U.S. relations. To some extent he regarded the proposed meeting as a form of penitence for past sins, and that was how Ambassador Grew regarded it.

"Prince Konoye bore the heavy responsibility for having brought the country to its present pass," he wrote, "but since Matsuoka was made the scapegoat, the Premier stayed on and was evidently far from reluctant to support and abet the new orientation of policy. Japan was rapidly drifting toward war with the United States and Great Britain, and we know that the Emperor had long ago told his ministers that whatever policy they pursued, they must on no account get Japan into war with either of those two countries. I think there can be no doubt that the Emperor was never happy about the Tripartite Pact and was persuaded to approve it only in the light of misrepresentations by Matsuoka that Japan was about to be strangled economically by the democracies and that Germany's victory over Great Britain was certain." [16]

Konoye's proposal to visit the President was made to Grew by Foreign Minister Toyoda on August 18, 1941, and he was impressed with it.

"For a Prime Minister of Japan thus to shatter all precedent and tradition," Grew wrote in his diary, "in this land of subservience to precedent and tradition, and to wish to come hat in hand, so to speak, to meet the President of the United States on American soil, is a gauge of the determination of the Government to undo the vast harm already accomplished in alienating our powerful and progressively angry country. . . . Prince Konoye's warship is ready waiting to take him to Honolulu or Alaska or any other place designated by the President, and his staff of the highest military, naval and civil officers is chosen and rarin' to go."

Toyoda told Grew that he was anxious that Konoye's proposal should not leak out, particularly to the Germans or the Italians, who would be very angry, and "he hoped that in my report to Washington no risk would be incurred of my telegram being read by others. I said that the telegram would be sent in a code which I hoped and believed was unbreakable." [17]

[16] Grew's diary, August 18, 1941.
[17] Grew did not tell Toyoda that he had been warned by none other than Konoye himself, a few months previously, that one of the American codes had been cracked by the Japanese military. The Embassy continued to use it, but only for innocuous messages or ones calculated deliberately to deceive. Nor, of course, did Grew reveal that the Americans had cracked Japan's top priority code.

As it turned out, the Japanese Ambassador, Nomura, inadvertently let the tiger out of the cage by mentioning to reporters in Washington as he emerged from the White House that he had been delivering a message from the Prime Minister to the President. As expected, the Axis ambassadors were furious; the Japanese envoy to Germany, the egregious Oshima, cabled that Hitler would be "pained and angry" when he heard about it; and the Japanese press, now completely subservient to the more militant factions in the Army, accused Konoye and Kido (whom they blamed for inciting him) of truckling to the British and the Americans.

Both of them began receiving threats of assassination. Kido wrote:

"Ever since August, 1935, when Major General Nagata was assassinated by Lieutenant Colonel Aisawa, the Metropolitan Police has continually protected me and my family from the militarists and rightists, by assigning five policemen for this purpose. One policeman constantly protected me while the others protected my home in shifts of two at a time. In August, 1941, after an attempt was made to assassinate Baron Hiranuma, the Metropolitan Police increased my guards from five to ten, doubling the number at each shift."

But if Grew was impressed with Konoye's proposal for a meeting, and if the Axis and the militarists were infuriated with it, Washington was unimpressed. From the start Secretary of State Cordell Hull had never believed in negotiating with Japan and regarded the search for new agreements as so much waste of time.

"I estimated right at the outset that there was not one chance of success in twenty or one in fifty or one in a hundred. Japan's past and present records, her unconcealed ambitions, the opportunity for aggrandizement lying before her while embroiled Europe demanded a large part of our attention, and the basic divergence between our outlooks on international relations, were all against the possibility of such an accord. The President and I agreed that the existing treaties relating to the Far East were sufficient, provided the signatories, meaning especially Japan, lived up to them. There was no real need for new agreements—but if new agreements would contribute to peace in the Pacific, we believed we should not throw the chance away, however microscopic it was." [18]

Hull persuaded the President that a meeting would be fraught with dangerous consequences if the two statesmen met without first having

[18] Cordell Hull, *The Memoirs of Cordell Hull*, Vol. 2. New York: The Macmillan Company, 1948.

ratified "essential points already agreed to in principle." He then summoned Nomura and suggested that before the President agreed to meet Konoye, Japan should indicate that she was willing to withdraw from the Tripartite Pact, signify her intention of abandoning the retention of her troops in North China and Inner Mongolia, and clarify the application (to which the Japanese had referred in a note to the U.S.) of the principle of nondiscrimination in international commercial relations.

There is no doubt that if Hull was stubbornly opposed, the President was also disinclined toward a meeting with Konoye. The fact that the United States had cracked the Japanese code was, at this time, both a boon and a bane. The United States Government knew a great deal of what the Foreign Office in Tokyo was thinking and of how it was instructing its representatives to act; but it was unaware of the seething conflict behind the scenes. It knew both too much and too little. For instance, it naturally presumed that all of the military were against any moves toward peace. In fact, General Tojo, the Minister of War, had given his backing to Konoye's proposal—but imposed a time limit. To do Konoye justice, he did try to ensure that if his confrontation with Roosevelt did take place, he would bring with him Army and Navy officers of sufficient caliber and influence to make sure that any decisions which were made would be carried out at home.

Hull's opinion was that no matter who came, the result would be the same. Konoye would make promises, and the Army would repudiate them. One feels from studying Hull's thoughts during this period that he had, in any case, come to the conclusion that Japan as a belligerent was rather less of a headache to the United States than Japan as an Axis-inclined neutral. Better a positive enemy than a doubtful friend. It was time to force her into a corner, to bully her into making up her mind. Once the decision had been taken, the embargoes imposed, the conflicts made clear, it was better to force the enemy into the open and begin the operation. In Hull's mind—and one suspects in Roosevelt's, too—this was a time when (to reverse Churchill's phrase) war, war, war was better than jaw, jaw, jaw.

Konoye waited for the reply to his offer to meet the President. It never came.

"The Emperor was very sad," Matsudaira reported.

Chapter Fourteen

The Emperor had learned a lesson from the Imperial Conference which ratified the Tripartite Pact. He had made his antagonism to the pact clear beforehand but had kept silent during the discussion, hoping that someone would support and argue out his convictions; but no one had. Obviously, silence did not pay. In the situations which were now confronting the state, the constitutional monarch which he had been trained since childhood to be would become a mere cipher unless *someone* made it clear at meetings with his ministers and military advisers exactly what he believed and how he felt. He was well aware of the fact that under the Japanese Constitution he could have demanded that his opinion be acted on rather than listened to; for was he not the supposedly all-powerful head of state, divinely appointed, whose person was sacrosanct and whose ideas infallible?

He knew that he had neither the tradition nor the personality to extract from his advisers this kind of dictatorial control. The time was past when he could exert overt influence. He was not trained for it and he was not backstopped by supporters sufficiently powerful enough to range themselves behind him even if he tried.

But he could at least make his opinion known this time, and on record rather than in the antechambers of the palace.

On September 3, 1941, the Liaison Committee of the Government and the armed forces met to discuss the situation, and drew up a draft plan which would be discussed at a new Imperial Conference to be held in the Imperial Palace on September 6, 1941. The day before, September 5th,

213

Konoye went to the Imperial Palace to discuss the draft with Hirohito.

Kido writes: "At four-thirty P.M., when Prince Konoye proceeded to the palace to submit the agenda of the Imperial Conference, he came to my room. The draft agenda consisted of the following three points:

"1. War preparations be made against America;

"2. In parallel, the negotiations with America be pushed very hard; and

"3. In case no prospect of an amicable conclusion of the negotiations with America came in sight by the tenth of October, Japan make up her mind to wage war with America and Britain.

"Up to this very moment, Prince Konoye had made no reference to the contingency which was thus abruptly advanced to me. I was astonished at its nature, which was grave indeed. I criticised him for submitting such a plan to the Emperor, particularly so suddenly. It would embarrass His Majesty who would have no time to think over it. I further told the Prince: 'This shows that the time limit is fixed for the first ten days of October. It is very dangerous to fix a time limit. Is it not possible to modify this point, if nothing else? Do you see your way to abandoning the plan altogether, since I feel it may lead to war?' In reply Prince Konoye said that the plan had already been agreed to by the Liaison Conference between the Government and the High Command. It was difficult to modify or give up the plan, adding that there would be no alternative left to him but to devote his all to bringing the negotiations to an amicable conclusion, now that things had come to such a pass."

Kido glumly watched Konoye proceed down the long corridors of the Administration Building to the Throne Room, where Hirohito was awaiting him. He had no doubt that the Emperor's reaction to the news that Konoye brought would be just as painful as his own.

Hirohito was in what for him was a belligerent mood. He listened to Konoye's recital with growing (and, for once, visible) concern, and immediately the Prime Minister was finished began bombarding him with what Kido called "strategical" questions, all of them designed to demonstrate the folly of going to war. Kido writes:

"September 5. The Premier says that as the Emperor asked many questions as to our policy toward the U.S.A. from the point of view of war strategy, he had advised the Emperor to summon the Chief of the Army General Staff and Chief of Naval General Staff. . . . At six P.M. they [Marshal Sugiyama, Admiral Nagano and the Premier] were granted an audience by the Emperor to answer the Imperial questions."

Kido was not present at the subsequent exchanges, but he was visited by Konoye afterward and told what had taken place.[1]

"This time Prince Konoye told me His Majesty put various questions to them, including that put to Marshall Sugiyama, Chief of Staff of the Army, as to when the projected Southern [that is, against Malaya and N.E.I.] campaign could be terminated once started. The Chief of Staff of the Army replied that it would be terminated in a short period of time. (Konoye, in his memoirs, mentions a definite period—three months.) Whereupon His Majesty reprimanded Marshal Sugiyama, reminding him that he had said a similar thing at the outbreak of the China affair, which was not yet settled. The Marshal pleaded that there was a difference between the two, China being a continent while the southern area consisted mostly of islands."

The Emperor was far from being impressed with this reply. It was all very well for Sugiyama to claim that the war which the armed forces proposed to make in the Southern area would be "mostly of islands." He said angrily:

"If you call the Chinese hinterland vast, would you not describe the Pacific as even more immense? With what confidence can you say 'three months'?"

At this point Sugiyama fell silent. The Emperor's wrath overawed him. But Admiral Nagano quickly came to his rescue, pointing out that the High Command was speaking from "a broad point of view." Nagano added:

"Something must be done quickly. If things go on as they are, we shall steadily lose the game. The situation between Japan and the United States is like a patient with an illness which might require an operation. Avoiding one could mean that the patient wastes away. But there is hope of recovery if a drastic act of surgery is undergone. That is war."

But, asked the Emperor, what about negotiations? He noted that in the draft agenda, the contingency of war was put first and diplomatic conversations second. Was this the priority which the government—and the armed forces—had in mind? No. They hastened to assure him that the draft just happened to have come out that way, but that the peaceful processes of diplomacy would still be pursued.

---

[1] The Lord Keeper, though not always present at Imperial audiences, almost invariably knew what had taken place at them—except in the case of service ministers, who were not as assiduous in keeping him posted. But he had other ways of finding out about their conversations, often from the Emperor himself.

But after the audience was over, the Emperor had no doubt in his mind as to the nature of the future Japan was planning for herself. Negotiations would go on and attempts would be persisted in to try to persuade America to accept Japan's policy—in China, in Indochina, and in the Pacific generally. But if they failed, Japan would make war even though neither Army Chief nor Navy Chief could hold out any hope that it would be a war that Japan could win. He recognized in the words of his military chiefs a fact of Japanese life which at least one Occidental was beginning to accept.

"While in Japan," wrote Grew, "there are groups who are entirely cognizant of the perilous possibilites inherent in the present positions and who are ready to make far-reaching efforts in an endeavor to avoid an armed clash with the United States, the possibility that the constructive statesmen of Japan will be able to counteract the increasing psychology of desperation is at present diminishing daily. Traditionally in this country a national psychology of desperation develops into a determination to risk all."

But this time Hirohito could at least try to bid the waves retreat. In the fourteen hours between the submission of the draft agenda and the convocation of the Imperial Conference he pondered and consulted as to what he should do.

At forty minutes past nine on the morning of September 6, 1941, Marquis Kido was summoned into the royal presence, and Hirohito told him what he had decided to do. This time he would speak. This time he would make it clear, to both his ministers and his service chiefs, that he would not sanction war so long as prospects for peace remained. When the Imperial Conference began, twenty minutes hence, he would adopt such tactics, he told Kido, that the Chiefs of the General Staff would be forced to push their war plans to one side and concentrate on diplomacy. He had a list of questions ready for them.

Kido listened to his royal master eagerly rehearsing his remarks, and then, with dull efficiency and total lack of imagination, burst them as if they were pretty pink bubbles. He had already anticipated His Majesty's wishes, he told him; he had arranged with the President of the Privy Council, Mr. Yoshimichi Hara, to ask questions along the lines of His Majesty's thinking, and thus elicit the answers without involving His Majesty directly in the discussion. When Hirohito made it clear that he wished to take part, that he felt it his duty to make his position clear, the Lord Keeper shook his head firmly. It would never do. Obviously he felt that, even in an emergency, an Emperor should be above such things. But, almost as if to mollify him and assuage his disappointment, he suggested that the Emperor "should wait until the end and then point out the importance of the Conference's decision, on which Japan's future prosperity will hinge and order the High Command to extend a full measure of co-operation in bringing diplomatic negotiation to an amicable conclusion."

The attendants came to call the Emperor to the meeting and Kido, who did not attend such occasions, watched him follow the flunkeys into Room No. 1 of the east wing of the palace, where the Cabinet, the Chiefs of Staff, the President of the Privy Council, the President of the Cabinet Planning Board and their aides were waiting. He had no fear that Hirohito would do anything other than follow his advice; the habits of nearly forty years were too ingrained for him to do anything other than what he had been told. But the Emperor nonetheless had a surprise for everyone, including Kido.

After the customary obeisances before their Emperor, the delegates sat at attention on their hard chairs and listened to the decisions that would lead them into war. Admiral Nagano spoke first and he was followed by the Army Chief of Staff Sugiyama. Then a retired General, Teiichi Suzuki, climbed to his feet and laboriously expatiated on the practical problems which would be involved in the event of war. It seems evident, in the light of what happened shortly afterward, that these speeches and all the others which followed, calmly accepting the inevitability of war, put Hirohito's mind in a turmoil. It was all so casual.

"In order to ensure her self-sufficiency and self-defense," read Suzuki, "Japan shall complete her preparations for war by the end of October, with the determination not to decline war with the United States, Britain and the Netherlands. Japan shall, in parallel with the above, endeavour to exhaust diplomatic measures to attain her demands vis-à-vis the United States and Britain."

He then listed the minimum demands which would need to be extracted from the two nations in order to ensure a guarantee of peace. The United States and Britain must neither interfere in China nor disturb Japan's disposition of this vexatious affair. The Burma Road must be closed by Britain and no more supplies for Chiang Kai-shek allowed to pass through. The United States must not take "such action in the Far East as to prejudice Japan's national defense." In other words, she must recognize Japan's "special position" in Indochina, refrain from establish-

217

ing any bases in Thailand, the Netherlands East Indies and the Soviet Far East, and maintain a status quo over the strength of her military forces in the area." At the same time, Suzuki stressed, the United States must end the oil embargo, and "restore trade relations with Japan and make available . . . materials indispensable to her existence."

In return Japan would agree to make no advances in Indochina except against China; would withdraw her troops from Indochina on conclusion of a Far East peace; and would be prepared to guarantee the independence of the Philippines. Precious little, in fact.

Suzuki went on to say that since everyone still believed in the approaching victory of Germany in the war against Britain, there would be no change in Japan's adherence to the Tripartite Pact, and added that there "is no intention on our side to resort to military action [against Russia] so long as the U.S.S.R. is faithful to the Neutrality Pact and refrains from taking actions such as menacing Japan and Manchukuo, in conflict with the spirit of the Pact."

The conference was asked to agree that "should there be no prospect, by early October, of attainment of our demands through the above negotiations, war against the United States (and Britain and the Netherlands) shall be forthwith determined upon."

It was clear enough to Hirohito that the mind of the delegates was made up; they had taken the idea of war in their stride; and talk of negotiation sounded no more than a rigmarole learned off by heart. True, the President of the Privy Council, Mr. Hara, bobbed to his feet immediately Suzuki had finished, bowed low to his Emperor, and then began to ask questions along the lines Kido had laid out for him. What steps were being taken to keep the diplomatic talks with the United States going? What new proposals had Japan discussed to meet the objections of the Americans? Did the High Command not agree that it was better to negotiate than fight?

To Hirohito's anger—and it is a measure of his feelings that he was angry at all, a rare emotion for him—the man who rose to answer the question was the Minister of Marine, Admiral Oikawa, whose opinions the Emperor knew only too well. He was a front man for the Navy and had no independent ideas of his own, merely mouthing what he believed to be the play-safe, well-tried formulae of his service. He repeated the well-worn phrases calculated to appease Mr. Hara—who parroted the questions and seemed not particularly interested in the replies—and re-marked that it went without saying, as everyone knew, that Japan was reasonable and realized the appalling hazards and hardships of war, and would much prefer to talk—but only if, of course . . .

The delegates relaxed, mentally if not physically, letting their minds sag even if their fingers still remained, out of deference to the Emperor, rigid along the seams of their trousers. It seemed to be all over. The decision had been taken. A little more of the futile talk—and then war for the glory, if not the aggrandizement, of Japan.

It was at this moment that Hirohito rose. No one had warned the conference that he would speak, except to say a few words to close the meeting. Could this be it? Was he about to give a benison to his policy-makers and wish them well in their approaching ordeals by fire?

They soon discovered that he had something altogether different on his mind. He had gone "very flushed in the face, which was unusual for His Majesty, and he had to rub the balls of his thumbs over his glasses, which seemed to have misted over in the heat which had started from his forehead." In the heavy hush which had fallen on the room "most of the members present suddenly seemed to feel a need to look down at their boots, a mark of respect which seemed to be more a mark of their shame by the end." [2]

The Emperor looked down from his seat before the golden screen to the place where Admiral Nagano was sitting, and then to Marshal Sugiyama. He said he had been most interested to hear the replies of the Minister of Marine to the inquiries of Mr. Hara, but was this enough? Should he not have heard the explanations of the chiefs of his armed forces on this vital question of which should have priority—war or diplomacy? Did they not have an opinion? If so, why had they not stated it?

He paused, and then added: [3] *As for myself, I have no doubt of the answer.* He put his hand in the pocket of his formal suit and brought forth a piece of paper. *I would like to read you a poem which was written by my grandfather, the great Emperor Meiji,* he said. And, in his high, abrasive, lapsed-chorister voice, he read:

[2] From a former court official who does not wish to be identified.

[3] Only a paraphrase can be given. No complete transcript of such meetings was ever made.

Yomo no umi
　　Mina harakara to
Omou yo ni
　　Nado namikaze no
Tachisawagaruramu [4]

(The seas surround all quarters of the globe
　　And my heart cries out to the nations of the world.
Why then do the winds and waves of strife
　　Disrupt the peace between us?)

This is a poem, he said, to a room whose stillness was now almost clamant with pained and embarrassed silence, *which has always been one of my favorites, for it expresses what is in my heart and was in my grandfather's when he wrote it—his great love of peace.*

He sat down. The room bowed to him and then sat to attention once again. There was no doubt in any of their minds what the Emperor was asking of them.

Eventually, after an agonizing pause, Admiral Nagano rose to explain the reason for his silence and that of his colleague, Marshal Sugiyama. In response to Mr. Hara's questions, Minister of Marine Oikawa had spoken for both of them. But of course, and he hastened to say it with all the force at his command, the High Command endorsed everything Oikawa had said. The priority in Japan's achingly urgent problems would continue to rest on diplomacy. Everyone, soldier, sailor, minister alike, would strive to bring the negotiations to a happy conclusion. War would be resorted to only when every other solution had been meticulously explored.

It was all over. The Emperor had had his say. But if he had stirred their emotions, he had not moved their minds. The decision of the conference stood—and so did the conditions. Japan was going ahead toward war.

[4] In Kido's affidavit to the IMTFE the poem is (incorrectly) given as:
　　Yomono umi
　　　　Minaharakarato
　　Omouyoni
　　　　Nado adanamino
　　Tachisawaguran.

The ears which heard their Emperor's words were, however, not entirely deaf. Their only trouble was that they heard too late. Konoye realized belatedly that sheer fecklessness and lack of leadership had led him into a trap. He had allowed the armed forces to push him into putting a time limit on the issue of peace or war. He had given them a date to shoot for. Now their military planners and their ordnance depots could be given the signal to go ahead. Requisition orders were prepared for the assembly of 400,000 tons of merchant shipping, for the deployment of 4 million troops and the conscription of thousands of others. The starting buttons had been pushed on the military and naval machines, and they were ticking over.

The Emperor's intervention had stunned Konoye and impressed the service chiefs. They were sufficiently in awe of him to heed his implied plea to continue to try for peace (though they must have thanked their gods that he had failed to give them a direct order) and when Konoye met with Tojo, the Minister of War, and Oikawa, the Minister of Marine, after the meeting, both of them gave him permission to do his utmost to heed Hirohito's plea. With the added concurrence of Sugiyama and Nagano, Konoye sent an emissary around to the United States Embassy.

That evening Ambassador Grew and an Embassy aide, riding in a car from which the CD plates had been removed, drove to a house in the suburbs of Tokyo. It was owned by Baron Ito, but he and all the servants had left for the evening and only the daughter of the house remained behind to serve the guests. It was a dinner à quatre (Grew and his aide, Doonan, Konoye and his secretary, Ushiba) and it turned out to be the Prime Minister's last attempt to persuade Roosevelt to meet him—and also, as it happened, his last attempt to preserve the peace. He told Grew that War Minister Tojo had agreed to send a full general and Navy Minister Oikawa, a full admiral, with him to Washington to ensure the full agreement of the armed forces in any settlement which might be reached. In the meantime, he gave the U.S. envoy the impression that his Cabinet and the service chiefs completely accepted (he called them "splendid") the four principles which had been cabled from Washington by Cordell Hull as a basis for negotiation.

These principles were:

1. Respect for the territorial integrity and the sovereignty of each and all nations;

2. Support of the principle of noninterference in the internal affairs of other countries;

3. Support of the principle of equality, including equality of opportunity; and

4. Nondisturbance of the status quo in the Pacific except as the status quo may be altered by peaceful means.

It was, of course, downright deception for Konoye to say to Grew that the government "conclusively and wholeheartedly" accepted them. For what else did the principles mean so far as Japan was concerned except—*quit* China, *quit* Indo-China, *restore* normal trading conditions in both countries, *and get back to the status quo?* Yet that very morning at the Imperial Conference—about which, of course, Konoye kept silent—the Cabinet and the High Command had without a dissentient enunciated a totally contrary set of principles.[5] And the Emperor had been the only person present to voice his dismay.

So what was accepted by Grew, in the conspiratorial atmosphere of a secret dinner party, as an important recantation on the part of Konoye and his administration was received rather more sceptically in Washington when his dispatch about the conversation ("probably the most important of my career") arrived. Later on Cordell Hull told Grew that if he had felt so deeply about encouraging a Konoye-Roosevelt confrontation he should have flown home to Washington and pushed the project personally. But in the circumstances prevailing, one feels that Grew could not have tried harder than he did. He sent a personal letter to Roosevelt. On September 29, 1941, he cabled a last plea that conversations should take place:

"Should the United States expect or await agreement by the Japanese Government in the present preliminary conversations to clear-cut commitments . . . almost certainly the conversations will drag along indefinitely and unproductively until the Konoye Cabinet and its supporting elements will come to the conclusion that the outlook for an agreement is

---

[5] To do Konoye justice, it is possible that Grew's hearing aid conveyed to him rather more than less of what was actually said on this occasion. Konoye's version of the conversation indicates that he accepted Hull's points only in principle, and said there would be difficulty in implementing them. But, in the circumstances, how could he have implied even general Japanese support for them?

hopeless and that the United States Government is only playing for time.[6] If the abnormal sensitiveness of Japan and the abnormal effects of loss of face are considered, in such a situation Japanese reaction may and probably will lead to unbridled acts."

He added: "There is a question that such a situation may prove to be more serious even than the failure to produce an entirely satisfactory agreement through the proposed meeting between President Roosevelt and Prince Konoye."

But Washington was in no mood to listen to such pleas. The urgent desire of both Grew and Konoye for a heads of state confrontation was still not answered.

Prince Konoye departed for Kamakura, a seaside resort some twenty-odd miles from Tokyo, where he indulged in one of his diplomatic illnesses and defied anyone to come near him with such crude matters as rough talk of war. But on September 26th, he came back to Tokyo. Time was running out. The Imperial Conference of September 6th had set a date. The armed forces had done it deliberately. They realized that the joint American-British-Dutch boycott was strangling their economy and grinding the machinery of state to a halt. Oil reserves were dwindling. Like the last, defiant swimmer in a municipal bath at closing time, they were splashing on while the cocks were open and the water draining away. At any moment they would be dry—and humiliated.

It was time to resign, the premier decided. "On September 26," wrote Kido, "Konoye came to my room and told me he could not but quit if the Army meant to start a full-blown war on October 15. He appealed to me for sympathy in his predicament, whereupon I chastized him as follows: 'You are responsible for the decision of the Imperial Conference. aren't you? It will be irresponsible for you to quit if you leave the decision of September 6th as it is. If you are in such a mess it would surely be better for you to propose a review of the Imperial Conference decision. Get together with the Army. If you cannot agree with them, then perhaps it would be better for you to quit. Otherwise it is surely irresponsible for you to leave things as they are.'"

[6] The U.S. Government was, of course, doing just that. She wanted to stretch the conversations in order to get her own military dispositions ready and allow the British to beef up the defenses at Singapore. In the event, neither Americans nor British did very well in this direction. The Japanese, of course, were pressing because oil supplies were ebbing away.

Konoye emotionally declared that such was not his intention. But with the heavy and uncooperative silence signalizing failure from across the Pacific and the increasing aggressiveness of the military, he was desperately determined to get out. He decided that the Emperor was the only one who could help him to run for cover. Hirohito, whose faith in Konoye's strength of purpose had at last begun to fade, accepted the inevitable.

The last meeting of the Konoye Cabinet took place (with the military leaders in attendance) at the Ogikubo on October 12, 1941, and raveled itself into such confusion that no one was sure, after it was over, whether war was now with them or still outside the door.

Wrote Kido: "Thus the situation was becoming more and more complicated. Everyone's opinion at the meeting hinged on the failure or otherwise of negotiations with America. . . . The political atmosphere became so tense that it was feared that a war would break out at any moment, under forcible pressure from the militarists."

The Emperor was concerned, for he knew what would be expected of him if hostilities commenced. An Imperial Rescript. An Imperial notification to his people that they would be fighting and dying in his name.

"October 13. Monday. Fair. On duty at 10 A.M. . . . Was received in audience by His Majesty from 10:35 to 10:45. His Majesty talked chiefly on Japan-United States problems. He said, 'The Japan-United States negotiations seem to be growing less and less hopeful. If it should end up in war, we should have to issue a proclamation of war. In the past Imperial Rescripts, especially in the one issued at the time of our withdrawal from the League of Nations, we emphasized the cause of world peace. But the people seem to have overlooked this point. It is highly regrettable that when the Rescript was issued at the conclusion of the Japanese-German-Italian pact, the people missed the point that the pact was proposed to bring peace, and took it as if it were our challenge to the United States and Britain. We therefore desire that if in future we should be obliged to issue a declaration of war we would like to have Konoye and Kido to assist us. Thus we would have our sincere thoughts well expressed in the proclamation.'"

It is clear that even by this date he had accepted the inevitable and, with it, war. He told Kido:

"In case we decide on war with the United States and Britain, we must closely study the conditions in Europe and the circumstances under which the peace talks between Britain and Germany and Germany and

Russia broke down. We must use every diplomatic strategy we can to stop Germany from concluding individual peace. We must have her assistance in our war with the U.S. From the beginning we must also make plans as to what to do at the termination of the war. For this we must adopt good-will policies, such as the exchange of envoys with the Vatican City."

It was too much for Konoye. When he was received in audience by the Emperor an hour later and heard these sentiments expressed, it was rather like the jet of cold water which jokesters sometimes direct on an unsuspecting bather emerging from the steaming heat of a Japanese bath. He was shocked. He suddenly realized that the political game which he had been playing with such casual sophistication over the past few months was one in which the guns the players held in their hands contained real bullets.

He procrastinated over the next few days, while he and Tojo, the War Minister, between them tried to promote a royal Prince (Higashikuni) as his successor as premier. Konoye naïvely thought that a prince of the blood would stimulate national unity. Tojo more shrewdly decided that a prince of the blood who could be persuaded to make war would involve the royal family in the decision—and force the Emperor to range himself wholeheartedly with the armed forces in favor of the war.

Kido, ever the guardian of Imperial *amour-propre*, quickly scotched that one. "True that Prince Higashikuni was talented," he wrote in his diary, "but he was lacking in political experience and training. Therefore it would be extremely difficult if not impossible for the Prince to grasp the situation which was so complicated, and work out a plan to cope with it. The result would be that the Prince would be reduced to a mere figurehead and actual power would be assumed by the deputy Prime Minister, and judging by persons available at the time, the person of deputy premier available would be concurrently assumed by the Minister of War [Tojo]. Such being the case, the possibility of averting war would be very slim under the Higashikuni Cabinet. Should war break out the direct responsibility therefore would have to be borne by the Imperial family. My outlook on the Japan-America situation was that no optimism should be warranted for a Pacific War, but on the contrary a very pessimistic view must be taken of its outcome. Should the worst eventually happen, I thought therefore that the Imperial family might become the target of hatred by the people, with the result that the question of national polity would be involved. The only case in which a Cabinet formed by a prince of the blood was permissible would be that of one organized as a result of the Army being convinced of its error and deciding to accept a volte face."

What Kido was making clear (and there is no doubt now that he was spurred on to do it by Hirohito) was that the Imperial family might be pushed into accepting and condoning the war, but that they would take no part in initiating it or shaping its course.

Konoye tarried no longer. With the collapse of the discussions with Tojo to promote a royal prince in his place, his relations with his War Minister deteriorated rapidly. Tojo was a short-tempered man who had never made much secret of the fact that he considered the Prince supine; now he was inclined to call him an outright coward for having led the nation to the brink of war but shuddered back from the vital decision. He refused to speak with him any longer.

"I am not sure that I can stifle my feelings," he said.

There was nothing for Konoye to do, therefore, but to tender the resignation of himself and his Cabinet. It was Kido who decided to recommend to the Emperor that General Tojo be appointed in his stead.

He did it, he was afterward to claim, because "his [Tojo's] character had changed" since he had left the Army to become War Minister and that "he much respected Imperial wishes." Kido was convinced that between them the Emperor and he could convert Tojo to their way of thinking. By an extraordinary process of thinking, he appears to have convinced himself that the very fact that Tojo believed in the Imperial Conference decision of September 6th, and wished to see it implemented, could be used to convert him into a proponent of negotiation.

"Respect for Imperial wishes was common to all soldiers," he wrote, "but it was stronger in Tojo. It was one of the reasons why Tojo was pressing for the execution of the decision of the Imperial Conference of September 6th, *which was held in the presence of the Emperor. If it was commanded by the Emperor to scrap the decision of the Imperial Conference in question, and review the situation on a fresh basis, I had sincere confidence that Tojo would change his policy in pursuance of Imperial wishes."* [7]

The peculiar processes of Japanese ratiocination have rarely been more salutarily illuminated.

Tojo became premier. And war became inevitable.

[7] My italics.—L.M.

Chapter Fifteen

Tojo represented the Army, and the Army, of course, was determined on war. Konoye himself summed up their attitude in the memorandum he submitted to the conference of the jushin which approved Kido's choice of successor.

"Judging by the situation prevailing in the negotiations with America in early October," wrote Konoye, "the Army has held 'that there is no prospect of our point of view being accepted,' and therefore they contend that it is a natural conclusion, based on the decision of the Imperial Conference of September 6th, that war should be commenced at the middle of October or the end of October at the latest."

The Army wanted action, and the sooner the better.

The Navy was, on the other hand, not so certain that precipitate action was called for. Konoye reported their attitude as follows:

"Japan now stands at the crossroads. Whether to stick to diplomatic negotiation or whether to go to war. If it is to be settled through diplomatic negotiation, Japan must stick to diplomacy to the finish. She must be confident enough to conduct diplomatic negotiation to an amicable conclusion. It is impossible to go to war after conducting diplomatic negotiations for two or three months, on the grounds that success has not yet been reached. Inasmuch as it is the government which decides whether to depend on diplomacy or go to war, it must be left entirely to the Prime Minister to decide whether to take the course to the port or to the starboard. It may be added that a strong opinion prevails among Navy circles that war should be avoided as far as possible. The best must be done to adjust relations between Japan and America through diplomacy."

In the circumstances, in the light of these statements—which accurately reported the attitudes of Army and Navy to the situation—why on earth did Kido persuade the jushin to recommend Tojo as premier instead of Toyoda? Why choose an Army man, nostrils flared belligerently, instead of a Navy man, anxious only to pour oil on troubled waters (especially if he could persuade the United States to resume supplying the oil)?

It is a mystery which has never been satisfactorily explained, and Kido is no longer alive to answer the questions one would like to ask. For here, surely, was a unique opportunity in which he could have involved both his Emperor and the Imperial Navy in a last attempt to pluck an olive branch from the fire. He could have persuaded the jushin to nominate a Navy chief for premier, knowing the Navy's reluctance for war. He could then have stimulated the Emperor into working with his new premier in a positive approach to the situation which could have broken the deadlock. There was only one real bone of contention between Japan and the West. China. If Japan would only withdraw its forces from China and signify its willingness to talk, Britain and America would be satisfied. It was not too much to ask. True, it would mean loss of face for the Army, forced to admit its failure on the Asiatic mainland, but this would be balanced by the gain in men, money and resources, all of which were being poured away in a fruitless war.

The opportunity was there, never to present itself again. Only a combination of the Imperial Navy and the civilians *plus the enormous influence of the Emperor* could overcome the intransigent and fanatical determination of the Army. Why did not Kido see his chance and seize it?

Alas, alas. The jushin at Kido's urging chose Tojo instead, and the Lord Keeper carried the recommendation to the Emperor. One can only presume that Hirohito was, by this time, feeling fatalistic, convinced that the times had become hopelessly disjointed and could not be reset by him. He summoned the General to an audience at the palace and told him:

"We direct you to form a Cabinet and to abide by the provisions of the Constitution. We believe that an exceedingly grave situation confronts the nation. Bear in mind at this time that cooperation between the Army and the Navy should be closer than ever before. It is our intention also to summon the Navy Minister and speak to him likewise."

Tojo asked permission to withdraw and think about the mandate he had been given. (He was afterward to say that he had been taken by surprise and never expected that the premiership would be offered to him.) Immediately after his departure, Admiral Oikawa arrived and was received in audience. He too was told to cease quarreling with the Army.

The Navy Minister promised and withdrew to the waiting room, where Tojo was sitting. The Lord Keeper came in. Though he had failed to grasp the obvious opportunity, he did have one idea buzzing in his head, and he had persuaded the Emperor to listen to it. It was an opportunity to "wipe the slate clean" not only in the matter of service rivalry, but in the matter of the September 6th decision to choose a date for going to war.

"I conveyed to them the orders of the Sovereign," wrote Kido, "thereby nullifying the resolution of the September 6th Imperial Conference. 'I presume you have just received Imperial words regarding cooperation between the Army and Navy,' I said. 'As regards the fundamental line of national policy I am commanded to convey to you the Imperial desire that careful consideration be taken by studying the internal and external situations more comprehensively and more deeply than ever, regardless of the resolution of September 6th.'"

The new premier and the Navy Minister agreed, and Kido was satisfied. Too easily. By expunging the date in the September 6th resolution, he appears to have believed—and the Emperor with him—that the situation was back to the starting point. But of course it wasn't true. The wheels had been set in motion, and mere words from the Lord Keeper and nods of the head from two ministers would not stop them.

True, in obedience to the Emperor's instructions, the new premier did cancel the decision of September 6th and tell members of his Cabinet that he would concentrate all his efforts on finding a peaceful solution to the problems dividing Japan and the West. He assured Mr. Shigenori Togo, whom he wanted as his Foreign Minister, that he would *not* be joining a War Cabinet, and it was upon this pledge that Togo consented to come in.

Tojo went to seek guidance for himself and the tasks he faced by praying at the shrine of the Emperor Meiji, at the shrine to the Empire's war dead, and before Amaterasu, the Sun Goddess, at Ise. He rapidly became known as The Premier on Horseback, for he took to riding about the city on a charger, exhorting the people to work harder. In the fish market, where supplies were scanty and the dealers complained of difficulties because of lack of gasoline for transport, he cried: "Gasoline, gasoline! Never mind gasoline! Get up earlier!"

For a short period, at least, tension eased. "A war which had threatened to break out at any moment," as Kido put it, was temporarily delayed. "His Majesty was exceedingly glad, and spoke to me about it on October 20th. . . . I had had only one motive in recommending Tojo and that was to avert war with America. I sincerely felt that war had been averted and that the situation had taken a new turn for the better."

As to Hirohito himself, he genuinely believed that he had brought off something of a revolution. He had spoken and the tide had turned.

"There is a saying, isn't there?" he said to Kido. " 'You cannot obtain a tiger's cub unless you brave the tiger's den.' "

Alas, tides have a habit not only of ebbing but of flowing again. And if it takes courage to brave a tiger's den, it also takes skill to get out again —especially if you are carrying the tiger's cub.

And if Tojo went through the movements of earnestly seeking peace in the next few weeks there were not many members of the armed forces who believed that he would get it. True, there was an Imperial Conference held at the Palace on November 5, 1941, which agreed to dispatch a special envoy to Washington to join Ambassador Nomura, who by this time was dispirited, downhearted and pleading to be recalled because of the failure of his mission. The envoy chosen was Mr. Saburo Kurusu, a skilled politician with an American wife and a son with American citizenship. Through the efforts of Ambassador Grew, a trans-Pacific clipper flying boat was held for two days at Hong Kong so that he could be transported to America by the swiftest means then available.

It seemed like a breakthrough. It would have been had Kurusu carried with him any new instructions. But of course he did not. The Japanese were still sticking to the same terms. So, for that matter, were the Americans, and it was a case of the immovable object meeting the irresistible force. Simplified, America wanted Japan out of China and Indochina before lifting the oil and trade embargo. Japan wanted the embargo lifted and the right to retain "peace-keeping" units in China for "police and protective work" and to "hold back the Communists." So long as each side insisted on these basic conditions, a settlement was impossible—and if the Emperor, Kido and Tojo didn't realize it, the armed forces did.

On the very same day that the Imperial Conference decided to dispatch Kurusu to Washington, Army Chief of Staff Sugiyama sent out instructions mobilizing the southern Army, and Navy Chief of Staff Nagano sent instructions to Admiral Yammamoto, Commander in Chief of the Combined Fleet of the Imperial Japanese Navy, telling him to prepare for war with the United States, Britain and the Netherlands, and accepting Yammamoto's plan for an opening attack on Pearl Harbor. There were no longer any illusions in this quarter.

"The atmosphere became a very ugly one," wrote Kido. "My house had been guarded by ten policemen, but about this time the number was increased to fifteen. At night my home was guarded by twenty-five men, including ten additionally detailed from the special guard. Furthermore, I had to follow a different route every day to and from my office. My views against war were the reason for increased protection. As days rolled on, the situation between America and Japan showed no indication of easing. In this country the solidarity of the young military and naval officers who formed the mainstay of the fighting services was further tightened with the result that an atmosphere was created in the fighting services themselves against the policy of those leaders of the Army and Navy who favored adjusting the relations between Japan and America."

Kido's reference to the Army and Navy leaders who "favored adjusting relations" meant Tojo and his new Navy Minister, Shimada. He did not know that the most active leaders of the armed services now, in fact, completely agreed with their junior officers in wanting to get the war started as soon as possible. It was now or never, in their view.

"Meanwhile," Kido wrote, "propaganda was spreading that if she further dilly-dallied, Japan would be attacked by America. Fretful impatience was the order of the day."

And, for the Emperor, sleepless nights.

For what could he do? Imbued with his success over the abrogation of the September 6th decision, it might be presumed that he could do plenty. If he could tell his warlords to delay the war, surely he could stop it.

But here none other than Kido, who agreed with him as to the foolishness and futility of war, was the very man who chastened him. Kido appeared to spend his *unofficial* moments dreaming of a perfect solution to the peace-or-war problem, but remembering every *official* minute of his life that he was a civil servant pledged to keep his Emperor in line.

(Pledged, in fact, is the wrong word. There was no pledge. There was only an unspoken agreement that the Emperor would fall into line with his government, even if he disagreed with it.)

Kido himself summed up his idea of his duties in this way:

"The official duties of the Lord Keeper dictated me not to interfere in national policies. Therefore I was not in a position to give voice to my opposition publicly. . . . Meanwhile the situation went from bad to worse. As one of those serving the Emperor, with official duties to offer close to him, I gave the most serious and constructive thought to enable the Emperor to do his best dispassionately, as sovereign, under constitutional government."

He added: "Put in another form, I made it a rule to petition the Emperor to make the government study the situation as cautiously as possible from all angles before making a decision. I also told him to caution the government about any matter which he thought was necessary, thereby putting forth all manner of effort so as to have nothing to regret later."

But Kido was a conformist. Even if war were threatened against all the hopes and beliefs of his Emperor, he still believed that Hirohito should accept. Or so he said about this time.

"Once, however, that the Government decided on a national policy," he wrote, "I used to counsel the Emperor to approve it by trusting the administration in accordance with constitutional government."

And Hirohito did as he was told.

Chapter Sixteen

What would have happened if Hirohito had refused to do as he was told? Could he have prevented the Pacific War? Was his influence powerful enough to have held his warlords in check?

There are ex-members of the Emperor's entourage who believe that as late as the end of November, 1941, it was within the range of the possibilities of the situation that he could have *ordered* his government to make concessions to the United States and that Tojo and his administration would have obeyed them. They also maintain that such was Tojo's influence with the armed forces that he could have forced them to obey a standstill order which would have muzzled their guns. The Imperial Japanese Navy, which was by this time at sea under the command of Admiral Yammamoto, had recall signals with them and were prepared to abandon the Pearl Harbor operation for which they had been rehearsing for so many weeks. Army and Navy had been keyed up to the point when they were ready for action; which meant that they were ready to obey orders; they would just as promptly have obeyed orders to hold their fire as to start the conflagration. Yammamoto ran a highly tuned organization, and it would have listened to his orders—even negative ones.

It has become the accepted formula of historians of this period to maintain that the question of peace or war passed out of Hirohito's hands once Tojo became convinced that the United States (which was, by this time, acting as negotiating power for both Britain and the Netherlands as well) would not knuckle under and make concessions—once he was sure that the embargo would not be broken, once he believed that the West would go on helping China. From conversations with those advisers—those at least who are still alive—who were close to him at the time, one begins to doubt this. One suspects that Hirohito himself now believes that, *had he only been stimulated into trying, had he only realized how really powerful was his influence for peace,* he would and he *could* have turned his nation away from war. He wanted, and he could have persuaded, Japan to make concessions. And had he demanded the acceptance of these concessions from his Prime Minister and his Cabinet, he would have got them—plus the influence of General Tojo in seeing that they were accepted by the nation too. When he drew up his Cabinet, Tojo had had himself made Home Minister as well as War Minister, and when he was asked why, he explained that the Japanese people were in a belligerent mood. In the event of an amicable settlement of the negotiations between Japan and America, there might be domestic trouble and strife from civilian and Army elements who objected to peace and conciliation. He wished to be Home Minister in order to take charge and see that the country accepted the settlement.

One feels, therefore, that Tojo would have obeyed Hirohito's demand that peace be secured *at almost any price* if only he had dared to demand it. The Emperor certainly wanted peace at almost any price. He was against the China war. He loathed the idea of war with the United States and Britain. He did not believe that Japan had the resources to win such a war.

American historians—including the present ambassador to Japan, Dr. Edwin Reischauer—seem to be convinced that Hirohito never had a chance. If he had insisted, as his divine prerogative, that his ministers make concessions and thus secure peace, he would—they say—have been arrested and his brother, Prince Chichibu, installed as Regent with the Crown Prince nominated as Emperor in his place. Most Japanese privately remark that this is nonsense. Chichibu was even more hostile to a war with the West than his brother, and neither mentally, physically nor emotionally prepared to usurp Hirohito.

The trouble was that, in 1941, the Emperor did not really appreciate his own strength or the potency of his influence. The American apologists say: "True, when the time came to make peace, the influence of the Emperor was paramount. But the situation was not the same in 1941 as it was in 1945. By 1945 the Cabinet was divided. Some wanted peace, others wanted war, and the Emperor had his opportunity—he could make his influence felt on the side of those who wanted to bring the conflict to an end. But 1941 was different. Everyone then was convinced that the only possibility was war. They refused to accept the American demands. They saw no possibility of peace. They were unanimous. And therefore the Emperor had no alternative, as a constitutional monarch, but to accept their guidance and issue the Rescript for War."

It is not true. There were several members of Tojo's Cabinet (Foreign Minister Togo, in particular) who paid lip service to the idea of war simply because no one was ardent enough to insist on peace. Their opinions could have been changed within the hour by an authoritative voice insisting that war was impossible, that peace—even a peaceful retreat—was mandatory if Japan be saved from disaster. More's the pity that Hirohito did not voice it. One senses that it is the festering scab of regret at which he picks even to this day.

"Donning the obligatory morning coat and top hat," wrote Otto D. Tolischus, *The New York Times* Tokyo correspondent, on November 26, 1941, "and commandeering the Embassy car of my Russian neighbors for lack of other transportation, I drove in style to the Diet building today to watch the Emperor formally open the extraordinary session of Japan's parliament. It was a very brief performance. Clad in the uniform of a generalissimo, and accompanied by Princes of the Blood and Household Ministry officials, the Emperor came in rather inconspicuously through a side door and ascended to the throne chair above the speaker's table while all the frock-coated peers and deputies bowed in silence." [1]

Ambassador Grew and his staff from the United States Embassy had decided, after some thought, that he would attend the special session, despite the fact that the situation was tense and Sir Robert Craigie, the British envoy, had decided to stay away. As usual Grew shook hands with the German and the Italian ambassadors in the entrance hall, but he did not fail to note that—for the first time—Okubo, the Master of Ceremonies, deliberately separated him from the Axis envoys in the gallery.

"Tojo, holding a scroll in his hand," wrote Tolischus, "advanced to the throne chair, and, keeping his head bowed, awkwardly hobbled up the steps by advancing only with his right foot and dragging his left

[1] Otto D. Tolischus, *Tokyo Record*, New York: Reynal & Hitchcock, 1941.

235

after him in exaggerated respect. With an almost impatient gesture, the Emperor stretched out his hand, and taking the scroll, read this message, which probably holds out all records for brevity:

"'We have commanded the State Minister to present to the Imperial Diet session various legislative bills and budget estimates necessary in connection with the current emergency situation. You are herewith commanded to fulfil your duties and help to conduct State affairs in a harmonious spirit, so as to meet our wishes.'

"But, the honourable frock coats who remained bowed throughout must have welcomed its briefness. Having read his two sentences in a clear voice, the Emperor stepped down. The ceremony was over. We went home."

But if the Emperor's official speech was deliberately short and dull, those which followed were not. The atmosphere of the special session had been set by a resolution submitted to what Tolischus calls the Throne-Aid League of Deputies (the writer probably means the Imperial Rule Assistance Association) by fifty-six of its members, in which they maintained:

"The haughty attitude taken by the United States against Japan is beyond words. Forming an anti-Japanese encirclement conspiracy together with Britain, Russia, the Netherlands and the Chiang Kai-shek regime, the United States is now not only hampering Japan's great ideal of establishing the East Asia Co-prosperity Sphere, but is also threatening Japan's right to existence. The Throne and the League should point out the unbearable attitude of the United States in the name of the 100,-000,000 Japanese people, so as to make the world understand Japan's just rights."

Tojo keynoted the session with a speech in which he summarized the points the United States must accept if the negotiations then proceeding in Washington were to prove fruitful and went on:

"The economic blockade resorted to by nonbelligerent Powers constitutes a measure little less hostile than carrying on armed warfare. Such an act not only impedes settlement of the China Affair, which Japan intends to bring about, but gravely affects the existence of our Empire, and we can by no means acquiesce in it. The Empire now stands at a crossroads of destiny unparallelled in its 2,600 year old history. The Government is resolved to fulfil with all its powers the responsibility of assisting the Throne."

It was as near to an ultimatum as Tojo had come, and though Smith-Hutton, the U.S. Naval attaché, whispered: "Well, he didn't declare war, anyway," it was little short of it.

The ultimatum was, in fact, being carried to Washington by Kurusu. He had arrived there on the day before the opening of the special session of the Diet, and he and Nomura were seen by President Roosevelt and Secretary of State Cordell Hull two days later, on November 17, 1941. Hull took an instant dislike to him.

"Kurusu, as Japanese ambassador to Berlin," he wrote later, "had signed the Tripartite Pact with Germany and Italy. . . . Neither his appearance nor his attitude commanded confidence or respect. I felt from the start he was deceitful. Knowing what I did of Japan's intentions from the intercepts . . . it did not seem possible to me . . . that he did not know . . . he was to lull us with talk until the moment Japan got ready to strike. . . . His only recommendation in my eyes was that he spoke excellent English, having married his American secretary. Nevertheless, I found that Nomura, despite his faulty English, understood the points I made much better than Kurusu, whose mentality was such that he could not appreciate our views." [2]

Kurusu was, in fact, persuaded by Nomura to ask Tokyo for an amelioration of the terms which he was supposed to deliver, and was resoundingly rebuked by Togo, the Foreign Minister, for going beyond his brief. Accepting the censure, he presented the Japanese terms for a settlement on November 20, 1941, and found them immediately regarded by the United States as an ultimatum. The terms were certainly tough and no one knowing the mood of the Americans and their allies at the time can surely have expected them to be accepted. They were the same as those which General Tojo had steered through the Imperial Conference of November 5th, and since the Americans had cracked the Japanese code, they knew that these were no doubt Japan's "final offer," for they had deciphered a code message to Nomura from Foreign Minister Togo saying that the Cabinet had set a time limit until November 25th for the successful (or otherwise) outcome of the talks. The terms Kurusu presented were:

1. Neither Japan nor the United States will move armed forces into

---

[2] Cordell Hull, *The Memoirs of Cordell Hull*, New York, The Macmillan Company, 1948.

South-East Asia or the South Pacific area, except that Japan may increase her forces in Northern Indochina;

2. Japan will withdraw troops from southern to northern Indochina as soon as an agreement is made with the United States, and will evacuate Indochina altogether when peace is concluded with China or "an equitable peace" is made in the Pacific area;

3. The United States and Japan will "cooperate" in securing for themselves commodities from the Netherlands East Indies;

4. The United States and Japan will release each other's assets, and the United States will "supply Japan a required quantity of oil"; and

5. The United States will cease to help China.

It was an ultimatum all right, and its acceptance would have amounted to an American surrender. Foreign Minister Togo, in his postwar memoirs, strenuously denied that it was to be regarded as such, even though he urged it on his envoys as "definitely our last offer." Such phrases, he maintained, were all part of the technique of expert bargainers.[3] But neither he nor his Prime Minister were prepared to regard the United States reply to their "last offer" with any such toleration.

Certainly, the service chiefs of both sides had no doubt of the significance of the Japanese message via Kurusu. After reading it, Admiral Yammamoto sailed the Imperial Japanese Fleet to sea and made for the northern waters of the Pacific. At the same time he put into operation the "camouflage techniques" calculated to deceive the United States Intelligence about his departure. A "ghost fleet" of radio sets remained behind in the Inland Sea to chatter messages to each other indicating to enemy listening posts that the big ships were still there—whereas, of course, they were on their way to the rendezvous (provided they got the right signal) with Pearl Harbor. Yammamoto certainly thought that this meant war.

So did Ambassador Grew, who cabled the State Department telling them to alert the armed forces of "possible unexpected attacks and assaults without warning." And on November 27, 1941, Navy Secretary Admiral Stark, Chief of Naval Operations, sent out from Washington to his chief subordinates in the Navy a message which said:

"This dispatch is to be considered a war warning. Negotiations with

[3] The argument over what was, at that time, an "ultimatum" and what was a "bargaining point" is rather like the argument over who is a spy and who is a secret agent: a spy if he is against you, a secret agent if he is on your side.

Japan looking for stabilization of conditions in the Pacific have ceased. An aggressive move by Japan is expected within the next few days. The number and equipment of Japanese troops and the organization of naval task forces indicates an amphibious expedition against either the Philippines, Thailand or the Kra Peninsula or possibly Borneo. Execute appropriate defensive deployment necessary to carrying out the tasks assigned in WPL 46." [4]

On November 27, 1941, the United States Government replied to Kurusu's "ultimatum" with a message which the Japanese Government chose to regard as an "ultimatum" in its turn. The only difference in the two is that the Americans made no attempt to suppress the contents of the Japanese "ultimatum" and did send a reply. On the other hand, the Japanese forbade the domestic Press to publish the American statement and replied to it with an act of war.

Summarized, the American reply was as follows:

1. A nonaggression pact should be signed among Great Britain, China, Japan, the Netherlands, Thailand and the United States, together with an agreement to respect the integrity of Indochina;

2. Japan should evacuate China and Indochina;

3. All the foregoing countries [with the exception, of course, of China] should agree to renounce extraterritorial rights in China;

4. Japan should recognize the Government of Chiang Kai-shek in Chungking;

5. A new Japanese-American trade agreement be signed, on a most-favored-nation basis, with raw silk on the free list, and reciprocal un-freezing of assets; and

6. Stabilization of the dollar-yen exchange.

It was not meant to be an ultimatum, but most senior American statesmen (particularly Roosevelt and Hull) suspected that it would be twisted into one by the Tojo Government. They prepared for war. Unfortunately, they guessed wrong as to where the Japanese would strike.

The Imperial Conference of November 5, 1941, had not only decided to send Kurusu to America with a "final offer." It had also decided on a "deadline" for the ending of negotiations and put it at November 25th, a date which was subsequently delayed by Tojo to November 29th. In

[4] *Pearl Harbor Attack*, Part 14, Hearings, Congress of the United States.

mid-November, Kido (who seems to be rather shocked that Hirohito said no word at all on the occasion of the November 5th Conference) approached His Majesty and "counselled the Emperor to deprecate strongly Japan's entering into a state of war with the passing of the end of November, as if it was a mere matter of routine business. Instead, I suggested, he should handle the matter with the most cautious attitude. 'When the premier solicits his final decision, if circumstances require,' I advised His Majesty, 'the premier should be required to hold the Council in the Imperial Presence with the participation therein of all the senior statesmen.' In other words, I felt that the mere fact that the end of November was approaching did not warrant the inevitability of war. I believed a re-examination should be made of the Imperial Conference [of November 5th] decision, depending on the state of the negotiations with America at that time. To be frank, I secretly thought that I could bring the negotiations to an amicable conclusion, by invoking Imperial intervention."

Just how Kido expected to do this is not now clear, and he is dead now. What he did go on to say in his diary was:

"November 26, 1941. I met Hara, President of the Privy Council, to consult with him about a Senior Statesmen's Conference. I saw the Emperor from 11:15 A.M. to 11:45 A.M. He said that as for the future of the Japanese-American talks it was feared, to Our regret, that the worst might come to the worst. Under these circumstances our final decision as to the war should be carried into practice after another Senior Statesmen's Conference, which should be convened in order to have broader and more complete discussions on the matter. The Emperor also said that he wanted to convey this idea to Premier Tojo."

Kido answered him as follows:

"*Majesty, once the final decision is made this time, it will truly be the last and irretrievably final one. Thus if there should be any doubt or any better idea which you may have to surmount the difficulties in Your Majesty's mind, I pray that Your Majesty be pleased to elucidate the same without the least reserve, so that appropriate steps which Your Majesty might not repent of afterward can be taken. I therefore pray that Your Majesty command the premier without reserve.*" [5]

It is known that Kido was not normally an emotional man, but that he delivered these remarks with a good deal of feeling—or so he informed

[5] My italics.—L.M.

members of the Imperial Household afterward. It was obviously meant as a goad to prick Hirohito into action. But he lost heart (or so he professed later) when Hull's message of November 27th arrived, for he too chose to consider it an "ultimatum."

Tojo, members of his Cabinet, elder statesmen and what Kido called "the primary vassals of the state" came to the Imperial Palace on the morning of November 29, 1941, and discussed the question of the American negotiations until one P.M. The Emperor was not present, but he afterward gave lunch to the statesmen and from two P.M. took them into his study and listened to their opinions.

Kido quotes the Emperor as remarking:

"The times have become very difficult, haven't they?"

He seems to have been waiting for the answers that would give him the mood of the meeting. Two of the former premiers, Baron Wakatsuki and Baron Okada appear to have had doubts about whether a war policy should now be followed.

"I am not worried about the spiritual strength of our people," Wakatsuki said, "but I am about material. The question whether we can really survive a long-range war deserves careful study."

Okada added: "I agree that today we are truly confronted with a critical situation. I am concerned as to whether we can put full confidence in our ability to supply necessary materials. There was an assurance by the government a short time ago, but I am still not convinced."

Prince Konoye, still regarded, particularly by Hirohito, as the indefatigable searcher for peace, as usual seemed to be facing both ways.

"I deeply regret," he said, "that I have not been able to do anything towards the adjustment of Japanese-American relations despite my efforts from last April onwards. I beg to express my appreciation to the present Cabinet for zealously striving to attain this end. To my great regret, I am forced to conclude, on the basis of this morning's explanation by the government, that further continuation of diplomatic negotiations would be hopeless."

One can picture the thin, languid body, shoulders hunched in a sort of frozen shrug, as he looked at the assembled statesmen. Almost certainly it was for the benefit of the Emperor that he added:

"Still, is it necessary to go to war at once, even if diplomatic negotiations have been broken off? Would it not be possible, I wonder, while carrying on matters as they are, to find a way out of the deadlock later by persevering to the utmost despite the difficulties?"

Then up spoke Admiral Yonai. Bowing to the Emperor, he said:

"If I may use a vernacular expression, let me say that in our efforts to avoid going broke in the future we are in danger of bankrupting ourselves at once."

It was a reference to the militarists' desire to adopt an all-or-nothing policy. And it was followed by cautious comments, deprecating the idea of immediate war, from three other jushin, former premiers Hirota, Hayashi and Abe.

There were allies here, if Hirohito were looking for them, and an indication that at this moment there was far from being a unanimity in favor of war; *and this was only nine days away from Pearl Harbor.* Wakatsuki, with the obvious intent of stirring his colleagues, rose to his feet again and said:

"We have today, I believe, arrived at a really important moment. I should like to say one thing. If it is necessary for the preservation and self-defence of the Empire, we must rise to arms *even if the country be reduced to ashes and though we can foresee defeat.*[6] But it is dangerous indeed to execute state policy or to make use of the national strength merely to achieve such ideas as the establishment of the Greater East Asia Co-Prosperity Sphere, or of the 'Stabilizing Power of East Asia.' I pray that Your Majesty will give careful consideration to this point. It is not worth it."

Was he looking to the Emperor for a lead, for someone whose abhorrence of war and determination to avoid it might crystallize the opposition to the Tojo policy? If so, he did not get it. Instead, Tojo himself arose and sarcastically asked if anyone else had "any brilliant ideas"? Brushing aside the expressed doubts and fears, he forecast that the military plans which had been made—all details of which he withheld from the meeting—would enable Japan to secure strategic points in the Pacific from which the nation could fight a long war. All military and political resources would be utilized to force Britain and the Chungking government out of the war, and sap the will of America to go on fighting.

He bowed to the Emperor and so did all the other primary vassals of the state. Hirohito impassively watched them file out and said no word. He appeared to think, in Kido's words, that the situation was "beyond control." But was it?

[6] My italics.—L.M.

Chapter Seventeen

What has never ceased to amaze students of the last days of peace in Japan is the complete silence of the Emperor, his failure to raise his voice against war. There is little doubt that, at this day and date, he is amazed at it himself. The decision to go to war was made at an Imperial Conference which was held at the palace on December 1, 1941. There were only two items on the agenda:

1. *The negotiations with the United States have finally failed of consummation;* and

2. *Japan will commence hostilities against Great Britain, the United States and the Netherlands.*

Hirohito had spent the past twenty-four hours brooding over the Elder Statesmen's Conference of November 29 in his study. Something had gone wrong there, he decided, though he did not seem to be sure exactly what. What he did sense was that there was not the total consensus of opinion in favor of war as Tojo, Togo (the Foreign Minister) and the militarists made out. He was therefore aroused when his younger brother, Prince Takamatsu, came to see him on November 30th and told him that he had heard—he did not say from whom—that the Imperial Navy was still not sure about the wisdom of going to war or of the prospects of winning.

As a result, Hirohito told Tojo that for the time being he would withhold consent for the Imperial Conference of December 1, and meanwhile sent for the Minister of Marine, Shimada, and the Navy Chief of Staff, Nagano, to find out how they were thinking. It is a measure of his

243

lack of knowledge of service affairs that no one had told him that, by this time, Japanese warships and troopships were at sea and awaiting orders. One fleet, under the command of Admiral Yammamoto, was on its way to northern waters in a secret creep across the Pacific toward Pearl Harbor while another was on its way toward Malaya and the Netherlands Indies.

Hirohito questioned Shimada and Nagano for some time. No one has since discovered what they told him, except that Prince Takamatsu was wrong; they *were* confident; they *did* believe that the fleet could win.

But what else?

Did they also tell him about Pearl Harbor? Did he ask them for details of the operations which would begin once war was declared?

At least this is certain. After he had talked with them, Hirohito called in Tojo, the Prime Minister, and gave his consent for the Imperial Conference of December 1, 1941, to take place.

"I was told," wrote Kido, "that they [Shimada and Nagano] had answered his questions with confidence. I do not know what they told him. He then told me to advise the premier to proceed with the Imperial Conference the next day as planned."

Kido went on to state:

"He told me to tell Tojo to proceed with the Imperial Conference—not with the war."

But it was for war that the Imperial Conference decided. This time there were no heavy doubts expressed. This time none of the ex-premiers got up to warn the conference that defeat lay ahead, and what they were fighting for was not worth it. Instead they listened in silence to a turgid lecture from Tojo.

Turning to Hirohito, he said:

"It is extremely regrettable that His Majesty must be troubled by the outbreak of this great war, when the China affair has already gone on for four years and more. When we think, however, that our national strength has several times multiplied since before the China affair, with the people drawn closer together and with the spirit of the fighting men of our Army and Navy higher and more vigorous than ever before, it is beyond doubt that this crisis will be survived by the whole nation's contribution, as one man, of its life to the country."

He ended: "We will now set His Majesty's mind at rest by speedily accomplishing, in perfect unity and with confidence in certain victory, the objectives of the war which Japan must now undertake."

The meeting nodded its approval to the premier and bowed to the Emperor. It was all over. Would the Emperor say a word? Disapproval? Approval? A blessing? *Anything?*

Not a word.

The fantastic situation was that the Cabinet, the elder statesmen, and all except the top service chiefs, had no notion when the war they had approved would begin or where it would strike. No one asked for information, though all the Army and Navy chiefs were present. Premier Tojo did not deign to enlighten them. As they left the conference chamber, it was as if the service chiefs were saying:

"Now it is out of your hands. Leave it to us. Don't interfere!"

The Foreign Minister, Togo, noticed this and said afterward that "I had the feeling that the members of the High Command were unwontedly carefree in their attitude, by contrast with their previous intenseness concerning an early commencement of the war." [1]

Togo was a pompous little man, puffed out with self-importance, who felt that the attitude of the armed forces represented a considerable loss of face to the civilians, and felt it his duty to do something about it. Rather like a senior civil servant in the War Office approaching Wellington, he bustled over to the Army Chief of Staff, Sugiyama, and demanded to know when hostilities would commence.

He replied "vaguely" that it would be "around next Sunday" (which would be December 8th, Japanese time, December 7th, American).

"This deepened the suspicion which I already felt of the High Command," wrote Togo, "and I therefore pointed out that *naturally we should give notice of the commencement of hostilities through usual procedures*" (meaning observance of The Hague Convention pertaining to the procedure to be followed in declaring war).

It was Navy Chief of Staff Nagano who intervened then and said:

"But we are going to make a surprise attack," and Vice Chief of Staff Ito followed by saying that the Navy wanted to leave the negotiations with America indeterminate until war had actually begun, in order to achieve the maximum possible effect with the opening attack.

Wrote Togo: "I then understood what the carefreeness in the attitude of the High Command had meant. I was equally astonished at the proposal of a surprise attack by a Navy which had professed such confidence

[1] Shigenori Togo, *The Cause of Japan*, New York, Simon and Schuster, Inc., 1956.

in its interceptive operations," and he was also "discouraged over the future of the war, as the proposal amounted to an admission that the Navy had no expectation of success, even in the initial stage of the war, unless it could achieve surprise."

Togo stressed to the service chiefs that the "notification of a declaration of war was absolutely necessary from the point of view of good faith. I pointed out that the action proposed by the Navy was entirely unallowable, being in contravention of the accepted procedure, and that it would be inauspicious for Japan at the opening of the war to commit irresponsible acts which would be hurtful to the national honor and prestige."

The Foreign Minister professed to be so disgusted with the attitude of the Navy and its sneaky plan for an unannounced attack that he stalked out of the room. He was followed by Vice Chief Ito who asked him whether a declaration of war couldn't be handed to the American ambassador in Tokyo. Wouldn't that fulfil the formula? Since it would have been easy to cut the telephone and cable wires immediately the message was handed over, this was rather like handing Grew a hand grenade with the pin pulled out and no place to throw it—and even Togo recognized this.

He said no. A real declaration of war. That was what was necessary. At last Ito agreed. He told Togo that "the Navy had no objection to the delivery in Washington of notification of termination of negotiations. It should be served, he said, at 12:30 P.M. December 7th, Washington time. All other participants in the meeting approved the proposal."

Togo demanded of Ito: "Will there be a proper interval between notification and attack?"

He was assured that there would be.

"I accordingly assented to his request," wrote Togo, "and it was so decided. I considered that I had succeeded through this controversy in confining the Navy's demands within the limits of legitimacy as recognised by international law."

He still did not inquire of either of the service chiefs exactly when war would start, or how. He knew nothing of Pearl Harbor. And a few days after insisting on an adequate time between act of war and presentation of ultimatum, he gave way to the armed forces—still desperately anxious to get in a sneak attack. He wrote:

"It had been decided to make delivery [of our declaration of war] to

246

the United States Government at 12:30 P.M. December 7th, Washington time. On December 5th, however, Tanabe and Ito, the Vice Chiefs of Staff of Army and Navy called on me at the Foreign Ministry, and Ito told me that the High Command had found it necessary to postpone presentation of the document *thirty minutes* beyond the time previously agreed upon, and that they wanted my consent thereto. I asked the reason for the delay, and Ito said that it was because he had miscalculated."

Togo asked how long this would leave between notification and attack. Ito refused to tell him, "on the plea that this was an operational secret." The Foreign Minister insisted, demanding assurance that "even with the hour of delivery changed from twelve-thirty P.M. to one there would remain a sufficient time thereafter before the attack occurred. This assurance Ito gave."

The documentation of what Emperor Hirohito did between the decision to make war on December 1, 1941, and the actual attack upon Pearl Harbor a week later is scanty. He stayed at home, and no doubt he prayed at the shrines in the palace grounds. Occidentals in Tokyo stayed home too. The city was full of jostling crowds and sulphurous talk and it was no place to be if your inclination was pacific. A couple of weeks earlier, Tojo had created a precedent by broadcasting for the first time over the radio and now the loud-speakers blared exhortations to martial valor and glory or martial music. Ships full of departing British and Americans had begun to sail from Yokohama, and those who remained behind, in the belief that the Japanese would treat them with decency and consideration, would live to regret their faith in the "civilized approach" of their hosts.

In Washington the cryptographers were busy deciphering and interpreting the significance of Japanese diplomatic telephone talks and cables. The United States has always made a special study of (and achieved an especial success in reading) the top-secret messages of other nations. Its Black Chamber operation in World War One told them most of what they wanted to know about Germany. Now, in 1941, they had access to the highest-priority codes and phrases which the Japanese used to conceal their instructions as they were conveyed over both cable and telephone.

They were therefore not deceived by the decision of Tojo's liaison conference in Tokyo, which decided to keep America guessing about

Japanese intentions. At the same time that he insisted that the armed services "obey the rules" about declaring war, Foreign Minister Togo was cabling his ambassadors in Washington to keep the negotiations going—and these exhortations the State Department learned from their cryptographers. But they also learned that, at the same time, Togo had instructed the Japanese Embassy to destroy all but one of its telegraphic machines equipped for receiving cryptograms, and to burn all but one vital book of codes.

They sent an FBI man around to the Embassy on Massachusetts Avenue, and there, sure enough, was a bonfire in the backyard and a couple of Japanese officials poking papers into it.

They were also listening to telephone conversations between Washington and Tokyo. The special envoy and the Foreign Minister had fixed up a verbal code for conversations, and this the Americans had also broken down. It was a pretty naïve set of phrases, anyway, and when Kurusu or Nomura used it they were apt to perform like amateur actors short of rehearsal time. The negotiations they were conducting were to be referred to as "the marriage proposal." Roosevelt was known as "Miss Kimiko" and a new turn in the crisis was "a baby is born." (In the circumstances, one feels that they might at least have called the President *Mrs.* Kimiko.) The Japanese Army was "Mr. Tokugawa" and the possibility of concessions or lack of them was to be referred to "in mountaineering terms," climbing up or down.

In some ways the conversations which passed over the wire must have sounded like passages from Gilbert and Sullivan's *The Mikado*:

"Is Miss Kimiko likely to come down the mountain?"

"I fear not. She is having a baby. How is Mr. Tokugawa?"

"He says he wants nothing more to do with the marriage proposal." [2]

The United States Government knew that the Imperial Japanese Fleet was at sea, and since they guessed that it was going to practically everywhere else, one might have hoped that someone in the Navy Department would guess that it might be going for Pearl Harbor. But that they didn't think of—not until too late, anyway.

[2] These, in fact, are not actual transcriptions, but they could have been. What Kurusu and Yammamoto (of the American Branch of the Japanese Foreign Office) actually said to each other included such phrases as "Does it seem as if a baby is being born?" "Don't break off the marriage proposal." "Miss Kimiko is leaving town tomorrow" and "Don't let him go up the mountain."

In the meantime, there were still some people who believed (even if he had ceased to believe it himself) that the Emperor could stop the war. Among them was a young Japanese Foreign Service official, Hidenari Terasaki. Terasaki had been in Shanghai during the first phases of the China affair and had been disgusted with the brutish arrogance of his fellow countrymen. Until September, 1941, he had been head of the American Section of the Foreign Office in Tokyo, and therefore intimately connected with the Japanese-American negotiations, and thereafter had been transferred as First Secretary to the Japanese Embassy in Washington. With either Nomura or Kurusu he had taken part in all the meetings with Cordell Hull and he was accepted by the Americans as a completely honest and sincere man who desperately wished to keep his country out of war.

It may have been the fact that both he and Kurusu had American wives, and therefore shared an outlook rather broader than that of most Japanese, which helped to establish a rapport between him and the special envoy. He was certainly able to talk to him in terms at once franker and riskier than would normally have been possible. Japanese officialdom is extremely stratified and bold remarks from a subordinate to a superior are extremely rare; normally a junior official bows to his senior, waits to be asked questions, and is carefully equivocal in his replies. But Mrs. Terasaki quotes her husband as having said to Kurusu, late in November, 1941:

"Ambassador, why don't you become a national traitor? Why don't you go ahead and say to the Americans: 'We *will* get out of China.' We can't remain in China for long, anyway. The war party knows that. They will have to leave China, but they would prefer war with the United States, as an excuse for leaving, to admitting they have made such a mistake. You may be executed, but they may honor the treaty. It would give them a way out, and we may get some concessions in exchange." [3]

Kurusu said he would consider it, but, of course, did not.

On November 29, 1941, Terasaki went to see Doctor E. Stanley Jones, a Wesleyan minister who had cordial relations with the President and was intently pursuing peace initiatives of his own. He asked Doctor Jones if he could introduce him to the President so that he could explain to him the Japanese position psychologically, so that he might be made

[3] Gwen Terasaki, *Bridge to the Sun*, University of North Carolina Press: 1957.

more receptive to their proposals. Jones got in touch with the White House and though he failed to get an appointment with the President, he did get a promise from one of Roosevelt's aides that a letter explaining Terasaki's ideas would be shown to the President. Terasaki wrote one on the spot and it was telephoned to the White House and taken down by a stenographer. In it the Japanese First Secretary said, in part:

"We Japanese have been four years at war. When one is in a war mentality he cannot think straight. The Allies were in a war mentality at the close of the last war, and made a bad peace. You help us from a war mentality to a peace mentality. Don't *compel* us to do things, but make it *possible* for us to do them. If you treat us this way, we will meet you more than halfway. If you stretch out one hand, we will stretch out two. Then we can not only be friends, we can be allies." [4]

That Roosevelt read the letter and took note of it became evident later that day, when he received Kurusu for a talk about the situation. The "psychology" of the administration in Tokyo formed a major topic of the conversation, and Kurusu was delighted. Later that day he called Terasaki into his office, carefully closed the door and said:

"You have suggested that I be a national traitor. How about being one yourself? I think we should approach the President through an intermediary, someone who has the President's ear, and suggest he send a cable directly to the Emperor appealing for peace. I must warn you that I have already asked permission of Tojo to do this, and have been ordered not to. The cable must be sent over Tojo's head direct to tenno heika."

Terasaki agreed to take the risk, and contacted Doctor Jones again, asking him to meet him but to tell no one except his co-worker, Doctor Robinson, about it. Mrs. Terasaki booked them a private room at a Washington restaurant called the Purple Iris, and there Jones (who had just come from the Chinese ambassador, whom he had urged not to block Japanese-American negotiations) agreed to use his influence with the President, and try to persuade him to send a personal cable to the Emperor.

Once more a White House aide agreed to get a note into Roosevelt's hands without delay, and once more Terasaki sat down to write it. He

[4] *Ibid.*

250

pointed out that the Emperor rarely interfered in state affairs, but that when he did so everyone was forced to listen, "even the War Ministry." This time, Doctor Jones assumed the responsibility of authorship of the note but insisted, at the same time, that there was a vital postscript missing from the message which could only be delivered by him personally and could not possibly be written down.

He was called to the White House to deliver his oral afterthought on December 3, 1941, being instructed to come in at the East Gate so as to attract least attention.

Mrs. Terasaki writes:

"The President told Doctor Jones: 'Two days before I got your note, I thought of sending the cable, but I hesitated to do it because I didn't want to hurt the Japanese here by going over their heads to the Emperor.' Doctor Jones replied:

"'Mr. President, that is the purpose of my visit. I have come to tell you that this suggestion of sending the cable did not come from me but from the Japanese Embassy. They have asked me to ask you to send the cable. But obviously they could not let me write that because there can be no written record, since they are going over the heads of their Government to the Emperor.'

"'Then that wipes my slate clean. I can send the cable,' Roosevelt then said." [5]

Jones then urged the President not to send the cable to the Emperor in the same way as, he believed, Roosevelt had sent one to him at the time of the *Panay* crisis.

"They told me that the reason you got no reply to that one," said Jones, "was that it never reached Hirohito, because it was held up in the Foreign Office. This time you must not send it through the Foreign Office, but direct to the Emperor himself. I don't know the mechanics of it, but that's what they suggest."

Roosevelt replied:

"I'm just thinking out loud. But I can't just go down to the cable office and say: 'I want to send a cable from the President of the United States to the Emperor of Japan,' can I?"

It is a pity that he didn't. If it had been as simply and straightfor-

[5] *Ibid.*

wardly worded as that, it might have reached its destination—and in time for the Emperor to do something about it. As it was, the all-important cable went astray.

December 1, 1941, was a bad day for the Japanese Intelligence Services.[6] They learned that one of their planes flying to Japanese Army Headquarters in China had crashed in Chiang Kai-shek territory. Aboard was an Intelligence major carrying in his briefcase information which a shrewd interpreter would realize indicated that Japan was about to make war on America and Britain. If the briefcase survived intact and its contents cabled to Washington or London, the cat would be out of the bag —and Japan's surprise attack anticipated by one from the Allies.

The following day, therefore, Admiral Nagano, the Navy Chief of Staff, was received in audience by the Emperor. He was accompanied by General Sugiyama, the Army Chief of Staff. They had decided to inform Hirohito that they had chosen December 8, 1941 (December 7th, American time) as the date for the opening of hostilities. They warned him at the same time that there was a danger of the United States anticipating them with an act of war of their own, and that December 8th was the latest possible date for action.

There has been an unwritten rule of silence until this moment as to how much the Emperor knew about the Pearl Harbor attack before it happened; and there has been a tendency to presume that, like most members of his Cabinet,[7] he was ignorant of it until after it was over. So long as rancor and hatred still existed against the Japanese over what Roosevelt called "the day of infamy," it was perhaps natural that efforts were made by the Japanese to dissociate their Emperor from the event. Hirohito is an honest man, and he has never denied that he knew about Pearl Harbor beforehand. But neither has he been allowed to admit that he did know about it. The Pearl Harbor attack has, until recently, been regarded as the supreme act of treachery and no words were vile enough to describe its perpetrators. The facts which are available today indicate that it was not, perhaps, such a "day of infamy" as it seemed. The dastardly Japanese villain made lots of warning noises before he broke

[6] It would have been a worse one had they known that their American counterparts were reading their code messages.

[7] Tojo and Admiral Shimada, the Minister of Marine, were the exceptions.

into the American maiden's bedroom, and there was really no excuse for her having left her chastity belt undone.

So the taint of treachery (as will be seen) need no longer cling to all those who were associated with Pearl Harbor, and there is thus no need for his protectors to insist that he knew nothing about it. They will still not confirm that he did, of course. But the indications have always been that *he knew*. For instance, at their audience on December 2, 1941, Nagano and Sugiyama pointed out that the night of December 8th (December 7th, American time) would be most propitious for their purposes. There would be reasonable moonlight from midnight to dawn, enabling their ships and planes to get close to the target. They also mentioned that the date they had chosen would be a Sunday, a day during which the Americans were apt to relax and when they would least expect to be attacked, when their warships would be in port and their personnel on leave.

Since December 8th, the day they mentioned, would be a Monday in Tokyo, the reference to the day being Sunday at the place where they planned to attack must, by itself, have alerted Hirohito to the fact that the target lay on the other side of the Pacific—beyond the International Date Line. And where else could that be but the great American naval base at Hawaii? It seems most unlikely that at this, and subsequent meetings, he did not ask; but if indeed he did not, then the Emperor surely must have guessed where his fleet was going.

At the meeting on December 2nd, Admiral Nagano, having explained that December 8th was the only appropriate day, asked for Imperial permission to confirm to the armed forces that this, indeed, would be the day. Hirohito signified his assent. He also made it clear—as he did subsequently to both Tojo and Togo—that "due notice should be given to the enemy before any belligerent move was made."

The Chiefs of Staff withdrew. That afternoon a cable was sent in code to Admiral Yamammoto, at sea with the Japanese fleet. It said simply:

"Ascend Mount Niitaka! 1208."

In the matter of crises and great events, the Japanese almost always thought in terms of mountains. Mount Niitaka was the highest peak in Japan and to reach it summed up the height of Japanese ambition. The code message meant: "December 8th has been selected as X-Day! Attack as planned!"

253

And attack as planned they did.

That part of the operation went through without a hitch. The fleet sailed to the rendezvous, ready to inflict at Pearl Harbor what Admiral Yamammoto called "the Waterloo of the war to follow." The radio operators tuned in for the signal—a simple message, merely "to-to-to"—that would mean that the operation was on, and the bomb-ready planes should make for their target. They were well rehearsed and ready.

But meanwhile, in both Tokyo and Washington, the Japanese civilians were getting themselves into a hopeless mess.

It will be remembered that both the Emperor and Togo, the Foreign Minister, had insisted that the armed forces give the enemy due warning, and to this the Chiefs of Staff had reluctantly agreed. But how long? At first they agreed to give the United States a warning of an hour. Then they looked up The Hague Convention and noted that no specific time limit was mentioned in this document; so they lopped thirty minutes off this, giving America thirty minutes' notice only. Since the reading of the note the Japanese planned to send would take about fifteen minutes to peruse and absorb, this would give the Americans at the most fifteen minutes to alert all stations, far too short a time to reach most of them overseas. But at least the Japanese would have obeyed the letter if not the spirit of the Convention.[8]

But through sheer idiocy and incompetence, even this scanty warning was not given. Togo writes:

"Another unpleasant incident, however, I cannot escape considering— the delay in the delivery of our final Note. The time of presentation having been decided [to Secretary of State Cordell Hull personally in Washington at one P.M. Sunday December 7th, Washington time] at the Liaison Conference, I instructed the bureau director in charge and the Chief of the Cable Section to use the utmost care to take measures such that our Ambassadors in Washington might without fail have the notification for delivery at the designated time. That those measures were in fact taken pursuant to my instructions is clear if we retrace the steps in the process."

Togo describes the sequence as follows:

---

[8] It should be noted, however, that in the case of Britain the Japanese did not even try to send notification. No note or ultimatum was sent at all. Japanese troops began operations against Khota Baru in Malaya an hour before the Pearl Harbor deadline.

"The Foreign Ministry transmitted to the Embassy [in Washington] on the afternoon of December 6th the instruction that as soon as the long note which followed had been received, the Embassy should make all necessary preparations, documentary and otherwise, so that it could serve the note on the United States Government *at any time upon receipt of further instructions.*[9] The text of the note was divided for transmission into fourteen parts, of which all with the exception of the fourteenth, consisting of the last several lines of the note, were dispatched from Tokyo Central Telegraph Office between 6:30 A.M. and 10:20 A.M. December 6th."

Togo uses Washington times throughout in his explanation, and goes on:

"The fourteenth part [and this was the vital one] was cabled between 3:00 A.M. and 4:00 A.M. on December 7th. To ensure safe receipt, it was sent by two routes. Finally, the instruction to make delivery of the note [to Cordell Hull] at one P.M. on the 7th was dispatched at 3:30 A.M. of that day, also by two routes. All these telegrams duly arrived at Washington and were received by the Embassy there [and] there was a sufficiency of time for deciphering and typing."

There was indeed. But from the moment the cables were delivered to the Embassy, things began to go wrong. In fact, so far as the Japanese in Washington are concerned, the last hours of peace were devoted to activities which can only be described as pure farce. Out in the Pacific the Imperial Japanese fleet was headed for Hawaii and the planes aboard the aircraft carriers were revving up and preparing for action. In the Japanese Embassy, the senior staff were behaving like dolts.

On Saturday evening (December 6th, Washington time) the first thirteen parts of the all-important note arrived and were sent down to the code room for deciphering. But after decoding the first nine parts,[10] the staff in the coding room adjourned. One of the Embassy staff was being posted to a new station, and there was to be a farewell party for him.

One wonders what can have been in the minds of Kurusu and Nomura

[9] Togo, *op. cit.* My italics—L.M.
[10] The note, incidentally, was dispatched in coded English and not Japanese, to save time. But the code room staff were lucky to have been able to decipher it at all. They had taken an earlier message instructing them to destroy one code machine to mean both, and were only just saved in time from wrecking their only means of decoding cables.

255

(and Terasaki, for that matter) in letting them go. All of them knew even before the note started to arrive that the sands of peace were trickling away. They had burned their code books. They had destroyed a cryptograph machine. They were trying desperately to persuade Roosevelt to send a last plea to the Emperor to preserve the peace. They must have realized, therefore, that the Note now coming over the cable wires from Tokyo was of agonizingly urgent importance. Yet they let the party go on, and they gave their code room staff permission to attend it.

Saké flowed freely. The Japanese head is notoriously susceptible to alcohol, and soon brains became woozy, in no condition to wrestle with the intricacies of a top secret code.

It was nearly ten on the evening of Saturday, December 6th, when they returned to the Embassy to resume work on the note. They were afterward to maintain that all of them were quite sober, and that they worked with such dispatch that they had finished the first thirteen parts of the note by midnight. But if their condition was one of sobriety, all the more mystery about what happened next.

Foreign Minister Togo had warned the Embassy in his earlier message that this was to be a note of urgent import. He had warned that the first thirteen parts would be sent early and the vital fourteenth part later. He had also instructed the Embassy to allow the note to be typed out *only by personnel with top security clearance.* This meant the elimination of the Embassy staff of typists, who did not possess the necessary clearance. One would have thought that the ambassadors, galvanized by the obvious significance of what was happening, would have rounded up a typist or typists with the necessary security qualifications and got them to work typing out the parts of the Note as they came in and were decoded.

Not a bit of it. The decoded thirteen parts lay around the cipher room all night while the cipher clerks waited for the arrival of the fourteenth section. The hours passed and still it did not arrive. Finally (and one must remember that the Embassy must have known this was a critical moment) the counsellor appears to have decided that part fourteen was not coming after all, and sent all but one duty clerk home to bed. The Embassy closed down for the night!

It was not until seven o'clock on Sunday morning, December 7th (Washington time) that the fourteenth section of the note arrived. Pearl Harbor was six and a half hours away. Since this final paragraph was the one in which the Japanese Government formally broke off negotiations with the United States, it had been held back by Tokyo until the last possible moment—in case of leakage.

This fourteenth part was followed by two other cables, both of top priority caliber. One was the message from Togo instructing the ambassadors to present the note to Cordell Hull personally at one P.M. Washington time. The other was a message of thanks to the envoys and their staff from the government for their hard work during the negotiations.

Now—at last—the Embassy heard the hiss of a burning fuse and realized that they were sitting on a bomb. Alerted by the duty officer, the cipherenes had staggered, bleary-eyed, back to duty but it was not until nearly ten A.M. on Sunday morning that the full complement was at work. The Oriental mask slipped. Panic took over. Pearl Harbor was four and a half hours away.

Kurusu telephoned the State Department and fixed an appointment with Cordell Hull for exactly one P.M.[11] Then he instructed his subordinates to prepare him at once a clean typescript of the all-important note which he was to take with him. It was one thing to ask for a typed copy, another to get one. The only Embassy official with sufficient security clearance who could also type was a junior secretary, Mr. Katsuzo Okumura, and he was strictly an amateur of the pick-and-peck order. He was handed the decoded transcripts of the first thirteen parts of the note and told to get on with it. From his apologetic demeanor in court after the war, when he was questioned about his part in the affair, it is possible to imagine the utter dismay which must have consumed him when he saw the task before him. Even without the vital fourteenth part, the note was nearly four thousand words long. He began plucking nervously at his machine, and the slow tick of doom must have been audible in his ear.

By eleven A.M. that Sunday morning (Washington time, of course) he managed by valiant endeavor to tap out a copy of the first thirteen parts. And then he made a fatal error. Instead of sending them in to the waiting ambassadors to be absorbed and assembled, he looked through them— and Japanese pride took over. Part fourteen had not yet reached him; it was still being deciphered. He decided that his first attempt on the preceding portions had not been up to his own exacting standard, and that he would lose face if he accepted them.

[11] The Secretary of State had been coming into his office regularly on Sundays since the start of the crisis.

He started to type them all over again.

The story of the last hours of peace in the Pacific is rather like a bad Western. One is tempted repeatedly to say: "Meanwhile, back at the ranch . . ."

Over in Tokyo, the cable authorities were engaged in some delaying tactics of their own. It will be remembered that Ambassador Kurusu aided and abetted by his First Secretary, Terasaki, was engaged in persuading President Roosevelt to send a personal appeal to the Emperor to intervene in a last attempt to secure peace.

Roosevelt eventually agreed, despite the objections of Cordell Hull.[12] But to send the message and ensure that it reached the target? Roosevelt said:

"If I can't send it direct from the President to the Emperor, I can at least send it to Grew. He has the right of audience to the head of the state and he can give it to the Emperor direct. If I don't hear about it within twenty-four hours, I can do something—I'll hand it to the press."

He went into conference with his advisers and prepared his message. He then sent it over to the Secretary of State with a note attached saying:

"Dear Cordell: Shoot this to Grew. I think can go in Gray code. Saves time. I don't mind if it gets picked up." [13]

There is a tendency on the part of American historians nowadays to treat Roosevelt's urgent plea to the Emperor as nothing more than a *geste*, written "for the record" and with no real belief behind it that war could be averted by its impact on the right target. This seems to me to be a disservice to Roosevelt. An imperious character himself, he was not given to tossing off futile gestures into the laps of his peers. He seriously believed that the message might well (despite the misgivings of Cordell Hull) find a formula for peace. He believed that this was a message which could break the log jam.

He wrote his message on December 5, 1941, and it was dispatched by cable to Ambassador Grew on Saturday, December 6th. To make sure (he

[12] "I felt that the Emperor, in any event, was a figurehead under the control of the military Cabinet. . . . They would therefore regard the message as our last recourse and a sign of weakness."

[13] A memorandum in the President's own hand. It seems likely that Grew had already informed him—via Konoye—that Gray code had been pierced by the Japanese.

hoped) that it did not go astray, President Roosevelt sent out a notification to the press that a personal message to the Emperor was on its way, though he gave no indication of the nature of its contents.

Like the Japanese ultimatum, it had a checkered career enroute. Once Doctor Jones and Mr. Terasaki had persuaded Roosevelt that a plea for the Emperor's cooperation might work, they faded from the picture. The cable went off. It was written in Roosevelt's most immaculate and dignified style, and it carefully eschewed polemics.

"Only in situations of extraordinary importance to our two countries need I address to Your Majesty messages on matters of state. I feel I should now so address you because of the deep and far-reaching emergency which appears to be in formation. Developments are occurring in the Pacific area which threaten to deprive each of our nations and all humanity of the beneficial influence of the long peace between our two countries. Those developments contain tragic possibilities. The people of the United States, believing in peace and in the right of nations to live and let live, have eagerly watched the conversations between our two Governments during these past months. We have hoped for a termination of the present conflict between Japan and China. We have hoped that a peace of the Pacific could be consummated in such a way that nationalities of many diverse peoples could exist side by side without fear of invasion; that unbearable burdens of armaments could be lifted for them all; and that all peoples would resume commerce without discrimination against or in favor of any nation."

The President then went on to illuminate the situation in Indochina as Japanese forces built up, and asked the Emperor to encourage a withdrawal so as to quiet the fears of the East Indies, the Philippines, Malaya and Thailand as to Japanese intentions, and offered a reciprocal guarantee of freedom from Western interference.

He ended: "I address myself to Your Majesty so that Your Majesty may, as I am doing, give thought in this definite emergency to ways of dispelling the dark clouds. I am confident that both of us, for the sake of the peoples not only of our own great countries but for the sake of humanity in neighboring territories, have a sacred duty to restore traditional amity and prevent further death and destruction in the world."

So there it was. *A desperate, last-minute attempt to avert a tragic war,* as the headlines might have put it. *President Pleads to Emperor.* And, as we now know, if it had reached its destination, it might have worked.

Only it didn't reach its destination; and even now, no one quite knows why.

Early on the morning of December 7, 1941 (Tokyo time), Ambassador Grew . . . but first let me clarify this business of Tokyo time, Hawaii time and Washington time. Japan is on the opposite side of the International Dateline to Hawaii and the United States. Twelve o'clock noon on Wednesday in Washington is 6:30 A.M. on Wednesday in Hawaii and 2:00 A.M. Thursday in Tokyo. The attack on Pearl Harbor actually took place at 7:50 A.M. on the morning of Sunday, December 7, 1941, in Hawaii, 1:50 P.M. the same day in Washington, and 3:20 A.M. Monday, December 8th in Tokyo . . .

Ambassador Grew was listening to the short-wave radio from San Francisco and heard an announcement that President Roosevelt had sent a message to the Emperor of Japan.

It "gave no information as to its substance or the channel of transmission," wrote Grew in his diary. "Late in the evening, however, a short triple-priority telegram came from Mr. Hull saying that a telegram was then being encoded containing a message from the President which I was to communicate to the Emperor at the earliest possible moment."

But for fourteen vital hours, the telegram went astray, to use a euphemism. No one (except Cordell Hull and the State Department) knew exactly how it had been sent or addressed. Cordell Hull did not confirm with Kurusu, Nomura or Terasaki that it had been sent via Grew—and all they could do, on the President's assurance, was cable the Gaimusho in Tokyo and tell them to watch out for a cable to the Emperor. They should have known about Roosevelt's remarks and realized that the message was going via the American Embassy, but they boobed on this (no doubt because they were, at the same time, so busy making a mess of the Japanese ultimatum then coming in from Tokyo).

Where was the message? How had it been sent? What did it say?

All through the day, Grew and his aides waited for the message to arrive and inquired when it did not. At the Japanese Foreign Office, certain high officials, including Mr. Toshikazu Kase, known to be sympathetic to the West, also got ready to deal with the President's appeal. Mr. Kase has written a book about his part in the events leading up to Pacific war, but on certain matters he has been as reticent as a British Foreign Office official bound by the Official Secrets Act. One has good reason to suspect, however, that he distrusted his chief and feared that they might be tempted to suppress the President's cable. He therefore alerted his staff and contacted the central cable office in Tokyo to let him know the moment the President's cable arrived. His mistake was that he appeared to believe that it was a direct cable literally addressed to: Emperor Hirohito, The Palace, Tokyo. A pity it was not. Hirohito would have got it had it been addressed that way and forwarded it to its destination. What Kase didn't guess was that it would go via the American Embassy. The central cable office promised to let him have—at once—any telegrams addressed to the Emperor. He did not ask for telegrams addressed to the American Ambassador, and it was these (along with all other cables) that a military censor held up for fourteen hours on the vital last day before the outbreak of war.

Pearl Harbor was only two hours away when Ambassador Grew eventually received President Roosevelt's message. He immediately asked for an audience with the Emperor.

Meanwhile, in Washington . . .

Mr. Okumura was still retyping the note, and though an assistant had now been rounded up for him, he began to lose his nerve. He kept making mistakes and starting a page again. The code room continued to send in corrections, or additions, and these had to be fitted in. One imagines that the sight of the ambassadors rushing in and out of the room, desperately trying to suppress their growing dismay, must have been most unnerving of all. *Clack, clack, clack. No, that won't do. Tear it up and start again.* The Embassy that morning must have been steaming like a kettle with seething frustration.

And, of course, with humiliation, too. For face was being lost. At 12:30 P.M., when it became obvious that the note would not be ready in time, Kurusu had an aide telephone to the State Department to inform the Secretary of State that he would be "a little late."

12:45 P.M. Out in the Pacific, Admiral Yamammoto had sent his pilots on their way, and the fighters, bombers and torpedo bombers were speeding toward Pearl Harbor.

1:00 P.M. Zero hour for the presentation of the note. The Japanese had calculated that it would take Cordell Hull fifteen minutes to read it, and perhaps another five minutes to realize its significance—that this was war. He would have another twenty minutes to alert his outposts of what was coming. Hardly long enough even for the fastest cables; but the chiefs of the Japanese armed forces were not worried about that. All they wished to do was satisfy the Emperor's demand that The Hague Convention be observed and the enemy be given due warning.

But at 1:00 P.M. the note still was not ready. It was still not ready forty minutes later, when the first bombs started dropping on Pearl Harbor and the war had begun.

It was not until 2:20 P.M. on Sunday afternoon that ambassadors Kurusu and Nomura filed sheepishly into Cordell Hull's room at the State Department and handed over their note. By that time Pearl Harbor was burning.

President Roosevelt, in his address to Congress and the nation on December 8, 1941, was to describe the previous day as "the date that will live in infamy." The civilized world recoiled, appalled, from the treachery of the Japanese, who had begun dropping their bombs, as the President said, "while negotiations were still going on between our two countries."

Had he made known all the facts, his wrath might not, perhaps, have sounded so righteous and the American people might not have reacted with such indignant determination to wreak revenge. By the bungling and delay in presenting their note, the Japanese Embassy did a considerable disservice to their country, for they roused even the diehard American isolationists and appeasers against them.

For, of course, the President and the United States Government knew, hours before Ambassadors Kurusu and Nomura, that the Japanese were breaking off negotiations at one P.M. Washington time. It has been mentioned earlier in this narrative that the United States had found the key to the most secret Japanese codes and read all messages which passed between Tokyo and Washington. When the first thirteen parts of the Japanese note started coming over the cable on Saturday, December 6th, they were at once deciphered by U.S. Intelligence and copies sent to the Secretary of State and the secretaries of Army and Navy. Coming on top of the news that the Embassy had destroyed one of its two code machines and was burning papers, it was possible to guess even from the first thirteen parts what the Japanese were intending. President Roosevelt himself, reading them, told Secretary for War Henry L. Stimson:

"This means war."

While the unfortunate Mr. Okumura was still pecking away at his typewriter, the note was being studied by the Americans, and precautions were being taken accordingly. The American Army Chief of Staff, General George C. Marshall, had little doubt that the note meant war, though he had some difficulty at first in convincing his Navy counterpart, Admiral Harold R. Stark. One of Marshall's aides pointed out to him that the note was supposed to be handed over to Cordell Hull at one P.M.

"Don't you think that is significant?" he asked. "One P.M. in Washington is sunrise in Hawaii."

Marshall, after consulting with Stark, dictated an urgent cable and ordered that it be sent to San Francisco, the Philippines, Pearl Harbor and the Canal Zone. It read as follows:

"The Japanese are presenting at one P.M. Eastern Standard Time today what amounts to an ultimatum. Also they are under orders to destroy their code machine immediately. Be on the alert accordingly."

This message was sent out from Washington at twelve noon, one hour and forty minutes before the attack began, and it should not have taken more than twenty minutes to reach its destinations. There was ample time to take precautions.[14] Alas, the Americans had their dolts and dunderheads too. (Didn't we all?) The Pearl Harbor base had gone off on its usual weekend leave. Marshall's vital message did not reach the Commander until after the attack was over. "Pearl Harbor was a sentry post, and the sentry was sleeping."

True, the Japanese note was far from being a declaration of war as such. Its first thirteen parts verbosely recited all Japan's grievances. The fourteenth part said:

"The Japanese Government regrets to have to notify hereby the American Government that, in view of the attitude of the American Government, it cannot but consider that it is impossible to reach agreement through further negotiations."

But when he read it through, Cordell Hull was in no doubt of its significance. So when Kurusu and Nomura shuffled into his office at 2:20 P.M. on December 7, 1941, to hand over their sheets of amateur typing, they brought stale news.

[14] It is significant that General MacArthur, in the Philippines, had presumed on hostilities even before this warning and put his forces on a war basis that weekend.

"I made a pretense of glancing through the note," Hull wrote afterward. "I knew its contents already but naturally could give no indication of this fact."

President Roosevelt sat down to write his speech about the "date that will live in infamy." The American public rose in fury against the unscrupulous little yellow men. The war had begun in such a way that the Emperor had lost face.

"The Emperor was very angry when he learned what had happened," wrote Foreign Minister Togo later.

And what of President Roosevelt's last appeal to Hirohito?

The sad thing about it is that it was sent in Gray code, which President Roosevelt knew the Japanese could read. It was a message appealing for peace, and therefore why not let the purpose of it filter through? Who cared if it could be read? It only made America's anxiety for a settlement more plain.

Unfortunately, the very fact that the Gray code was used defeated the President's purpose. If he had sent it in *plain English* the military censorship would have felt bound to send it through, knowing its source and its destination, and knowing that it could not produce any excuse for delaying a message of such purport. If it had been sent in a *top priority code* they would not have been able to read it, and would have sent it on. But since it was in Gray code—which they could read, but didn't know that the Americans knew that they could read—they first deciphered it and then referred it to their Army chiefs. Tojo, during his interrogation before the International Military Tribunal, Far East, professed complete ignorance of the existence of the presidential cable until after it reached the American Embassy. This may be true. Foreign Minister Togo also said that he didn't know about it until too late. This may also be true. For both of them, it was also extremely convenient, as will be seen.

The truth was that since the beginning of December, the military censorship at the Tokyo cable office had been holding up all foreign cables. On December 4th, they began to alternate the delays—holding back messages for four hours on one day and ten hours for the next. Saturday, December 6th, when Roosevelt's cable was in transit, was one of the ten-hour-delay days. But this applied only to ordinary foreign cables. Incoming diplomatic cables were exempt. It is too late now to produce any proof, but one feels that only the fact that the President's

264

message was read by the Army censor and referred to the Army High Command—both of whom didn't realize that the Americans knew the code was vulnerable—stopped them from sending it through.

For the appeal would, of course, have been a considerable embarrassment. Arriving in good time, it could not have failed to have produced a positive reaction from Hirohito. His zeal for peace was such that he would undoubtedly have ordered his armed forces to pause. It was not too late. The Japanese fleets steaming towards Pearl Harbor, Malaya and the Philippines, had recall messages built in to their orders, and were ready to call the whole thing off. No one outside the Japanese High Command need ever have known. The possibility of a last-minute abandonment had been prepared for.

But what was possible twelve hours before the time planned for the attack was not possible ten hours later. If Grew had been able to present Roosevelt's appeal to the Emperor at the time it was received in Tokyo— at four o'clock on the afternoon of December 7, 1941 [15]—he would have had a good chance of persuading the Emperor to take steps. It was highly convenient for the armed forces, who were adamant against a postponement, that this leeway did not exist. From their point of view, the one thing to be desired was that the message to the Emperor should go astray. And it did.

Nevertheless, Ambassador Grew did his best, even in the short time at his disposal. But by the time he had the President's message in his hands, the odds (and the Japanese Government) were against him. He had already indicated to the Gaimusho that he wished to exercise his privilege as an ambassador extraordinary and be received by the Emperor. When the President's cable was at last in his hands, he had his aide, Doonan, telephone Tomoda, Foreign Minister Togo's secretary, and asked for an interview at once. He reached the Gaimusho about 12:30 A.M. December 8th, Tokyo time, and there read the President's message aloud to Togo, afterward asking that he be allowed to repeat it to the Emperor personally.

"The Department had left to my discretion the appropriate method of communication," Grew wrote, "and I felt it important to give it the maximum weight by asking to see the Emperor myself—and to make sure that it got to him personally. Togo at first said that he would study the docu-

---

[15] This is Tokyo time again. It will be remembered that the Pearl Harbor attack, Tokyo time, occurred at 3:40 A.M. December 8th.

ment, but when I asked if that meant some doubt as to whether he would ask for an audience for me, he replied that he would present the matter to the Throne. . . . I left him at 12:30 A.M."

Grew, of course, had no idea that the outbreak of war was only three hours away, and Togo did not enlighten him.

Togo appears to have telephoned Kido as soon as Grew left, for the Lord Keeper wrote in his diary for December 8th:

"At 12:40 A.M. Foreign Minister Togo telephoned me and said that Ambassador Grew had brought a personal telegram from President Roosevelt to the Emperor, and asked my advice as to the manner of handling same. I therefore advised him to deliberate carefully with the premier as to its diplomatic effect and procedure. Also said that with regard to an audience with His Majesty, His Majesty would graciously grant an audience even at midnight. . . . At 1:30 A.M. Matsudaira, Minister of the Imperial Household, called me up about the aforesaid matter, so I gave him my opinion. I was notified that Togo had proceeded to the Imperial Palace. I also proceeded to the Imperial Palace at 2:40 A.M."

By this time, of course, Pearl Harbor was only an hour away. Why had Togo taken so long to get to the palace with the President's message? His department, for one thing, seems to have taken an unconscionable time translating the President's message into Japanese. Then he went to see Prime Minister Tojo about it. Tojo immediately asked whether the message contained "anything new." Togo's reaction to this question was a strange one indeed. Here was the head of one state appealing to the head of another for a last-minute effort to stop war breaking out between the two of them. But to the Japanese Foreign Minister, this seemed to be of no consequence. Can he really have expected President Roosevelt, in such a message, to have enumerated specific proposals? He must have, because he told Tojo that no, the message contained nothing new, and the Prime Minister said:

"Well, then, nothing can be done, can it?"

Togo, who obviously regarded the message as nothing more than a scrap of worthless paper, remarked:

"It seems a pity to go around disturbing people in the middle of the night."

Tojo, however, looked relieved. "It's a good thing the telegram arrived late," he said. "If it had come a day or two earlier, we would have had more of a to-do."

266

It was not until three A.M. that he went into audience with Hirohito and read him the President's message. By then, of course, it was far too late, and no one knew it better than the Emperor. He was dressed in naval uniform. The planes of the Imperial Japanese fleet were already in the air and speeding for Pearl Harbor. The outbreak of war was twenty minutes away.

Would the President's appeal have done any good had it arrived in time? American historians prefer to believe that it would not.

"The nature of the Japanese decision-making process in 1941 was such that the Emperor could have intervened at the last moment only if he had been prompted to do so by the government," writes Robert C. Butow. "Presumably the influence of the throne would have been necessary to control the reaction of the fanatics to a *volte-face* in national policy. The government itself would have reconsidered its decision to use force only if the President's communication had indicated an American readiness to capitulate to Japan's demands. In such an eventuality, even the supreme command would have been willing to forego the risks and hardships of the battlefield for the enticements of the diplomatic chamber. The prestige of the throne could then have been employed against various fringe elements which might otherwise have been slow to grasp the advantages of a change in direction." [16]

But this argument ignores certain facts. It ignores a postwar statement by Tojo himself that the war would have had to be delayed if Cordell Hull's last message had been "a little more conciliatory" and the President's message had arrived "a few days earlier." It ignores the fact that Hirohito, having stopped the war once—or, at least, succeeded in postponing it—as he did after the Imperial Conference of September 6, 1941, still remained convinced that hostilities were wrong, that war with Britain and the United States was mistaken, that China should be evacuated, and that Japan would eventually lose if she decided to go to war. It was true that, during October and November, he lost heart. But if Roosevelt's message had arrived in time, he might have found it again.

After the war, when Hirohito received Doctor Stanley Jones—the Wesleyan minister who had helped to stimulate Roosevelt into sending the personal appeal—he told him frankly that "if I had received the cable-

[16] Robert C. Butow, *Tojo and the Coming of War*, New Jersey: Princeton University Press, 1961.

gram from Roosevelt a day sooner, I would have stopped the attack." [17]

It wouldn't have done any good, the historians say. But Emperor Hiro-hito still wishes that he had been given the opportunity—and encourage-ment—to try.

[17] Gwen Terasaki, *op. cit.*

Chapter Eighteen

The Emperor had put his seal to the Imperial Rescript proclaiming a state of war, and at 11:40 A.M. on December 8, 1941, it was issued to the nation. News of the success at Pearl Harbor had already spread and there were special editions of the newspapers on the streets. "The people were intoxicated with victory," wrote Kido. The Imperial Rescript had been written by Hirohito's advisers and was presented to him for his seal but not for his criticism. Nor did he have any to make. But he did insist on one addition to the wording, which he wrote out himself. It seems obvious that the insertion was a deliberate attempt on his part to indicate that the declaration of war was a decision of his ministers and not of himself, for what the extra sentence said was:

"It has been truly unavoidable and far from Our Wishes that Our Empire has now been brought to cross swords with America and Britain."

Kido was received in audience by the Emperor immediately after the Rescript was promulgated, and found him "calm and collected even though Japan was now locked in a struggle which would determine the fate of the nation." He made no secret—at least to Kido—of his distress at what had happened, and the knowledge that the ultimatum to the United States had been bungled made him both angry and humiliated. The decision to declare war on his old friends, the British, and to make enemies of the English royal family in particular, had been "heart-rending" enough without having it accompanied by an act of treachery.

But the significance of the extra sentence was for posterity and was missed by the Japanese public. What they appreciated more keenly were the phrases extolling the patience and forbearance which they had shown in the face of British and American intransigence. They nodded their heads over the paragraphs which told them that if they had waited any longer the very existence of the nation would have been in danger.

"The situation being such as it is," the Rescript concluded, "Our Empire for its existence and self-defense has no other recourse but to appeal to arms and to crush every obstacle in its path. The hallowed spirits of Our Imperial Ancestors guarding Us from above, We rely upon the loyalty and courage of Our subjects in Our confident expectation that the task bequeathed by Our Forefathers will be carried forward, and that the source of evil will be speedily eradicated and enduring peace immutably established in East Asia, preserving thereby the glory of Our Empire."

One of Japan's best known poets, Kotara Takamura caught the mood of the hour in a poem he wrote for the occasion:

> Remember December the Eighth!
> This day world history has begun anew.
> This day Occidental domination is shattered,
> All through Asia's lands and seas.
> Japan, with the help of the gods
> Bravely faces white superiority.
>
> All Japanese are soldiers now,
> Ready to fight
> Until the enemy corrects his way.
> World history has begun anew.
> Remember December the Eighth!

The poem was, in its way, a warning too. It voiced none of the jingoistic flights of venom which disfigured the Japanese press in the next few weeks. It had a built-in cautionary note to the nation that they were facing a foe with superior resources. But the people were cock-a-whoop and, as Foreign Minister Togo wrote later, "the intoxication with victory was no less apparent in the Diet, as an incident will illustrate. In February 1942 at a meeting of the Budget Committee of the House of Representatives, Uehara demanded a statement of the attitude of the Foreign Minister toward the prospects of peace. I replied that it was equally natural and necessary to stop war as to start it, and that I was consequently fully prepared and resolved to that end. This drew protests from members that the purpose of war being to destroy the enemy, the Foreign Minister should not be heard to say that he was preparing for peace, and they demanded that I retract my statement. I refused on the ground that no retraction was called for, what I had said being axiomatic. Nevertheless, even with the Cabinet there was opinion that the Representatives were right—Japan might well, if she kept on at the present pace, occupy Washington, they said—and the Premier suggested that a compromise be somehow found. It was finally decided to strike my statement from the record of the Diet proceedings—a practice not infrequently resorted to in those days." [1]

The Japanese people (and, of course, the Japanese armed forces) were convinced that the whole of Asia was now open to them. Singapore fell, and so did Hong Kong, the Netherlands Indies, and the Philippines. There were even rumors current in Asia that Britain had made an offer for peace after the fall of their Malaysian bastion. It is perhaps typical of the attitude of the Japanese toward the British that, even in a moment of triumph, they never believed that this was so. Togo wrote:

"I want to leave no room for doubt that the Japanese Government received no such offer at that time. A negative can be proved only circumstantially, but the utter implausibility of this rumor is, I think, rendered sufficiently clear by the fact alone of the British Government's having throughout the Pacific war fallen in completely with the United States design. In view of this it is impossible to believe that she should have tried to make a separate peace with Japan. The following episode, moreover, will, I believe, serve to evidence the absence of any ground for the British peace offer. When [Sir Richard] Craigie [2] was leaving for home, some time after the commencement of the war, I sent my private secretary to convey to him my regret that the Japanese-American negotiations had ended in failure and the war had ensued. I also sent him the message—asking that, if he thought appropriate, he communicate it to the British Government—that now that war had come it was to the advantage of both Parties to end it whenever either side should have lost the hope of victory. It was reported to me that the Ambassador answered that he could not convey my suggestion to his government at the mo-

[1] Shigenori Togo, *The Cause of Japan*, New York, Simon and Schuster, Inc., 1956.
[2] The British Ambassador.

271

ment, when the war was going unfavorably for Great Britain, but that he was appreciative of the intention of the Japanese Foreign Minister. I thought at the time that the Ambassador's words were quite a natural expression of the indomitableness of the Englishmen." [3]

But practically everything else was possible, and, as Togo wrote, "the successes in the initial stage of the war were, as I have indicated, spectacular." How could Japan go wrong?

In fact, however, no intelligent Japanese really believed, even while floating on the scented pink clouds of initial triumph, that Japan was going to win the war. Not by fighting it out, anyway. Those who talked of an invasion of the Hawaiian Islands and, even, the eventual occupation of Washington, were madmen living a dream. Tojo and his ministers had their blinkered view of the situation, but even they had their sights set on something more tangible than overwhelming victory. They were after less conclusive conquests which, though not overwhelming, would convince the enemy of their power and determination, and persuade them to sue for peace and consent to concessions.

Shortly after the capture of Hong Kong and Malaya, the German Ambassador to Japan, Ott, cabled his government that there were several indications that the push of the Japanese forces would be in a southerly direction. He forecast the capture of Port Darwin and the neutralization of Australasia, and told Hitler that the Japanese were wary of conquering India because they feared it would drive that country to Bolshevism.

A year after the victory at Pearl Harbor, the Japan *Times* could boast in an editorial (December 8, 1942):

"From the icy rocks of the Aleutians, across the vast expanse of the Pacific and among its countless islands, down the littoral of the Asiatic continent, through the fabled lands of the Indies to the very gates of the Antipodes, and then around into the Indian Ocean, the undisputed power of Japan has been established. The sting of Japan's lash has been felt as far afield as the mainland of America, in the harbors of Australia, off the coast of Africa, and even in the Atlantic. Over tens of thousands of miles, from the arctic to the tropics, over the seven seas and the five continents, the land has rumbled to the tread of Japan's legions and the skies have thundered to the roar of Japan's winged knights of the air."

[3] Togo, *op. cit.*

But by August of the same year, the rap of American knuckles could be heard at Japan's door. The U.S. Army landed on Guadalcanal. President Roosevelt cabled to Stalin: "We have gained, I believe, a toehold in the Southwest Pacific from which the Japanese will find it very difficult to dislodge us."

The painful, bloody, heroic and agonizing fight along the road back had begun.

For almost eighteen months after Pearl Harbor, Hirohito ceased to play any part in the affairs of his nation, except as a symbol. He was, of course, invoked in every patriotic speech. The Empress sent a message to the wife or relatives of every soldier who was killed. He journeyed to Ise to beseech his divine relative, Amaterasu, to bring victories to Japan. He sent messages of exhortation and encouragement.

And he worried. But what could he do?

Trying to piece together from the accounts of those who were with him what his wartime life was like, one gets a picture of dreadful dullness and frustration. At least outside the walls of his palace, men and women were doing something positive—dying or killing, feeling pain, making love, making money, cheating, getting drunk, exploiting patriotism, black marketeering, pandering, prostituting. The government had instituted a great campaign of puritanism to "show our sons on the battlefield that we are making sacrifices too," and, as usual in Japan, it was the respectable portion of the female sex which suffered the most from the restrictions which were introduced. They were dragooned into abandoning Western clothes or kimonos and donning a shabby smock and a sort of plus fours called mompei which did very little for their sex appeal; but since the prohibition on costume did not (at least until later) apply to geishas or to that section of the female population which needed no clothes at all during its working hours, only the housewives were turned into drabs.

There came a time when geisha houses were closed down and the ten thousand and one places of entertainment in the cities were shuttered by official order. But, like every other place in the world in wartime, this did not stop Japan from finding its fun in between its bouts of pain and horror. The Japanese who lived through the war in the homeland will mention its hardships and its agonies, but will always admit that it was never for a moment without its excitements.

273

On the other side of the moat, behind the wall of the Imperial Palace, however, Hirohito was to suffer all the hardship with none of the excitement which went with it. His advisers considered it unseemly, while his subjects were valiantly dying for him, that he should be concerning himself with crustaceans, and his laboratory was shut for the duration. Sagami Bay had been fortified and most of the houses at Hayama requisitioned for the expanding naval personnel working out of the base at nearby Yokosuka, and there were no more interludes at sea, diving for specimens. In the Imperial Palace he instituted a regime of austerity to set an example to his people, and even abandoned his beloved English breakfast of bacon and eggs; he ate brown rice instead.

So long as the Japanese armies were chalking up victories in Singapore, Malaya, Indonesia and the Philippines, Tojo's government and the militarists were content for Hirohito to remain in the background, a vague symbol of the divine purpose behind the war. The military, in any case, did not entirely trust him, for there were rumors that even as early as February, 1942, he had called in the premier and discussed with him the question of making peace. But once the tide turned—and most experts now consider the Battle of Midway, which Japan lost, as the moment when her chances of victory began to ebb—both Tojo and the armed forces saw the advantage of utilizing his prestige. They did not need him in victory, but he could prove a magic name to conjure with to persuade the people to fight on despite defeat. From Midway onward, the armed forces began to use his name and his influence as part of the campaign. It was like 1936 all over again.

An intelligence document issued by the Office of Strategic Services in 1944 called *The Emperor and the War* described the increasing invocation of the Emperor's name in all public pronouncements as part of "a deliberate policy" to "reassure the people of the sacred nature of the war, and that the Emperor's divine destiny will assure victory."

But there was another reason, too. "More fundamentally," the document went on, "the increasing use of the Emperor's name tends to make him share with the military the responsibility for the war. The firmly established identification of the Emperor with the cause and the war would tend to frustrate any attempt by the Allies to dissociate the Emperor from the military group."

To protect themselves, the militarists were even willing to risk discrediting Imperial rule and to see the very structure of Japanese polity threatened. Tojo was told to organize the royal family and get its members out into the country, visiting factories, schools and bases. Almost every week there was an expression by the Emperor of his "deep concern" about the progress of the war.

The more the Allies advanced, the more the Army sought to involve Hirohito. It was as if they were determined that, if they were smashed, the Emperor be smashed too. From 1943 onward, barely a month went by without the issuance of an Imperial Rescript exhorting the people to gird themselves for total war, assuring them in Hirohito's name of certain victory. And a few months later, at the direct behest of the Supreme Command, Tojo presented to the Emperor for his seal an Imperial Rescript which, for the first time, committed him personally to a tissue of lies. The Emperor announced to his people and commended his armed forces for their "great victory" in the battle for the Solomon and Gilbert Islands. It was, in fact, one of Japan's most decisive defeats and put the Allies well and truly forward along the road to Tokyo. But it was not until many months later that even highly placed Japanese statesmen learned the truth, and were appalled that their Emperor had been deceived into giving currency to lying propaganda. The mighty impact of the Imperial Rescript had been made suspect. As much as anything else, it was this act of corruption which turned the senior statesmen against the men who were now running their country in the Emperor's name, and theirs.

It is no part of this biography to enumerate, step by step, the triumphs of the Allies and the progressive deterioration of Japan in the war in the Pacific. I am concerned only with the Emperor's part in it, and until 1945, his was a minor role. True, his name was in large type at the top of the playbill, but the words he had to utter signified nothing.

He was well aware of this, of course. It should have become clear by this time that Hirohito was not only against the war for idealistic reasons—for he has always been philosophically antiwar—but because he simply did not believe that Japan could win it. There is evidence today[4] that for the first few weeks after the outbreak of hostilities, he seriously believed not that Japan would win the war but that she could get herself into such a dominating position that an advantageous peace could be

[4] From a former adviser who does not wish to be named.

secured. But by February, 1942, he had changed his mind, and his pessimism was reinforced by some words of Kido, who was received in audience on February 5th of that year.

"The enemy has an indomitable fighting will, though he has suffered a series of reverses," the Lord Keeper quotes himself as saying to Hirohito. "The Pearl Harbor attack has signally served not only to strengthen the feelings of hostility against Japan but also to unify the public opinion of America. Therefore the Pacific War will not easily end. The shortest way will be to fight it out but at the same time we must pay due attention to construction. No less necessary will it be to seize the occasion to return to peace as soon as possible, for the purpose of minimizing the ravages wrought by the Second World War. . . . The Army and Navy have recently vauntingly stated that they have gone through elaborate preparations and training, but it is highly problematical if the picked troops which have gone through special training can be maintained for long in the future with replacements. It is inevitable that the time will come when the differences of the resources of the contending powers counts. Full consideration should be paid by the Army and the Navy to this right now." [5]

In other words, what Kido was saying was: "We can't win."

Hirohito seems to have been so impressed by this that he talked at length about it to the Empress, who confided in turn with Baron Osanaga Kamroji, then Deputy Grand Chamberlain. It was as if, Kamroji said later, the Emperor had for the first time come face to face with the facts of the war.

There was no avoiding them in the months to come. One by one, the islands fell. Step by step, the armies retreated in Burma. By 1944, there was so little oil that training had ceased in the Air Force: there was no gas to fuel the planes. Ships were being built of wood because there was no more steel, and as they wallowed slowly across the Pacific the submarines of Britain and America were waiting for them. Food was scarce and growing scarcer. Even the fire-eating General Tojo, once so sure of victory, had gone—and been replaced by a less belligerent but much more incompetent premier, General Kumaki Koiso. It was a measure of Koiso's inability to grasp the facts of the situation that he went on record, shortly after assuming office, as saying that the Battle of Leyte,

[5] The English used is Kido's own.

276

then being fought, would decide the outcome of the war. He did not appear to be aware that Japan never had had any real chance of winning it, fanatically though the Japanese soldiers fought.

On New Year's Eve, 1944, the Cabinet under Koiso met at the Imperial Palace and faced, for the first time since 1941, the possibility that Hirohito was once more about to take an active part in their deliberations. He had been well primed by Kido and Marquis Tsuneo Matsudaira, his Lord Chamberlain, both of whom had been involved in "peace discussions" with Prince Konoye, Mr. Mamoru Shigemitsu and Admiral Okada [6] over the past few months. The Emperor had a series of questions which he desired the Cabinet to answer, and considering the politeness and circumlocutions of Japanese language and usage, they were direct in the extreme. Present at the Cabinet meeting was Mr. Toshikazu Kase, a high official of the Japanese Foreign Office, and he wrote afterward:

"The fate of the Cabinet hung in the balance in consequence of an inquiry from the throne. This took the form of a blunt question as to what General Koiso meant to do toward retrieving the deteriorating situation both at home and abroad. The Emperor said he could not understand why, in spite of the Prime Minister's repeated assurances that Leyte would be effectively defended, there now remained, it seemed, small chance of holding it against growing enemy pressure. The Emperor pointed out that although the Prime Minister frequently and frantically exhorted the nation to stake everything on Leyte in order to make a last stand there, the battleground was now shifting to Luzon, endangering the Philippines as a whole. Would not the nation, he asked, be shocked to learn the desperate situation? Would not the people's disillusionment result in the deterioration of morale, thus hampering the production of war material which was already falling far short of expectations? What measures did General Koiso contemplate for coping with such a dire eventuality?" [7]

It might have been as well if the people *had* known the truth of the situation, but they did not. An iron control of the press and radio by the armed forces and a rigid censorship saw to that. As for measures which Koiso might contemplate for restoring the situation, the Emperor knew only too well that the old man had no answers for him. As long as the Army had an iron grip over the nation, and as long as they could bam-

---

[6] The same Okada who had so narrowly escaped assassination in 1936.

[7] Toshikazu Kase, *Journey to the Missouri*, New Haven, Conn.: Yale University Press, 1952.

boozle the nation into believing in victory, there was nothing he or the Cabinet could do. It was only outside the Cabinet (in the private parlors of the elder statesmen and Court officials) that moves could be made which might start an impetus toward peace. The intervention of Hirohito was his way of letting it be known that he was no longer content to fret in the background. It was in this way that his intervention was important. He was announcing his intention to participate in the affairs of the nation once more—and there seemed a good chance that this time there would be no hesitation and irresolution, as there had been in 1941.

New Year's Day, 1945.

As Hirohito returned from family prayers that morning the sickly sweet scent of smoke drifted across the gardens of the Imperial Palace, from bodies and buildings burning across the city. The Flowers of Edo (as the people of Tokyo called their frequent fires) were blooming again, with the same fierceness and savagery as they had during the days of the Great Earthquake. The bombers had been over the night before, and Tokyo was ablaze.

For if the Supreme Command could keep from the people the dire facts of Japan's strategic situation, they could not conceal from them the truth of what was happening at home. For two months now the B-29 bombers of the United States Air Force (the Bi-ni-ju-ku, as the Japanese called them) had been visiting the Japanese homeland and meeting little opposition, for the air defenses were puny. A combination of Japanese optimism and fatalism had persuaded the High Command that the enemy's planes would never get through in any serious force. True, there had been the Doolittle raid from an aircraft carrier early in the war, but it had wrought little damage; and those Japanese who had been terrified by the appearance of the American bombers had been appeased by what seemed to them—despite the outraged protests of the Allies—the condign punishment which had been meted out to them. The pilots and crews captured after the Doolittle raid had been tried for murder, and a number of them executed. The masses were persuaded that this would teach the white barbarians a lesson, and they would not come again.[8]

---

[8] The Japanese continued to execute enemy fliers as murderers until as late as June, 1945. Each death sentence was "confirmed" by the Emperor and a number of condemned air crew were reprieved in his name. In fact, the decision was usually taken by the War Minister in consultation with the High Command.

But since September, 1944, they had been regular visitors. The incendiary bombs rained down, and the houses burned like tinder. They would burn even more disastrously in the days to come. Since 1942 the government had begun building great towers in all parts of the city. They were called churei kensho-to (or War Dead Towers) and were memorials to the fallen. Yoshio Kodama wrote about them:

"With the material used for the construction of churei kensho-to antiaircraft emplacements could be constructed in all the cities of Japan." He suggested this to the High Command and "immediately incurred the displeasure of the Japanese military. . . . However, when huge formations of B-29's began to raid and bomb the principal cities, only Tokyo, Nagoya and Osaka were provided with flak defenses and other cities did not even have an antiaircraft gun. This was, of course, not due to War Dead Towers alone, but the point is that the highest military leaders of Japan could not understand the glaring, self-evident truth that museum-piece war memorials could not defend Japan's cities against enemy planes. This inability of the military to grasp such fundamental and common-sense facts was due to their illusions of self-grandeur." [9]

Kase echoed the mood in an entry in his diary for Monday, January 1, 1945:

"Fine weather. Early in the morning a small number of planes raided the Tokyo area. Toward the direction of Ueno the sky was ablaze with fire. Poor helpless people rendered homeless on New Year's Day! This is the year of decision. This year will see the end of the war both in Europe and Asia. Sad though it is, we must face realities squarely. We have lost the war."

Kase had been to a meeting that day with Admiral Okada and Matsudaira, Kido's secretary, and their general pessimism about the future had convinced them that some drastic action must be taken soon if chaos and (as Konoye believed) communism was not to take over in Japan.

"Defeat now stares us stark in the face," wrote Kase. "There is only one question left: how can we avert the chaos attendant upon a disastrous defeat and how shall we seek the reconstruction of Japan, so defeated? The preservation of my Fatherland, that is the paramount task assigned to me by fate. The hostile attack is developing so surprisingly swiftly that it may be diplomacy cannot intervene before it is too late. I shudder

[9] Yoshio Kodama, *I was Defeated*, Tokyo: Booth & Fukada, 1951.

to think of such an eventuality. I must therefore redouble my efforts to expedite the restoration of peace."

Kase, who had some influential friends, resolved on that New Year's Day: 1) to cultivate closer contact with Kido and with the jushin (senior statesmen); 2) secure friends in the Army who would collaborate with him secretly; 3) enlighten public opinion through wider exchange of views with politicians, publicists and press representatives.

"Chances are that the reorientation of our policy is yet feasible," he wrote. "If so, the nation will escape annihilation. Even so, it will probably be accompanied by civil disturbances. Much blood will flow—and who knows that mine, too, will not be spilt? I do not, of course, hesitate to sacrifice my life for the cause of the country. On the contrary, I consider it my privilege. But I do not like to die meaninglessly. I must hold on to my life tenaciously in order to exert my utmost efforts to save my country and people. That, in short, is my New Year's Day prayer." [10]

Kase was not the only one who thought that the elder statesmen might have some ideas for extricating Japan from her situation. The Emperor's mind was working in the same direction. His brother, Prince Chichibu, had been ill for some time and had been moved to a country palace near Hakone, not far from Mount Fuji, but he wrote frequently to Hirohito at this time, giving his ideas on the situation. He too by this time felt that the war was lost and believed it was time for peace feelers to go out across the Pacific. But he warned the Emperor that the situation was fraught with danger should the approach be too recklessly made, if the efforts leaked out too soon, and if the utmost precautions were not taken to keep news of any negotiations from "unsympathetic" Army elements. He advised his brother to consult the jushin and find out if these "men of great experience and calmness of judgment" could not find a way across the lava fields to firmer ground. [11]

Prince Chichibu obviously rarely or never attended a meeting of the elder statesmen, for he would otherwise hardly have called them men of "calm judgment." Reading through their discussions during times of emergency is a disheartening proof of the charge that a Japanese can speak for forty minutes about a question requiring a specific answer, and leave you at the end unsure whether he has said yes, no or maybe. The accounts of Imperial conferences at which they spoke reported pathetic

[10] Kase, op. cit.
[11] Information supplied by one who does not wish to be identified.

indecision. Nevertheless, the Emperor told Kido on January 6, 1945, that he felt it urgently necessary to summon an Imperial conference of the jushin to give him guidance, and it was rather like asking the veteran members of a home for the blind to lead him across a minefield.

Perhaps Kido was of this opinion too. At any rate, he persuaded Hirohito to call the elder statesmen separately rather than together, on the grounds that this would arouse less suspicion among the military; and this the Emperor agreed to do. He saw them all in turn during the early part of February, and it could hardly be said that, one conversation aside, they gave him much enlightenment. Former premier Wakatsuki at one moment suggested that Japan should extricate herself from the war before either the Japanese people or the enemy realized that they were defeated; and then changed his mind and said that of course Japan must fight on until the enemy was convinced that she would never give in. General Tojo was as bombastic as ever. What did the air raids matter? They were only light ones and America was in no position to increase them, nor was she capable of increasing the rate or strength of her counteroffensive.[12] He thought the war was going reasonably well.

The Emperor asked him what about Russia? Tojo thought that there was an even chance of keeping the Soviet Union out of the war. And anyway, what did it matter if she did come in? She was too busy fighting Germany to spare any large forces. No, things were not too bad. The worst enemy Japan faced was defeatism. He said the people needed inspiring. An Imperial Rescript spurring them on would be the best idea. "With determination, we can win!" he told the Emperor, and with a clank of spurs, bowed his way out of the room.

Mr. Hirota, who had preceded Tojo, was even more hopeless. He thought that the American people were flagging, and that Roosevelt wanted to get out of the war both with Germany and Japan. Otherwise, why had the President made Stettinius, whose grandfather was a German, and Grew, who was a friend of Japan, members of his Cabinet?

Prince Konoye was the only statesman consulted who calmly and straightforwardly admitted—alas—sigh—that the war was lost. But far from counselling the Emperor to start overtures for peace before it was too late, he cautioned him to do nothing precipitate. He had brought with

[12] The High Command seems to have briefed him on these matters. When the assault on Okinawa was made later, they were dumbstruck. It had come at least a month before they expected it.

him a long memorandum [13] in which he maintained that the greatest danger Japan faced was not defeat in the war but the usurpation of the national polity by a communist *coup d'état* on the part of the younger elements in the Army. "Since Japan's professional military men—at least a majority," he wrote, "hail from families below the middle class, their whole environment of life has been such that it is easy for them to fall prey to communist doctrine. At the same time, however, their military education has thoroughly inculcated them with the spirit of our national polity. The communist element, therefore, is endeavoring to captivate these militarists with the claim that the national polity and communism can stand side by side."

Konoye maintained that before any peace moves were started the Army must be purged of its fanatics, but he had no answer as to how this should be done. The Emperor mildly suggested that possibly the only way would be for the Japanese Army to win a considerable victory. This would bolster the reputations of the military leaders and enable them to suppress the rebels in their ranks.

But where were the victories to come from? All the Japanese armed forces were experiencing now were defeats. He sighed.

> Sublime is the moment,
>> When the world is at peace
> And the limitless deep
>> Lies bathed in the morning sun.

It was a verse the Emperor had once written, and this (he told Konoye) was the moment when he thought of it again.

[13] In the preparation of which Mr. Shigeru Yoshida, a postwar premier of Japan, had collaborated.

Chapter Nineteen

On May 25, 1945, the Imperial Palace in Tokyo burned down—or, at least, many of its buildings and pavilions were completely destroyed by fire. There had been a heavy raid on Tokyo the night before and fire bombs had gushed down upon Marunouchi and Chiyoda-ku, two districts abutting the palace, setting all but the old Meiji brick buildings aflame.

Just before dawn the Emperor and Empress, who had spent the night in the air raid shelter built beneath the palace grounds, were warned that the conflagration, for the first time since the bombing began, had encroached on Imperial territory. The central administration building was ablaze and so was the small wood surrounding the Empress's pavilion; and the flames were spreading fast.

"We have been bombed at last!" Hirohito said. "At least now the people will realize that I am sharing their ordeal with no special protection from the gods." [1]

In fact, the palace had not been bombed at all. Flames from the burning buildings around it, flying debris and drifting paper, had leaped the moat and set fire to the dry brushwood on the other side of the wall, and it was from this that the flames spread and engulfed the palace buildings. Fire squads from the city and the palace fire wardens fought the flames for nearly fourteen hours before getting them under control, and in that time twenty-eight members of the palace staff died. [2]

[1] From a former palace official who does not wish to be identified.
[2] They included a dozen palace firemen in the forecourt of the administration building. They could easily have escaped but no one gave them direct orders, and they died at their posts.

283

The rumor spread through the city that the palace was aflame, and that the Allies had decided to include the Emperor in the targets which they were now attacking. But when the truth was discovered, the Emperor quickly countermanded an announcement which the government propaganda department planned to issue which was designed to whip up resentment against the barbarians who dared to attack him. He insisted that the facts be made known to the people—that he had not been bombed, but that he had been burned. He could hardly explain to them the irony of the situation—that he had been informed, through neutral sources, that the palace would be regarded as forbidden ground by the B-29's and left alone, and that he had let it be known that he resented any special treatment, and would prefer to share the bombs with his people.

The Allies, of course, had no intention of bombing the Emperor, even though there was some agitation—in Britain, America and Australia—for reprisal raids against him. The mere fact that the palace buildings caught afire was of some embarrassment to the strategists at MacArthur's headquarters, where there was certainly no desire to incinerate the Emperor. And not because he was so greatly admired and respected above his fellow countrymen by the Allied strategists.

"The point has been advanced in some quarters," wrote Joseph C. Grew in 1944, "that merely by bombing the Imperial residence we would rid the Japanese people of the myth of the invincibility of the Emperor and of his alleged protection by the sun goddess, and that the Emperor would thereby lose caste and be discredited in the eyes of the people. This in my opinion is a very shortsighted view, and a view based upon an inadequate understanding of Japanese psychology. On the contrary, I believe that such an act on our part would weld the Japanese people together more firmly than ever in a solid wall of hatred, and would rally all shades of opinion against us." [3]

Hirohito was astute enough to make use of the blazing palace as a reminder that he was there beside his people, sharing their hardships, while at the same time absolving the Allies from a deliberate attempt to kill him.

But how, how, how to get out of the war?

[3] General Doolittle told Grew that he had been encouraged, during his carrier-borne raid on Tokyo, to bomb the Emperor's Palace, but had refused. "A most fortunate decision," said Grew.

Everything was going wrong now. Premier Koiso had resigned office at last after nine months of footling and futile attempts to pretend that he was in command of the situation, when he knew only too well that the military were his masters and were calling the tune.[4] The ring was closing round Japan. American bomber bases were now so close that round-the-clock bombing of the Japanese mainland was possible, and there was hardly a fighter plane or ackack gun left to make a pretense of defense. Food supplies were running down and starvation-diseases were spreading. The Imperial Japanese Navy, which had once so proudly sailed to seek battle, had now practically no surface vessels left and was almost out of oil.

The armed forces were now relying on nothing more than "a wing and a prayer" to pull them through. One of Hirohito's more melancholy duties at this time was to take the salute at a parade of kamikaze pilots. The planes were old and were filled with only enough fuel for a one-way trip. They were loaded with explosives and their inexperienced young pilots were instructed to crash them into the ships of the Allied navies in a series of desperate suicide attacks. This was the kamikaze, or Divine Wind, which was supposed to save the Japanese Empire from destruction in 1945, as it had done in 1281, when Amaterasu sent it to blow away from Japan the invading fleets of Kublai Khan.

As he looked at the brave young men going out to die, what could the Emperor say except the words Admiral Onishi (father of the kamikaze corps) proudly repeated to his eager boys:

"Your divine Emperor said to me: 'Was it necessary to go to this extreme? They certainly do a magnificent job.'"

In two sentences it summed up the magnificent futility of the enterprise.

These airborne charm bracelets and a nation-wide issue of bamboo spears were to save the Japanese, if not from annihilation, then from the shame of defeat. Led by such characters as Onishi and General Anami, an Army fanatic, the cry of national seppuku was being raised. Japan must not give in. Japan must wait for the invader to arrive and meet him on

[4] To do him justice, it must be admitted that he did try on several occasions to take charge; and his resignation was, in the end, mainly due to his failure to be given the dual role of premier and Minister of War. As War Minister he would, of course, have had access to military information denied him as premier.

the shore with bamboo spears. Ten million people willing to die would turn the tide and wash the enemy away. It was as simple as that. All that was necessary was that the volunteers, willing to die for the Emperor, should come forward.

In fact, as Hirohito knew only too well, they were dying already in the thousands without even being asked to give their lives. The raid which had set fire to his Imperial Palace had been a heavy one, but it was a night attack of a few weeks earlier which had demonstrated to all with eyes to see the flames, ears to hear the shrieks and groans, and noses to smell the reek of burning flesh what was in store for Japan as long as she fought on.

Of that raid, which inflicted more damage in one night with 139 B-29 bombers, than the Nagasaki atom bomb, Kodama wrote:

"Out of the dark night a shower of incendiary bombs fell to the earth, riding a stiff wind which was blowing in Tokyo that night. A fountain of brilliant sparks rose skyward and in no time the city was in a welter of belching smoke and roaring flames, the incarnation of purgatory itself. The nation experienced the horrors of night bombing for the first time. In one night the major part of the city was transformed into a vast plain of scorched earth, and 200,000 citizens of Tokyo had become seared corpses."

Some pathetic attempts were made after this raid to organize some sort of civil defense, "but in face of this first large-scale air raid," Kodama wrote, "the government had had nothing prepared, no countermeasures formulated; there were neither relief facilities nor even crematoriums where the bodies of the dead could be disposed of. This because the Government had not been able to imagine the effects of such an air raid and led the people into false security by making them believe that they could cope with incendiary bombs with crude pumps and buckets of water."

Into this succession of ordeals by fire came Admiral Kantaro Suzuki as the new Prime Minister with the task of saving the nation. It was no time for a Churchill to take over the premiership, for Japan was long since past the moment when the call to blood, sweat and tears could be calculated to save them. What was needed was a leader with a forthright sense of purpose and a cool appreciation of the desperation of the situation. If Winston Churchill had been a win-the-war premier when he took over the British nation in 1940, Admiral Suzuki should have been the win-the-peace premier who extricated his people from their agonies in 1945. A strong hand and a clear head were needed to control the armed forces and calm the people while the nation embarked on negotiations. It must be made clear to everyone that there was no hope. Germany was out of the war. The Allies were free to concentrate all their might upon Japan; and might be joined at any moment by Russia. Peace—any sort of peace—was needed now if the nation was not to be torn to shreds.

The amazing thing is that Suzuki, in accepting the mandate from the Emperor did not understand that this was what he was expected to achieve. *He was there to make peace.* Nor did Kido or any of the senior statesmen who recommended him to the Emperor tell him that this was his duty. "Not, at any rate," Kido said afterward, "in so many words."

He presumed that Suzuki was so well aware of the situation that he must realize that this was the only thing he must do, and quickly. But he over-estimated the intelligence of this shy, timid, amiable, lame and deaf old man. So did Hirohito—for he too had accepted Suzuki as the apostle of peace, and was giving him the mandate to form a government for that purpose.

The old man explained to his sovereign that he was an old man un-schooled in politics, and nowadays so deaf that he feared that he would never be able to hear the instructions which His Majesty might give him. The Emperor (perhaps because he had learned to make himself audible to Ambassador Grew) cheerfully reassured him, and said:

"Your unfamiliarity with politics is of no concern, nor does it matter that you are hard of hearing. Accept this command."

Judge the astonishment of the Emperor, therefore—and of the elder statesmen too—when Suzuki hobbled in front of the Diet a few days later to rally that ignorant and corrupt body of stooges with a militant speech telling them that unconditional surrender was out of the question, that peace under such terms would mean the destruction of Japan and the Imperial system, and that Japan had only one choice—*to fight to the very end.*

He preceded this with a call to the people, telling them that he had come forth prepared to give up his life to defend the Emperor and the State. "Should my services be rewarded by death," he said, "I expect the hundred million people of this glorious Empire to swell forward over

287

my prostrate body and form themselves into a shield to protect the Emperor and this Imperial land from the invader!"

It was definitely *not* what anyone had expected.

When you ask the statesmen who survived those times why Japan did not surrender at the time of the German capitulation, they still do not cite Suzuki's bombastic ignorance for the reason, but put the blame on the fanatic intransigence of the military. "The answer is that we could not," wrote Kase. "The domineering militarists were still directing our national destiny at their pleasure, and they stubbornly refused to entertain for a moment the thought of giving up the struggle. Yet it was unmistakably clear that even their confidence was being rapidly undermined. Germany was gone. . . . It was only common sense that continuing the war would be entirely futile. Yet the military wanted to carry on. The military position was indeed desperate. . . . Although defeat stared them in the face, [the military leaders] frantically exhorted the people to brace themselves for the final struggle. If they themselves were to perish, the nation might as well perish with them."

But this is exactly what Suzuki, the head of the civil government, was telling the people too, at the very moment when he should have been preparing them for capitulation. With almost senile complacence, he caused to be issued, on the day following Germany's collapse, an official statement saying:

"The surrender of Germany, which had pledged to fight as one with Japan, is indeed regrettable. Our war aims are based on self-existence and self-defense. This being the unshakeable faith of Japan, the dire change in the European situation will not cause the slightest change here."

To those elements around the Emperor who saw hope for Japan's survival only in a swift end to hostilities, it became hourly more evident that in choosing Suzuki to stamp out the fire they had picked a man who just liked spreading sparks. Kido compared notes with one of his old friends, Mamoru Shigemitsu, a former member of the Tojo and Koiso Cabinets,[5] and found that his view of the situation was even more pessimistic than his own. Kido believed (and had hinted as much to the Emperor) that Japan could still get terms from the Allies which would

[5] And subsequently a signatory of the surrender terms aboard the *Missouri*.

mean that not everything would be lost in losing the war. Shigemitsu, on the other hand, maintained that Japan's straits were so dire that she would be lucky to get anything at all beyond unconditional surrender. Both of them agreed that, for the moment, at least, they could expect nothing from the Government.

Like a few other members of the jushin and certain members of the Cabinet—Foreign Minister Togo, in particular—they were beginning to realize that conspiratorial plotting and secret meetings in each other's houses were but a preliminary. One of these days one of them would have to pluck up enough courage to go out and throw the bomb called capitulation. But which one?

And here we get a clue to the reason for the hesitation, even by those who saw the need for an immediate peace. There was a tendency among the Allies to condone the dilatoriness of the so-called liberal statesmen of Japan in working for an end to the war because, they believed, the Army militants were rampant in Japan at the time and either imprisonment or assassination faced them if they pursued their aims too openly.

This is not true. The pro-peace element did not fear assassination because the murder gangs and bully boys were all out on active service, and were far too busy worrying about their own skins to be ready to hunt political scalps. That sort of danger was over. True, there had been a short-lived terror campaign organized by Tojo during which four hundred suspected "liberals" had been arrested and imprisoned, and they included such statesmen as Shigeru Yoshida; [6] but Mr. Yoshida was soon released. The Japanese police never would have dared to arrest any member of the jushin, especially those close to the throne; they were much too distinguished.

It was not the kempei-tai and the dread of arrest and torture which inhibited the elder statesmen searching for a way out, but the knowledge that in saving Japan—even, in saving their Emperor—they might be putting *themselves* in jeopardy. For few of them, not even Kido, Konoye, Shigemitsu, Togo, Okada, Koiso, Yonai, had a record of opposition to the war sufficiently documented to convince the Allies of their sincerity. All of them had served in cabinets which had propagated war as an instrument of national policy. They knew that atrocities had been committed by the Army against Allied prisoners of war during the period during

[6] Japan's most distinguished and effective postwar premier.

which they had held office, that there were war crimes charges facing all Japanese politicians who had served in the Cabinet from 1936 onward. The more worldly of them did not even deny that, by association, they might well be guilty, and that a victorious force with a score to pay off, hundreds of thousands of vengeful prisoners and their relatives to appease, would not be too choosy in differentiating between the degrees of war guilt. In seeking peace, they were possibly—even almost certainly—handing themselves over to a war crimes tribunal.

And yet, if they were truly patriotic, peace they must secure. It was easy enough to die for the Emperor. It was much more difficult to risk punishment and humiliation as a result of securing him peace.

It would do an injustice to Premier Suzuki to suggest that he spent all his time brandishing a torch and looking for an altar on which to immolate himself. He had his theories too about how the situation might be ameliorated. There were the Russians, for example. The Russians had signed a nonaggression pact with Japan in 1941 which was to last until 1946, and so far they had stood by it. The Soviet Government had not helped her allies, Britain and America, in the war against Japan, and in turn the Japanese had not helped her ally, Germany, in the war with Russia. In fact, both countries had kept their hands off each other because they were very much otherwise occupied: it was an arrangement which worked as long as Japan wanted her Manchurian frontier with Russia neutralized, and as long as Russia was too busy with Germany to bother about Siberia.

Now the situation had changed. Germany was defeated, and Russia no longer needed her vast armies in the West. She could start planning about the east again. The Soviet Union gave what should have been a broad hint of her intentions when she announced, in the spring of 1945, that the Neutrality Pact with Japan, due to end in 1946, would not be renewed. Neither Suzuki nor the Japanese Supreme Command seemed to have realized the significance of this. The Army proposed bribing the U.S.S.R. to stay neutral by promising them a rearrangement of the status quo in the North Pacific and on the Asiatic mainland. The Navy wanted to do a straight swap whereby Japan would exchange cruisers and escort vessels in return for Russian oil and aircraft. Suzuki even had hopes of enticing Russia into the war against Britain and America in return for a share of the colonies and riches of Southeast Asia.

The Foreign Minister, Togo, pointed out to Suzuki that he had been an ambassador to the Soviet Union and knew the way Stalin's mind worked. It was most unlikely that he would back the losing side, even had he sympathized with it. Japan was now the pariah of civilization; it seemed almost certain that at the Yalta Conference, just concluded, Russia had agreed to enter the war not with but against Japan, in return for the very tangible rewards which the Allies could offer. Unfortunately, this was a shrewd guess on his part which he could not confirm—and neither Suzuki nor the Supreme Command believed him.

The Prime Minister (with Togo's reluctant cooperation) appointed a former premier, Mr. Koki Hirota, to "sound out" the Russians. The Russian ambassador to Japan was Mr. Jacob Malik, who, now that American bombing of Tokyo had begun in earnest, had moved himself to the cool, secluded and leafy heights of a hotel at Hakone. With elaborate casualness, Mr. Hirota was instructed to set off for the region on a walking tour during which he would "drop in" on the Soviet envoy and get him into conversation.

One has a picture of Mr. Hirota, a fussy little man, turning up in his plus fours, walking stick in hand, and pretending to be surprised as he traps the dour Mr. Malik beside the waterfall in the garden of the Gora Hotel.

"Ah, so! You are happy here in lovely Hakone, Excellence? Not as beautiful as Nikko, perhaps. But the hot springs, and the geisha, they are even better, neh?"

"Da."

"Perhaps tonight we have geisha party, Excellency? Many things to talk about. Our lovely country. Mount Fuji. A new haiku I have heard about the cherry blossom. And the question of the neutrality pact, neh?"

It was the beginning of a series of conversations which were to last almost until the war was over. Malik listened. He listened while Hirota tried to bribe him. He listened while he offered ships, and then islands, and then tracts of Southeast Asia. He listened as the bribes changed to pleas. He listened as Hirota—and later, much more important people—beseeched him to help Japan get out of the war, act as an intermediary, forward proposals to the Allies. And to give him his due, he did pass on all he was told to his masters, Molotov and Stalin, in Moscow.

One wonders how the Japanese could have been so naïve as to imagine, in that last summer of war, that the Russians, of all people, could help them in their desperate dilemma. "We put great faith in the integrity of Secretary Stalin," the Emperor was afterward to say. The result was that the Russians, from June, 1945, onward, played the Japanese like a fish on a hook.

Chapter Twenty

The air raid shelter at the Imperial Palace had been built as a sort of underground annex to the Emperor's quarters in the building known as the Obunko (library).[1] There was a door from Hirohito's study which connected, by a thick steel door, to a flight of stairs, below which was a conference hall, an engine house and kitchen, a small bedroom and bathroom, and a telephone switchboard.

As the raids grew more frequent and started to come in by night and day, the Emperor and Empress spent much of their time in the shelter. They were sometimes joined by two of his brothers, Takamatsu and Mikasa, and by his uncle, Higashikuni, all of whose homes had been damaged by fire. The children were in the country and so was the ailing Prince Chichibu; though even there, as the raids began to proliferate over Japan, they were not particularly safe from incineration.

One godsend for the Japanese during the period of trial through which they were now passing was their ability to sleep. They have always had the knack of being able to drop off for short periods, even in the noisiest and most uncomfortable surroundings, and it must have saved the sanity of thousands of them at this time. Unfortunately for Hirohito, he had never shared the boon of easy and automatic sleep with his people, and from April onward he had been racked with insomnia; he could hardly sleep at all. Whenever possible, he wandered around the gardens picking specimen flowers and plants and bringing them back to study through his

[1] In which he had been living and working since the night of the fire.

portable microscope before pressing them into books. He devoured whatever books he could still lay his hands on which dealt with undersea flora and fauna; and one of his officials, Marquis Kamroji, had dug up from somewhere an old file of copies of the *National Geographic Magazine* which he found a great comfort.

In the darkest hours of the night, he picked up from beside his bunk a copy of a small volume of Aesop's Fables, which he had cherished since childhood, and always read in moments of stress. One imagines him perhaps contemplating Japan's own situation—her grandiose ambitions crumbling to dust—as he read the Fable of the Fir-tree and the Bramble:

"The fir-tree treated with contempt the bramble that grew at its foot. 'I am put to many high and noble uses,' he said boastfully. 'I furnish taper spars for ships and beams for the roofs of palaces. You are trodden underfoot, and despised by everybody.' Replied the bramble: 'You talk very finely now, but for all that, when once you feel the axe applied to your root, you'll wish you had been a bramble.'"

He had been convinced ever since April and the collapse of the Koiso Cabinet that the time would come when he must intervene. Kido and his Lord Chamberlain, Matsudaira, had kept him in touch with the secret colloquies of Konoye, Okada, Shigemitsu, Yonai *et al.* (though no one, yet, had told him of the approach to the Russians) and both to him and to Kido it became increasingly obvious that for all their anxious conspirating, none of the plotters seemed capable of throwing the bomb. If they could not, who must throw it instead?

It was Kido who first put the idea of Imperial intervention down on paper. He wrote:

"June 8, 1945. Drafted a tentative plan for solving the crisis. 1. It is apparent that the fighting at Okinawa will, contrary to our expectations, end most unhappily on our part. Moreover, it is obvious that the end will come in the very near future.

"2. The statistics appended [for the perusal of the Emperor] reveal that after the latter half of the year we shall completely lose our power in every way for prosecuting war.

"3. Needless to say, layman as I am in this field, I am not in a position to judge what strategy the enemy will take in the future. Judging, however, by the formidable power displayed by the enemy air force—mass attacks with incendiary bombs—it would not take much time to make a holocaust of all towns and villages in this country. The enemy resorts to tactics of destroying houses, resulting in loss of spare clothes, and stocks of food. Farmhouses are not used to these tactics, and it will prove extremely difficult for them to disperse their belongings and stocks in advance. . . .

"4. If my above assumption is not much mistaken, a keen shortage of food and clothes will occur throughout the country in and after the latter half of this year. This coupled with the advent of winter will cause social unrest of alarming proportions. I fear that the situation may get out of control.

"5. From the above point of view, I think Japan is called upon to take a resolute move for restoring peace by terminating hostilities. By what method and steps shall this object be attained, then? This is what calls for the most anxious study.

"6. It is almost certain, in the light of various announcements, speeches and essays made public by the enemy, by way of a peace offensive, that it is the enemy's major object to overthrow the so-called gumbatsu or militarists in this country.

"7. I believe, therefore, that the orthodox way of opening peace negotiations will be to propose peace on behalf of the fighting services, and then to decide on a peace plan and open peace negotiations on behalf of the government. But it will be almost impossible to do so at this juncture, judging by Japan's actual conditions. Further, if we wait for the opportunity to be ripe for it, it may become possible too late, and Japan may share Germany's fate, so that even the security of the Imperial family and vindication of the national polity—*Japan's minimum demands* —may not be guaranteed."

And here Kido reached the heart of his plan. He wrote:

"8. In the light of precedents it will be exceptional, and we shall be struck with awe and trepidation to do so, but I believe there will be no other course left for us but to petition for Imperial intervention, for the sake of the people, and make peace moves."

He went on to explain that a message should be sent via an intermediary power which had been personally written by the Emperor. He went on:

"9. It may be a good idea to open peace negotiations with America and Britain directly, if possible, but it may be advisable to ask the Soviet Union, which maintains neutrality with Japan, to mediate between the Allies and Japan, with some latitude allowed to this country.

"10. The keynote of the Emperor's personal message would follow that of the Imperial Rescript on the declaration of war, emphasizing His Majesty's constant concern for peace and his decision to conclude peace with general terms, in view of war ravages and for the sake of world peace, by bearing the unbearable."

Kido did not envisage unconditional surrender at this juncture. His idea of "terms" included withdrawal of all Japanese troops from the territories at present occupied by them, provided that, in return, the future independence of these territories was guaranteed; the drastic reduction of Japanese arms; and the transformation of the Pacific region into one which genuinely lived up to its name.

While he was in process of drawing up his plan, an Imperial Conference was held (on June 8, 1945) at which, to his astonishment, Suzuki once more huffed and puffed with senile belligerence. To the delight of the militarists, the premier exhorted his Cabinet to prepare for the worst. The invasion was coming and soon the blood would begin to spill on the Japanese homeland; but what better fate than to die resisting? The people were ready. They had their bamboo spears: they had their pockets filled with explosives, ready to throw themselves beneath the enemy tanks; they had their planes—alas, only training planes were left now—loaded with bombs and willing kamikaze pilots waiting in the cockpits. His old eyes filled with tears as the words "death" and "destruction" and "blood and pain suffered willingly for the Emperor" tumbled from his fluttering lips. And yet, at the same time, he still talked of victory.

"There is only one way to win, and that is by determination," the old man quavered. "When the whole nation possesses this will, then we shall be able to achieve victory."

He had spoken. *It was to be a fight to the end, and no surrender.* He looked around at his colleagues. Did any of them have any objections?

Silence. Not one minister raised his voice against the decision.

Nor did the Emperor. He sat stonily through the whole proceedings and did not say a word. It is hardly surprising. He must have been stunned.

After the sorry affair was over, however, he received Kido in audience and listened to his plan, and immediately told him to take it and discuss it with the Prime Minister and the ministers of War, Navy and Foreign Affairs. The daily reports of bomb damage were on the desk in front of

Hirohito, and he played with them nervously as he spoke. He was deeply distressed, he told his Lord Keeper, that more towns and villages had been reduced to rubble, and innocent people made homeless.

"It cannot go on," he said.

But so long as the policy of fighting to the bitter end was followed, go on it would.

"At 3:30 P.M.," wrote Kido on June 13, 1945, "Prime Minister Suzuki came to my room [in the Imperial Palace] and I had a talk with him about the war situation. I asked him how long he thought Japan's fighting power would last. The Prime Minister replied that August would witness a sharp drop in Japan's fighting potential. Thereupon I told him my idea. After telling him about my report to the Throne of my tentative peace plan, which was approved by His Majesty, I laid bare my heart to him and urged him to do his best to terminate the war, for the sake of the Imperial Family's security and the safeguarding of the national polity. My plea struck a sympathetic chord in the Prime Minister, who emphatically promised to do his bit. I felt greatly reassured."

So he should have been; and surprised too. The old man who had been roaring like a lion only five days before was now cooing like a dove. It seemed that he too was desperately anxious for peace, and assured the Lord Keeper that he always had been. He did not explain, possibly because it was beyond explanation, why he had spent so much time brandishing his sword if he did not wish to fight.

That same afternoon there was another surprise for Kido. The dumb men of war at the Imperial Conference of June 8th were also beginning to speak up for peace.

"My gracious!" he wrote in his diary for June 13th.

"Had an interview with Navy Minister Yonai in His Majesty's library [the Obunko] and talked with him about countermeasures to save the situation." And, two days later: "Talked to Foreign Minister Togo and found him 'not opposed' to my peace plan, but pointing out the vigorous war decision just recently adopted at the Imperial Conference in the presence of the Emperor, and wondered how to adjust the peace plan with it."

On the other hand, he found War Minister Anami, though prepared to admit the necessity of seeking peace, obsessed with the idea that Japan should "win one more victory" before surrendering, on the grounds that this would enable the nation to ask for better terms; though he saw no prospect of such a victory being secured. Like one or two other members of the High Command, Anami, rather than admit the harsh reality, and the utter defeat which went with it, was conjuring battles out of the air which could not possibly be fought, and potential victories which had no chance whatsoever of being won. Anything to delay the inevitable end.

Even Kido still felt that "terms" were possible, and he must have been jolted by a memorandum from Mr. Toshikazu Kase which reached him about this time. He had consulted Kase about his peace plan, and here was his reaction to it. Among other things, he wrote:

"Since it is likely that we will have to terminate hostilities by unconditional surrender, or on terms virtually similar, we must be prepared to accept this fact in embarking upon diplomatic negotiations and must take necessary measures on the home front in anticipation of the worst. Consequently, the 'peace with honor' envisaged by the Lord Keeper of the Privy Seal is too optimistic, being incompatible with the grim realities.

"We may conduct diplomatic negotiations either directly with the enemy powers or through neutral countries. Logically speaking, the direct course [that is, negotiations with Britain and America] is simpler, but the Army will not countenance it, as it will involve a loss of face on its part. On the other hand, the minor neutral countries are of limited influence. Therefore Moscow seems to offer a convenient channel."

But Kase, a career member of the Japanese Foreign Office, was less naïve than most of the Imperial advisers about this solution to Japanese dilemma. He wrote:

"However, to rely on the Soviet Union at this critical juncture, when the very fate of our nation hangs by a thread, may, as some point out, be liable to cause later complications by introducing subversive influences into the highly complex and combustible situation. It is in a sense like crossing a dangerous bridge. But as there is no other way, we are obliged to risk it. Only it seems wiser to approach Great Britain and the United States also at a later stage in a propitious moment in order to counterbalance the Soviet influence by conducting a parallel negotiation."[2]

It was wise advice, but it was not taken.

[2] Toshikazu Kase, *Journey to the Missouri*, New Haven, Conn.: Yale University Press, 1952.

The Prime Minister, Suzuki, had been to the Shrine of Amaterasu at Ise to seek the advice of the Sun Goddess and her relatives as to what he should do. The divine progenitors of the Japanese Imperial Line appear to have lost touch with the situation and become hopelessly overoptimistic. At any rate, Suzuki returned from his pilgrimage with sulphur flaring from his nostrils and the air around him filled with fire and brimstone. He seemed once more convinced, along with his Minister of War, Anami, and the Army Chief of Staff, Umezu, that what Japan needed at the moment was a good, honest-to-god, bloodletting battle on the Japanese mainland—during which, at the sacrifice of a million lives on either side, an amelioration of terms might be secured from the Allies.

When he heard this from his Lord Chamberlain, Matsudaira, Hirohito let his nerves momentarily snap and gave vent to an outburst of rage. He had just learned for the first time of the "negotiations" which Mr. Koki Hirota had been conducting at Hakone with Mr. Jacob Malik, the Soviet ambassador—Suzuki having, through a lapse of memory, forgotten to inform him of them—and he found both the progress and the tenor of these talks little to his liking. For Mr. Hirota was concentrating his efforts more on making a bargain with Russia rather than seeking her services as a mediator; offering bribes in return for oil, for instance. It came to the knowledge of Hirohito that Mr. Malik was so bored with these overtures that he even yawned or glanced at a newspaper while they were being made to him; that, having been urged to send proposals to Moscow, Malik had reluctantly agreed, and then dispatched them by courier instead of cable; and was now, when Foreign Minister Togo attempted to intervene in the talks, feigning sickness.

The Japanese did not know, of course, that none of the bribes they were offering to the Russians to stay out of the war were anything like the bribes Roosevelt and Churchill had promised them at Yalta for coming in. But they might have guessed from Malik's deliberately rude lack of interest that he was acting on instructions from Moscow and that Stalin was not really interested in mediating the end of a war from which, as a neutral, he had most to gain from its prolongation.

Hirohito, however, like all the other Japanese,[3] preferred to rely on the good faith of the Soviet Government and ascribed Malik's lack of

[3] With the exception of Foreign Minister Togo, who suspected that Russia had been bribed at Yalta, but couldn't prove it.

interest to his—and Stalin's—contempt for Japan's attempts to wriggle and bargain rather than ask outright for mediation. At the suggestion of Kido, he called a meeting of the Supreme War Council on June 22, 1945, and decided this time to speak his mind. Unfortunately, not frankly enough.

He tried. Alas, the Japanese find it difficult to deliver clear, concise and simple statements of fact, and Japanese Emperors seem to be born with plums in their mouth. What Hirohito wanted to tell the Council was that the June 6th decision to fight to the bitter end was now a dead letter, that surrender was the only alternative, and that the sooner they sought and got it the better. Unfortunately, he veiled his thoughts in complicated phraseology about "established principles" and the danger of relying on "traditional methods." Only Togo seemed to realize what he was getting at and said (in response to a question from the Emperor) that a special envoy could be sent to Moscow to solicit on-the-spot mediation by the Soviet Government, *but that he had better go quickly, before Stalin and Molotov departed for the Potsdam Conference.* Among the Cabinet members, only he and Navy Minister Yonai seemed to have any idea of the importance of the approaching Potsdam Conference and to be aware that it was not just a conference about Germany, but one likely to decide the fate of Japan. Suzuki, still charging around his private Valhalla, did condescend to come down from the clouds for a moment to say that, of course, he was ready to obey anything the Emperor suggested.

But what did this mean? What *was* the Emperor suggesting? As Suzuki interpreted it, Hirohito had no thought of suing *at once* for peace. He decided, quite wrongly, that the Emperor wished to battle on. It so happened that at the very moment the Emperor was speaking to his ministers, Okinawa, a Japanese island within easy flying distance of the Japanese mainland, was falling to the American forces. Suzuki chose to salute this disastrous defeat—when the time came for him to admit it, four days later—with a pugnacious speech announcing that the enemy had lost "ten times" the men and ships as the Japanese in conquering the island, and had suffered not only material losses but a "severe spiritual blow."

The old man was once more flexing his biceps and preparing for battle.

"Who will not be filled with confidence of victory," he cried, "when

300

we think of the hundred million people impressively marshalling themselves in their respective fields of occupation, and upon the fields of battle as well, for the sake of the country!" Now, he said, was the time to "decide the rise or fall of the Empire, our country being confronted with the gravest crisis since the Mongol invasion. . . . How can we ever permit the sacred land to be outraged by a foreign foe?"

It was just, of course, the mad raving of a silly old man, but how were the Japanese people—or, for that matter the Allies—to guess that? Suzuki was still Prime Minister. They had every reason to believe that he spoke for his Cabinet and his country. They listened to his windy rhetoric, and unfortunately took it seriously.

In the midst of his worst crises, Hirohito always had the same instinct—to call in Prince Konoye. He felt that the Prince would never let him down, even though he almost always did.

Konoye had been spending the summer in a state of gentle melancholy at Karuizawa, breathing the cool mountain air and sadly contemplating the collapse of his country, but on July 12, 1945, he and his wife descended to Tokyo, with its muggy smell of fire and death, and he was summoned to the Imperial Palace for an audience with his Emperor. He saw Hirohito alone, but afterward he came to Kido and described their talk. It contained a typical example of the Konoye rigmarole. He told the Lord Keeper:

"At the audience His Majesty asked me my opinion of the question of putting an end to the war. I replied as follows: 'Recently I have heard explanations from Army personnel of the possibility of a successful outcome of the war. These explanations might not be wholly groundless providing that the figures cited by the exponents be trustworthy. But on the other hand the explanations by the Navy suggest the untrustworthiness of such figures. Meanwhile, the morale of the general public cannot be said to be high. The only hope for the people is that the Emperor may do something for them, some way or other, as a last resort. However, there are signs, though as yet sporadic, that [some people are showing] resentment toward His Majesty. In view of these tendencies, I believe it imperative to terminate the war as early as possible.'"

Hirohito seized upon these remarks as a cue, and said it was his intention to ask Konoye to journey to Moscow as his special envoy and ask the Russian Government to mediate with the Allies on Japan's behalf.

301

"I respectfully accepted," was what the prince told Kido, but the Emperor's version was slightly more romantic.

"He said he is ready to sacrifice his life in order to comply with my will," the Emperor said to Kido, "making me recall how I told him, at the time of the formation of the second Konoye Cabinet [in 1941] to share both joy and grief with me. This time he seems to be most firmly determined."

It was a secret mission after Konoye's own heart, and one which might, in part, make up for his failure in 1941 to bring off the meeting with Roosevelt. He could not guess that this one, too, was fated to be abortive. He gathered his friends among the statesmen together and picked the members of his mission. Since there was some danger of assassination attempts by fanatics should the nature of the venture become known, extraordinary steps were taken to keep the projected journey a secret. The plane would take off from a secret airfield on Shikoku and fly to Manchuli, in Mongolia, where, it was hoped, a Soviet plane would be waiting to take the envoy to Moscow.

In the meantime, Foreign Minister Togo on July 12th cabled to Mr. Naotake Sato, the Japanese ambassador in Moscow, asking him to deliver the following message "urgently" to the Soviet Commissar for Foreign Affairs, Mr. Molotov:

"His Majesty is extremely anxious to terminate the war as soon as possible, being deeply concerned that the further continuation of hostilities will only aggravate the untold miseries of the teeming millions of innocent men and women in the countries at war. Should, however, the United States and Great Britain insist on unconditional surrender, Japan would be forced to fight to the bitter end with all her might in order to vindicate her honor and safeguard her national existence, which, to our intense regret, would entail further bloodshed. Our government therefore desires to negotiate for a speedy restoration of peace, prompted as we sincerely are by solicitude for the welfare of mankind. For this purpose Prince Konoye will proceed to Moscow with the personal message of the Emperor and it is requested that the Soviet Government be good enough to accord travel facilities to him." [4]

Sato realized at once the tremendous significance of the message and

[4] Toshikazu Kase, *ibid.*

302

hurried to the Kremlin to ask for a meeting with Molotov. He was extremely excited and did not fail to convey to the officials in the Russian Foreign Office the extreme importance of the message he had been given. It is easy to understand why. His Emperor had spoken, and was intervening to terminate the war. To a Japanese it was an event of world-shaking importance.

Nor should its significance have been missed by the Soviet Union. They still maintained relationships with the Japanese which were superficially friendly; they had an ambassador and an embassy in Tokyo, and an efficient Intelligence service operating throughout Japan; they knew the state of the nation, and they also knew that the Emperor would not have intervened had he not decided that the war must end. Yet to his astonishment, Sato found it extremely difficult to persuade anyone in Moscow of the vital nature of the mission he was endeavoring to sponsor. Molotov sent word to say that he was too busy to see the Japanese ambassador before leaving for Potsdam, and he was shuffled aside into the care of a vice commissar, Lozovsky. He did, however, promise to see that Molotov got the gist of the Imperial message and also read a personal letter from Sato explaining the Emperor's attitude and the significance of the Konoye mission. That was on July 13, 1945. Though Sato urged the necessity for haste, it was the last he heard of it until July 18th.

It would not be true to say that the Soviet Government was embarrassed, for it does not react that way, but it was certainly irritated by the Emperor's appeal. They had never had any intention of acting as mediators between Japan and the Allies in terminating the war, for reasons which the Japanese could not have known but should have guessed. The offers of territory and concessions made by Roosevelt (with Churchill reluctantly concurring) at Yalta had been made contingent on Russia's entry into the Far East war. *No come in, no get booty.* Stalin and Molotov realized only too well that they must break their neutrality pact with Japan and declare war in order to collect the spoils they had been promised. They therefore had a vested interest in *keeping the war going* until the moment when they could most conveniently—and at least cost—intervene.

So long as Japanese approaches were being handled by the mealy-mouthed Mr. Koki Hirota and the frozen-faced Mr. Malik at Hakone, it was easy to brush them aside without even the dignity of an official reaction. A message from the Emperor of Japan was different, in that it could hardly be ignored. Something would obviously have to be done about it—but slowly, slowly.

First of all, Mr. Lozovsky asked Ambassador Sato to whom the Emperor's message was addressed: to Foreign Commissar Molotov, Secretary Stalin or President Kalinin? And here poor Sato was confronted by the kind of inefficiency which is characteristic of the Japanese in an unexpected situation. When they are asked to do something unusual, they almost always make a mess of it. In this case, any message from the Emperor should, of course, have been officially addressed to the Soviet President, and if Sato had kept his wits about him, that is what he would have told Lozovsky. Instead he blurted out the truth, that the Imperial message was not addressed to his opposite number in the Soviet Union nor to anyone in particular, but would, he hoped, be seen by Kalinin, Molotov *and* Stalin.[5] It gave Lozovsky the opportunity he had been seeking to murmur about protocol and diplomatic usage, and procrastinate.

The Imperial message itself also played into Soviet hands, for it contained the unfortunate statement that if the United States and Britain insisted on unconditional surrender, Japan would be forced to fight on to the bitter end. It was just what Stalin needed. At Potsdam he could make a show of frankness by telling President Truman and the British premier, Clement Attlee, that the Japanese had asked him to mediate, but at the same time suggest that the terms they were asking were unreal.

Secretary of State Byrnes, who accompanied Truman to Potsdam, later wrote:

"At a later meeting [it was actually on July 17, the first day of the Conference] Stalin told the President and me that the Japanese Ambassador in Moscow had asked whether the Soviet Union would agree to act as mediator to bring about the settlement of the war. This request, Stalin said, did not indicate a willingness to surrender unconditionally as the Allies demanded; it was phrased so generally that Mr. Molotov simply told the Ambassador he would discuss the matter with him later. Subsequently, Stalin said, the Japanese Ambassador presented another

[5] Sato's inability to lie, even for his country, was well known in the Japanese Foreign Office, where there was a saying about him: "If Sato tells a lie the sun will rise in the West."

message. This stated that the Emperor wished to send Prince Konoye to Moscow with a message saying *that Japan wanted to end the war but had decided to fight on with all its strength as long as unconditional surrender was demanded*. Stalin added that a letter was then sent to the Ambassador stating that the character of the indicated message was general, contained no specific proposal, and therefore, it was impossible to give a definite reply. President Truman expressed his approval of Stalin's action." [6]

This flawed gem of information was intended to convince the Allies that the war in the Far East was far from won, and that the Soviet Union's help was still needed. Stalin was out to fool both victor and vanquished and to make sure that they would not come together and make terms.

With the Japanese, he succeeded in both objectives. He gave orders to Lozovsky to inform Sato that the Imperial message contained nothing specific, and that, under the circumstances, there seemed no reason why Prince Konoye should journey to Moscow as the Emperor's envoy. Sato doggedly kept on trying, with both his own government and the Kremlin. He cabled to Foreign Minister Togo pleading for more details, and strongly suggesting that only unconditional surrender would be accepted by the Allies. He was curtly told by Togo not to intervene with his personal feelings and ideas, and to continue to make it clear that Japan could *not* accept unconditional surrender, and that if it were persisted in, Japan would fight to the death. These words were music in Stalin's ear, for they meant that Japan would not give in too easily—or so the Allies, with Soviet encouragement, would go on thinking.

But were President Truman and the United States Government equally deceived by the disingenuousness of Stalin's statements at Potsdam? The unfortunate truth seems to be that they knew the truth anyway, and still allowed themselves to be deceived. For the Department of Navy Intelligence which had deciphered the Japanese codes was still in operation, and by a combination of remarkable circumstances was able to read the enciphered, top secret messages passing between Foreign Minister Togo in Tokyo and Ambassador Sato in Moscow, a facility which the Soviet

[6] J. F. Byrnes, *Speaking Frankly*, New York: Harper & Row, 1947. My italics.—L.M.

305

Government did *not* enjoy. President Truman and his advisers therefore knew all about Hirohito's attempt to send Konoye to Moscow and exactly why he was going, and they were not bamboozled by Stalin's offhand comments about the motives behind it.

Nevertheless, they did nothing about it and President Truman "expressed his approval of Stalin's action." Why? It is one of the baffling tragedies of the last stages of the Far East war, this failure on the part of the American administration to make use of the information at its disposal, think about it, act on it. True, the Japanese Government was still insisting, in the secret cables which Washington was decoding, on its adamant opposition to the idea of "unconditional surrender." But one wonders what can have been happening to United States Intelligence agents in Japan at this time, that they so signally failed to inform Washington of what Japan feared from unconditional surrender and why it was so strenuously opposed to the last.

Did Truman not realize that the only thing the Cabinet was really worried about was the position of the Emperor, and of the Imperial system? That they believed "unconditional surrender" would mean his overthrow? Everything else they were willing to abandon, but not the national polity. The American historian, Mr. Robert C. Butow, in a quietly stated but nevertheless devastating indictment of the Truman administration, has put the position quite plainly. He writes:

"Secretary of War Stimson has raised the question of whether an earlier surrender of Japan could have been achieved had the United States followed a different diplomatic and military policy during the closing months of the war. In the light of available evidence, a final answer in the affirmative seems possible, even probable." [7]

He goes on to summarize the situation in July, 1945, in the three vital capitals where the fate of Japan was being decided, Washington, Tokyo and Moscow. In the first two capitals, everything hinged on what was to happen to Emperor Hirohito.

In Washington, unfortunately, the war leaders were at loggerheads. [8] They could not decide among themselves what to do about the Emperor,

[7] Robert C. Butow, *Japan's Decision to Surrender,* California: Stanford University Press, 1954.

[8] Stimson thought a limited promise to preserve the Imperial system, as a constitutional monarchy, would satisfy the Japanese, and Grew agreed with him. Byrnes and Cordell Hull did not, and they influenced Truman—who didn't care very much, either way.

and therefore were unable to make their position clear. They were equally confused about whether they really wanted to get the Soviet Union into the Far East war or not. "After many delays a decision was eventually reached to define 'unconditional surrender' to a point," Butow writes, *"but to maintain silence on the Emperor* and to insist on continuing the fiction that a *conditional* surrender was unconditional." [9]

In Tokyo, "the ruling elite was caught between desire and necessity. The Government, especially its civilian members, would readily have ordered a cessation of hostilities if the Allies would have hedged 'unconditional surrender,' with a proviso to the effect that Japan's distinctive polity, the Imperial System, would not be destroyed. Without such a guarantee there was no alternative but to fight on. At the same time, the government recognized the pressing need of keeping the Soviet Union from entering the war, and, in desperation, decided to employ the Kremlin as broker."

In Moscow, what Stalin urgently needed to do was get his armies involved in the Far East war—and thus collect his promised loot—before Washington, London and Tokyo settled for peace. "While the Americans were piling huge spoils at the front door of the Kremlin to induce a Soviet entry into the war, the Japanese were at the back door with offerings with which they hoped to purchase continued Soviet neutrality and eventual Soviet mediation."

And Butow adds:

"Here was the spectacle of Washington sacrificing what it did not own but should have claimed for itself or China, and of Tokyo dispensing what it had once held but no longer could maintain. Under the circumstances, it could not have been too difficult for Stalin to foment plans whereby both the victors and vanquished would later have cause to regret their common folly." [10]

Folly is the word. For as it turned out, the Proclamation signed at Potsdam on July 26, 1945—by Truman for America, Attlee for Britain and Chiang Kai-shek for China—did not ask for the unconditional surrender of Japan, but only for the "unconditional surrender of the Japanese armed forces," thus differentiating between the militarists and civilian administration. True, and, as it turned out, alas, the Proclamation made no mention of the position of the Emperor. Had it done so,

[9] Butow, *ibid.* First italics mine—L.M.; second—Butow's.
[10] *Ibid.*

307

history might have turned a different corner. There were those in Washington (and neither the British nor the Chinese objected) who wanted to see a statement in the Proclamation defining, in general terms, the attitude of the Allies toward the Emperor and the Imperial Family, and stating that they would have no objection to the continuation of the line as a constitutional monarchy, provided the parliament and people of Japan agreed. Unfortunately, this suggestion (backed mainly by Stimson) aroused the strongest objections from Cordell Hull, who thought that this was "kowtowing" to the Japanese royalty, and he argued so persuasively with Truman that all reference to Hirohito and the Imperial Family was deleted. Hull's solid and unrepentant republicanism prolonged the war and made the dropping of the atom bombs inevitable.

Even without the reference to the Emperor, however, the Potsdam Proclamation stated terms in such a way that one still boggles at the failure of Truman, Attlee, Chiang Kai-shek and their advisers to seize the opportunity for peace presented by Hirohito's decision to intervene in July, 1945. As Butow says of the Potsdam Proclamation:

"The Allies thus had here, in late July 1945, the very document which Japan finally accepted in mid-August. Had Prince Konoye, as the fully empowered personal representative of the Emperor of Japan, been permitted to travel to Moscow (or anywhere else, for that matter) and had he there been handed the text of this proclamation *prior* to its release to the world at large, he conceivably could have resolved speedily the very issues which government leaders in Tokyo spent the next three weeks in debating, without result. Had the Allies given the Prince a week of grace in which to obtain his Government's support for acceptance, *the war might have ended towards the latter part of July or the very beginning of August without the atomic bomb and without Soviet participation in the conflict.*" [11]

It was not to be. Prince Konoye, with a sad sigh, called for his wife and his servants and departed for Karuizawa. His last chance to serve his Emperor had come and gone, and he had failed him once more—though this time through no fault of his own. He took to his bed to brood on Japan's fate and his own lost opportunities. It would be another six months before he killed himself, but in a sense this effete prince, whose ineffectiveness had helped to hasten Japan's downfall, was already dead.

[11] *Ibid.* My italics.—L.M.

Chapter Twenty-one

Foreign Minister Togo arrived at the Imperial Palace on July 27, 1945, carrying with him a copy of the Potsdam Proclamation as it had been monitored over shortwave radio. Though it made no mention of the Imperial Family, it did guarantee the Japanese people freedom of speech, religion and thought, asked for the unconditional surrender of the armed forces and not of Japan, and advised the government and people to eschew the militarists and "follow the path of reason." Otherwise, the Proclamation went on, the "alternative for Japan is prompt and utter destruction."

One of the paragraphs stated:

"Following are our terms. We will not deviate from them. There are no alternatives. We shall brook no delay."

Togo was shown into the library where Hirohito was awaiting him and handed over the Proclamation, which the Emperor read through. Then he and the foreign minister discussed the terms clause by clause. Togo thought that they were the most reasonable they could expect in the circumstances, and said so. Hirohito agreed. In principle, he said, he thought they were acceptable.

It was an opinion most of the nation shared by the following day, when parts of the Proclamation were published in the newspapers. The Army at first tried to have the document suppressed, but were prevailed upon by the Foreign Office to agree to partial publication—on condition that certain liberal-sounding phrases, such as "we do not intend that the Japanese shall be enslaved as a race or destroyed as a nation" and "they

[Japanese troops] shall be permitted to return home . . . to lead peaceful and productive lives," were eliminated. Even so, Kase wrote, "the popular reaction . . . was that the terms were far more lenient than had been generally expected. The people were exhausted by war and tired of the militarists' rule; despairing of the future, they began to murmur approval. If the acceptance of this proclamation could save our homeland from utter devastation . . . was it not a reasonable price to pay?" [1]

Why then, if the Emperor and the people thought the Proclamation reasonable, did the Cabinet not at once signify a willingness to accept? The answer, once more, lies in the slavish attachment of the Japanese to protocol and their inability to improvise in an emergency. How could they accept the Potsdam Proclamation, or even signify their willingness to talk about it, when (officially) they hadn't even received it yet, but had merely monitored its text over the shortwave radio? They must wait until they were formally approached. (It was rather like a young lady demanding an introduction to her rescuer before allowing him to save her from drowning.)

In any case, some of the Cabinet (and a large part of the armed forces) were still, amazing though it may seem, relying upon the Russians. Had not the Emperor approached the Soviet Government and asked for their intervention? [2] At any moment now, Moscow would reply to say that she would respect Japanese integrity, stay neutral, and mediate a reasonable surrender. To accept Potsdam would be to insult Russia. Or so they reasoned. It was not just the Soviets who were deceiving the Japanese now; they were deceiving themselves.

It was at this juncture, while the Allies waited to hear the Japanese reaction to their Proclamation, that the bumbling old man who was Japan's prime minister intervened once more, and brought the roof crashing down on the nation. What Premier Suzuki thought he was doing is a mystery, even to this day, for even his own postwar explanations make no sense of the incredible stupidity which he displayed at this time. It is possible that he feared assassination from military fanatics if he showed any signs in public of wanting an end to the war, and spoke to appease potential killers. It is possible that he was drunk—as many a Japanese

---

[1] Toshikazu Kase, *Journey to the Missouri*, New Haven, Conn.: Yale University Press, 1952.

[2] By this time, the secret had gained partial circulation and the approach was known to certain high officers in the Army and Navy as well as to members of the Cabinet.

statesman, shattered by bombs and shame, was at this time. What he did was to call a press conference at which, by prior arrangement, a reporter asked for his comments on the Potsdam Proclamation. There was a gasp of amazement when he looked at the notes in his trembling hand and said:

"I consider the joint proclamation of the three powers to be no more than a repeat of the Cairo Declaration.[3] The government does not regard it as a thing of any great value. The government will just ignore [mokusatsu] it. We will press forward resolutely to carry the war to a successful conclusion."

Japanese apologists were afterward to explain that Suzuki was merely trying to say that his Cabinet was "marking time" and were "ignoring" the Potsdam Proclamation only while they waited to hear the results of Soviet mediation. They claim that the main trouble caused by his statement resulted from a mistranslation of the word "mokusatsu" in the report of the premier's statement sent abroad by the official Japanese news agency, Domei. In their shortwave bulletins they translated mokusatsu as "reject" instead of "ignore" and therefore gave the Allies a completely wrong impression.

This really won't do. The working and the context of Suzuki's statement was such that, no matter how you translate "mokusatsu," the meaning of the message comes out clearly as a contemptuous brushing aside of the Proclamation and the ultimatum it offered.

That was how it was received abroad. And that was how the United States Government regarded it. Secretary of War Henry L. Stimson wrote:

"In the face of this rejection, we could only proceed to demonstrate that the ultimatum had meant exactly what it said when it stated that if the Japanese continued the war, 'the full application of our military power, backed by our resolve, will mean the inevitable and complete destruction of the Japanese armed forces and just as inevitably the utter devastation of the Japanese homeland.'"

He added:

"For such a purpose, the atomic bomb was an eminently suitable weapon." [4]

---

[3] Which, in fact, had been much shorter and tougher.
[4] Henry L. Stimson, *On Active Service in Peace and War*, New York: Harper & Row, 1947.

On August 6th, the first atomic bomb dropped on Hiroshima. On the following day, hurtling into the war before it was too late, Russia broke her treaty with Japan and sent Red Army troops and planes into Manchukuo.

Premier Suzuki and his use of the word "mokusatsu" may not have been the cause of it all; but they certainly helped.

The bomb had obliterated Hiroshima at 8:15 A.M. and Hirohito was walking in the palace gardens when news of it reached him. He had spent much of the night in the air raid shelter, discussing the situation with his brother, Prince Takamatsu, and there had not been much time for sleep. In his highly emotional state, word of the Hiroshima disaster had an immediately physical effect, and tears came into his eyes. "He was overwhelmed with grief for the innocent civilians who were its victims," said Kido later.[5] In great agitation, he told his Lord Keeper:

"Under these circumstances, we must bow to the inevitable. No matter what happens to my personal safety, we must put an end to this war as speedily as possible, so that this tragedy will not be repeated."

He made the reference to his "personal safety" because the bitter-end fanatics were still citing the Potsdam Proclamation's silence over the fate of the Imperial Family as reason for fighting on. "It is the only way to save the Emperor!" was their cry. But Hirohito was sick of them and beyond worrying about himself. He no longer cared—except to stop the bombing and the killing.

News of the atom bomb, followed by the Soviet declaration of war, had had its effect upon the Japanese premier, too, although, as it proved, not yet enough. But at least some sense was beginning to filter into his muddled mind. Kido writes:

"When I arrived at the Imperial Palace at approximately ten on the morning of August 9th, I was informed that the Emperor had been waiting for me. Therefore, without even entering my room, I went immediately into the Imperial presence. The Emperor informed me of the start of hostilities with the Soviet Union and ordered me to meet immediately with Premier Suzuki and to urge him to work for the speedy

---

[5] While being interrogated at Sugamo Prison, where he was held on war crime charges.

312

termination of the war in accordance with the policy already discussed."

Fortunately, Suzuki had just about that time arrived at the Imperial Palace. "I immediately saw him and conveyed to him the Emperor's wishes. He stated that he was of the same opinion as the Emperor and that he believed there was no other way to deal with the situation than by accepting the Potsdam Declaration. He promised immediately to call a session of the Supreme War Direction Council and then a Cabinet meeting to determine the policy and thus strive to fulfil the Emperor's wishes. He departed in great haste."

But when the Supreme Council met later that day, haste was the last quality they displayed. Events seemed to have stunned them and frozen their minds, so that they were unable to absorb facts and face up to realities. Around the table, with Suzuki doddering at the head, sat the statesmen and soldiers of Japan upon whom the fate of the nation rested. These were the men who had hurled Japan into the war and learned, by hammerblow after hammerblow, of the folly to which they had committed their people. But now their minds were atrophied. They knew the war was lost, that Japan could be saved from doom only by urgent and desperate resolution to accept defeat; but like Pavlov's dogs, they went on making the same reflex actions, still talked of "last attacks" and "fights to the death" and "victory yet!" Only Togo seemed to be alive to the agonizing nature of the emergency they were facing, but the icy words of truth which he aimed at his colleagues fell off them like summer hail, and they relapsed into their stupor.

They talked all morning, and then adjourned for lunch. They talked all afternoon and into the evening. The air was heavy with the muggy heat of a Tokyo summer and the ominous feeling of disaster in the air. But they got nowhere. They were not even galvanized when a messenger came in to inform them that a second atom bomb had dropped—on Nagasaki, this time. The knowledge not only did not frighten them, it did not seem to affect them in any way, and they showed neither fear nor indignation, neither sorrow nor pity. It was like a conference of the walking dead.

Eventually, at ten in the evening, it was obvious that they were getting nowhere. A small majority was for accepting the Potsdam Proclamation in its entirety, provided the maintenance of the Imperial Line was guaranteed. The rest, including service ministers and their chiefs of staff, were for insisting on an amelioration of the terms: *no* occupation of Japan, *no* prosecution of war criminals except by the Japanese themselves, *no* humiliation of the armed services. Otherwise they wanted to fight on and die gloriously. Or so they monotonously repeated.

The Council was adjourned, the deadlock complete. It was then that Togo and Suzuki, after conferring together, decided that there was only one man left who could solve the problem and save the nation. The Emperor. They hurried to the Imperial Palace and were received immediately in audience. They rehearsed their dilemma to the silent monarch, and asked permission to call an Imperial Conference over which he would be asked to preside. He realized the significance of what they were asking, and this time he knew what he must do—become what he had always tried not to be, though his courtiers insisted he was: A Divine Monarch, speaking with the voice of the gods, whose words must be obeyed.

It was now or never.

The air raid shelter which had been built as an underground annex of the Obunko, the Emperor's library, where he was now living, had a conference room which was only thirty feet long by six across.[6] A long table rimmed with chairs, and a throne at the head, took up most of the space, and by the time the delegates to the Imperial Conference had taken their places the room was stifling. It was a hot night, there was no air-conditioning, and one delegate noticed that even the wooden panels on the thick stone walls were sweating.

The conference began at 11:50 P.M. when Hirohito quietly entered and took his seat. The whole room rose and congealed into bows until the Emperor indicated that they should be seated. Then they began to talk.

Except that they were now in the presence of their Emperor, it was the earlier meeting all over again. The same arguments were rehearsed, the same attitudes struck, the same pleas for peace and exhortations to resist. Once more the Army Chief of Staff, Umezu, advocated a final battle, and once more Navy Chief of Staff Toyoda backed him up.

[6] It still exists, though the door leading from the library to the stairs has been blocked up, and the only ingress is through a door and staircase hidden in a palace copse.

"We cannot say that final victory is certain, but neither do we believe we can be finally defeated," he declared.

Once more Foreign Minister Togo put the case for surrender, and heard the murmurs of "defeatist!" from the sweating statesmen around him.

It did not need Suzuki to state the obvious—that here was unbreakable deadlock once more—but that did not prevent the Prime Minister from saying it. It gave him his excuse, anyway. He glanced at his watch. It was nearly two A.M. Collars were wilted and there were pools of moisture on the table where hands were resting. A mosquito had got into the room and was buzzing around the head of General Anami, the Minister for War, but he did not dare to move it away.

"Gentlemen," said the premier, "we have spent hours in deliberation without coming to a decision and yet agreement is not in sight. You are fully aware that we cannot afford to waste even a minute at this juncture." He paused and then went on:

"I propose, therefore, to seek the Imperial guidance and substitute it for the decision of this conference."

The time had come.

"The announcement, sudden as it was, electrified the whole gathering and the participants gasped," wrote Kase later, "not having anticipated such a step . . . an extraordinary deviation from time-honored practice." [7]

Hirohito was well aware of it. Marquis Yasumasa Matsudaira, the Lord Chamberlain, who had seen the Emperor in the hour and a half before the convening of the conference, later said:

"The Emperor must have felt that this was a national crisis and that it was far more serious than any matter to do with the constitution of Japan. Since the outcome would decide whether Japan would cease to exist as a nation or not, it seems that he took a drastic step in view of the situation, and discarding all his previous convictions, *gave his opinion.* He made a statement to the effect that the members of the Council should abide by his views. This was altogether an unprecedented case. It was the one and only time in his life that he talked so long and in such a manner in public. However, this Cabinet did not merely listen to

[7] Kase, *op. cit.*

315

His Majesty's opinion and accept it as his order on the spot. The Cabinet listened to the Emperor's opinion—and held a Cabinet meeting. They deliberated on the future course on the basis of what His Majesty said. The result was that his wishes were complied with." [8]

Hirohito was very nervous as he rose to speak. He had some notes in his hand but it was obvious that he could not read them very well, either because there was sweat and steam on his glasses or because his perspiring fingers had smudged the ideographs. For a few moments his Adam's apple gulped so much that it got in the way of the words, and what came out at first was high and strained and abrasive. And then, slowly, he took courage and calmed down.

"I have given serious thought to the situation prevailing at home and abroad, and I have concluded that continuing the war can only mean destruction for the nation and a prolongation of bloodshed and cruelty in the world. I cannot bear to see my innocent people suffer any longer. Ending the war is the only way to restore world peace and to relieve the nation from the dreadful distress with which it is burdened."

The do-or-die fanatics had dwelt at some length on the bloodshed they hoped to inflict on the Allies once they disembarked on the shores of the homeland, and talked clankingly of waiting kamikaze pilots, loaded ships and impregnable beach defenses.

The Emperor went on, with his voice now drained to a monotone: "I was told by those advocating a continuation of the hostilities that by June new battalions would be ready for action in the impregnable positions at Kujukurihama when the enemy began to land. It is now August and the fortifications have still not been completed.[9] Not only that. The equipment for these battalions is insufficient, and, I am told, will not be ready until at least the middle of September. As for the promised additions to our air strength, these are not forthcoming, and, I understand, will not be."

He paused to swallow and wipe his wet and pallid face. "I am told that there are those who say that the answer to the survival of our nation

[8] Part of a statement by Yasumasa Matsudaira to Military Intelligence Section, GHQ, Far East Command.
[9] The Emperor knew whereof he spoke. For the past few weeks he had had attached to his personal staff a trusted naval officer whose sole duty was to watch and report on the activities and preparations of the armed services and report direct to him.

lies in the outcome of one last battle, to be fought here in our homeland. Do we have a plan for this? How is it to be carried out? The experiences of the past show that there has already been a grave difference between our plans and our performances. In the case of impregnable positions at Kujukurihama, which are not impregnable, I do not believe that the difference between what is and what should be can be rectified. And this is the shape of things. How can we repel the invaders?"

Another pause. An uncomfortable one, this time, because Hirohito was obviously near to a breakdown. But he shook himself slightly.

He went on: "I cannot help feeling sad when I consider the people who have served me so loyally, the soldiers and sailors who have been killed or wounded in the battlefields overseas, the families who have lost their homes and so often their lives as well in the air raids here. I need not tell you how unbearable I find it to see the brave and loyal fighting men of Japan disarmed. It is equally unbearable that others who have given me devoted service should now be threatened with punishment as the instigators of the war. *Nevertheless, the time has come when we must bear the unbearable.*[10] When I recall the feelings of my Imperial Grandsire, the Emperor Meiji, at the time of the Triple Intervention [11] I swallow my tears and give my sanction to the proposal to accept the Allied proclamation on the basis outlined by the Foreign Minister."

It was done. The god-king had spoken at last.

"The Imperial verdict was announced and the issue was now clear," wrote Kase. "It was to be peace! The nation whose fate had hung by a hair was saved by the explicit command of the Emperor to terminate hostilities at once."

Hirohito rose and so did the rest of the room, bowing almost cringingly toward him as he left the air raid shelter. He climbed the stairs slowly and passed through the darkened library into the park, where it was very still. There was no air raid that evening and save for the hum of mosquitoes and the phosphorescent flash of fireflies, all was quiet and heavily, almost languorously, peaceful.

The delegates filed out of the air raid shelter, the first of them Togo, who hastened to the car in the palace courtyard where Kase was waiting

[10] A crib from Kido's statement to the Emperor of a month before.
[11] A reference to successful pressure on Japan by Russia, Germany and France in 1895 to relinquish the Liaotung Peninsula to China.

for him.[12] They hurried to an emergency meeting of the Cabinet, which, with only one hesitating voice, unanimously accepted the Emperor's advice and endorsed the decision of the Imperial Conference, to accept the Potsdam Declaration. Kase then went on to the Foreign Office where he hastily drafted a note in English which he ordered to be cabled off at once —to the Swiss Government in Berne for transmission to the United States and China, and to the Swedish Government in Stockholm for transmission to Britain and the Soviet Union. It said:

"In obedience to the gracious command of His Majesty the Emperor, who, ever anxious to enhance the cause of world peace, desires earnestly to bring about a speedy termination of hostilities with a view to saving mankind from the calamities to be imposed upon them by the further continuation of the war, the Japanese Government several weeks ago asked the Soviet Government, with which neutral relations then prevailed, to render good offices in restoring peace vis-à-vis the enemy Powers. Unfortunately, these efforts in the interest of peace having failed, the Japanese Government in conformity with the august wish of His Majesty to restore the general peace and desiring to put an end to the untold sufferings entailed by war as quickly as possible, have decided upon the following:

"The Japanese Government are ready to accept the terms enumerated in the joint declaration which was issued at Potsdam on July 26, 1945, by the heads of the Governments of the United States, Great Britain and China, and later subscribed by the Soviet Government, with the understanding that the said declaration does not comprise any demand which prejudices the prerogatives of His Majesty as a Sovereign Ruler. The Japanese Government sincerely hope that this understanding is warranted and desire keenly that an explicit indication to that effect will be speedily forthcoming."

It was all over.

Or was it?

---

[12] He had taken refuge there from the omnipresent mosquitoes.

318

Chapter Twenty-two

The telegram accepting the Potsdam Proclamation (with the proviso about the status of the Emperor) had been sent from the Foreign Office in Tokyo in the early hours of August 10, 1945. For forty-eight hours of fretfulness, doubt, mounting tension and proliferating chaos, there was silence from the capitals of the Allied powers.

The diehard militarists made good use of the time to fan fanaticism, and the government unwittingly played into their hands. It was necessary to give the Japanese people some indication that the end was near, and a statement was written and distributed to the newspapers. But its real meaning was so camouflaged by circumlocutions and parentheses—and no language can better conceal real meaning, even when an effort is being made to be plain—that the readers of it completely failed to realize that the government was suing for peace; the more so since side by side with the administration's statement appeared a message ostensibly from the Minister for War, Anami, exhorting the armed forces to fight on to the death for the glory of Japan.[1]

As the hours ticked slowly by—to the thump of bombs, since there was no letup in the Allied air raids—Hirohito could be forgiven his agonized groans of impatience, for both he and his advisers realized the danger of procrastination. The fanatics were being given invaluable time to organize and wreck a peaceful surrender.

[1] In fact, Anami never actually signed the message, which was dug out of his wastepaper basket and issued by a subordinate.

Unfortunately, however, just as members of the Japanese administration were divided over the question of peace or a battle to the death, so were the American Government and her allies divided over what should be done about the Emperor. The schism was particularly wide inside the United States Administration. Mr. Cordell Hull, as has been indicated, was fundamentally opposed to any promise that might preserve the Imperial system in Japan, and he was backed by many a Republican to whom the idea of any sort of a monarchical institution was inimical. On the other hand, there were those like Mr. Joseph C. Grew, Secretary Stimson and Admiral Leahy, the President's aide, who maintained that any attempt to abolish the Imperial system and dethrone the Emperor, sacred, inviolable, the divine heart of Japanese life, would antagonize every section of the community and make a war to the finish inevitable, with all that meant in loss of life to the armies which must fight it out.

Grew wrote:

"August 10th was hectic in Washington. Radio reports from Japan announced the surrender before official notification reached Washington by way of Switzerland. At nine o'clock Stimson was called to the White House, where the President was holding a conference on the surrender terms. All those present seemed eager to make the most of this great opportunity to end the war, but there was some doubt as to the propriety of accepting the Japanese conditions."

Truman asked Grew what his opinion was.

"I told him I thought that even if the question had not been raised by the Japanese, we would have to continue to accept the Emperor ourselves under our commander's supervision, in order to get him to surrender the many scattered armies of the Japanese who would own no other authority, and that something like this use of the Emperor must be made in order to save us from a score of bloody Iwo Jimas and Okinawas all over China and the New Netherlands. He was the only source of authority in Japan under the Japanese theory of the State." [2]

Like Leahy, he was for accepting the Japanese surrender as worded in their cable, and for smoothing out the wrinkles when the Allies were in Tokyo. But Secretary of State James Byrnes persuaded President Truman (who, good Kansas City politician though he was, seemed not to appreciate the importance of the "boss" system as applied to Japan) that the Allied

[2] Joseph C. Grew, *Turbulent Era*, New York: Houghton Mifflin Company, 1952.

reply must take note of those elements who considered Grew and his supporters as "appeasers" and "royal lickspittles." The reply, which was broadcast over San Francisco radio, said (in part):

"From the moment of surrender, the authority of the Emperor and the said Japanese Government to rule the state shall be subject to the Supreme Commander of the Allied Powers who will take such steps as he deems proper to effectuate the surrender terms. The Emperor will be required to authorize and ensure the signature by the Government of Japan and the Imperial Japanese General Headquarters of the surrender terms necessary to carry out the provisions of the Potsdam Proclamation, and shall issue his commands to all the Japanese military, naval and air authorities. . . . The ultimate form of government of Japan shall, in accordance with the Potsdam Proclamation, be established by the freely expressed will of the Japanese people."

Secretary Stimson was afterwards to call it a "masterful paper" which avoided any direct reference to the Japanese condition "but accomplished the desired purpose of reassuring the Japanese."[3]

That is what *he* thought. Many Japanese were, in fact, far from reassured, and the fanatics saw in the Allied reply an immediate opportunity to cry: "Our terms have been rejected. Let us fight to the death!"

Kido wrote:

"On August 12th at 9:45 A.M. the reply from the Allies was received. At 11:00 A.M. Foreign Minister Togo proceeded to the palace to submit the Allied reply to the Throne. After withdrawing from the Imperial presence, the Foreign Minister anxiously told me that opposition to a reference in the Allied reply, paragraph 4, to 'the free will of the people' might raise its head among those Japanese who were anxious to guard the national polity jealously. When I asked him what interpretation the Foreign Office put on the paragraph in question, he replied that the Foreign Office saw nothing objectionable in the paragraph in question."

But others did, as Kido quickly discovered.

"As feared by Foreign Minister Togo, not only the paragraph in question became a serious issue with these Japanese who were jealous of safeguarding national polity, but the military stiffened their attitude once the Allied reply was received."

[3] Stimson, *On Active Service in Peace and War*, New York: Harper & Row, 1947.

The President of the Privy Council, Hiranuma, thought that the Emperor's position was left in an equivocal state by the Allied reply; and, inevitably, of course, Premier Suzuki, always ready to fizz every time someone struck a match near him, also expressed his belief that there was only one way out left for Japan if the Emperor was to be saved—fight, fight, fight! He was no longer interested in the why or the how.

When Kido heard about this he was furious, and immediately telephoned to the Prime Minister's office and asked to see him. The time had obviously come to call a halt to the old man's foolishness. He had been indulged too long. Kido said to him:

"I have no intention to belittle the arguments of those who are anxious to guard the national polity jealously, but, on the basis of his careful study, the Foreign Minister assures us that there is nothing wrong with the paragraph four in question. It would get nowhere if our opinions were allowed to be swayed by the opinions of individuals. Therefore I think that there is nothing left to us but to trust to the interpretation of· responsible bodies, that is, the Foreign Office. . . . Otherwise, it means the loss of a million lives. Is this your wish?"

The premier (as reported by Kido) replied fervently:

"Let us do!"

One takes it that by such an expression he meant: "You are quite right. Let us get on with it!"

But, of course, he did not.

The reply from the United States had thrown the whole question of peace or war back into the ring again, and Suzuki's lamentable display of irresolution, as he made clear at conference after conference during the next forty-eight hours, once more brought Japan to the brink of utter disaster. The Supreme Council met again, and yet again flogged all the old arguments. It was as if the Emperor had never spoken. The arbiters of the nation's destiny (all speaking, of course, on the Emperor's behalf, hand on heart) were once more ranged against each other.

August 14. In Hiroshima the surviving inhabitants, picking their way out of the scorched plain where a city had been, wondering why some of them were brown on one side and black on the other, were pleading for help from those with no idea of what sort of help to give. In Nagasaki, the victims died or suppurated not knowing that, if the weather and the cloud formations had been different, it would have been somewhere else and someone else; and they could not guess that, compared with the people of Hiroshima, they would become second-class atom bomb victims, anyway.

In any case, the effect of the atom bombs upon the consciences of the Japanese Government had been remarkably light. If the two cataclysmic explosions had been intended to stop the war at once, they had failed. The cosmic horror was too great to be properly understood.

The Allies seem to have decided that if obliterating the Japanese people was not going to have its effect, then informing them of the facts might do so. They decided to substitute pamphlets for atom bombs (possibly because they had, at this time, no atom bombs left).

"When I got up from my bed on the morning of August 14th," Kido said, "a chamberlain showed me a propaganda leaflet containing the terms of the Allied Powers translated into the Japanese language. These leaflets had been scattered by the B-29's. One look caused me to be stricken with consternation. In the past two or three days, the military services (both Army and Navy) had gradually stiffened their attitude. Because of military opposition, the convocation of the Supreme War Direction Council had been postponed. At this juncture these leaflets were being distributed. If they should fall into the hands of the troops and enrage them, a military *coup d'état* would become inevitable and make extremely difficult the execution of the planned policy. It would bring about the worst possible situation for our country."

Kido sent a message through to Hirohito at once requesting an audience and was shown into the library, where the Emperor was pensively breakfasting off brown rice, at 8:30 A.M.

"I advised him [the Emperor] to remain firm in his resolution and to summon the members of the Supreme War Direction Council and of the Cabinet to inform them of his wish for the *immediate* cessation of hostilities. The Emperor grasped the situation fully and ordered me to make arrangements with Premier Suzuki."

Kido, who had become the winged messenger of peace in Japan by now, flew off to find the Prime Minister and on discovering him just arriving at the Imperial Palace, inquired when the Supreme Council was going to meet.

A harried expression flitted across his face at this question. He replied: "I'm having a hard time. The Army wants to wait until thirteen hundred hours, while the Navy asks me to postpone it without setting a specific time!"

Kido, who by now had had his fill of Suzuki's hesitations, prevarications, procrastinations and apprehensions, asked him sharply whether he had seen the American leaflets. Of course, he had not. The Lord Keeper told him:

"The American planes are apparently scattering the Japanese translation of the reply of the Allied Powers all over Japan. If these are to fall into the hands of the troops and arouse their wrath, internal chaos will result, beyond all hope of salvaging. I have informed the Emperor of the urgency of the situation and advised him to summon the members of the Supreme War Direction Council and the Cabinet in order to direct them to accept immediately the reply of the Allied Powers and bring about peace. His Majesty agreed and instructed me to consult with the premier. If you have no objection, let us make arrangements toward that end."

Suzuki hesitated, fluttered, sighed heavily, said: "Let me hear it from the Emperor's own lips," and eventually agreed.

The Japanese engine of war, which had wheezed to a halt on August 9th, when the Emperor applied the brake, had been cranked up again by the diehards and had rattled on for another five days. This time it would be necessary to cut the ignition.

On August 14, 1945, another Imperial Conference was convened in the air raid shelter in the Imperial Palace, and at eleven A.M. that morning Hirohito walked in. It was hotter than ever and everyone in the room looked uncomfortable, possibly because the meeting had been summoned hurriedly and the delegates were in disarray; the Imperial Protocol Section had consented to waive the rules for the occasion, and did not insist on the striped trousers and tails which were usually *de rigueur*, but they had specified that ties should be worn. The ties had been borrowed at the door and were carelessly looped. But it was the internal untidiness of the delegates which made them feel most uncomfortable.

Premier Suzuki (in morning dress; he knew all about the meeting) rose to state the reasons for the summons. As they all knew, the Allied reply had come, but there were those who objected to it. Therefore there could not be a unanimous decision to accept it. He called on the objectors, for the last time, to state their views. At this Anami, Minister for War, Umezu, Army Chief of Staff, and Toyoda, Navy Chief of Staff, all rose and once more emotionally aired their views. They were so emotional that it was difficult to understand what they were saying, except that they did not think the Emperor was being given sufficient guarantees, that the Imperial polity was in danger, and they were prepared to die fighting.

All through their perorations, Hirohito sat on his throne at the head of the table, fixedly and determinedly staring at his feet. Now, rather like a dog climbing out of a pool and shaking off the water still clinging to him, he rose. He seemed quite relaxed and calm, though in fact he was constricted with emotion. He said:

"I have listened carefully to each of the arguments presented in opposition to the view that Japan should accept the Allied reply as it stands. But my own thoughts have not changed. Let me restate them. I have surveyed the conditions prevailing in Japan and in the world at large, and it is my firm belief that a continuation of the war promises nothing but more and more destruction. I have studied the terms of the Allied reply and I have concluded that they constitute a virtually complete acknowledgement of the position we maintained in the note dispatched some days ago."

A pause.

"In short, I consider the reply to be acceptable."

The delegates, heads bent, sweat dripping from their noses, shuffled and shuddered, but did not speak.

"I realize that there are those of you who distrust the intentions of the Allies. This is, of course, quite natural, but to my mind the Allied reply is evidence of the peaceful and friendly intentions of the enemy. The faith and resolution of this nation as a whole, therefore, are factors of paramount importance."

Another pause. A sip of the green tea on the table beside him.

"I appreciate how difficult it will be for the officers and men of the Army and Navy to surrender their arms to the enemy and see their homeland occupied. Indeed, it is difficult for me to issue the order making this necessary and to deliver so many of my trusted servants into the hands of the Allied authorities, by whom they will be accused of being war criminals. In spite of these feelings, so difficult to bear, I cannot endure the thought of letting my people suffer any longer. A continuation of the war would bring death to tens, perhaps even hundreds, of thousands of persons. The whole nation would be reduced to ashes. How then could I carry on the wishes of my Imperial ancestors?"

Those ministers sufficiently in possession of their emotions to keep

325

tab on what was happening remember that it was at this time that Hirohito's voice began to falter, and he gulped for moisture to salivate his throat between every sentence.

"The decision I have reached is akin to the one forced upon my grandfather, the Emperor Meiji. I say it once more. As he endured the unendurable, so shall I, and so must you. It is my desire that you, my ministers of state, accede to my wishes and forthwith accept the Allied reply. In order that the people may know of my decision, I request you to prepare at once an Imperial Rescript so that I may broadcast to the nation. Finally, I call upon each and every one of you to exert himself to the utmost so that we may work together in the trying days to come." [4]

There are those who were present who afterward said that by the time he had reached the last sentence, Hirohito was weeping; but this is not true. His time for weeping had come and gone days before. The tears belonged to his ministers. All of them were crying openly, and some of them quite audibly.

The Emperor had spoken. This time there was no gainsaying what he had said. The war was over, no doubt of it. It was Hirohito's finest hour.

Tears Hirohito did shed later, when he received Kido in his library that evening and told him what had happened. But they did not last long. The Lord Keeper, ever the brisk and practical aide, indicated that now the vital decision had been taken, there were arrangements to be made.

First of all, the Imperial Rescript by which the Japanese people would learn their fate must be issued. To secure its widest circulation and acceptance, Kido had already discussed with Hirohito the idea of having it broadcast by radio—and by the Emperor himself. It would be the first time in the history of the dynasty that an Emperor of Japan had ever spoken directly to his people. Hirohito had agreed to this method of making his views known beyond all doubt.

Just before midnight on August 14, 1945, he was driven from the Obunko to a room in the Imperial Household Building where he began the recording of a disc which would inform the Japanese people of the

[4] Text based on the recollections of those who were present. There was no official stenographer present, but there is a record at the Imperial Palace.

nature of their future. The text had been prepared by the Cabinet but it incorporated much of Hirohito's own words as he had spoken them at the Imperial Conferences of August 9th and 14th. In view of the awesome nature of the occasion, the text had then been passed on to three Chinese scholars for their approval and emendation, so that the Rescript, destined for history, should contain no literary solecisms. Hirohito was nervous and so complete a stranger to the microphone that the radio engineers had to remind him to speak in his ordinary voice, and not try to reach his millions of subjects by shouting to them. But the first disc was satisfactory, and it was only at the Emperor's insistence that a second one was made as an insurance.

It was during the recording of this second disc that a messenger reached the room where the Emperor was speaking with vague news of trouble brewing. No one quite knew what was afoot, but it was thought better to get Hirohito back to his quarters as quickly as possible. His car had been brought around to a side door and in this he drove quickly back to the Obunko along the twisting tarmac road through the woods, and there the Empress was waiting for him, with a cup of green tea. While he sipped it, the record was played over for Nagako's approval and she heard it through with tears in her eyes.

By this time the vague rumors had crystallized into ugly truth. Word reached the Obunko that a battalion of the Imperial Guard was in revolt, and, led by a number of fanatics, had crossed the moat and was at large in the grounds of the Imperial Palace.

"I cannot believe it!" the Emperor said. "I do not believe my men would betray me!"

He was quite right; they had no intention of doing so. But they had been tricked. A group of bitter-enders, led by a certain Major Hatanaka and an Air Force captain, Uehara, had got wind of the fact that the Emperor had made a disc of his Imperial Rescript announcing the surrender, and that it would be broadcast to the nation the following day. They were determined that the broadcast should never take place. One group was sent off to occupy the main radio station in Tokyo, where the engineers were questioned and beaten until they convinced the insurgents that they had passed the disc into the custody of court officials. Another group, with Hatanaka as their spokesman, went to the headquarters of the Imperial Guard, where they were seen by General Mori, its commander. Hatanaka appealed to him as a patriot to join their revolt, insisting that Hirohito was no longer a free agent and was being forced to issue a surrender Rescript under pressure from evil, corrupt and cowardly politicians. When Mori refused to join, he was asked if he would take an "inactive" role in the coup by putting his seal on an order, which Hatanaka produced, ordering his men to support the rebels. His refusal caused Hatanaka to lose his patience, and he took his pistol and shot the commander; and his aide, who tried to come to his rescue, was cut down with a sword by Uehara. Then the rebels put Mori's seal on the forged order and were afterward led by members of the Guard, who were unaware of their commander's murder, across the moat.

Fortunately, there was an air raid alert on at the time, and the palace grounds and buildings were in total darkness. The rebels were short of flashlights, and they did not quite know where to look. But they made first for the Imperial Household Building, and once inside found their way to Kido's office. They decided that he must have the disc.

Kido had had little sleep during the past three or four days, and he was dog tired. As soon as the Emperor's recording session was over, he returned to his office, slipped on a kimono, and went to sleep on the floor, leaving the radio playing—for it kept going through the night in order to announce air raids if and when planes approached the city. It was not the sound of the radio but the silence of it which awoke him. The radio had gone off the air.

He scrambled to his feet and was getting dressed when Ishiwata, a court official, burst in to tell him of the revolt. The Lord Keeper, ever a quick-thinking and practical man, emptied his drawers of his most important documents, went with them down the corridor to the lavatory, and there tore them into little pieces and flushed them away down the benjo. After which he and Ishiwata descended to the Imperial Household vaults and had themselves locked in. They escaped just in time. Ten minutes after their departure Hatanaka and his men burst into Kido's office and ransacked it, and then set about the servants with their swords and pistols in an attempt to discover where the Lord Keeper had gone. They didn't know so they couldn't tell.

It would have been unthinkable, of course, for such royalist fanatics to have disturbed the Emperor himself; and the Imperial Guard, tricked though they might be, would never have allowed it. But a cordon of troops was thrown around the Obunko to see that Hirohito did not leave

328

and no one got in to see him.[5] As it turned out, the Emperor's faith in his Guard was less than their awe of him, and he had taken no chances. At the suggestion of the Empress, the all-important disc was given to one of her ladies-in-waiting, who took it across to the ladies-in-waiting pavilion, where she hid it in a safe concealed behind an old Chinese scroll. She and three companions slept, or pretended to sleep, beneath it for the remainder of the night.

The search went on, to no avail. And then, just before dawn, help came.

The fanatics had made one mistake. They had cut all the telephone wires from the Imperial Palace except one, which was connected directly with naval headquarters in Tokyo. It was over this that a call was sent for help. While the rebels were still pointing their flashlights into likely corners, looking for the disc, General Tanaka, Commander of the Eastern Army, stormed across the moat. He upbraided the rebel leaders for daring to humiliate the Emperor by doubting his decision, and did it so effectively that Major Hatanaka immediately stepped forward and apologized for the shameful actions of himself and his men. They moved across the moat into the palace plaza, where they bowed in the direction of the Emperor over the wall, and then ceremonially fell upon their swords in a salutary act of contrition.

They were not the only ones to die by the sword in the next few hours. General Anami, the War Minister, after writing an apology to the Emperor and imbibing an inordinate amount of saké—on the theory that a heavy intake of alcohol makes bleeding easier—cut open his abdomen in the ritual act of seppuku, and was finished off by his brother-in-law. Vice Admiral Onishi, the commander and "inventor" of the kamikaze corps, was rumored to have taken a plane and flown out to sea until his gas supply ran out. In fact, he too disemboweled himself, after apologizing to his men for taking an easy way out. They, in turn, complained that the Navy had shamed their leader by providing him with a casket five inches too short for his body, and carting him to the crematorium in a truck.

But the disc was intact. The Emperor was safe. And at one minute

[5] He could have left quite easily, as it turned out, by going through the air raid shelter. The rebels never thought—or didn't even know—of the entrance in the park.

before noon on August 15, 1945, the Japanese people—who had been issued a special ration of electricity for the purpose—turned on their radios and heard their Emperor speak for the first time.

The nation paused, bowed to their loud speakers, and waited in awe to hear what the descendant of the Goddess of the Sun would have them do.

"To Our good and loyal subjects," he began. "After pondering deeply the general trends of the world and the actual conditions obtaining in Our Empire today, We have decided to effect a settlement of the present situation by resorting to an extraordinary measure. We have ordered Our Government to communicate to the Government of the United States, Great Britain, China and the Soviet Union that Our Empire accepts the provisions of their joint declaration. . . ."

There was more to it than that. There were strange phrases over which the nervous Hirohito seemed to stumble, phrases such as "the war situation has developed not necessarily to our advantage" and "the general trends of the world have all turned against her [Japan's] interest."

But it was not the words that the people listened to after those first two sentences, but to the voice of their divine monarch. His voice! They were hearing his voice! He was speaking to them directly as a father to his children.

And he was telling them that the war was over.

Chapter Twenty-three

"We climbed the gangway," wrote Kase, "Shigemitsu leading the way, limping heavily on his cane. He walks with a wooden leg, having had his left leg blown off in a bomb outrage in Shanghai some fifteen years ago. It was as if he took each step with a groan and the rest of us echoed it with a sigh."

It was the morning of September 2, 1945, aboard the U.S. Battleship *Missouri*, and at 9:04 A.M. precisely, Shigemitsu, as leader of the Japanese delegation, signed the formal instrument of surrender. Hostilities between Japan and the Allied powers were officially at an end.

Now the Japanese would begin to feel the humiliations of defeat and possibly some of the horrors which their enemies had experienced in the past four years, and a shudder of premonitory terror passed over the nation. How would the conqueror behave—like a raging, vengeful beast, raping, looting, killing?

In the days before the first American troops arrived at Atsugi Airfield on August 26th, the heads of families gathered in anxious colloquy and seemed to reach a general conclusion, that lust would be the greediest appetite of the occupying forces. Temptation must therefore be removed at once from their line of vision. Mothers with nubile daughters were packed off to the country and told to go into hiding. Those who could not leave were warned to stay at home, or, if they must go abroad, do their utmost to eschew attire calculated to arouse sexual desires in the white barbarians. For instance, the prevailing female uniform of wartime, the baggy-trousered mompei (which, as Mrs. Terasaki remarked,

331

actually made the Japanese women "look like frogs") was banned as "too provocative. It may possibly persuade the enemy soldiers that it is pajamas, the kind of night attire worn in the West, and thus provoke evil thoughts." The women were urged instead to don kimonos, preferably in drab colors, and to be particularly sure that they also wore tabi (white socks) because "Westerners consider bare feet to be lascivious." But above all, they were told to hide. The Terror was about to descend. The Beast was coming.

As many a German fraulein could have told them by this time, it was not the ferocious grimaces of the GI's which made them so dangerous but their open smiles, not their desire for vengeance but their eagerness to be liked. Within a week of the arrival of the first Allied troops, daughters had begun to disobey their parents and creep out of the hovels and cellars in which most of bomb-racked Tokyo was now living, and had begun to bring back the first packs of Luckies, the first cans of Spam.

Japan was not even to be put under military occupation. On the evening of the signing of the surrender an order was forwarded to Suzuki (who had been dispatched to Yokohama as Minister-liaison) from General MacArthur's headquarters informing him that Japan was about to be subjected to military government. At once Shigemitsu hastened to Yokohama to see the United States Commander in Chief to plead with him to change his mind. He recounted the story of the capitulation, stressing the Emperor's part in it.

"His Imperial Majesty has declared that the spirit of the Potsdam Declaration must be observed and to ensure its observance, he has taken the unusual step of appointing an Imperial Family Cabinet,[1] which has taken all the necessary steps. But that Declaration assumes the existence of the Japanese Government and we did not anticipate that you would substitute military government for it. Japan's case is different from that of Germany."

He stressed the willingness of the Japanese Government under the Emperor's guidance to cooperate to its fullest extent in helping the conquerors to rule Japan, but prophesied disaster should it be thrust aside.

"It may well be that utter confusion will result, the responsibility for which will not be that of the Japanese Government. The latter has

---

[1] Immediately after the capitulation, Suzuki had resigned the premiership in favor of H.I.H. Prince Higashikuni. Other royal relatives were dispatched to outlying battlefields to "carry the Imperial word" to Japanese armies overseas.

already taken steps to put the Directive No. 1 into effect. It has begun the disbanding and disarming of Japanese troops on all fronts. Orders have been issued already for the cessation of operation of all factories that have any connection with munitions."

It was a bland threat served on a velvet platter, and MacArthur was realist enough to accept it. He knew only too well that there were 2,685,000 armed troops still on duty in the Japanese islands. (As the first Allied troops had driven into Tokyo from Atsugi Airfield, Japanese soldiers with rifles under their arms stood shoulder to shoulder every twenty-two miles of the way, with their backs to the conquerors—not to insult them, but to see that no Japanese interfered with them.) He knew that another 4 million troops were overseas. With the puny forces at his disposal, MacArthur was at the mercy of Japanese good will to sustain his role as conqueror. One false move—or one word from the Emperor— and he was in trouble.

With a great show of magnanimity, he consented to allow the Japanese Government to go on governing—so long as it obeyed the directives sent to it by Supreme Commander Allied Powers (SCAP). There was to be no military government. The civil power would remain (officially, at least) in control. Japanese face had been saved.

But what of the Emperor?

For twenty days, since his historic broadcast of August 15th, Hirohito had been immured inside the Imperial Palace, waiting for the conqueror to arrive. In the interregnum between the capitulation and the landing of the first American troops, he had been kept in touch with events by Kido and his ministers—of the wave of suicides among the Army and Navy high commands, of the abortive revolt of the young Air Force pilots at Atsugi,[2] of the action of young fanatics at Atagoyama in blowing themselves up with their own hand grenades. He had watched for himself, from beyond the moat, the mass act of seppuku committed by ten young soldiers in the palace plaza, who first bowed toward him, and then ripped open their bellies as "an act of sorrow and of penance for having failed our divine Emperor."

But over all, the Emperor could feel that his words had been taken to

[2] They dropped leaflets over the city declaring that the Emperor had been "tricked" and threatened to bomb the American fleet when it arrived, but were persuaded to obey the Imperial surrender order by a personal plea from Hirohito's brother, Prince Takamatsu.

heart, that the anger and frustrated violence of the few was not shared by the bulk of the populace. Japan, a wounded beast and an exhausted one, but one with claws left to rip and teeth to tear, had obeyed his command and marched almost humbly into captivity.

On September 4, forty-eight hours after the surrender ceremony aboard the *Missouri*, the special gate in the Imperial Palace, which is used for ceremonial occasions only, swung open for the first time since the capitulation, and Hirohito drove across the famous Niju-bashi (or double-bridge) to address the Diet. A special session had been called to receive the Emperor's personal report on the events, and he was on his way to it. There were no crowds in the streets to cheer him on the way, and there were only subdued demonstrations in the Diet itself, for the members of that body, lickspittles all, were not quite sure what to do when they saw him; it might be dangerous, many of them figured, to grovel at his feet now when there were better-shod feet striding across the horizon, ready to be licked.

Hirohito himself regarded this engagement, before the so-called elected representatives of his people, as probably his final appearance in public as Emperor of Japan. He had little doubt in his own heart of what was going to happen to him. If the address he had given on the radio on August 15th was, as it came to be called, the Voice of the Crane,[3] now came his swan song. He had worked hard with Kido, Shigemitsu, Kase, Konoye and Togo to make it an address worthy of the occasion, and when he rose to deliver it he was less nervous than he had ever been before in his life.

He spoke in court Japanese, using many archaic phrases, and sounding very much like a medieval king.

"We issued some days ago a proclamation of the cessation of hostilities, and We dispatched Our plenipotentiaries and caused them to sign the documents relating thereto. It is Our desire that Our people will surmount the manifold hardships and trials which attend the termination of the war, and make manifest the innate glory of Japan's national polity, win the confidence of the world, establish firmly a peaceful state and contribute to the progress of mankind. Our thoughts are constantly directed to that end. In the consummation of that great task, beware most strictly of any outbursts of emotion which may engender

[3] The crane is regarded in Japan as being the voice of the Emperor and the Throne.

needless complications, or any fraternal contention and strife which may create confusion, lead you astray and cause you to lose the confidence of the world. At home, cultivate the ways of righteousness, foster nobility of the spirit, and work with resolution so that you may enhance the innate glory of the Imperial State and keep pace with the progress of the world."

He exhorted his representatives to remember the sick and wounded, and called for a united nation to serve and aid them, and then he bowed stiffly, and walked swiftly out of the Chamber. He did not even stay to listen to the isolated cheers. He went back to the Imperial Palace—to wait. There was nothing else he could do, now.

On September 8, 1945, General MacArthur, the Allied Commander in Chief, arrived in Tokyo and took up his abode in the American Embassy. The era of SCAP had begun.

What would be the attitude of the Allied Commander in Chief toward the Emperor? The vultures were gathering over the Imperial Palace, scenting the prospect of royal carrion; and they were encouraged when they noticed that Hirohito's enemies had their knives out and were creeping in from all sides. The Emperor's princely cousin, Premier Higashikuni, for instance, had privately advocated the immediate abdication of the monarch on the grounds that "he was captain of the ship and must take responsibility for its going aground." (Prince Higashikuni, no friend of Hirohito but a perfervid admirer of "strong" leaders, advocated the substitution of Crown Prince Akihito—now twelve years old—as Emperor and Prince Chichibu as Regent. How he could possibly have expected such a setup to be "strong" is not known, unless, of course, he envisaged himself as the power behind the throne: for, of course, Prince Chichibu was a sick man.) [4] The Australians and the Dutch, and to a lesser extent the British, were looking for scapegoats upon whom to blame the brutal atrocities of the war, and General Tojo and his cohorts did not seem to be sufficient. Why not the Emperor too, since everything had been committed in his name? They were aided and abetted in this desire to "Get the Emperor!" (as other men in another generation had once cried "Hang the Kaiser!") by a powerful clique in Washington who were antipathetic to the whole idea of monarchy and believed that an Imperial usurpation

[4] Information from a source who does not wish to be identified.

would be a salutary lesson to the Japanese people, who would then learn the benefits of republicanism.

All of them (some unwittingly, some deliberately) were playing into the hands of the Soviet Government, which wanted Hirohito's removal for much more practical motives. His abdication at such a juncture, they believed, would create such chaos and confusion among the Japanese people that Communism would benefit. Especially if they were given, as they had been in Germany, an equal say in the administration of conquered Japan and a third of its territory under their control.

Even at MacArthur's headquarters, the general opinion seemed to be one of apathy or contempt toward Hirohito. No one in the organization (including MacArthur himself) appeared to be sufficiently well-informed in Japanese history to appreciate the Emperor's significance and his enormous potential as an ally. Opinion was divided between those who thought of him as a royal war criminal deserving of condign punishment, and those who considered him a pathetic, myopic little puppet to be thrown away now that his manipulators had been captured.

Fortunately, the Russian delegation in Tokyo seemed to be unaware of the opportunity presented to them by this general mixture of prejudice and ignorance. Had General Kuzma N. Derevyanko, chief of the Soviet delegation, been adequately briefed, he might have been able to bring the monarchy to an end in Japan in the first few weeks of the Occupation—a result which would almost certainly have delivered Japan and the Far East into the Soviet camp. All he had to do was rally the anti-Emperor elements among the Allies and get them working, at the same time fomenting huge anti-Emperor demonstrations among the Japanese populace. The combination might have been too much, even for MacArthur.

As it was, a crop of anti-Hirohito articles began to appear in the Japanese press in which he was not only accused of being a warmonger and an atrocity-monger, but as a womanizer and lecher, too. An old scandal was raked up about a "legitimate" heir to the throne who had been suppressed in Hirohito's favor, and the American Forces newspaper, *Stars and Stripes*, even fell for it and printed details. There were demonstrations outside MacArthur's headquarters in the Dai-Ichi Building and before the Imperial Palace calling for Hirohito's removal.

The situation was saved from disaster by the same vanity, power-complex and dictatorial determination of General MacArthur which was to excite so much criticism—for other reasons—in the days to come.

MacArthur had arrived in Tokyo resolved to let no one—no individual, no monarch, no party, no nation—interfere with his plans for administering Japan. As the man on the spot, he believed he knew more than Washington about how to deal with the situation, and he was determined that Japan should not become another Germany, divided up among the victorious powers, and between the East and West. Japan was to be an American bailiwick. And in fending off the Russians and making sure that they had no say in Japan's administration, he was even prepared to offend the British and other Commonwealth allies, too. And he did. He told them brusquely to keep off. With the Soviet Union he was much ruder—and threatened to lock up the whole Soviet delegation if they tried to resist him.

As to the position of the Emperor, he didn't really care very much at first. He was not in possession of all the facts, and sceptical of much of what he had been told, and was inclined to believe that Hirohito was as bad as the rest of the warlords.

"I came here prepared to be stern with him," he said later.

He had on his staff one officer, General Courtney Whitney, who did all in his power to exacerbate this feeling by priming his chief with carefully selected stories of Japanese feudalism and horror tales about the influence of the Emperor as a symbol of Shintoism. He urged the Commander in Chief to summon the Emperor at once to his headquarters and give him his orders. "Make him come in, crown in hand, and plead for his throne," was the way he put it.

MacArthur had a better idea. He wrote afterward:

"Shortly after my arrival in Tokyo, I was urged by members of my staff to summon the Emperor to my headquarters as a show of power. I brushed the suggestion aside. 'To do so,' I explained, 'would be to outrage the feelings of the Japanese people and make a martyr of the Emperor in their eyes. No, I shall wait and in time the Emperor will voluntarily come to see me. In this case, the patience of the East rather than the haste of the West will best serve our purpose." [5]

What he really meant was: "Let him sweat it out!"

It may not have occurred to MacArthur—but it had certainly occurred to some members of his staff—that the situation was not unlike the times of the Tokugawas. A powerful shogun in the shape of MacArthur had

[5] From REMINISCENCES by Douglas MacArthur, Copyright © 1964 by Time, Inc. Used by permission of the publisher, McGraw-Hill Book Company.

come back to Edo, and all that was needed was a malleable and acquiescent Emperor safely tucked away behind a palace wall to make it just like the old days.[6]

The scurrilous attacks and the demonstrations against the Emperor went on all through September, and to Hirohito, upon whom the strain of the past few weeks was beginning to tell, the pressure became unbearable. What did the Allies, what did the people, what did MacArthur want of him? All he wished to do was retreat into the background. He was tired and unwell, suffering from a mild attack of jaundice—a notorious producer of gloom and depression—and he was under the care of the court physician. His spirits were momentarily lifted by the Empress, who came into the Obunko one day to tell him about her experiences on her first venture outside the palace since the surrender. She had been on a visit to her mother-in-law, the redoubtable Dowager Empress Tei-mei (the former Empress Sadako). On returning she had heard the sounds of shouting coming from the direction of the palace; it was yet another of the anti-Imperial riots organized by the communists. She ordered her driver to proceed and her car skirted the edge of the screaming crowd. At once the demonstrators noticed the flag on the bonnet and passed the word to their comrades. The Empress, eyes sparkling, described the hush which had fallen on the palace plaza, and of the fear suddenly clutching her heart. And then, almost as one man, the crowd turned toward her, and bowed—after which they went on with their meeting.

As the days passed, and Hirohito's sleeplessness by night and gloom by day increased, it became obvious that something must be done to ease the tension. It was decided at last that there was only one thing to do. If MacArthur would not summon the Emperor, the Emperor must go to him instead. Arrangements were begun through Terasaki for him to be received. (Terasaki was the Japanese foreign service official who had been First Secretary to the Embassy in Washington at the time of Pearl Harbor. He and his American wife had spent the war in Japan, and, shortly after the surrender, he had been appointed to the Emperor's liaison staff, obviously because of his perfect English, his pro-American sentiments,

[6] Some cynic later suggested that the parallel would be complete when MacArthur's son—who was in Tokyo with Mrs. MacArthur—contracted a dynastic marriage with one of the Emperor's daughters.

and just possibly because one of his wife's cousins, General Bonner Fellers, was an important member of MacArthur's staff.)

On September 26th the Nijubashi gate once more swung open and the Emperor's venerable (1930), canvas-topped Rolls Royce—which was later to become known to SCAP as "the Cement Mixer"—slid silently across the handsome double bridge over the moat. The confrontation was on at last.

MacArthur wrote later:

"In cutaway, striped trousers and top hat, riding in his Daimler [sic] with the Imperial Grand Chamberlain facing him on the jump seat, Hirohito arrived at the Embassy. I had, from the start of the occupation, directed that there should be no derogation in his treatment. Every honor due to a sovereign was to be his." [7]

It all depends on what you mean by "every honor." It is certain that the circumstances and the reception would have been very different had it been the King of England. But who can blame the Allied Commander, and who could have expected him to be anything but frigidly correct? He had tried to ban the press from the meeting—and those who got wind of it were roughly treated when they tried to get into the Embassy—but he knew that the world would be watching him. The Australians and the Russians wanted Hirohito deposed and tried as a war criminal. There were plenty of Americans and British who would have liked to see him in the dock "even though," as Grew wrote, "that does not necessarily mean he would be convicted." Even if MacArthur himself was by this time beginning to realize that Hirohito was no war criminal, he still regarded him as a possible source of embarrassment. Any suggestion of deference or too much respect would inevitably bring the charge of "toadying to royalty."

For someone as nervous as Hirohito had always been on public occasions—even when the circumstances were happy ones—the ordeal was a shaking one. He had brought with him Marquis Matsudaira, his Court Chamberlain, Terasaki as his interpreter, and his doctor, and he looked pale and nervous as he descended from the old Rolls and walked into the Embassy. The glances turned in his direction were, not unnaturally, hostile; there was neither love nor reverence here—only cold, if controlled, contempt.

[7] MacArthur, *op. cit.*

Except, as it turned out, in the heart of one man. General Bonner Fellers, MacArthur's aide, was waiting beside the elevator which would take the Emperor up to the Allied Commander's apartments. As he watched Hirohito, so slight and pale beside the strapping, sunburned bodyguard of GI's, so incongruous in his cutaway in contrast with the khaki uniforms, he felt a sudden surge of pity not unmixed with admiration for this Daniel walking into the lions' den. "MacArthur even frightens his friends," he said afterward. "Imagine what he must have done to his enemies."

Fellers made a gesture which Hirohito was always afterward to remember, with the deepest gratitude. Amid the frozen faces, his broke into a smile. Amid the rigid formality, he unbent, and walking forward he thrust out his hand—and shook the hand of the Emperor of Japan.

"Welcome, sir," he said.[8]

Hirohito smiled for the first time in days, braced his puny shoulders, and marched in to meet the American shogun.

Exactly what took place at that first interview between the Emperor and MacArthur will not be known until the Allied Commander's papers are posthumously published. Hirohito considers that it is the privilege of General MacArthur (or, now that he is dead, his biographer) to release the full story; and in the meantime the version as given in the *Reminiscences* should be accepted as roughly authoritative.

"I met him cordially," wrote MacArthur, "and recalled that I had at one time been received by his father at the close of the Russo-Japanese war. He was nervous and the stress of the past months showed plainly. I dismissed everyone but his own interpreter, and we sat down before an open fire at one end of the long reception hall. I offered him an American cigarette, which he took with thanks. I noticed how his hands shook as I lighted it for him. I tried to make it as easy for him as I could, but I knew how deep and dreadful must be his agony of humiliation."

It is a measure of MacArthur's failure to realize the nature of the man who had come to meet him that he suspected Hirohito—and believed he had asked for the interview solely in order to plead with him on his

[8] "Who was that general who shook my hand as I came in?" Hirohito asked Terasaki the moment he got back to the palace. When told it was Bonner Fellers, he sent him a photograph signed in English, and marked him down as a friend.

own behalf and persuade the Allied powers not to have him indicted as a war criminal.

"There had been considerable outcry from some of the Allies, notably the Russian and the British, to include him in this category," MacArthur wrote. "Indeed, the initial list proposed by them was headed by the Emperor's name. Realizing the tragic consequences that would follow such an unjust action, I had stoutly resisted such efforts. When Washington seemed to be veering toward the British point of view, I had advised that I would need at least one million reinforcements should such action be taken. I believed that if the Emperor were indicted, and perhaps hanged, as a war criminal, military government would have to be instituted throughout all Japan, and guerilla warfare would probably break out.[9]

Hirohito, in any case, had come not to plead for himself but to be branded. He had heard rumors that most of his ministers and several of his palace servants were to be indicted as war criminals, and in this case he felt that the responsibility, if not the culpability, was definitely his.

"What he said was this," wrote MacArthur. "'I come to you, General MacArthur, to offer myself to the judgment of the powers you represent as the one to bear sole responsibility for every political and military decision made and action taken by my people in the conduct of the war.' A tremendous impression swept me. This courageous assumption of a responsibility implicit with death, a responsibility clearly belied by facts of which I was fully aware, moved me to the very marrow of my bones."

He let the tension relax and allowed a smile to appear.

"He was an Emperor by inherent birth," he wrote, "but in that instant I knew I faced the First Gentleman of Japan in his own right." [10]

After that first interview, MacArthur indicated to Washington that there must be no question of arresting Hirohito on a war crimes charge. The Truman Administration accepted his decision, reluctantly. But they insisted that the indictment of all other war criminals cited by them and

[9] General MacArthur seems to have been misinformed as to the attitude of the British Government at this time toward the Emperor. In fact, the Office of Strategic Services (OSS) was at this time circulating a document in Washington rather proudly announcing that the Australians felt more rapport with the U.S. authorities than with Britain, because Australia and the U.S. wanted the Emperor punished, and "Attlee and Bevin don't even care." See OSS Archives, Washington.

[10] MacArthur, *op. cit.*

the Allied Governments should be set in motion without delay.[11] Hirohito, who had been willing to face trial, found himself in the humiliating position of being safe while all around him were his servants being snatched away and put under arrest. There were some about whom he cared little, and some he believed were scapegoats chosen simply to appease the ignorant or malevolent. He was particularly wounded by the indictments of his Lord Keeper of the Privy Seal, Kido, and of his Foreign Minister, Togo, for what had they done but strive, not always too wisely, and not always too well, but certainly as hard as he had done himself, to keep the nation out of war?[12] He had no criticism to make of the arrest of General Tojo, for he had never forgiven him for allowing the High Command to include false victories in the Imperial Rescripts during the war.

Over the death of Prince Konoye, however, he grieved. It had become gradually apparent to him that his faith in the prince as an arbiter of the nation's destiny had brought Japan nothing but harm. Could Japan have been saved from war if, in 1940 and 1941, a dilettante prince had not dabbled in politics, thrown everything into the brew, and then confessed that he did not know the magic formula? Hirohito preferred not to think about it. More than anyone else during his adult life, more than Kido, more than his brothers, more than Saionji, Makino and Suzuki, he had trusted Konoye—and admired him, too, for his worldly manners, his sophisticated outlook, his super-abundant self-confidence. It came as a shock to him when he heard the circumstances of his death. Such a shoddy way to die! For when they came to tell the prince in December, 1945, that he was shortly to be arraigned as a war criminal, Konoye went home and swallowed poison.

It was Konoye's revelation of his own sense of inadequacy, his innate lack of confidence, which surprised Hirohito, for whom Konoye had always been such a model of self-sufficiency, whom he had always admired for the very quality which the Emperor felt he lacked himself,

[11] MacArthur actually had the list on the desk before him as he talked to the Emperor.

[12] He did himself a certain injustice here. Though Kido and Togo were, at times, against war with the Allies, they both voted for hostilities when he remained against them. Kido was sentenced to life imprisonment by the IMTFE and released on parole in 1955. He died in 1961. Togo was sentenced to twenty years' imprisonment by the IMTFE and died in prison in 1950.

imperial arrogance. On the Prince's deathbed was a copy of a book which he had borrowed from Toshikazu Kase. It was Oscar Wilde's *De Profundis,* and he had underlined certain passages:

"I must say to myself that I ruined myself, and that nobody great or small can be ruined except by his own hand. I am quite ready to say so. I am trying to say so, though they may not think it at the present moment. This pitiless indictment I bring without pity against myself. Terrible as was what the world did to me, what I did to myself was far more terrible still."

He also left a note which said:

"I have made many political blunders since the China Incident, for which I feel deep responsibility, but it is unbearable to me to be tried in an American court as a so-called war criminal. Since I felt responsibility for the China Incident, I arrived at the conclusion that the only way left for the settlement of the China Incident was to seek an understanding with the United States, and I have made my utmost effort for the negotiations with the United States. It is regrettable that I was suspected as a war criminal. I believe God knows what my intention was. I believe that even in America there are some friends who understand me. The excitement and resentment that accompany war, an excess of boastfulness by the victors and extreme servility and intentionally false accusations by the loser, and rumors due to misunderstanding—all these things together form public opinion; but I believe so-called public opinion will calm down and return to normalcy. Then I hope that in the court of God a judgment of justice will be given to me."

It was obvious that there was at least one Imperial virtue which Konoye lacked and Hirohito had already shown he possessed, in submitting himself to the War Crimes Tribunal.

Humility.

It was a virtue that would prove to be an insurance policy in the years to come.

Chapter Twenty-four

To lose face in Japan is to lose everything.

But to lose everything is not necessarily to lose face. And this, in the next few months, Hirohito most humbly, and superbly, demonstrated.

Under the direction of General Courtney Whitney, the process began of "cutting the Emperor down to size." So far as Whitney was concerned, there was no room for General MacArthur and a divine monarch in the same country, and the sooner Hirohito knew his place the better. Was it true that there was a staff of 7,500 retainers attached to the Imperial Household? It was indeed true. "Then get rid of them!" roared Whitney to Terasaki. "We've no room for royal parasites here."

So the palace staff was cut to the bone. Six thousand servants were thrown on to the streets at a time when food and jobs were practically nonexistent. The ration was so basic that one well-known Japanese judge, who announced his intention of actually living on it as a test of his ethical integrity, died of starvation in a few weeks. "Of course, everyone lived on the black market," said Mrs. Terasaki. "One sold what precious possessions one still possessed, article by article, in exchange for food. We called it onion-skin living. An appropriate description. Each layer of your belongings you peeled off and sold made you weep."

For the laid-off employees of the palace, Hirohito and his family did what they could. Their own regime was frugal in the extreme. SCAP had put the Imperial Family on the ration strength and sent regular sup-

344

plies of canned goods to the palace, but Hirohito refused to allow any of his family to touch them; they were passed on to the older members of the dismissed staff.

In the meantime, the vast palace grounds swiftly became a tangle of weeds, and the pathways sprouted grass in the wet season, dust and rubble when it was dry. As news of the Whitney axing operation spread, village councils met all over the country and the elders gravely discussed the "misfortunes" which were besetting their divine Emperor.

"We hear that His Imperial Majesty's money and property have been taken from him," [1] they said, "and that he is now so poor that He lives in his palace in untidy squalor. This must not be."

Volunteers were called for and began arriving in batches in Tokyo from the villages and the islands, old women and men mostly, carrying their own brooms with them. They had come, they said, to sweep the palace clean. Soon these "sweeping parties" arrived in such numbers that steps had to be taken to organize them, and a roster was set up under Matsudaira's direction. Thereafter twenty thousand Japanese came in batches to the palace each year; they were paid for by their village councils and they worked hard and eagerly, for what had begun as a sympathetic chore soon developed into a pilgrimage, and waiting lists of volunteers built up.

If Whitney had visions of profligate plenty at the palace while the ordinary people starved, he could not have been more wrong. It must have been difficult for Hirohito to cut down his intake of food and drink, for he had always (except for that self-indulgent bacon-and-egg breakfast of prewar years) been a man of most ascetic tastes, but he nonetheless instituted a regimen at the palace which was monastic in the extreme. He learned that the Crown Prince, Akihito, who was living in a small house in the woods outside Tokyo, had begun to learn the delights of Spam and Hershey bars sent in to him by some members of the staff of SCAP. He was summoned to the Emperor's presence and rebuked. He must learn to live like his people, and share their privations. From that moment on, the twelve-year-old Prince learned, like his father, to appreciate the qualities of plain brown rice and the occasional sweet potato.

[1] All his properties, at SCAP's behest, were taken over by the State and his personal fortune (estimated at $100,000,000 in 1945) sequestered and subjected to a capital levy. Hirohito's personal holdings in 1951 were estimated at $70,000.

What else could be done to diminish the stature of the Emperor and the Imperial Line?

It did not take Whitney's department long to get around to the question of his "divinity." It was pointed out to MacArthur that he had, from the moment of his arrival in Japan, guaranteed that every Japanese could worship as he wished. But how could he as long as there was Shinto— "the ancient, backward, state-controlled subsidized faith known as Shintoism," as the Allied Commander wrote. "The Emperor himself was the High Priest of Shinto, and, by the precepts of a mythological holdover from primitive times, derived his spiritual power from his Imperial ancestors who had become gods. The Japanese people were told that the Emperor was divine himself and that the highest purpose of every subject's life was death in his service. The militarists who had led Japan into war had used this religion to further their efforts, and the state still subsidized it." [2]

In November, 1945, MacArthur sent a SCAP order to the government telling them to cease all subsidies of Shintoism from that moment on. Since the shrines would henceforth have to rely on voluntary contributions—at a time when no Japanese had money to spare for upkeep or food to spare for the priests—it seemed obvious that they would quickly fall into ruin. Unless, of course, "sweeping parties" could be found for them, too—and they were. At the same time, the Allied Commander "told visiting Christian ministers of the need for their work in Japan. 'The more missionaries we can bring out here, and the more occupation troops we can send home, the better.' The Pocket Testament League, at my request, distributed 10,000,000 Bibles translated into Japanese." [3]

General MacArthur maintains in his *Reminiscences* that "it was without any suggestion or discussion with me" that Hirohito decided to take the hint and publicly renounce his own divinity. This does not jibe with information from Imperial circles, who insist that it was at the direct request of SCAP that the Emperor acted. Ironically enough, at the moment that MacArthur banned the subsidies on Shinto, Hirohito was visiting the Grand Shrine at Ise and the Imperial Mausoleums at Uneba and Momoyama where he had been to report to his ancestors on the outcome of the war. He had gone there at the behest of the Japanese Government who promptly recalled him in some embarrassment. To the

[2] From REMINISCENCES by Douglas MacArthur, Copyright © 1964 by Time, Inc. Used by permission of the publisher, McGraw-Hill Book Company.
[3] *Ibid.*

SCAP request that he go before the Japanese people and publicly "de-god" himself (as the GI's termed it) seemed to him, at first, to be absurd.

"I have never considered myself a god," he said. "Nor have I ever attempted to arrogate to myself the powers of a divine being."

He might have quoted, not without a conscious sense of irony, the words of Richard the Second:

"Throw away respect,
Tradition, form and ceremonious duty,
For you have but mistook me all this while:
I live with bread like you, feel want,
Taste grief, need friends: subjected thus,
How can you say to me I am a king?"

All that was necessary was to change the word god for king, and you had Hirohito's situation.

But if SCAP wanted him "purged" of his divine pretensions, purge himself he would. On New Year's Day, 1946, Hirohito issued an Imperial Rescript in which he said:

"We stand by the people and we wish always to share with them in their moments of joy and sorrow. The ties between us and our people have always stood upon mutual trust and affection. They do not depend upon mere legends and myths. They are not predicated on the false conception that the Emperor is divine and that the Japanese people are superior to other races, and fated to rule the world."

There! It was done. And to the Empress, Hirohito said:

"Do you see any difference? Do I look more human to you now?"

To the Allied Commander, if not to the Japanese, he certainly did, and MacArthur commented:

"The Emperor's New Year's message pleases me very much. By it he undertakes a leading part in the democratization of his people. He squarely takes his stand for the future along liberal lines. His action reflects the irresistible influence of a sound idea. A sound idea cannot be stopped."

"On a February morning in 1946," reported *Time Magazine*, "the Emperor of Japan drove across the palace moat in his black Mercedes Benz sedan on his way to meet the people of Japan. . . . Hiro-hito's first attempts to 'democratize' the throne were of such an awkwardness as to make foreign spectators uncomfortable. There were few traces left of the earnest and well-schooled young Crown Prince who in 1921 had known just the right things to say to Lloyd George, the President of the French Republic or a Scottish gamekeeper. Hirohito now asked questions perfunctorily and with great nervousness, a tense, shuffling figure in a gray overcoat and a crumpled gray hat."

It was his first venture abroad to meet his people, thought up as a popularization move by members of his palace staff, and encouraged by General Whitney, who believed that one look at "the myopic, apologetic little man" would kill the monarchic idea stone dead for ever. It was a typically transatlantic misunderstanding of the nature of royalty and its appeal to the masses.

Hirohito's visit was as pathetically ineffective as Whitney hoped. Hirohito wandered rather ineptly among the workers of the Kawasaki factory holding out his hand to be shaken, listening to the fumbled words of the workers, and repeating the automatic reply which caused him to be dubbed in coming days by the opposition newspapers as "King Is it Really?" For every time a worker said something to him, he automatically replied: "Ah, so desuka? (Is that so?)"

Far from doing any harm, this propaganda seemed to make him increasingly popular with the populace, who were apt to say: "Ah, so, desuka?" at the end of every sentence themselves, and were relieved to discover that the Emperor was one of them.

In the visits which followed, he grew less strained. "The crumpled gray hat became in time the badge of a successful political campaigner," wrote Time correspondent Frank Gibney. "The monosyllables in which Hirohito had conducted his early interviews with the common folk grew into coherent questions and intelligent replies. The shy man waved his hat in the air to acknowledge greetings. He smiled. Slowly the sense of a personality behind the walled moat of the Imperial Palace communicated itself to the people of Japan."

By 1950 it could be said that Hirohito was established as Emperor of Japan more solidly than he had ever been before, even though the people no longer bowed in fear when he ventured abroad. To the definite discomfiture of Whitney (but not entirely to the dissatisfaction of several members of his staff), Hirohito as a democratic monarch turned out to be more popular than he had been as a mythical, divine and autocratic god-king "in the clouds."

Harry Emerson Wildes, a former member of MacArthur's staff, reported: "In January 1946, a public opinion poll showed that 90.1 per cent favored Hirohito, and that all but four of the eighty-nine political parties registered in Japan supported him; a similar poll in 1951 gave him 90.3 per cent support, with only the communists opposing him. Twice yearly, on New Year's Day, and on April 30,[4] his birthday, several hundred thousand people thronged the Imperial Palace Plaza to sign his visitors' guest books, regardless of the weather. The crush was so great on New Year's Day, 1954, that sixteen persons were trampled to death and thirty were injured when 380,000 people, half of those who visited the Palace, suddenly rushed forward to enter the grounds."

The Emperor of Japan remained the Emperor of Japan, even if the public image of him was rather different in the postwar period to what it had been before. To Hirohito, in fact, it made no difference. In the convulsive changes which rocked Japan in the postwar period, bringing votes to women, outlawing war, demolishing the tyrannies of family life, he changed little of his routine. True, no one objected any longer to his laboratory inside the Imperial Palace. True, the world recognized his skill as a marine biologist and he was encouraged to fish for specimens beneath the waters of his beloved Sagami Bay.[5] He had merely ceased to be a figure of awe and an object of veneration. That, as he said to one of his advisers, was what he preferred; as to his freedom:

"I am like a canary whose cage has been opened and someone says: 'Fly away!' Where should I fly to? If I have a song to sing, why should I waste it on places where the wind may blow it away?"[6]

There would be trials and insults and humiliations in the years to come, for the legend of his war guilt died hard and few Japanese paused to defend him. They had no time. They were too taken up with the mad rush to exploit the postwar (or rather the Post-Korean War) boom. The newspapers and magazines tucked him away and gossiped instead about his son, the Crown Prince Akihito, of his courtship and marriage, the birth of his sons, his first trips abroad.

[4] Actually, April 29.
[5] His latest book about the crustaceans of the Pacific, published in 1965, includes several important discoveries, including two new species of crab found southwest of Jogashima Island, at the entrance of Sagami Bay.
[6] From a palace servant who does not wish to be identified.

Hirohito faded into the background, and was thankful for it. He was simply Ohoribata, the Honorable across the Moat, a forgotten monarch stripped of power. It was the way he wanted it. He emerged for one happy moment in 1964 during the Olympic Games and relished the privilege of being able to sit in the grandstand, watch the athletes, meet the champions face to face.

"Do you know," he said to the United States Ambassador, Edwin O. Reischauer, "this is the happiest moment of my life. I fear I have been cut off too much from my people. This is the first time I have been to a public spectacle since 1957,[7] and it is most enjoyable." And then he hastily added:

"But don't think I am out of touch. I am very keen on television. I do not need to envy any more people who travel to different places. It has made all the difference to my life."

The American envoy nodded his head.

"Ours too," he said. "I never thought I would get the habit. But do you know what my wife and I watch now—and love it? *Bonanza*."

"Ah, so desuka?" said Hirohito. "Now, the Empress . . ."

[7] In 1957 he took the Empress to see a performance of *Kabuki*. It was the first time they had ever been to a theater or an entertainment together.

350

Appendices

I. THE YALTA AGREEMENT

Signed at Yalta February 11, 1945

The leaders of the three Great Powers—the Soviet Union, the United States of America and Great Britain—have agreed that in two or three months after Germany has surrendered and the war in Europe has terminated the Soviet Union shall enter into the war against Japan on the side of the Allies on condition that:

1. The status quo in Outer-Mongolia (The Mongolian People's Republic) shall be preserved;

2. The former rights of Russia violated by the treacherous attack of Japan in 1904 shall be restored, viz:

(a) the southern part of Sakhalin as well as all the islands adjacent to it shall be returned to the Soviet Union,

(b) the commercial port of Dairen shall be internationalized, the preeminent interests of the Soviet Union in this port being safeguarded and the lease of Port Arthur as a naval base of the USSR restored,

(c) the Chinese-Eastern Railroad and the South-Manchurian Railroad which provides an outlet to Dairen shall be jointly operated by the establishment of a joint Soviet-Chinese Company it being understood that the preeminent interests of the Soviet Union shall be safeguarded and that China shall retain full sovereignty in Manchuria;

3. The Kuril islands shall be handed over to the Soviet Union.

It is understood, that the agreement concerning Outer-Mongolia and the ports and railroads referred to above will require concurrence of Generalissimo Chiang Kai-Shek. The President will take measures in order to obtain this concurrence on advice from Marshal Stalin.

The Heads of the three Great Powers have agreed that these claims of the Soviet Union shall be unquestionably fulfilled after Japan has been defeated.

For its part the Soviet Union expresses its readiness to conclude with the National Government of China a pact of friendship and alliance between the USSR and China in order to render assistance to China with its armed forces for the purpose of liberating China from the Japanese yoke.

> J. STALIN *
> FRANKLIN D. ROOSEVELT
> WINSTON S. CHURCHILL

February 11, 1945

II. THE POTSDAM PROCLAMATION

July 26, 1945

(1) WE—THE PRESIDENT of the United States, the President of the National Government of the Republic of China, and the Prime Minister of Great Britain, representing the hundreds of millions of our countrymen, have conferred and agree that Japan shall be given an opportunity to end this war.

(2) The prodigious land, sea and air forces of the United States, the British Empire and of China, many times reinforced by their armies and air fleets from the west, are poised to strike the final blows upon Japan. This military power is sustained and inspired by the determination of all the Allied Nations to prosecute the war against Japan until she ceases to resist.

(3) The result of the futile and senseless German resistance to the might of the aroused free peoples of the world stands forth in awful clarity as an example to the people of Japan. The might that now converges on Japan is immeasurably greater than that which, when applied to the resisting Nazis, necessarily laid waste to the lands, the industry, and the method of life of the whole German people. The full application of our military power, backed by our resolve, *will* mean the inevitable and complete destruction of the Japanese armed forces and just as inevitably the utter devastation of the Japanese homeland.

(4) The time has come for Japan to decide whether she will continue to be controlled by those self-willed militaristic advisers whose unintelligent calculations have brought the Empire of Japan to the threshold of annihilation, or whether she will follow the path of reason.

(5) Following are our terms. We will not deviate from them. There are no alternatives. We shall brook no delay.

(6) There must be eliminated for all time the authority and influence of those who have deceived and misled the people of Japan into embarking on world conquest, for we insist that a new order of peace, security and justice will be impossible until irresponsible militarism is driven from the world.

(7) Until such a new order is established *and* until there is convincing proof that Japan's war-making power is destroyed, points in Japanese territory to be designated by the Allies shall be occupied to secure the achievement of the basic objectives we are here setting forth.

(8) The terms of the Cairo Declaration shall be carried out and Japanese sovereignty shall be limited to the islands of Honshu, Hokkaido, Kyushu, Shikoku and such minor islands as we determine.

(9) The Japanese military forces, after being completely disarmed, shall be permitted to return to their homes with the opportunity to lead peaceful and productive lives.

(10) We do not intend that the Japanese shall be enslaved as a race or destroyed as a nation, but stern justice shall be meted out to all war criminals, including those who have visited cruelties upon our prisoners. The Japanese Government shall remove all obstacles to the revival and strengthening of democratic tendencies among the Japanese people. Freedom of speech, of religion, and of thought, as well as respect for the fundamental human rights shall be established.

(11) Japan shall be permitted to maintain such industries as will sustain her economy and permit the exaction of just reparations in kind, but not those which would enable her to re-arm for war. To this end, access to, as distinguished from control of, raw materials shall be permitted. Eventual Japanese participation in world trade relations shall be permitted.

(12) The occupying forces of the Allies shall be withdrawn from Japan as soon as these objectives have been accomplished and there has been established in accordance with the freely expressed will of the Japanese people a peacefully inclined and responsible government.

(13) We call upon the government of Japan to proclaim now the unconditional surrender of all Japanese armed forces, and to provide proper and adequate assurances of their good faith in such action. The alternative for Japan is prompt and utter destruction.

III. JAPAN'S FINAL NOTE

The Japanese Government would like to be permitted to state to the Governments of America, Britain, China and the Soviet Union what they most earnestly desire with reference to the execution of certain provisions of the Potsdam Proclamation. This may be done possibly at the time of the signature. But fearing that they may not be able to find an appropriate opportunity, they take the liberty of addressing the Governments of the Four Powers through the good offices of the Government of Switzerland.

1. In view of the fact that the purpose of occupation as mentioned in the Potsdam Proclamation is solely to secure the achievement of the basic objectives set forth in the said Proclamation, the Japanese Government sincerely desire that the Four Powers, relying upon the good faith of the Japanese Government, will facilitate discharge by the Japanese Government of their obligations as to forestall any unnecessary complications.

It is earnestly solicited that:

(a) In case of the entry of Allied fleets or troops in Japan Proper, the Japanese Government be notified in advance, so that arrangements can be made for reception.

(*b*) The number of the points in Japanese territory to be designated by the Allies for occupation be limited to minimum number, selection of the points be made in such a manner as to leave such a city as Tokyo unoccupied and the forces to be stationed at each point be made as small as possible.

2. Disarming of the Japanese forces, being a most delicate task as it involves over three millions of officers and men overseas and having direct bearing on their honour, the Japanese Government will, of course, take utmost pains. But it is suggested that the best and the most effective method would be that under the command of His Majesty the Emperor, the Japanese forces are allowed to disarm themselves and surrender arms of their own accord.

Disarming of the Japanese forces on the Continent be carried out beginning on the front line and in successive stages.

In connection with the disarming it is hoped that Article 35 of the Hague Convention will be applied, and the honour of the soldier will be respected, permitting them, for instance, to wear swords. Further, the Japanese Government be given to understand the Allies have no intention to employ disarmed Japanese soldiers for compulsory labour. It is sincerely hoped that shipment and transportation facilities necessary for the evacuation of the soldiers to their homeland will be speedily provided.

3. Since some forces are located in remote places, difficult to communicate the Imperial Order, it is desired that reasonable time be allowed before the cessation of hostilities.

4. It is hoped that the Allies will be good enough quickly to take necessary steps or extend us facilities for the shipment of indispensable foodstuffs and medical supplies to Japanese forces in distant islands, and for the transport of wounded soldiers from those islands.

IV. JAPAN'S FIRST SURRENDER OFFER

August 10, 1945

THE HONORABLE
JAMES F. BYRNES
Secretary of State

SIR:

I have the honor to inform you that the Japanese Minister to Switzerland, upon instructions received from his Government, has requested the Swiss Political Department to advise the Government of the United States of America of the following:

"In obedience to the gracious command of His Majesty the Emperor who, ever anxious to enhance the cause of world peace, desires earnestly to bring about a speedy termination of hostilities with a view to saving mankind from the calamities to be imposed upon them by further continuation of the war, the Japanese Government several weeks ago asked the Soviet Government, with which neutral relations then prevailed, to render good offices in restoring peace vis a vis the enemy powers. Unfortunately, these efforts in the interest of peace having failed, the Japanese Government in conformity with the august wish of His Majesty to restore the general peace and desiring to put an end to the untold sufferings entailed by war as quickly as possible, have decided upon the following.

"The Japanese Government are ready to accept the terms enumerated in the joint declaration which was issued at Potsdam on July 26th, 1945, by the heads of the Governments of the United States, Great Britain, and China, and later subscribed by the Soviet Government, with the understanding that the said declaration does not comprise any demand which prejudices the prerogatives of His Majesty as a Sovereign Ruler.

"The Japanese Government sincerely hope that this understanding is warranted and desire keenly that an explicit indication to that effect will be speedily forthcoming."

In transmitting the above message the Japanese minister added that his Government begs the Government of the United States to forward its answer through the intermediary of Switzerland. Similar requests are being transmitted to the Governments of Great Britain and the Union of Soviet Socialist Republics through the intermediary of Sweden, as well as to the Government of China through the intermediary of Switzerland. The Chinese Minister at Berne has already been informed of the foregoing through the channel of the Swiss Political Department.

Please be assured that I am at your disposal at any time to accept for and forward to my Government the reply of the Government of the United States.

Accept [etc.]

GRASSLI
Chargé d'Affaires ad interim
of Switzerland.

V. THE IMPERIAL RESCRIPT OF AUGUST 15, 1945

To Our good and loyal subjects:

After pondering deeply the general trends of the world and the actual conditions obtaining in Our Empire today, We have decided to effect a settlement of the present situation by resorting to an extraordinary measure.

We have ordered Our Government to communicate to the Governments of the United States, Great Britain, China and the Soviet Union that Our Empire accepts the provisions of their Joint Declaration

To strive for the common prosperity and happiness of all nations as well as the security and well-being of Our subjects is the solemn obligation which has been handed down by Our Imperial Ancestors, and which We lay close to heart. Indeed, We declared war on America and Britain out of Our sincere desire to ensure Japan's self preservation and the stabilization of East Asia, it being far from Our thought either to infringe upon the sovereignty of other nations or to embark upon territorial aggrandizement. But now the war has lasted for nearly four years. Despite the best that has been done by everyone—the gallant fighting of military and naval forces, the diligence and assiduity of Our servants of the State and the devoted service of Our one hundred million people, the war situation has developed not necessarily to Japan's advantage, while the general trends of the world have all turned against her interest. Moreover, the enemy has begun to employ a new and most cruel bomb, the power of which to do damage is indeed incalculable, taking the toll of many innocent lives. Should We continue to fight, it would not only result in an ultimate collapse and obliteration of the Japanese nation, but also it would lead to the total extinction of human civilization. Such being the case, how are We to save the millions of Our subjects; or to atone Ourselves before the hallowed spirits of Our Imperial Ancestors? This is the reason why We have ordered the acceptance of the provisions of the Joint Declaration of the Powers.

We cannot but express the deepest sense of regret to our Allied nations of East Asia, who have consistently cooperated with the Empire towards the emancipation of East Asia. The thought of those officers and men as well as others who have fallen in the fields of battle, those who died at their posts of duty, or those who met with untimely death and all their bereaved families, pains Our heart night and day. The welfare of the wounded and the war-sufferers, and of those who have lost their homes and livelihood, are the objects of Our profound solicitude. The hardships and sufferings to which Our nation is to be subjected hereafter will be certainly great. We are keenly aware of the inmost feelings of all ye, Our subjects. However, it is according to the dictate of time and fate that We have resolved to pave the way for a grand peace for all the generations to come by enduring the unendurable and suffering what is insufferable.

Having been able to safeguard and maintain the structure of the Imperial State, We are always with ye, Our good and loyal subjects, relying upon your sincerity and integrity. Beware most strictly of any outbursts of emotion which may engender needless complications, or any fraternal contention and strife which may create confusion, lead ye astray and cause ye to lose the confidence of the world. Let the entire nation continue as one family from generation to generation, ever firm in its faith of the imperishableness of its divine land, and mindful of its heavy burden of responsibilities, and the long road before it. Unite your total strength to be devoted to the construction for the future. Cultivate the ways of rectitude; foster nobility of spirit; and work with resolution so as ye may enhance the innate glory of the Imperial State and keep pace with the progress of the world.

(Imperial Sign Manual)
(Imperial Seal)

The 14th day of the 8th month
of the 20th year of Showa.

Bibliography

Blond, Georges, *Admiral Togo*, trans. by E. Hyams. New York, The Macmillan Company, 1960. A biography of the great naval hero of Japan.

Busch, Noel, *Two Minutes to Noon*. New York, Simon and Schuster, Inc., 1962. An expertly researched account of the great Kanto Earthquake of 1923.

Bush, Lewis, *The Road to Inamura*. England. One man (a lover of Japan) tells what it was like to be a prisoner in the war. An anguished tale told without anger or hate.

———, *Land of the Dragon Fly*. London, 1959.

Butow, Robert J. C., *Japan's Decision to Surrender*. California, Stanford University Press, 1954. Another fascinating minute-by-minute account of the last days of the Japanese Empire.

———, *Tojo and the Coming of War*. New Jersey, Princeton University Press, 1961. A masterly account of the events leading to the downfall of the Japanese Empire, meticulously documented, grippingly told.

Close, Upton, *Behind the Face of Japan*. New York, Appleton-Century-Crofts, 1951. A polemical account of the nation in the era before the war.

Craigie, Sir Robert, *Behind the Japanese Mask*. London, Hutchinson & Co., (Publ.) Ltd., 1945. An account, to be read in parallel with the memoirs of Mr. Grew, of how the British Ambassador to Japan saw the events leading to Pearl Harbor.

d'Anethan, Baroness, *Fourteen Years of Diplomatic Life in Japan*. London, 1912.

Earl, David Mafarey, *Emperor and Nation in Japan*. Seattle, Wash., University of Washington Press, 1964. A treatise on political thinking during the Tokugawa period, prior to the Meiji Restoration.

Grew, Joseph C., *Ten Years in Japan*. New York, Simon and Schuster, Inc., 1944. The diaries of the able United States Ambassador to Japan in the years up to Pearl Harbor. Indefatigable but realistic worker for better American-Japanese relations.

———, *Turbulent Era*. New York, Houghton Mifflin Company, 1952.

Ickes, Harold L., *The Secret Diary of Harold L. Ickes*. Three volumes. New York, Simon and Schuster, Inc., 1954.

Imamura, Akitsune, *Theoretical and Applied Seismology*. Tokyo, 1937.

James, David H., *The Rise and Fall of the Japanese Empire*. London, Allen & Unwin, Ltd., 1951. A provocative, knowledgeable, intensely personal but fascinating sweep through Japanese history from mythical times to 1945 by a Japanese-speaking Welshman who became a POW of the Japanese.

James, Grace, *Japan: Recollections and Impressions*. London, Allen & Unwin, Ltd., 1936.

Kodama, Yoshio, *I was Defeated*. Tokyo, Booth & Fukada, 1951. Memoirs, sometimes whining with self-justification, of a former member of the pre-war Japanese secret societies.

Kurihara, Ken, *Tenno: Showa-Shi Oboegaki* (The Emperor and Showa History). Japan, Yushindo, 1955. A Japanese account of the Emperor's part in the events of his reign (from a translation specially made for the author).

MacArthur, Douglas, *Reminiscences*. New York, McGraw-Hill, Inc., 1964. Not quite all he could have told, one feels, but what there is makes absorbing reading.

Morison, Samuel Eliot, *The Rising Sun in the Pacific*, Volume 4. Boston, Mass., Little, Brown and Company, 1948. Part of the multi-volumed story of United States disasters, mistakes and glorious triumphs of the Pacific war at sea.

Morris, Ivan, *The World of the Shining Prince*. New York, Alfred A. Knopf, Inc., 1964. A delightfully evocative reconstruction of Court Life in Ancient Japan.

Piggott, General F. S. G., *Broken Thread*. London, Gale & Polden, Ltd., 1950. A memoir from the 1880's until 1938 of a former British military attaché in Tokyo, a friend of the Emperor and the Imperial family, intensely pro-Japanese.

Price, Willard, *Son of Heaven*. New York, Duell, Sloan & Pearce, Inc., 1945. A wartime sketch of the Emperor and a plea for his removal by an American who was once Hirohito's next door neighbor.

Reischauer, Dr. Edwin O., *Japan Past and Present*, revised edition. New York, Alfred A. Knopf, Inc., 1964. A condensed history of the land and people written with clarity, vigor and insight, by a Japanese-speaking historian who is at present United States Ambassador to Japan.

Riddell, Lord, *Intimate Diary of the Peace Conference and After, 1918-1923*.

Saito, Yoshie, *Azamukareta Rekishi* (The Distorted History), Tokyo, 1955.

Sansom, Sir George, *A History of Japan*. Three volumes. California, Stanford University Press, 1958, 1961, 1963. A masterly, readable standard history by a great scholar of Japan from the earliest times to the nineteenth century.

————, *Japan, A Short Cultural History*. New York, Appleton-Century-Crofts, 1962.

————, *The Western World and Japan*. New York, Alfred A. Knopf, Inc., 1950. A brilliant account of the impact of European civilization on Japan.

Statler, Oliver, *The Black Ship Scroll*. Rutland, Vt., Charles E. Tuttle Co., 1964. Another account of the beginnings of Japanese-American relations, splendidly illustrated by a contemporary Japanese's sketches of how the American "invaders" looked to him.

Stimson, Henry L., *On Active Service in Peace and War*. New York, Harper & Row, 1947.

Storry, Richard, *A Modern History of Japan*. New York, Penguin Books, Inc., 1960. A short study of the last century of Japan whose every sentence betrays the wealth of knowledge and research which has been compressed into it. Most readable and reliable.

―――, *The Double Patriots.* New York, Houghton Mifflin Company, 1957. A perceptive insight into the right-wing movements in Japan during the 1930's.

Sugimoto, Etsu Inagaki, *A Daughter of the Samurai.* 1926.

Takeuchi, Tatsuji, *War and Diplomacy in the Japanese Empire.* Chicago, Ill., University of Chicago Press, 1935. A study of Japanese policy in the twenties and early thirties.

Tanaka, Ryukichi, *Niho Gumbatsu Anto Shi.* Tokyo, 1947.

Terasaki, Gwen. *Bridge to the Sun.* University of North Carolina Press, 1957.

Tolischus, Otto D., *Tokyo Record.* New York, Reynal & Hitchcock, 1941. The day-to-day record of the last months of peace in Japan by a United States reporter.

Walworth, Arthur, *Black Ships Off Japan.* New York, J. B. Lippincott Company, 1960. An account of Perry's expedition and the opening up of Japan to the outside world.

Wildes, H. E., *Typhoon in Tokyo.* New York, The Macmillan Company, 1954. A breezy, no-holds-barred, informative account of how Japan looked to an American occupationeer on General MacArthur's staff.

Young, Morgan, *Japan Under Taisho Tenno.* New York, William Morrow and Company, Inc., 1929. A crisp, sometimes abrasive account of life during the reign of Hirohito's father.

Some of the many studies of the years leading up to the death of the Emperor Meiji in 1912:

Ike, Nobutaka, *The Beginnings of Political Democracy in Japan.* New York, Alfred A. Knopf, Inc., 1950.

Kosaka, Masaaka, *Japanese Thought in the Meiji Era.*

Norman, E. H., *Japan's Emergence as a Modern State.* Vancouver, B.C., Canada, Institute of Pacific Relations, 1940.

Okuma, Shigenobu, *Fifty Years of New Japan.*

Yanaga, Chitoshi, *Japan Since Perry.* New York, McGraw-Hill, Inc., 1949.

Two absorbing and spendidly documented personal accounts of life in the capital as seen by two top foreign correspondents:

Byas, Hugh, *Government by Assassination.* New York, Alfred A. Knopf, Inc., 1942.

Fleisher, Wilfred, *Volcanic Isle.* New York, Doubleday, Doran, 1941.

Studies, all of them excellent, of the policies, rivalries and plots which preceded the outbreak of war:

Feis, Herbert, *The Road to Pearl Harbor.* Princeton, N.J., Princeton University Press, 1950.

Jones, F. C., *Japan's New Order in Asia.* New York, Oxford University Press, Inc.

Maxon, Y. C., *Control of Japanese Foreign Policy*. California, University of California Press, 1960.

Young, Morgan, *Imperial Japan, 1926-38*. London, Allen & Unwin, Ltd., 1938.

Some versions of how Allied statesmen saw the coming of war with Japan:

Beard, Charles A., *President Roosevelt and the Coming of War*. New Haven, Conn., Yale University Press, 1948.

Byrnes, James F., *Speaking Frankly*. New York, Harper & Row, 1947.

Churchill, Winston S., *The Second World War*. Six volumes. New York, Bantam Books, Inc., 1962.

Hull, Cordell, *The Memoirs of Cordell Hull*. Two volumes. New York, The Macmillan Company, 1948.

Some versions of how Japanese statesmen saw the coming of war with the United States and Britain:

Kase, Toshikazu, *Journey to the Missouri*. New Haven, Conn., Yale University Press, 1952.

Konoye, Fumimaro, *Memoirs*. Asahi Shimbun, 1946.

Shigemitsu, Mamoru, *Japan and Her Destiny*. New York, E. P. Dutton & Co., 1958.

Togo, Shigenori, *The Cause of Japan*. New York, Simon and Schuster, Inc., 1956.

Yoshida, Shigeru, *Reminiscences*.

The first, a clock-ticking account of the attack; the second, an account of the events preceding and following the attack on Pearl Harbor:

Lord, Walter, *Day of Infamy*. New York, Holt, Rinehart and Winston, Inc., 1957.

Millis, Walter, *This is Pearl!* New York, William Morrow and Company, Inc., 1947.

A varied series of accounts of the development of Japanese affairs from 1945 onward:

Ball, W. Macmahon, *Japan—Enemy or Ally?* New York, John Day Co. (Institute of Pacific Relations), 1949.

Brown, Delmer, *Nationalism in Japan*. California, University of California Press, 1951.

Martin, Edwin M., *The Allied Occupation of Japan*. California, Stanford University Press (Institute of Pacific Relations), 1948.

Morris, Ivan, *Nationalism and the Right Wing in Japan*. New York, Oxford University Press, Inc., 1960.

Two charming reminiscences by the American Quaker tutor of Crown Prince Akihito:

Vining, Elizabeth Gray, *Return to Japan*. New York, J. B. Lippincott Company, 1960.

————, *Windows for the Crown Prince.* New York, J. B. Lippincott Company, 1952.

Documents:

Dull, Paul S. and Michael Takaaki Umemura, *The Tokyo Trials.* A Functional Index to the Proceedings of the International Military Tribunal, Far East. Ann Arbor, Mich.: University of Michigan Press, 1957. An indispensable guide to all those traveling through the 40,000 pages of evidence given at the IMTFE.
Government Printing Office. *Mission Accomplished.* Interrogations of Japanese Military, Industrial and Civil Leaders of World War Two. United States Army Air Force, Washington, D.C.
Library of Congress. *Pearl Harbor Attack.* Hearings before the Joint Committee of the Investigation of the Pearl Harbor Attack. Congress of the United States, Washington, D.C.
National Archives. *Biographical Notes on the Japanese Cabinet, 1945.* O.S.S., Washington, D.C.
————, *The Brocade Banner.* The Story of Japanese Nationalism. United States Army, GHQ, SCAP, Counter-Intelligence Sector, Washington, D.C.
————, Interrogation of Japanese Officials, Washington, D.C.
————, Interrogations of Koichi Kido, Koki Hitoa, Yosuke Matsuoka, Kenryo Sato, Mamoru Shigemitsu, Shigetaro Shimada, Shigenori Togo, Hideki Tojo, Fumimaro Konoye, Tsuneo Matsudaira, among others. Washington, D.C.
————, *The Japanese Emperor and the War.* O.S.S., September 8, 1944, Washington, D.C.
————, Nikki, *The Diaries of Koichi Kido.* Washington, D.C.
————, The Record of the Affidavits, Charges, Evidence and Cross-Examination of the Accused at the International Military Tribunal, Far East. Washington, D.C.
————, Translation of Japanese Documents. 4 Volumes. United States Army, FE Command, Washington, D.C.
————, United States Strategic Bombing Survey, Washington, D.C.

Correspondence.
Private Interviews.
Japan Year Book, 1946-48.

Index

Abe, Gen. Nobuyuki, 193, 242
Air raids, 278-79, 281, 283-84, 286, 296-97, 328
  atomic, 311-12, 313, 322-23
Aizawa, Lt. Col., 136, 211
Akasaka Detached Palace, 1, 2, 30, 79-80, 81, 89, 93
Akihito, Prince, 335, 349
  birth of, 127-29, 207n
  rebuked by Hirohito, 345
Allenby, Field Marshal Viscount, 55
Amakasu, Capt., 84
Amaterasu, 16, 32, 94, 101, 273, 299
Amsterdam, 64
Amur Society, see Black Dragon Society
Anami, Gen. Korechika, 285, 297-98, 299, 315, 319, 324, 329
Ando, Capt. Teruzo, 135, 138, 146n
André Lebon (liner), 78
Anethan, Baroness Albert d', 1
Anti-Comintern Pact, 156, 170
Anti-semitism, 186
Aosta, Emanuele, Duc d', 65
Araki, Gen. Sadao, 115, 121, 122, 124, 131-32, 137, 150, 151n, 172
  birth of heir to throne and, 128, 129
Arita, Hachiro, 189, 190
Army:
  belligerent policy of, 99, 228
  in China, see China
  Choshu control of, 23, 41, 118
  domination of government by, 121-22, 153-54, 157-62, 187, 191-92
  Hull's opinion of, 212
  Meiji Rescript on, 178-79

Army (*Cont.*)
  opposes Hirohito's liberalism and popularity, 72-74, 85, 109-10
  plots and mutinies by
    Febr., 1936, mutiny, 134-48, 151, 172
    Inukai assassination, 119-21
    Oct., 1931, plot, 112-15
    Shimpeitai plot, 125-27, 128, 131
    at surrender, 327-29, 333
  in Siberia, 68n
  unpopularity in 1920's of, 96
Arsené-Henry (French Ambassador), 202
Arthur, Duke of Connaught, 14, 57
Assassinations, 109, 135-36
  in Feb., 1936, mutiny, 137-41
  of Hamaguchi, 109-11
  of Hara, 47n, 69
  of Inukai, 119-21
Atami, 78, 158
Atholl, 8th Duke of, 61-62, 71
Atomic bomb, 308, 311-12, 313, 322-23
Attlee, Clement, 307, 308
Australia, 97, 335, 341n

Bathing, 11
  by Hirohito, 182
Belgium, 12
Benedict XV, Pope, 65
Black Dragon Society, 152
  Hirohito's betrothal and, 46-48, 50
  opposes Hirohito's liberalism, 73-74
  program of, 68-69
Briand-Kellogg Pact, 110

363

365

369